C000041498

STARLING BENSON

OF

SWANSEA

by

Dorothy M Bayliffe and Joan N Harding

1996

D Brown & Sons Limited

Cowbridge and Bridgend

ISBN 1 872808 42 5

Printed and published by D Brown & Sons Ltd., North Road, Bridgend Industrial Estate, Bridgend, Mid Glamorgan.

Dedicated to his Great-nephew,
Colonel J R E Benson of Dorchester

Starling Benson in his early twenties from a drawing in the possession of Col. J R E Benson

Contents

Abbreviations

The following are the abbreviations used throughout 'Starling Benson of Swansea' for recurring personal names and references to companies, locations, sources, etc:

UCS/BC: Unpublished family letters and other material from the Benson Collection in the Swansea University College Archives

JREB: Unpublished material in the possession of Col J R E Benson, Dorchester

D/D SB: Documents from the office of Strick & Bellingham, Swansea solicitors, WGRO

EMB: Elizabeth Meux Benson
HRB: Henry Roxby Benson
MHB: Mary Henrietta Benson
RMB: Richard Meux Benson
SB: Starling Benson
TSB: Thomas Starling Benson

BA: British Association
C Cambrian
CRL: Cardiff Reference Library
GWR: Great Western Railway
L&NWR: London & North Western Railway
MR: Midland Railway
NMW: National Museum of Wales
N&BR: Neath & Brecon Railway
NLW: National Library of Wales
PRO: Public Record Office
RISW: Royal Institution of South Wales
SCL: Swansea Central Library
SHT: Swansea Harbour Trust
SSJE: Society of St John the Evangelist
SM: Swansea Museum
SVR: Swansea Vale Railway
Sw and Glam Herald: Swansea and Glamorgan Herald
SWR: South Wales Railway
SWWIAS: South West Wales Industrial Archaeology Society
UCS: University College of Swansea
WGRO: West Glamorgan Record Office
WMR: Welsh Midland Railway

List of Illustrations

Foreword

Amongst my earliest memories is one of being taken by my father one Sunday morning in Swansea to 'the docks'. The Second World War had started so the docks east of the river were out of bounds, but we walked around the North Dock Basin (now Sainsbury's) to the quay wall beside the grey and choppy river. There we watched the only two ships to be seen, as they manoeuvred with the tide against the wind. They were both tugs and one of their names remained in my mind ever after. It was the 'Benson'.

To a seven year old a name was a name and needed no origin, though my father would have known it. Many years later I came to read W. H. Jones' History of the Port of Swansea and there I learnt that the man whose name was borne by my tug had been a leading figure in the affairs of Swansea and Swansea Harbour in the middle years of the last century and that he had been Chairman of the Harbour Trustees for twenty-two of them. Beyond that, Jones' work gives little detail, for his was the story of the Port, a subject too large to leave much scope for individual biography. Even had he had space to expand on Starling Benson's activities, he could have dealt with only one aspect of them, for like many of his contemporaries, Benson's involvement with Swansea Harbour and its docks was but part of his many public and business activities.

Until now no other author has pursued the story of this Victorian's life, family and commercial ventures, though Dr Joan Harding had provided an indication of its potential interest in her book *From Fox How to Fairy Hill*. Happily, she and Dorothy Bayliffe, another assiduous worker in the same field, have together gone on to research the subject in much greater detail. The result is this very full and careful study of one of the makers of modern Swansea which, in telling of Starling Benson's life and work, also illuminates many aspects of local society and business in a period of remarkable economic expansion. It should find a place on the bookshelf of all who work in the many fields of study which explore the history of nineteenth-century Swansea.

Bernard Morris
President,
The Royal Institution of South Wales,
Swansea
September 1995

Authors' Note

We had little idea, when we first began compiling material for this book, that our researches would take so long or that, even when we were already meeting our publisher, fresh material, crucial to the study, would still be emerging.

Of those who helped us in the early stages one is no longer with us. We much regret the passing of Mr W C Rogers with whose kind permission we were allowed to use some of the illustrations from his 'Pictorial History of Swansea'. We benefited greatly from the early support given us by Miss Betty Nelmes before her retirement from the curatorship of the Swansea Museum. We are grateful to her, as well as to the present staff under the leadership of Rosalind Gee and Jenny Sabine and to the Education Officer, Gerald Gabb. We are equally indebted to Susan Beckley and the staff of the West Glamorgan Record Office for the invaluable help they have given. Another source of information has been the 'Cambrian Index' at the Swansea Reference Library, so willingly put at our disposal by Marilyn Jones, while the staffs of both the Reference Library itself and of the Swansea University Library have always been most helpful when approached.

We particularly wish to acknowledge the consistent interest of the President of the Royal Institution, Bernard Morris, who kindly consented to provide the Foreword, while in all matters relating to railways we have been guided by Michael Hale of Dudley who has also assisted in reading, checking and criticising our manuscripts, of which, over the years, there have been quite a few varied versions! We are most grateful for his long-suffering vigilance. We should also like to thank Ralph Tutton of Teddington for his generosity in providing us with valuable information about that area. Nearer home, we have been helped by a number of people, too many to be mentioned by name, who have furnished us with useful details about their own localities, including the Swansea Valley and Gower, particularly Penclawdd.

Above all, our special thanks must go to Colonel J R E Benson of Dorchester who has so graciously offered us hospitality at his home and allowed us to ferret among his books and papers to our hearts' content in pursuit of what we considered relevant to our work. Consequently, it gives us the greatest pleasure to dedicate to Colonel Benson this tribute to his great-uncle's memorable contribution to the history of Swansea.

Because of the many facets of Starling Benson's activities, we found it easier to adopt a thematic rather than a strictly chronological approach as this allowed us to follow through the development of single interests rather than become entangled in the multiple concerns engrossing him at one and the same time.

The dictates of modern technology eventually decided our usage of punctuation (not without reservations on occasions). In other ways we have been more faithful to nineteenth century practice. The spelling of local place-names may, as a result, vary considerably according to the whim of the writer of a particular document. This means that occasionally the same word is spelt differently in different contexts, depending possibly on the date, as with 'Llanelly' and 'Llanelli', or, more frequently, the degree of the writer's acquaintance with the Welsh language, eg 'Abercedi' and 'Aberkedy'.

Similarly, we have in general allowed other personal eccentricities of spelling and abbreviation to remain, as in the correspondence of the older members of the Benson family. It may afford some comfort to younger readers to discover that unorthodox spelling is not an entirely modern phenomenon!

BENSON FAMILY TREE

Thomas Benson
m. Joan Slee

Henry Roxby
m. Margaret Sanderson

Richard Meux
of Avery Hill
m. Mary Brougham
(aunt of Lord Brougham)

Thomas Starling
b. 1775
d. 1858
m.

Margaret
m. Revd. Th. Maude*

Elizabeth m.
b. 1773
d. 1836

Richard
b. 1768
d. 1824

Henry
(later Sir Henry
Meux, Bart)

Thomas

Henry
m. Augusta Bruce

Jane
m. Henry
Roxby Maude
(later Roxby)
son of Revd. Th. Maude*

Elizabeth

m. (1) Elizabeth Newberry
m. 1800

(2) Hannah Newbury
m. 1803

(3) Elizabeth Meux
b. 1793 d. 1859
m. 1816

Thomas
b. 1801
d. 1834
unmarried

Starling
b. 1808
d. 1879
unmarried

Sarah
Jane
b. 1812
d. 1854
unmarried

Emma
b. 1813
d. 1836
m. T. H. Usborne of
Gillwell House, Essex
1831

Florance John
b. 1815
d. 1853
unmarried

Henry Roxby
b. 1818
d. 1892
m. Mary Henrietta
Wightman

Richard Meux
b. 1825
d. 1915
unmarried

Starling Meux
b. July 20, 1846
d. 1933
m. (1) Elizabeth
Tawke
(2) Eleanor
Viscountess Gort

William Denman
b. Mar. 21, 1848
d. Feb. 1919
m. Jane Penrice of
Kilvrough, Gower

Alice Elizabeth
Frazer
b. June 16, 1850
d. 1922
unmarried

Mary Florance
b. Feb. 20, 1852
d. 1895
unmarried

Margaret
Elizabeth
b. Sept. 11, 1853
d. 1955
unmarried

Henry
Wightman
b. July 22, 1855
d. 1935
unmarried

Charlotte
Leonora
b. Dec. 3, 1857
d. 1915
unmarried

Richard Erle
b. Oct. 4, 1862
Killed in action
Sept. 1914
m. Janet Florence
Armour

Florance John
b. Jan. 3, 1865
d. 1945
unmarried

Richard
Arthur
Starling
(died of
dysentry
Boer War
1902)

John Penrice
b. 1877
Killed in action,
Aug. 1914
m. Laura Annette
Rideout

Gladys May
b. 1878
m. Prof. Bowhay

Wilfred Starling
b. 1880
d. 1898

Knightley
Henry
b. c.1885
m. Jocelyn Margaret

Florence
Marguerita Erle
m. Mervyn
Wingfield
1919
d. 1990

Mary Alice Erle
m. Lord Basing
1924
d. 1970

John Roxby
Erle
b. 1903

* denotes double reference to the Revd Th. Maude

Introduction

'Never, we believe,' wrote 'The Cambrian' of January 16 1857, 'in the previous history of Swansea has there been a ball on such a grand scale as that at our Assembly Rooms last evening.'

It was, according to the other contemporary newspaper, 'The Swansea and Glamorgan Herald', 'a brilliant gathering of rank, beauty and fashion of Swansea and neighbourhood.'

The event referred to was the annual Bachelors' Ball, hosted by the bachelors of the district, of whom the senior was Starling Benson. After welcoming the guests with 'a few appropriate remarks', he opened the dancing with Mrs H H Vivian, the wife of the leading industrialist in the area who was also one of the two MPs for Glamorgan.

By this time Starling Benson was forty-eight years old. Born at Dulwich on August 30 1808 to Thomas Starling Benson, a prosperous London merchant, and his second wife, Hannah (née Newberry), he had come to Swansea in 1830 to be responsible for his father's interests in the copper smelting business trading as Benson, Usborne and Company. He made his mark quickly on the municipal life of his new place of residence, being elected to the Town Council in December,1835, to represent the Upper Ward where his father's business interests mostly lay. By 1843, he had become Mayor of Swansea at the early age of thirty-five, one of the youngest Mayors in the town's history, although, before the 1832 Reform Act, Gabriel Powell the Younger could have laid claim to being Portreeve, largely through his father's influence, at an even earlier age.

About the same time as his election to the Town Council, Starling had become a member of the Swansea Harbour Trust, taking over as its Chairman in 1856 upon the resignation of another leading industrialist, Pascoe St Leger Grenfell, and steering its fortunes through a critical period in the development of Swansea as a port until his retirement in 1878.

The significance of Starling Benson's social and official progress can only be appreciated in the light of the hostility the young man had had to overcome in order to be fully accepted by a body of people who had all too good a reason to regard his father with a deep-seated suspicion.

Thomas Starling Benson's insistence on his pound of flesh in payment for the loss of part of his newly acquired Tyrllandwr Estate in order to form the New Cut necessary for the diversion of the River Tawe had made him one of the most unpopular men in Swansea.

In the words of 'an intelligent communication' received by the thrustful barrister and self-appointed guardian of the public interests, W H Smith of Hen

Dderwen, who quoted them in a letter to 'The Cambrian' of August 11 1838:

> ... it has ever been the bane of Swansea that her improvement has been left to parties who cared little for the public good, provided their private interests were attended to.

Although W H Smith was no more scathing in his criticism of Thomas Starling Benson than of the rest of the Harbour Trustees, whom he condemned for their dilatoriness, undoubtedly his words would have been taken by many of his readers to apply especially to T S Benson.

It must, therefore, have been difficult for his son not to be affected by the prejudice aroused by the family name during the late 1830s and early 40s, especially as his only Christian name was the same distinctive 'Starling' as was borne by his father as a middle name. There was to be no disguising his parentage for the earnest, rather retiring, young man who found himself drawn into a public controversy which he would probably have preferred to avoid.

Yet during this inflammatory period, Starling Benson continued to serve on both Town Council and Harbour Trust, as well as identifying himself fully with the social, cultural and philanthropic activities of his adopted town. His father's withdrawal to new pastures in Teddington in 1838 undoubtedly made it easier for his son to be appreciated for what he was in himself. He had already, during the time from the family's arrival in Swansea in 1830 to the unfortunate Tyrllandwr episode in 1838, become known for a quiet integrity in business matters linked with a strong zest for the lighter side of life, and had been able to draw on this personal reservoir of goodwill among those who knew him best even when his family was the target of public contumely.

The fact that Starling Benson never married may well have been the result of the double life thrust upon him from the time of his father's removal from Swansea, for, in addition to being fully immersed in the business affairs of his own company as well as local public life, he became increasingly the mainstay of his extended family with its ramifications stretching well out from its centre in Teddington Manor.

Before considering his contribution to the development of Swansea, it is necessary, therefore, to look at this family background to understand Starling Benson in the context of the many and sometimes conflicting domestic pressures behind the scenes which he combined, seemingly unobtrusively, with his ongoing role on the public stage.

Chapter I

Benson Background

There are still people in Swansea, mostly former employees of the Docks and Railways, in whom the name of Starling Benson evokes an instant reaction although he has been dead well over a hundred years. Perhaps it is his unusual name that has kept alive his memory, for little has been done officially to preserve it. What follows is an attempt to rectify that omission by showing that Starling Benson was not only an interesting figure in himself but also a catalyst for many of his contemporaries.

It is difficult, however, to evaluate Starling Benson's character and the impact he made on the Swansea of his day without knowing something of his family background with its somewhat complicated structure. He began his adult life in South Wales as very much the representative of his father and yet, throughout his dealings with his contemporaries, fortunately succeeded in remaining a personality to be reckoned with in his own right.

The family can be traced back to North Yorkshire. There the first Thomas Benson lived at Loftus Hill near Stavely. His son, also a Thomas, married a Mary Jackson, the youngest daughter of a prosperous bacon and butter factor who had been Sheriff of the County. Largely through her social pretensions, the feckless young couple had run through their resources and, as a result, the husband had to leave Yorkshire for London. There he obtained a 'trifling situation' at a guinea a week as a tide-waiter with the London Customs House. He found a place to live at the Hermitage, Wapping, where he was joined by his wife and youngest child, Thomas, Starling Benson's grandfather, the five other children having been parcelled out among friends and relatives in their native district of Stavely and its surroundings. The parents' links with those left behind became increasingly attenuated, although some contact must have been retained since 'Starling', the married name of Martha, the youngest but one, was to be adopted by future generations of the family.[1]

Thomas, the father, continued to work on the Thames until he eventually met his death by drowning. In the meantime, young Tom had gone to sea and later married, as his second wife, Joan Slee, whose family had sea-faring connections with the West of England.[2]

The son of this marriage was the Thomas Starling Benson whose connection with Swansea began in the 1820s. Like his paternal grandfather, several of his mother's relatives had also met death by drowning, a fact which may have

---

1 Unpublished Family Letters, Benson Collection, Swansea University College Archives (UCS/BC), Mrs Gilbertson to TSB, Oct 3 1825
2 *Ibid*

influenced him, with his strong instinct for self-preservation, to choose the life of an inland merchant rather than the more dangerous existence of a sailor.

It is interesting to note in passing that, about this time, there was a notorious smuggler named Thomas Benson, the MP for Barnstaple, who made Lundy Island in the Bristol Channel his rendezvous. One of his captains was apprehended by the King's men and hanged, whereupon the rest of the smugglers dispersed. Among the ships owned by Benson was 'The Nightingale Brig', the boatswain of which was one named James Bather. He, in 1761, published a pamphlet entitled 'The Life of James Bather', ostensibly to purge his conscience.[3]

It would be fascinating to imagine some family connection between the daring MP for Barnstaple and his namesake working for the Customs and Excise in the Port of London. Unfortunately there is no evidence for such a swashbuckling fantasy but, be that as it may, Thomas Benson of London certainly had West Country connections through his wife. This knowledge of ports on the Western seaboard may well have diverted the young Thomas Starling's thoughts to that area, particularly Bristol, as he pursued his business interests in conjunction with the Usbornes, his first partners in the import of copper in the early part of the nineteenth century.

The Drapers' Company Records give details of a somewhat varied preparation for T S Benson's introduction to the non-ferrous metal industry. He had been apprenticed on August 11 1790 to John Brett, a Camberwell surveyor, and freed on September 26 1797 by John Slee (possibly a relative) a brandy merchant in Southwark, although earlier, at the time when the young Benson was transferred to him, he had been described as a barber. By 1801, Thomas Starling had himself taken on an apprentice. That was in the capacity of an iron merchant; by 1809, he had become, according to the Records, a timber merchant, and from 1821 on, a copper smelter.[4]

He had been admitted to Livery in the Drapers' Company in 1806. Through his contacts there he would have known men already involved in the industrial development of South Wales. John Smith, the son-in-law of Chauncey Townsend and inheritor of a share in mineral leases in Llansamlet and Llanelli, had been clerk to the Company of Drapers as well as solicitor to the East India Company. Although he had died in 1797, nine years before T S Benson's association with the Company, it is not hard to imagine that talk of the industrial potential of South Wales might well have fired the ambitions of his fellow members of the Drapers' Hall.

Thomas Starling Benson was married three times. His first wife, née Elizabeth Newberry, died after less than three years of marriage, leaving her husband with two young children, Thomas and Elizabeth. The little girl died soon after her mother. Left alone with Thomas, the young father remedied his difficult situation by marrying his dead wife's sister, Hannah, a course not yet forbidden by legislation.

---

3 James Bather, Full and Faithful Account of the Life of James Bather, late Boatswain of the Nightingale Brig, Thomas Benson Esq, Owner - 1751; Biographical Tracts (London; printed for Griffiths, Paternoster Row, 1754)

4 Drapers' Company Records from Drapers' Hall, London, ref. no. 27155

Elizabeth and Hannah were the daughters of William Newberry, a London brewer, in whose firm Thomas Starling Benson had become a partner. At first Hannah seemed even less fortunate in her childbearing than her sister. She had lost three children in infancy before the birth of Starling on August 30 1808, and was to lose yet another after him. There was therefore quite a gap between Starling and his half-brother Thomas who, by the time Starling was ready for Eton, was already in the Light Dragoons, a difference in age highlighted by the fact that, during Starling's first term in Eton, his master was Thomas's friend and contemporary, Tom Belcher.[5]

Although born at Dulwich, Starling was, like the earlier members of his family, christened at St John's, Southwark. Beyond that entry in the family Bible there is little record of young Starling's early days, with the exception of one recollection mentioned by his half-brother, Henry Roxby, when he was serving in the 17th Lancers in India at the time of the Indian Mutiny. In one of his letters home to his mother Henry wrote:

> I have just got a new pay master appointed to the Regiment of the name of Belcher - he says he remembers when a little boy going to drink tea with Starling Benson at Denmark Hill who was then a little boy in petticoats - his name is George. I always thought there had been a Tom Belcher who was Tom's friend - he says he does not know any one of that name? - do you remember him?[6]

In 1807, the year before Starling's birth, Thomas Starling Benson had been appointed Deputy Lieutenant of Surrey, and in 1812, he became High Sheriff of the County. The Drapers' Company Records give his address between 1805 and 1813 as Tooley Street, close to London Bridge, but growing affluence had made him look elsewhere for a residence in more secluded surroundings. Just prior to his becoming High Sheriff, he had, in 1811, in accordance with a practice common among the gentry of his day, rented, rather than purchased, an impressive mansion standing in its own grounds on Denmark Hill.

This was Champion Lodge, belonging to Claude de Crespigny. Here in 1804, the year before he was given a baronetcy, Mr and Mrs de Crespigny had entertained the Prince of Wales at a *fête champêtre* in the grounds of their home. It was obviously the sort of house T S Benson required for his growing family, and he was happy to remain there until Claude de Crespigny signified his desire to resume occupation, whereupon, in 1821, the Bensons moved to Bolton House, Russell Square, and later, in 1823, to Sandersted Court near Croydon.

Starling's early years at Champion Lodge must have been a pleasant time as he enjoyed the privilege of being the son of a well-to-do and generally respected merchant with an established position in county society. Undoubtedly those early years coloured many of his later attitudes, lending him the calm confidence which marked his relations even with the most tiresome of his contemporaries.

5   Unpublished Family Letters in the possession of Col. J R E Benson (JREB), Dorchester, EMB to Nicholas Newberry, Ghent, June 20 1821
6   UCS/BC, HRB to EMB from India, April 24 1859

During the remaining years at Denmark Hill three other children were born to Hannah Benson, Sarah Jane, on July 9 1812, Emma, on July 29 1813, and Florance John, on March 19 1815. Mrs Benson did not long survive the birth of her youngest child, and the bereaved husband was left once more with a family of motherless children. Fortunately he found a young woman, almost half his age, who was prepared to accept this heavy responsibility and who, by her capacity for love and sympathy, was able, despite her comparative youth, to overcome much of the bitterness of her stepchildren's loss. Elizabeth Meux was twenty-three at the time of her marriage, and the bridegroom forty-one, only a few years younger than her mother.

Elizabeth was the only child of the ill-fated eldest son of Richard Meux, the founder of the Griffin Brewery, Liquor Pond Street, London. The family had originated in the Isle of Wight, and in 1641 John Meux had been made a baronet, although the title became extinct within two generations in 1705. The Meuxes of Liquor Pond Street and Avery or 'Aviary' Hill, as it was spelt in family correspondence, had descended from a younger branch of the family, headed by a Bartholomew Meux who had married into the family of Sir Thomas Moulson, an Alderman of London with a seat at Theobald or Tibald's Park, Hertfordshire, later the home of Elizabeth's uncle, Sir Henry Meux.

Richard Meux's three sons were all involved in the family brewery, but not long after the father had gone into semi-retirement, his eldest son, also named Richard, suffered a severe mental breakdown, from which he never recovered.[7] This may have been partly the result of stress caused by infighting over the conduct of the business. Nevertheless, in spite of personal differences, the two remaining brothers continued to feel concern for Richard's wife and daughter - especially Thomas, the younger brother, whose strong evangelical fervour, which developed comparatively late in his life, made him a kindred spirit of his sister-in-law.

Thomas's new-found piety tended, on the other hand, to alienate him from his second brother, the more worldly Henry. The latter was, in 1831, to become a baronet through the good offices of his cousin, the dynamic Whig statesman, Lord Brougham. Sir Henry's lifestyle was henceforth on a scale of luxury which the more ascetic Thomas had now repudiated.

It would be interesting to know how Thomas Starling Benson first met the young Elizabeth Meux. It might have been through her uncles whose brewery connection would have brought them into touch with the Newberry family or, even more likely, through her maternal grandfather, Henry Roxby, who was himself a member of the Drapers' Company and whose brother-in-law, Sir James Sanderson, a former Lord Mayor of London, would, as a Southwark hop merchant, be known to both Meux and Newberry families.

Soon after his last marriage, stimulated undoubtedly by his new wife's prestigious connections, the ambitious London merchant obviously felt it was time to find some titled connections of his own. One of his enquiries was addressed to a relative, a Mrs Gilbertson of Bath, who passed on to him the information we have already seen about his Benson forebears. This result must

7 Peter Mathias, The Brewing Industry in England, 1700-1830 (Cambridge, 1959) p 61; *cf* p 96

4

Drawn by B. DelaCour.

Engraved by S.W. Reynolds.
Engraver to the King

THOˢ STARLING · BENSON. ESQʳ

1   Thomas Starling Benson with the Benson Coat of Arms   Courtesy of JREB

have been somewhat disappointing. He was unable to prove, as he had hoped, any family connection between his grandfather and Robert Benson, Lord Bingley.[8] Nevertheless, by his own enquiries in the areas of Stavely, Knaresborough and York itself, he was able to establish a claim to armorial bearings, granted on September 4 1828. This family crest Starling later used when, in 1843, he became Mayor of Swansea.

Thomas Starling's third marriage proved a very happy one despite the difference in age between him and his wife. The feelings of her new family towards their young stepmother are reflected in a fragment of a poem in Starling's writing on the back of an unfinished letter to his business partner, William Edmond Logan, obviously composed soon after his sister Emma's early death in childbirth in 1836:

> Reverting to thy childhood's early day,
> The first commencement of thy brief career,
> We see a helpless infant ...
> ... a youthful mother on her bier.
> God heard the mother's prayers, another came
> Who took the trembling infant to her breast
> Became a mother to the helpless child ... [9]

Elizabeth Benson was soon to have children of her own but there was again the sorrow caused by deaths in infancy, especially the loss of her two little daughters, Margaret Sanderson and Elizabeth Meux. Her first-born son, Richard Henry, died at ten months, but within six months of his death on May 30 1818, she gave birth to a second son, Henry Roxby, named after her mother's father. Seven years later, shortly after the death of her own tragic and much-loved father, another son was born, to be named after him, Richard Meux.

In all her voluminous correspondence over the years there was never any difference in the warmth with which Elizabeth Benson referred to her five step-children and her own two sons. Thomas's recurrent absences from his Army duties on health grounds helped to keep him in close contact with the rest of the family. His stepmother explained to his uncle, Nicholas Newberry, in a letter of June 1821, her reasons for agreeing to Thomas's being her baby daughter's Godfather:

> He is so affectionate of late to his younger Brothers and Sisters & everything that cements affection in a large Family is desirable, & the difference between their ages makes it very proper.[10]

By this time Starling had started at Eton, and in the same letter, Elizabeth Benson went on to say:

> Starling I suppose you know is gone to Eton, which he is delighted with, he is in the middle of the fourth year, which is considered very

8 UCS/BC, TSB to Henry Maude, April 14 1827
9 JREB, fragment on a discarded envelope to W E Logan, no date
10 JREB, EMB to Nicholas Newberry, June 20 1821

high for his age, a young Belcher is his master, so you may suppose he is not very much fagged, the latter being a very amiable young man and Tom's old schoolfellow. They are under a Tutor's care, which is much better than under a Dames *(sic)*.[11]

His father was obviously missing him as he had written from Brighton on July 10 of that same year to find out when Starling's holidays would begin, and also to find out if any of the boys were coming home for the Coronation of George IV.

Give my compliments to Mr Knape and ask him if you can have permission to come home the day before the Coronation. You can if necessary return again the day after.[12]

He explained that, had he not been so busy, he would have been down to see Starling at Eton, and it was only indisposition that had kept Tom from going down to see his brother and his friend Belcher.

This was apparently not the first time for Starling to be away from home. His younger sister, Emma, wrote home in 1818 from Tunbridge Wells where she and her sister and brother, Sarah and Florance John, were staying with their governess and nurse in a cottage rented by their parents. She expressed the hope that 'Brother Starling will be home when we return and that he will breakfast, dine and drink tea with us.'[13]

There is little to show that Starling distinguished himself at Eton. The School Lists for 1791 - 1850, compiled by a master named Stapylton, give, for 1823, simply his name, form (Lower Division of the Vth Form) and address. Nothing has been added about his future career, as was the practice with those who had excelled in their chosen professions. After his address, given as North Cray Place, there is a question mark, as though confirmation were required for future reference.[14] North Cray was again given as his address when, following in his father's footsteps, he was admitted to Livery in the Drapers' Company on November 5 1829, testimony being given by his father and Jacob Wrench, gent. of North Cray.[15]

The question of Starling's future now loomed large. There seems to have been no question of his following Tom into the Army. That he had had nascent literary leanings is suggested by a satirical short story about a wealthy Countess of Charlesberg written in a notebook during a stay in Fribourg in Switzerland in September 1828. He shared too something of the artistic skill which was to become so highly developed later on in his half-brother, Henry. In another copybook, there are mischievous drawings of family scenes with monkeys' faces on human bodies, suggesting a wry sense of humour as he viewed his surroundings.

Such escape from reality soon yielded to the sterner business in hand. In that same copybook exercises in chemistry are interspersed with finely sketched

11 *Ibid*
12 JREB, TSB to SB at Eton, July 10 1821
13 JREB, Emma Benson to EMB, July 22 1818
14 Eton School Lists, 1791-1850, compiled Stapylton (British Museum)
15 Draper Company Records, Ref. 27155

2 Starling at 13

3 Monkeys: a small music party
Courtesy of JREB

4 Sketch of coal drops and specimen of Starling's handwriting
Courtesy of JREB

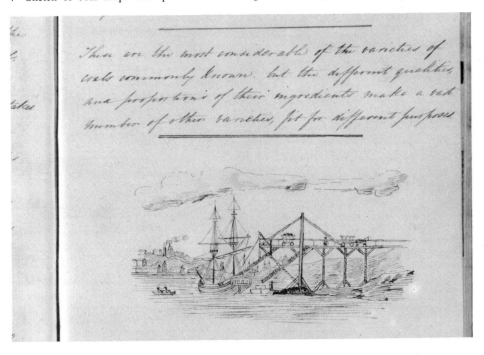

views of ships, presumably on the Tawe, with copper works in the background. Henceforth Starling was to be immersed in the world of industry.

During the 1820s, Mrs Meux's indifferent health had meant that her daughter's family spent ever longer periods at her home at North Cray Place in Kent. The tragedy of her husband's illness had left her permanently scarred and in spite of, or sometimes even because of, her strong religious faith, the victim of severe nervous tension. The bond between mother and daughter, often expressed in terms of intense endearment, was exceptionally close though never exclusively so. Mrs Meux's affections had been consistently extended to Elizabeth's stepchildren as well her own grandchildren.

For Starling she had a particular tenderness, and when it was proposed that he should move to Glamorganshire as his father's representative in the copper smelting venture which Thomas Starling was undertaking with his business associate, Henry Usborne, Mrs Meux was anxious to be near him, her thoughts focussing on Swansea as a rather more permanent home than her son-in-law had envisaged.

By Christmas 1830, the whole Benson family, including Mrs Meux, had taken up residence at Sketty Park, a Swansea mansion let to them by Sir John Morris. Mrs Meux's niece, yet another Elizabeth, Thomas Meux's daughter, was writing from Bloomsbury Square to wish them well in their new home and send them the season's greetings:

> I hope dearest Aunt Meux continues to derive benefit from her new abode & that she has lost the neuralgic affection in her face - I cannot say it has left me. Have you had any snow - we have had it here two or three times & this morning it laid (*sic*) on the ground but is now nearly melted and the sun shining ... I conclude with united kindest love to your family circle & every good wish at this happy Season. May each return of it find us more prepared for the 2nd Advent wh. will truly be a most blessed period.[16]

Mrs Meux remained at Sketty Park with Starling, Dicky, his younger half-brother, and her friend, Miss Salmon, after the rest of the family had returned to London but she found it difficult to settle in what was, at the best, temporary accommodation. By the middle of 1831 she obviously felt the time was ripe to open discussion about her acquiring a more permanent residence, either in Swansea or elsewhere. In June of that year she wrote from Sketty Park in reply to a letter from her son-in-law at his London office in New Broad Street.

> My dear Sir,
> I receiv'd your kind letter yesterday for which I return you my thanks tho' really I find it very difficult to answer its contents to my own satisfaction - or perhaps to yours - but I will sincerely state my opinion. I think with you, under all the circumstances, perhaps North Cray is on too large Scale, for my state of health makes it expedient for my comfort - and probably, under divine Providence! for my life -

16 JREB, Miss Elizabeth Meux of London to EMB, Dec 1830

that I should at least be in a mild and salubrious Climate near the Sea for six Months in the Year.[17]

She was quite ready to leave North Cray permanently, even though it would possibly mean seeing her daughter less frequently if she herself stayed most of her time in Swansea to be near Starling. The image of Swansea as a fashionable seaside resort, the Brighton of Wales, had not yet been completely obliterated by the vision of blazing copper furnaces belching forth obnoxious fumes, but even so, for this delicate woman in her late fifties to contemplate moving to comparatively unknown territory speaks volumes for the strong attachment which existed between her and her step-grandson. She obviously still considered him to be sufficiently vulnerable to need her care and protection as he took up his new position of responsibility in his father's South Wales business interests.

How long Mrs Meux would stay at Sketty Park was still in the balance and so it was now necessary to put her point of view on the question of having 'two establishments':

> ... the point to be determin'd is whether you prefer or find it most convenient to have a House in the Regents Park or London and have some Place here; or whether you prefer some situation in a dry healthy Air and cheerful situation within ten miles of London, and for me to go to Hastings, D.V., for the six Winter months.
>
> Since we have been here, Mr & Mrs Vivian and their family have been two or three times to London. At Hastings many families resid'd there for the winter months, the gentlemen going to Town on business occasionally. Now, with regard to your being here, Starling must reside here if he continues in the business, so that, if you preferr'd this Place and the Regents Park, you and the family might make it very easy by coming twice only a year, with the interval of three or four Months between, and one or two remain with Starling and me, and so, me go up once a year when I can. But all of this I leave entirely to your arrangement, praying God to direct you for the best! I have no doubt, if circumstance permit, I shall be content.[18]

She could not resist trying to tip the balance in favour of Swansea:

> This Place looks more lovely every day! Sir John Morris has no intention of selling it and is expect'd in Swansea next week, but, I dare

---

17   UCS/BC, Mrs Elizabeth Meux to TSB, June 1 1831
18   *Ibid*

say, he would lett *(sic)* it for a year or two if you wish'd it. The Brynn *(sic)* is also to lett next September, a very shelter'd, nice situation but a Mr Eaton has requested the first refusal. We went to see Woodlands Castle yesterday, a very beautiful situation and shelter'd - and the only Room I went into, the Library, delightful. Miss Salmon went all over - and lik'd it much, but not more than this (i.e. Sketty Park).[19]

Woodlands Castle had been the home of General George Warde, becoming known later, in 1860, as Clyne Castle, the bachelor residence of William Graham Vivian, and finally, in 1965, a University Hall of Residence.

As it happened, Sir John Morris was prepared to let Sketty Park for more than a year or two, and consequently the rest of the family took up residence there with Mrs Meux. Nevertheless, Mrs Meux and her son-in-law were still looking for a suitable property to purchase in the area.

The wily Benson took his time but eventually, in 1834, he decided on an estate on the eastern bank of the River Tawe. Tyrllandwr was perhaps hardly the home Mrs Meux had dreamed of when she had visited Woodlands Castle although it was advertised in 'The Cambrian' of May 22 1830 as 'an eligible residence for a genteel family' with 'five best bedrooms and three servants' ditto'.[20]

At that time it had been to let; and later, after it had been bought on behalf of Mrs Meux with her money, it was re-advertised in October 1834 as being again to let.[21] Obviously the Bensons had no intention of moving in while they could continue to rent the superior accommodation of Sketty Park. The Tyrllandwr estate had been secured primarily as a commercial venture although to the pious Uncle Thomas Meux, 'the late purchase of that very important portion of land' was seen as 'God's reward to the Benson family' for Elizabeth's good works.[22] It was probably only Thomas Starling and his son who knew the full significance of the transaction, both for their own family fortunes and for the future development of Swansea.

Mrs Meux lived less than two years after the completion of the sale. In her long and detailed will of January 30 1835, the property 'lately purchased of the Reverend Henry Sharpe Pocklington', as well as all her other real estate, was entailed upon her daughter and after her death, upon 'all the children of my said daughter living at my decease.'[23]

The loss of Elizabeth's mother on April 25 1836, followed a month later by the death in childbirth of Starling's younger sister, Emma Usborne, at the early age of twenty-two, may well have had an unsettling effect on the older Bensons. In addition, their tenure of the Tyrllandwr estate produced problems which we shall later consider in much more detail. By the early summer of 1838 they had left Sketty Park and soon afterwards had settled in the Manor House at Teddington

19 *Ibid*
20 Cambrian (C) May 22 1830, *cf* Aug 9 1833
21 C Oct 4 1834; also May 14 1835 & Sept 19 1835
22 JREB, Thomas Meux to Mrs Elizabeth Meux, c 1834
23 Last Will & Testament of Elizabeth Meux, 'proved at London', June 8 1836

5   Sketty Park (rear) based on a photograph by Mr W C Rogers   DMB

which was to be their home for the rest of Thomas Starling Benson's life.
   Starling, on the other hand, was to spend the rest of his life in the Swansea area, firmly pursuing his own interests as well as those of his father's business, and generally contributing to the life of his adopted home.

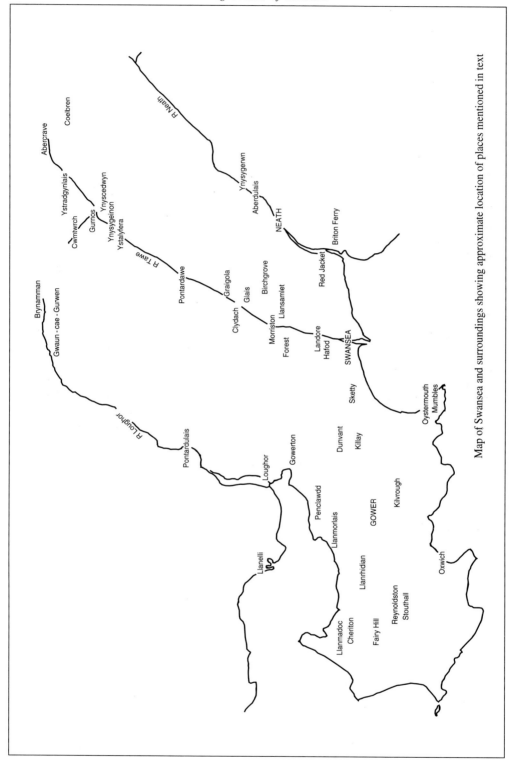

Map of Swansea and surroundings showing approximate location of places mentioned in text

Chapter II

Copper and Coal

Starling Benson's initiation into the commercial life of South Wales was through the copper trade, but it did not take him or his father long to realise that prosperity in that field was closely linked with the coal industry. One important reason for the growth of the coal trade in the Swansea area was the demand for fuel from the increasing number of copper works then being established in the vicinity. Copper-smelting depended largely on imported ores and cheap coal and had necessarily to be located where the coalfields were easily accessible to the sea. The ore was brought by ship from Anglesey, Cornwall and Ireland, though soon there were sources overseas, notably in Cuba. For the return journey to Cornwall, cheap local coal, exempted from coastal duties, would be piled into the hold, thus giving both Neath and Swansea an advantage over other districts.[1] This advantage could only be fully exploited by an improvement of the harbour, and plans for such an improvement were being discussed as early as 1827.

Both father and son knew enough of foreign trade to realise that Swansea's maritime position held possibilities which needed to be developed. Their immediate concern was with the future of their own copper smelting business at the Forest Works situated on the banks of the Tawe between Landore and Morriston. To have the river made navigable as high up as their works would have far-reaching effects upon the prosperity of their enterprise; this was a part of a plan being discussed in the early 1830s.

The first copper smelting works had been established on the banks of the River Tawe by Dr Lane and his relative, John Pollard, who, like many of the later entrepreneurs, had Cornish connections. They set up the 'Llangavelach Works' (sic) at Landore on ground subsequently covered by the Turnpike Road to Neath. In 1726, the time of the South Sea Bubble, their business failed and their works went into the receivership of Robert Morris who later, with Thomas Lockwood and Edward Gibbon, grandfather of the historian, purchased them, trading as Lockwood, Morris and Co.[2]

At first, the new firm bought their coal from Thomas Popkin, a man who drove a hard bargain, but before long, to escape his stranglehold and have easier access to coal, they left the 'Llangavelach Works' and moved upriver, near the Morris mine in Trewyddfa where ample supplies were available. By 1748 they were well on the way with the construction of the new Forest Works. In that year Joseph Harris, the Assay Officer of the Royal Mint and a brother of the famous Welsh evangelist, Hywel Harris, visited the works and in his testimony helped to give

1 A H John, 'Glamorgan 1700 - 1750', The Glamorgan County History Vol V, p 24
2 A H John, Industrial Development of South Wales, 1750 - 1850, (Cardiff; University of Wales Press, 1950) p 30

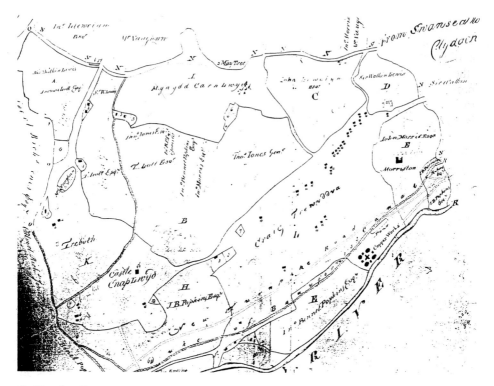

6   Beaufort Estate Map 1761 showing Copper Works at Forest   D/D Beau E/1, WGRO

a clearer picture of what was planned.[3] He said that the new works were circular
in design, but of the four furnace buildings commissioned, so far only one had
been completed. The rest of the work was later carried out with, eventually, the
addition of a battery mill and by 1761, the pioneer Llangyfelach works were no
longer in commission. The two views of the Forest Works, looking downstream
(1792), and looking upstream (1794) show the works situated on both banks of
the river and fully operating.[4]

The 1761 Beaufort Estate map of Trewyddfa[5] corresponds to some extent with
the description given much later in a letter from a Mr William Edmond of Clase
to George Grant Francis. He recalled that, in 1834, the works had consisted of
four large circular constructions. On the outside of the circular walls had been
fireplaces, with the furnaces within them arranged in such a way that whatever
was going on was concealed from view. In the centre of the four circular houses
had been an octagonal-shaped Refinery. A public road 'anciently went under an
arch at the Refinery and crossed the river at the Hen Bont ... '[6]

3   Peter Wakelin, 'The Founding of the Forest Copper Works', SWWIAS Bulletin 32, p 4
4   J W Smith, Watercolour, 1792, NMW; Thomas Rothwell, Views of Swansea, 1794, SM
5   D/D Beau E/1 No. 27, WGRO
6   G G Francis, The Smelting of Copper in the Swansea District of South Wales (Charing Cross; Willis &
     Sotheram, 1867) p 80

The works described above were transferred in 1793 to Harford's Bristol Brass Wire Company. Their occupancy is noted in a document dated 1833,[7] but was earlier referred to in a contemporary letter from William Padley to his nephew: 'the Morris Copper works are sold to the Bristol Brass Wire Co... and' (they, presumably Morris) 'are building a new works at Landore'.[8] In 1813, according to J G Woods, there were 'adjoining rolling mills where a great deal of copper is rolled for the use of the navy'.[9]

This occupation of the premises (probably continuous) can be traced up until 1826. Between 1824 and 1826 Richard Janion Nevill, originally from Birmingham but by this time deeply involved in the industrial development of Llanelli, was conducting an interesting correspondence with both Morris & Lockwood and Harford's. He made an agreement with Morris & Lockwood which enabled him to select copper slag from the working of the Forest Copper Works on the east side of the Tawe and on part of Lower Forest Farm adjacent to Lower Forest Bridge. It appears that the slag banks on the eastern side of the river still belonged to that firm. Nevill also purchased slag from Harford's on the western side of the river and had an agreement with them to use some of their furnaces for resmelting the copper deposits from the slag selected until December 31 1825. The new works at Landore were likewise being used for re-smelting.[10]

By September 13 1825 Nevill had heard that 'a gentleman' had been inspecting Harford's works the previous day on behalf of would-be purchasers. He was quick to respond to this news, being curious to discover their names and intentions. Since he was engaged in using the furnaces, he was anxious to know when they would be required as he would need time to remove 'the Bottom' from them. The 'Bottom' contained the deposits of copper after smelting had taken place.[11]

The prospective buyer of the works in 1825 was a Richard Edmonds who, in conjunction with his solicitor and agent, John Hodgson, completed the purchase on March 1 1826.[12] Edmonds had bought 'the Forest Copper Works, the Slag Banks and the Ground' and had also contracted an agreement for the Lower Forest Farm for the remainder of the term of which 18 years were unexpired - ie until 1844. On April 4 1826 a contract was signed by Edmonds and Nevill[13] whereby Nevill was allowed to use the one building he already occupied and the furnaces in it, three of the calciners and the wharf and blacksmith's shop until at least September 25 1826. He also had the right to select slags on the north or Morriston side until March 25 1828 and slags on the east side until March 25 1836.

Another industrialist interested in the processing of slag was Nicholas Troughton. His experience as a lieutenant in the Navy had undoubtedly made him aware of the importance of copper to shipping. On entering civilian life,

7 D/D SB 12/6. The source of all documents in this collection is WGRO
8 W H Jones, History of the Port of Swansea (Carmarthen; Spurrell & Son, 1922) p 353
9 J G Woods, The Principal Rivers of Wales, 1814
10 Nevill Correspondence, 1025 (13 Sept 1824), 1027 (22 Feb 1825), 171 (13 Sept 1825), NLW
11 *Op cit*, 171 (13 Sept 1825), 243 (Oct 12 1826)
12 D/D SB 12/6
13 Nevill, *op cit*, 1028 (April 8 1826), NLW

Troughton had developed a process for the treatment of slag which he in turn tried out at the Forest Works. Grant Francis in his account of copper smelting in Swansea states, somewhat vaguely, that, after the Harford epoch, 'Forest came into the hands of a Mr Troughton - a gentleman of some chemical and mechanical skill' who had been occupied in crushing, mixing and re-smelting slag.[14] The evidence indicates, however, that Nicholas Troughton's experimentation was carried on in close association with Edmonds and Hodgson. His experiments were concerned not only with the processing of copper slag but also with the production of metallic cement for which he was granted a patent in 1832.[15]

It is interesting to note that, in 1831, at a vital stage in the early negotiations for floating the river in order to provide Swansea with improved harbour accommodation, Troughton was one of those invited to represent the local copper interests.[16]

The occupancy by Edmonds was short-lived as, on May 11 1827, the Forest Works had been purchased by the firm of Usborne & Benson.[17] A third member of the partnership was Aristides Franklin Mornay who, like Troughton, was experimenting in the processing of copper slag, and on September 27 of that year he was granted a patent for 'smelting slag'.[18]

About 1828, according to W E Logan's biographer, Bernard Harrington, 'the inventor of a process for extracting copper from slag (discovered in Wales but abandoned as useless) gave the secret for a consideration to a certain gentleman who soon bought up, at very little cost, millions of tons of slag and began smelting operations in the neighbourhood of Swansea.'[19] The inventor was probably Mornay; the 'gentleman', a representative of the new owners, possibly one of the Bensons. Between May 1827 and July 1829 the Company had certainly made agreements to purchase slag from neighbouring copper smelters, Freeman & Copper Co., Fox, Williams, Foster & Co. and, further afield, to lease premises and slag at Melincryddan, Neath. An agreement was also made with C H Smith for the use of his canal to transport the slag from White Rock.[20]

Mornay's involvement with Usborne & Benson, however, ceased on April 25 1828. He had invested £1050 in the business and received, on his departure, £800 for his share in the Company including his patent, the other two partners accepting responsibility for the payment of three outstanding bills of exchange for a total of £4500.[21]

Troughton's connection with the firm continued. His latest attempts at rolling instead of stamping the copper slag had been tried out at Clydach. Now other sites were being considered. William Kirkhouse, the prominent engineer, had been consulted early in 1830 and reported the trials to his employer, George

14 G G Francis, *Op cit*, p 80
15 D/D SB 12/8
16 SHT Minute Book 1825-35, PRO RAIL 877/5, April 11 1831
17 D/D SB 12/6
18 D/D SB 12/8
19 B J Harrington, The Life of Sir William E Logan, Kt, Ll D, FRS, FGS (Montreal; 1883) p 52
20 D/D SB 12/8
21 D/D SB 12/6

Tennant.[22] By this time Usborne & Benson had set up an engine at a new site at Red Jacket, having leased the area of Truman's Hole in Briton Ferry near the Tennant Canal in September 1829.[23] Here also they intended to place rolls. Kirkhouse expected the engine to start on May 31 and he proposed to ask 'Mr Houghton' to bring down a barge load of Blaenhonddan coal for it.[24]

T S Benson hoped shortly to acquire the Tennant Works at Ynysygerwn near Aberdulais, yet another site for the firm's new project. Kirkhouse considered it would be 'an excellent situation for them to bring the Melincryddan slag to be rolled likewise the Mines Royall *(sic)* if the rolling will answer better than stamping'. He had taken Troughton to look at the Ynysygerwn Works, by now badly run down. From the Tennant-Kirkhouse point of view, the whole affair had to be discreetly handled, and Kirkhouse was most anxious for Mr Tennant not to appear to know what was going on if he was approached about the matter.[25]

A month later, Kirkhouse was able to report that everything had been fixed. All his recent efforts had been concentrated on bringing Ynysygerwn up to standard for the Benson firm to try out their experiment there. He wrote to Mr Tennant to explain this: 'I thought it was of more importance to you to get rid of that old ruin than anything else I could have done for you.'[26] The lease of Ynysygerwn mills was signed on September 16 1830 by George Tennant, Henry Usborne, Thomas Starling Benson, Hart Logan and James Dyke.[27]

The creation of an industrial dynasty, like that of the leading copper smelters in the area, the Vivians, was very much the ambition of the successful businessmen of the day. To achieve this in the interests of Starling and possibly his younger sons may well have been in T S Benson's mind when he had set his face towards South Wales in 1826. To consolidate his enterprise he was glad to enlist, towards the end of the decade, the support of the London business man, Hart Logan.

The Logan family originated in Stirlingshire but had emigrated to Canada. There Hart carried on a prosperous importing business, frequently returning to Britain where he later resettled. He now became involved in a number of highly lucrative enterprises. In 1817, his nephew, the young William Edmond Logan, broke off his course at Edinburgh University to join his uncle in his large London counting house at 44 Cross Street, Finsbury Square, where he remained for ten years, freeing Hart Logan to lead the life of a country gentleman at his home in Kentwell, Suffolk.

Early in 1819, there had been a connection between Hart Logan and Henry Usborne when Logan's nephew was despatched to Ireland 'to superintend the shipment of some provisions on account of a contract which my uncle, conjointly with Mr Stewart and Mr Usborne, has had with Government.'[28] Mr Stewart was

22 Kirkhouse Correspondence, Jordan Collection, MS 466, April 20 1830, WGRO
23 D/DT 285, Sept 15 1829, WGRO
24 Kirkhouse, *op cit*, MS 466, May 30 1830
25 *Op cit*, MS 466, April 20 1830, WGRO
26 *Op cit*, MS 466, May 30 1830, WGRO
27 D/D SB 12/8
28 Harrington, *op cit*, p 20

a neighbour in Finsbury Square who had married young Logan's sister, Agnes.

Some time after Usborne, Benson & Co. took over the Forest Works, another nephew of Hart Logan's, William Logan Edmond, was employed in a supervisory capacity. The Edmonds formed one branch of the Logan family and there is a possibility that the Richard Edmond(s) mentioned earlier might also have been related. William Edmond was joined in the spring of 1831 by his cousin, William Edmond Logan, later to become the distinguished geologist. Sent to the Forest Works as his uncle's personal representative, W E Logan was initially in charge of the accounts, but such was his enthusiasm that before long he was concerning himself with the full process of copper smelting as well as investigating the essentials of coal mining.

For the greater part, Hart Logan's interest was purely financial. He supplied a 'substantial part of the capital, in fact £10,000, in return for which he acquired an eighth-share in the business.' In addition, in the terms of his co-partnership, he reserved the right of giving his nephew part of his own share. The young man, however, cannily preferred to accept a salary - preferably £1000, though he 'would settle for less.'

William Logan's reasoning was that he had nothing to lose and, being unwilling to undertake the responsibility of a partnership, he preferred not to accept a share until he had become acquainted with the business and was able to satisfy himself 'from experience and personal observation that it is of the profitable nature his friends represent'. If 'when the business is ultimately proved to be so profitable, those concerned will not give me a share...I cannot help it; but I hope to make myself so useful that they will not refuse.'

He obviously had no illusions about the toughness of the people with whom he would be dealing. He now found himself working in the counting house of the Forest Works from 6 or 7 in the morning until midnight in order to establish 'a proper and regular system of accounts'. Conditions were obviously rough. Soon after his arrival there he wrote to his brother, Henry, asking for his old clothes. 'This will be a famous place to wear them out at ... a sin and a shame to wear anything else.' He also wanted his scientific books, especially of chemistry and mechanics.

At first it seemed a confined and isolated existence. 'Here I am out of the world altogether and attending to nothing else but the making of copper and digging of coal from morning to night.' As an outlet for his stifled talents he turned to making a detailed study of the geological structure of the coalfield of which the firm's mines formed a part, a work so accurate and far-reaching that it was adopted by Sir Henry de la Beche as part of his Government-authorised survey.

By the spring of 1833 Logan was so involved in this research that he very much resented having to lose valuable 'working' time (more than likely, time he wanted for his geological investigations). Reluctantly he had had to go to London to attend to affairs concerning the Copper Company. There he became frustrated while waiting 'until the lawyers have brought to a conclusion the arrangement that is on foot to push Mr … out of the Forest Copper company'.[29]

A deed of March 30 1833 confirmed the dissolution of the Company, with Henry Usborne being paid £4000 with interest for relinquishing his 3/8th share.[30] The new Company, formed on April 20 1833, was known as Benson, Logan & Co., with T S Benson transferring part of his shareholding to Starling, and Hart Logan part of his to his nephews, William and Henry Logan.[31]

This change in management coincided with the proposed modernisation of the works. The following year, 1834, the old buildings were replaced by new structures. William (Logan) Edmond had been asked to be present at the demolition and later in 1867 provided Grant Francis with information about the removal.[32] The need for development may well have been the result of the growing involvement of the younger generation.

Some three years earlier, Starling Benson had entered the business as his father's representative. Still in his early twenties, he probably had much to learn about industry, and must have welcomed the contact with another young man already versed in the ways of commerce. Their mutual interest in geology, as well as in the developing cultural life of Swansea, brought them together outside as well as at the Forest Works. Possibly, as Logan was at this time living in Cambrian Place without being himself a ratepayer, he may even have been sharing the house which Starling had taken there in 1833.[33]

In April 1838 tragedy struck the Logan family with the deaths of both Hart Logan and his nephew Henry. This brought about a change in the constitution of the Company. W E Logan now held all the Logan shares, amounting to 21/48ths, while Starling held the remaining 27/48ths, his father having transferred his own holding 'in natural love and affection to his son'.[34]

Within a few years Logan was to relinquish an active part in the conduct of the Company. Through his investigations into the geological structure of the South Wales coalfield, he had laid the foundation for the career to which he naturally aspired. By 1840, he had gone on a visit to Canada. Shortly afterwards, upon the recommendation of de la Beche and other eminent geologists, he was appointed as the first Director of the Geological Survey of Canada, and in August 1842 he left to embark on his new career.[35] As a result Logan was less actively involved with the Company. The Gower family, however, related to Logan through the marriage of his sister Elizabeth to Abel Lewes Gower, played a significant part in the affairs of Benson, Logan & Co., as we shall see in a later chapter.

By 1831, when Logan had joined Starling at the Forest Works, it was already becoming apparent that they needed to extend their supplies of coal if they were to meet the growing demands of industry and shipping.

29   *Op cit*, pp 49-55
30   D/D SB 12/8
31   D/D SB 12/11
32   *Vide* p 16, n6
33   Swansea Rate Books, WGRO
34   D/D SB 12/11
35   Harrington, *op cit*, p 126

Previously, in 1830, Usborne & Benson had leased from George Tennant the Wenallt Colliery near their Ynysygerwn copper mills.[36] Particularly attractive, however, were the Graigola coal seams in the parish of Cadoxton, only four miles from their Forest Works. On March 25 1831, with the consent of William Meyrick, the Merthyr solicitor who had widespread interests in the county, John Parsons, of Graig Cottage, Cadoxton-juxta-Neath, leased seams of coal, culm and fire clay under the Cwm Cyrnach and Llwyn Erch Edwal farms to Henry Usborne of Portland Place, Thomas Starling Benson of North Cray Place, Kent, and Hart Logan of Kentwell, Suffolk, for the term of sixty-two years.[37]

Parsons also agreed to construct a tramway to connect the pits at Graigola and Ynysymond with the Swansea Canal. It was stated in the agreement that in 1830 a survey had been carried out for a railway from Ystradgynlais to Swansea. This was undoubtedly the first survey undertaken for what was to become the Swansea Vale Railway.[38] It was either to pass between the Canal and the River Tawe or take a route on the east side of the river. The length of the tramway needed and the subsequent tolls levied would vary according to the route taken by the proposed railway if completed. If a bridge were built and later found unnecessary, the Company would have to pay a sum of £300 compensation to Parsons.[39]

The following June Kirkhouse was surveying the area and presented an account to Usborne, Benson & Co. of the time he had spent at the Graigola level above Tyr Eynon Farm - 'taking stock' from the 8th to the 11th and 'making out dect *(sic)* and taking in' on the 12th. There follows an estimate of the work to be done at the level and on the tramway from the pit to the Swansea Canal.[40] The route of the tramway was across the river Tawe and the Lleche brook where he says the bridges were in need of repair. This, together with the stock available, suggests that a tramway already existed there before Kirkhouse's survey and, since Richard Parsons and later his son John were the original owners of coal seams in the area, they were responsible for it. Part of the track of the tramway is shown on the 1840s tithe map and on the plan of the proposed Swansea Vale Railway of 1845, and can be traced today on either side of Ynysymond Road. The farms through which the tramroad passed, Tyr Eynon and Noyadd Wen, were purchased by Messrs Benson & Price when the Neath Abbey lands came up for sale in 1838.[41]

From the 1820s on, Graigola coal had been very much in demand to supply a network of coaling stations from the West Indies to the Middle East. This demand grew with the advent of steamboat companies, both at home and abroad. George Huxham, the Graigola Colliery agent, had on one occasion shipped 400 tons of Large Forest Graigola to Lisbon alone at 9/- a ton. At the same time he was selling the 'best hand picked at 11/- and unscreened coal, used by Swansea packets, at 5/- a ton'.[42]

36 D/DT 443 1-4, April 15 1825, WGRO
37 D/D SB 12/7
38 C Nov 24 1846, later published as a pamphlet, Dec 1 1846
39 D/D SB 12/7
40 Kirkhouse, *op cit*, MS 466, June 1841, WGRO; C July 21 1838, p 3
41 Tithe Map and Apportionment, Cadoxton 1841, WGRO
42 A H John, Industrial Development of South Wales, 1750-1850, p 120

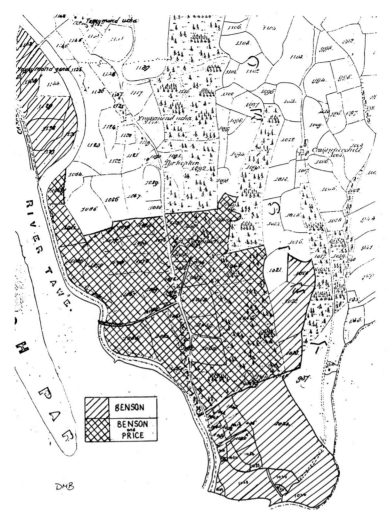

7   Land in the Glais area acquired by Benson and Benson & Price.
Based on the Tithe Map (1841), WGRO

As Starling took on increasingly the role of a coal shipper as well as a copper smelter, his twofold capacity acted as a spur to the family's plans for extending C H Smith's tramroad up the Swansea Valley as far as their pits. George Tennant was interested in the progress of this project, and on January 13 1835, William Kirkhouse, Tennant's engineer, was writing to his employer to apologise for his failure to contact Mr Smith who was 'absent either sporting, visiting or electioneering or such other things', while Mr Price was away from home. Visiting Sketty Park he found the young Mr Benson was also away and 'the old Gentleman very unwell.'[43] Contact was eventually made, however, to the good effect that 'the old Gentleman' was able to enlist Kirkhouse's services in finding out about various lots of the Duke of Beaufort's property then on the market, the

43   Kirkhouse, *op cit*, MS 466, Jan 13 1835, WGRO

disposition of which might interfere with the plans for the projected railroad.[44]

Starling was now virtually in control of his father's business, combining his copper and coal interests to good effect. In Pigot's Directory for 1836, the Swansea section gives two Benson entries. Benson, Logan & Co. are included under the heading of 'Copper Smelting Works', with premises at the Forest Works and F D Michael as their agent, but Benson and Logan also figure as 'Coal and Culm Proprietors and Merchants' with an address on the Strand, Swansea.[45] George Huxham, their agent, had already been involved with the Graigola Coal company at the time of the meeting of the coal interests to discuss the creation of the town float in January 1832.[46]

By the late 1830s the Forest Works was experiencing difficulties, in spite of the earlier updating of their premises in 1834. The Company continued to buy in ores from Chile, Cornwall, Ireland and North Wales, but they were now finding it a struggle to compete with the major firms of Vivian, Williams and Grenfell. Nevertheless, up until 1838, they were still holding their own. In 1839, however, 'The Mining Journal' was reporting their expenditure at the Cornish and Welsh ticketings as £9,243 for 1,966 tons of ore. When compared with the Vivians' £250,117 for 38,536 tons, the Grenfells' £177,362 for 26,833 tons and Williams, Foster and Co.'s £347,651 for 47,966 tons, the amount purchased certainly did not augur well for their future.[47]

It is significant, as A H John pointed out, that the great copper masters of the nineteenth century all came from the ore side of the industry or were financed by those interested in the copper mines, notably in Cornwall or North Wales. The small entrepreneur of the opening decades of the century was already doomed.[48]

There were troubled times ahead but one source of obvious gratification to the firm of Benson & Logan was their successful application at the Forest Works of Nicholas Troughton's patent to allay the effects of the emission of sulphurous and other noxious vapours. The problem of air pollution is far from being a purely modern concern. Towards the middle of the last century increasing criticism of the adverse effects on the property, as well as the personal health, of those living in the vicinity of the copperworks had in some instances led to prosecution, as in the case against the Vivians in 1833.[49]

In a letter to 'The Cambrian' of April 6, 1839, a correspondent named John Francis wrote enthusiastically in praise of the efficacy of Mr Troughton's patent process operating in the newly constructed calciners at the Forest Works of Messrs Benson and Logan, where the smoke visible was only the amount issuing from any cottage chimney.[50] Later that year, however, some of the comments in 'The Mining Journal' of December 14 seemed to cast doubt on the success of this process. A fortnight later, in the issue of December 28, there appeared a reply

44 *Op cit*, MS 466, April 22 1837, WGRO
45 Pigot's Directory 1836
46 *Vide* pp 30, 32
47 The Mining Journal, Sept 28 1839
48 A H John, Industrial Development of South Wales, 1750-1850, p 30
49 C March 3 1833, p 3
50 C April 6 1839, p 3

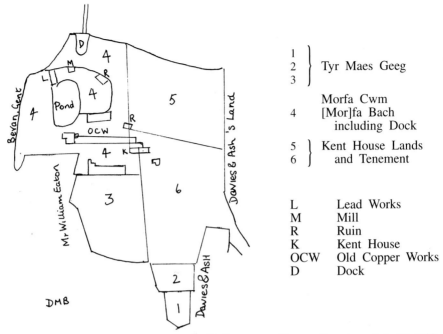

1 ⎫
2 ⎬ Tyr Maes Geeg
3 ⎭

      Morfa Cwm
4   [Mor]fa Bach
      including Dock

5 ⎫ Kent House Lands
6 ⎭   and Tenement

L   Lead Works
M   Mill
R   Ruin
K   Kent House
OCW   Old Copper Works
D   Dock

8   Penclawdd - site of Copper Works leased by N Cameron to Benson & partners July 12 1827
Based on plans attached to documents D/D SB 12/1 and 12/2, WGRO

9   Penclawdd - land acquired by Benson & partners. The tramway from the Penlan pit to the docks
is marked   Based on Tithe Map and Apportionment (1840s), WGRO

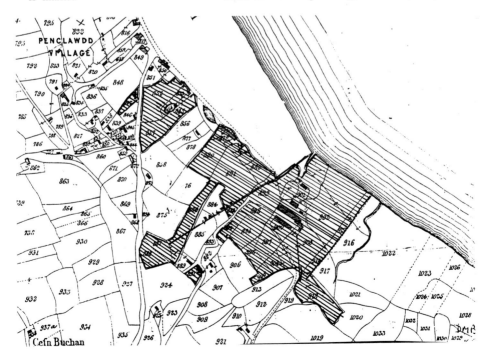

from Benson and Logan, defending their reputation. In order to avoid any accusation of bias, they included a copy of the report by the celebrated chemist, Mr Richard Phillips, and by Mr William Carpmael of Lincoln's Inn, both well known as men of practical science. Both had been satisfied with the perfect success of the process. Moreover, Benson & Logan had intimated to other proprietors of copper works in the vicinity their readiness to treat with them for the use of the invention but there is no record of any takers.[51]

There was yet one other area in which the Bensons showed a keen interest. Even before their purchase of the Forest Works in 1827 they had begun to acquire land and mineral rights on the Gower Peninsula. As early as September 1826 Usborne, Benson & Co. had leased land in Penclawdd from Nathaniel Cameron,[52] and afterwards from William Eaton, Paul Bevan, Sir John Morris and William Ash.[53] On part of this land stood the copperworks previously owned by the Cheadle Co. in which John Vivian had become a partner in July 1800. His involvement had brought welcome financial relief at a difficult time, but with the Vivians opening up their own Hafod works in 1809, the Cheadle Co. was once more faced with money problems.[54] This had led to the abandonment of the works and, by 1833, they were described as 'now neglected'.[55]

In addition, there were extensive opportunities in this area for coal mining. Between 1826 and 1827 the Bensons and their partners had leased over 550 acres of land for its coal seams, pits, iron ore and iron mine with power to develop further mines.[56] This land included Penlan, Rhean Fawr, Caer Ithyn, Cefn Bychan and Abercedy and the veins of coal included Pomfald *(sic)*, Clements, Glylid *(sic)* and North Veins. This property was part of the Gellihir estate and belonged mainly to Nathaniel Cameron and his wife, Letitia. To assess the possibilities of all their acquisitions, Benson & Logan, in July 1831, engaged William Kirkhouse to survey the collieries already in existence. In his letter reporting his findings, Kirkhouse recommended re-opening

> the old Ivy Engine Pit, sink it 10-12 fathoms deeper, then drive from thence toward the dip of the vein about 15 fathoms. You would meet the vein again and gain thereby a new range of coal abt 20 fathoms wide and a mile in length ... and would produce abt 75,000 tons of coal, which would last you at a rate of 50 tons a day abt 5 years. The other veins could be worked from the same pit.

He also recommended sinking a pit to the north of Ivy Engine Pit on the flat ground near the beach, probably the land leased from Sir John Morris. From there, he said, all the coal could be worked under Starling Benson's possessions in that neighbourhood.[57]

51   C Dec 28 1839, p 3; Mining Journal, Dec 21 1839, p 197
52   Cameron Estate Sale Catalogue 1852, UCS Archives, p 274/4
53   D/D SB 12/6, 12/8 and 12/11
54   R R Toomey, Vivian and Sons 1809-1924 (Thesis UCS) pp 10-12
55   Lewis's Topographical Dictionary of Wales, 1833
56   D/D SB 12/1-5
57   Kirkhouse, *op cit*, MS 466, July 15 1831, WGRO; *cf* Stephen Hughes, Brecon Forest Tramroads (The Royal Commission on Ancient and Historical Monuments in Wales, 1952) p 128

The expense would be as follows:

Cleaning out the Ivy Pit and putting up an engine £650

Sinking the pit 10 fathoms £l00

Laying down a railroad to shipping place £220

15 Ton trams @ £7 each...£105 etc

Total........................ £1450

The cost of working the coal and delivering to ships 2/6 a ton or 25/- a day.[58]

On November 1 1834, Kirkhouse was reporting to Messrs Benson, Logan & Co. at the Forrest *(sic)* Works that he had been over to Penclawdd on the previous Wednesday to examine their 'new Pit now sinking'. He had to inform them that

according to my judgment of the ground which I have seen, there is no men *(sic)* that can sink more than a fathom a week in it and as far as I can see it appears to be the same sort of ground the whole distance to the coal, therefore I am of opinion that it will take from 12-15 months at least to get the pit in a proper manner to the intended Vein of Coal. This would cost, in sinking alone without any other expenses, from £10 to £12 per fathom.[59]

The Bensons obviously rose to the challenge of the expense of pits in the area, in particular, the pit at Penlan on the land leased from William Ash and Paul Bevan. From this pit a tramway was constructed to run down to the dock. This can be clearly seen on the 1840s tithe map.[60] In addition, orders were later sent to the Neath Abbey Works, in November 1842 and in February 1843, for parts for a 65" engine.[61] It is quite possible that these were for the engine that was set up at the Penlan pit.

Also in the early 40s Benson, Logan & Co. proceeded to re-open and develop the copper works. A plan of c 1840 shows a well-ordered range of buildings, a furnace, a calciner, a refinery, a brick kiln and a lime kiln. There was also a terrace of cottages known as Barracks Row to provide accommodation for the workers. The tramway from the Penlan Pit to the dock, now with a branch to the copperworks, can be seen also on this plan.[62]

So involved did Starling become with these developments that he found it necessary to have a residence in the district in addition to his Swansea home in the Burrows. His Penclawdd house, however, according to R N Cooper in 'A Dark and Pagan Place', was sufficiently far from the works for its occupant not to experience the worst discomforts of copper fumes.[63] Such discomforts would

58   Kirkhouse, *op cit*, MS 466, July 15 1831, WGRO
59   *Op cit*, MS 466, Nov 1 1834, WGRO
60   Tithe Map and Apportionment for Llanrhidian, SCL
61   Neath Abbey Iron Works Collection, WGRO
62   Plan of Copperworks area, Penclawdd, D/DP 858, WGRO
63   R N Cooper, A Dark and Pagan Place (Bridgend & Cowbridge; D Brown & Sons Ltd, 1986) pp 55-57

have been insignificant compared with the financial difficulties the Company was soon to face in both the pits and the copperworks.

There could, however, be problems other then those of industrialisation. The age-old difficulty of establishing a right to property involved Starling in what appears to us now a mere quibble. To Starling it was a matter of principle. A case of trespass, although brought later, in 1855, reveals the conditions concerning the development of the tramway.

An argument had arisen concerning a field called Coity which was being claimed by a certain Evan John of Penclawdd as his property, although Starling had in fact purchased the freehold of it in 1850. In June 1855 one of Starling's employees, Thomas Leyshon, had driven Evan John's cattle out of the field but almost immediately afterwards he saw John's servant remove the locks and drive the cattle back in. Following this, Starling brought a charge of trespass against Evan John of Penlan Farm.

The colliery tramway had been constructed partially through Penlan farm, occupied by William and Margaret Lewis whose daughter, Ann, married Evan John after her parents' death. The Lewises had been allowed use of the Coity field as compensation for the land taken for the tramway, although Evan John assumed they had actually been given the field in return for sinking pits on their land. Upon his marriage to Ann Lewis in May 1850, he believed he had a right to the property, including Coity. Coity, however, was not part of Penlan Farm.

Starling, it emerged, had approached Ann Lewis two months earlier about accepting money as compensation instead of the use of Coity. This she had refused, preferring to pay rent. In a subsequent letter she had asked for a long lease. She later claimed that she had been helped to write this by her future husband but Evan John could not recall any such involvement. Relations between Starling and Evan John must previously have been harmonious since they had purchased Penlan Farm between them, Starling taking the tramway and the land to the west and Evan John the farm buildings and the land to the east.

When the case was heard, Evan John's evidence was so vague and contradictory that it was difficult to reach a conclusion. The magistrates in any case had to admit that they had no power to decide on the entitlement. Strangely neither side had produced the relevant title deeds. Eventually a compromise was reached whereby Evan John gave up his claim to possession while Starling agreed to forego an action for the four years' rent due to him.[64]

This case is evidence of the Bensons' continuing connection with the Penclawdd area even though by 1847 they were no longer operating the copperworks themselves. The firm had also run into difficulties in connection with its mining interests although we know that it was still operating the Penlan Colliery (also known as the Penclawdd Colliery) in 1844 from a reference to a tragic accident in which an 'Edward Hughes, a collier in Messrs Benson & Logan's employ', fell to the bottom of the pit and was killed.[65] The colliery and part of the copperworks land were, indeed, still in the possession of the Bensons at the time of Starling's death in 1879.

64 C June 6 1855, p 6
65 C Jan 20 1844, p 3

The fortunes or misfortunes of the Penclawdd properties, the Forest Works and the Graigola collieries during the difficult years of the 40s will be dealt with fully in a later chapter. For the moment, however, we have to pass to a consideration of Thomas Starling Benson's struggle against a Harbour Trust only slowly awakening to the urgency of developing Swansea as a port capable of handling the demands of its varied industries.

Chapter III

The New Cut

The history of the port of Swansea has been fully traced by W H Jones in his book of that name. As early as June 24 1791 as the result of 'an Act for repairing, enlarging and preserving the Harbour of Swansea in the County of Glamorgan', those with landed rights in the area, such as the Duke of Beaufort, the Earl of Jersey and their officers, had been appointed to serve as Trustees. In addition twelve representatives of business interests in the Port, the 'Proprietary or Representative Trustees', and twelve burgesses serving on behalf of the Corporation had been chosen to conduct the affairs of that harbour.

An important step forward came at the time of the 1827 Bill in Parliament which sought to amend the Glamorgan Turnpike Act of 1823 by 'giving powers to make a road across the Crumlyn Burrows from Briton Ferry and to erect bridges over the Neath and Swansea rivers'. Mr J H Vivian, the local MP, saw this measure as an opportunity for implementing plans for deepening and 'floating' the river and had put forward three options, two of which involved a navigable cut through the adjacent Tyrllandwr estate. At that time, the estate was owned by the Revd Henry Sharpe Pocklington who had inherited it from his father, an East Anglian banker of the same name.[1]

At a meeting of the Swansea Harbour Trust on April 8 1831 it was resolved to accept the principle of a Floating Harbour.[2] This involved the erection of bridges across the cut and the river. A premium of 200 guineas was offered for the best plan submitted to carry out the scheme for not more than £60,000. That by Jesse Hartley, the Chief Engineer of the Liverpool Dock Company, particularly attracted Mr Vivian who was anxious to see it adopted in a slightly revised form, even though the cost would be well in excess of the sum stipulated. Mr Hartley's plan was accordingly approved on November 28 1831, with the Harbour Board expressing a desire to secure entire control over what was then Mr Pocklington's land.[3]

By January 1832 the Trustees had agreed to accept Mr Pocklington's proposal of the sale of Tyrllandwr for £13,000 and had also, by that time, realised that an Act of Parliament would be needed to continue with their plans for the Harbour.[4]

The various interested bodies of the town were already being consulted. Some disagreement, however, occurred at a meeting of the Copper Interests at the Town

---

1 W H Jones, History of the Port of Swansea, p 157*ff*
2 SHT Minute Book 1825-35 PRO RAIL 877/4
3 W H Jones, *op cit*, p 165
4 Swansea Harbour Reports, 1831-2 (Swansea; Murray & Rees) Meeting of Copper Interests, Jan 23 1832

10 Pocklington's Farm by G Shepherd *c*1820

From a personal copy, given to J N H by Mr W C Rogers, January 1990

Hall on January 23 1832 with Mr Vivian in the Chair.[5] On the list of those present Starling's name is given as 'Sterling' Benson, perhaps, in retrospect, a Freudian slip in the days before Freud; for if Starling was anything in his personal relationships, he certainly was 'Sterling' by nature, if not by name.

The issue under discussion was an additional tax of one farthing on copper to defray the costs of the proposed new channel through the Tyrllandwr estate. The proposition, however, soon ran into difficulties and it was decided to abide by the earlier resolution of January 10. On that date it had been carried that the advantages of a float would not be sufficient compensation to those engaged in the copper trade for the extra tax. The Bensons, with sea-faring in their blood, must have shuddered at such shortsightedness.

Another party to be consulted was, of course, the Duke of Beaufort who owned a sizeable portion of land 'immediately contiguous' to the Pocklington estate. (see Appendix A)

From the start Mr Vivian had been in favour of a navigable cut, in accordance with the findings of such eminent civil engineers as Henry Habberly Price, William Kirkhouse and others who had investigated the feasibility of such an idea.

The Harbour Trustees of that time, however, were men of entrenched views who were slow to adopt sweeping changes and also reluctant to involve the Trust in such enormous debt. Mr Vivian was to remind his audience at a public meeting on January 25 1841,[6] almost ten years later, that, had the arrangement made by him, on behalf of the Trustees, with the Pocklington family to purchase the whole Tyrllandwr estate been confirmed at the time, the work on the New Cut might have been carried out on highly advantageous terms. The subsequent appreciation of the land, he added, would almost, if not completely, have offset the initial outlay. Such an 'appreciation', however, could only have been achieved by the sale of a large part of the land, a course which the Harbour Trust would hardly have considered at that time.

Discussions dragged on. Meantime several advertisements appeared in 'The Cambrian' stating that Tyrllandwr was 'to let'.[7] Henry Sharpe Pocklington had married in 1827,[8] the furniture in his house had been sold immediately[9] and by 1831 the Pocklingtons had moved away from Swansea,[10] although still having an interest in its affairs. By this time they were, no doubt, anxious to find a buyer for the estate.

To an astute man of business like T S Benson, the purchase of Tyrllandwr presented itself as an ideal opportunity for investing in the future prosperity of Swansea. Its importance had been confirmed earlier when, on April 8 1831, the Harbour Trustees had resolved to accept the principle of a Floating Harbour. Furthermore, by 1834, Mrs Meux's property in North Cray had been sold and Thomas Starling had the ready money for purchase. By October he was in

---

5 SHT Minute Book 1825-35 PRO RAIL 877/4
6 C Jan 30 1841, p 3
7 C May 22 1830; Nov 5 1831, both p 2
8 C Aug 11 1827, p 3
9 C Sept 15 1827, p 2
10 C March 3 1831, p 3 & April 2 1831, p 4

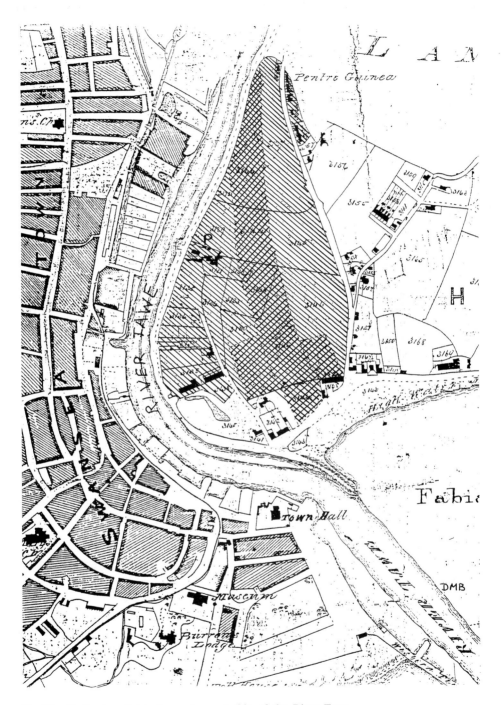

11   The Tyrllandwr Estate is on the east side of the River Tawe
P - Pocklington Farm; Heavily shaded area - land purchased by SHT for the New Cut
Based on Tithe Map & Apportionment 1837/8, WGRO

possession of Tyrllandwr[11] for the sum of £11,000 and Tyrllandwr was again advertised as 'to let.'[12]

It was not until 1835 that the Harbour Trustees took positive action when an application was made to Parliament for an Act to allow them to go ahead with the projected Harbour scheme. In the ensuing Act of 1836, which set out to 'alter and amend several Acts for the improvement of the Harbour of Swansea', they were authorised to proceed in three stages.[13] The first allowed them 'to make a navigable Cut or Canal, or Cut for Waste Water, from Fabian's Bay to communicate with the River Tawe at or near Pentreguinea....' and to this end, they were empowered 'to borrow Eighty thousand Pounds and to levy and collect such Tolls' as were specified in the Act. The second phase would be to form a Wet Dock which would communicate with both the New Cut and the Half-tide Basin, which was also authorised in this part of the Act. For this the Trustees were allowed to borrow a further 'Forty thousand Pounds'. In the third place, they were authorised 'to further deepen and improve the Bed of the said River Tawe and to make it navigable for Ships and Vessels as high as the Forest Works near Morriston in the Parish of Llangevelach'.

In view of 'the Increase in Trade ... and the Extent of the Improvements thereby contemplated', it was considered expedient 'that the Number of Proprietary or Representative Trustees acting under and by virtue of the Powers of the said recited Acts should be increased to Twenty-four.' In order to become one of the additional Trustees, the new holder of office had to 'be possessed of one or other of such Qualifications as are required by the said recited Acts, or be possessed of a Wharf or Warehouse on the Banks of the River Tawe or of an Interest in any Canal or Railroad terminating at or communicating with the River Tawe, of the full Value of Two thousand Pounds at the Least.'[14]

By now, Mr Benson, by virtue of the aforementioned requirements, had himself qualified as a Proprietary Trustee, as had Starling.[15] Negotiations for the ground needed for the Cut had now to be opened with the new owner and, at first, it looked as though an agreement could be reached on 'fair and equitable terms'.[16]

Later, in a letter of February 6 1841 in response to criticism from Mr Vivian, T S Benson explained that he had been prepared to offer the Harbour Trust all the land necessary for the proposed development at the same price per acre as he had given for it.[17] What he had not been prepared to do was to sell them the whole of the estate. According to Mr Benson, a subsequent attempt by the Trustees before the Committee of the House of Commons to enforce this had failed in view of his offer of the land needed for their purpose at cost price. Moreover, he had expressed his willingness for the Harbour Trust to share in the benefit from the completed wharfs. Although Parliament would not allow the Trustees one foot beyond the area required without his permission, it had been

11 W H Jones, *op cit*, p 178
12 C Oct 4 1834, p 2
13 Swansea Harbour Act 1836, 6 & 7 William, *cap* cxxvi, Section 1
14 *Op cit*, Section 2
15 SHT Minute Book 1825-35 PRO RAIL 877/4
16 C Feb 13 1841, p 4
17 *Ibid*

arranged for 700 feet of frontage (ie more than three acres above the requisite quantity) to be selected by them in any part of the New Cut, and the agreement signed by both parties was still in their possession.

Unfortunately, on October 2 1837, a resolution was passed by the Trustees which proved fatal to all hopes of an early implementation of their plans.[18] In the meeting held that day, a decision was reached to make the New Cut a waste-water cut only, thereby destroying T S Benson's vision of a river offering far greater potential for commercial purposes than existed at the time. This would have helped Swansea to compete with the rival South Wales ports of Cardiff, Neath and Newport, creating, in turn, an increased demand for the wharfs he hoped to set up on his own land.

This latest development seriously frustrated T S Benson's plans. When he was next approached in the November, he repeated his former offer but pointed out that, in view of the 'various disjointed resolutions tending to the injury of (his) property in adjoining lands', he would now expect to be paid £5000, the increase being for 'severance'.[19]

The Trustees were obviously dumb-struck. No reply was forthcoming from them until May 1838. Mr Benson now suggested that, if the Board could not agree on the value of the land, it might be better to have it ascertained by disinterested assessors, possibly one for each of the two parties involved, with a third to be chosen by the Trustees. In the event of failure to agree on the value of the land, Section 33 of the 1836 Act stated that the Trustees were empowered to apply to the Sheriff of Glamorgan or his representative to 'impannel summon and return a Jury' of at least 'Twelve sufficient and indifferent Men ... to appear before the Justices of the Peace for the said County ... '.[20]

However, to avoid further delay, Mr Benson was prepared for the Harbour Trust to take immediate possession of the land and commence operations, provided both parties agreed to abide by the award or verdict when it was given. This offer, put forward by Starling on behalf of his father, was seen by his opponents as a sinister attempt to hustle the Trustees into a premature commitment.[21]

This must have been a gruelling episode in Starling's life, both private and public, and his father was well aware of the strain being imposed on his loyal representative in the ongoing battle with his fellow Trustees. From their London home in Russell Square, Thomas Starling had written to his son on March 1 1838 're allowance for trouble and time in attending to Tyrlandwr (sic)'

> My D Starling
> In the Parcel herewith you will receive various papers, also the Catalogue of the Neath Abbey Sale some lots of which it would be desirl (*sic*) to Buy on the part of the Trust. But referring To this, & the enormous trouble & anxiety (independent of the expense) which you have had with the Tyrlandwr Business - I really know not how you are

18 *Ibid*; *cf* W H Jones, *op cit*, p 169
19 C Feb 13 1841, p 4
20 Swansea Harbour Act 1836, 6 & 7 William, *cap* cxxvi, Section 33
21 C Dec 15 1838, p 3

to be paid. We will put it on this footing (I will engage on the part of the Trustees that you shall receive Commn for management), say 5 per Cent - on whatever we may Receive, I mean 5 per Cent on the amt to be Received (whatever it may be) from the Trustees for Compensation - & also as We must pay the Collector 5 per Cent on the Rents, for Collection, whenever you choose to take the Collection into your own hands you shall Receive 5 per Cent on the Amt thereof instead of paying him. The same comn will of course apply to the Farms, if We Buy any. I trust this will be satisfactory, however of that I entertain no doubt - & as you are fully entitled to It say no more abt It - but take it - & I hope our forthcoming verdict will satisfy all parties—

believe me my D S
yrs afft

Tho S Benson[22]

The first two references to Trustees would appear to be to those administering the estate of the late Mrs Meux with whose money Tyrllandwr had been bought; the last is obviously to the members of the Swansea Harbour Trust.

In the event, the Board decided to ask for a Jury in accordance with the provision of Section 33 of the 1836 Act. The case was heard at the adjourned Glamorgan Quarter Sessions on July 14 1838. In the light of hindsight, the Trustees came to regret their action. It was felt the Bensons had had an unfair advantage in that John Gwyn Jeffreys, the Deputy Sheriff on whom devolved the task of summoning the Jury, was their solicitor.[23] Moreover, they had objected to any Juryman thought to be inimical to their interests, while the Trustees ignored the fact that two or three of those serving were known to have connections with the Benson family.[24]

The Benson side was adroitly handled by the rising advocate, Mr E Vaughan Williams, who was warmly praised for his skilful presentation of his client's claim.[25] Several highly competent witnesses confirmed the valuable nature of Mr Benson's property, including Robert Beaumont, at one time mineral agent to the Marquess of Bute but now resident in Swansea. According to his calculations, the 'quantity of land required for the wider cut would be 35,410 yards which, at 2s.3d. per yard, would amount to £3983 12s'. Documents dated July 13 1838, showing the total value of the part of the Tyrllandwr Estate under discussion, signed by Beaumont, are among the Bute papers in the Cardiff Reference Library, and merit a more detailed consideration than is possible here. It is sufficient to say that Robert Beaumont's calculation of the potential value of the land to Mr Benson was £19,132 3s. 0d.[26] This figure was roughly confirmed by the London auctioneer and land agent, Adam Murray, who gave an estimate of £21,743 6s. 0d.

22 JREB, TSB to SB, March 1 1838
23 C April 27 1839, p 3
24 C Nov 26 1842, p 3
25 C July 21 1838, p 3
26 Bute Papers, MS 75 50 (D), Cardiff Reference Library (CRL), March 25 1831

The projected railway up the Tawe Valley was referred to by William Kirkhouse who explained that it had been delayed pending the sale of the Neath Abbey lands. Had it been built, it would have increased the demand for wharfs as Tyrllandwr was the only land available for this purpose, a point emphasised by George Huxham in his evidence. William Meyrick also referred to the proposed railway in his evidence, adding, 'The Neath Abbey lands have since been purchased by Mr Price and Mr Benson and thus every difficulty of carrying on the railway has been removed.' Another witness, a builder by the name of Richards, considered the land well suited for building purposes, whereas Mr Brough felt the part required by the Trustees was purely agricultural; 'there was no prospect of its being used for any other purpose.' He valued nine acres at £120 per acre, with £50 for severance per acre, resulting in £1530, and three acres for warehouses, £1000, making a total of £2582, 'which I consider its full value, for unless it was near a large town, it would not fetch anything like it.'

The Jury came to a very different conclusion. The Trustees' minute book, recording that fatal resolution of October 1837 to make the New Cut a waste-water cut, had been presented at the hearing. This evidence had been seen as sufficient testimony to the injury Mr Benson was likely to incur by the division of his land, and the Jury accordingly awarded him £10,341 - £2865 for the land and £7476 for the severance.[27]

Trust and town were stunned. The columns of 'The Cambrian' buzzed with correspondence from a large cross-section of Swansea residents, many of them blaming the Harbour Trust for their prevarication resulting in what was seen as 'mismanagement of public funds'. According to W H Smith of Hen Dderwen, they had failed lamentably in not having shown more discretion in their negotiations. It seemed to him the time might well come when their only course of action would be to memorialise the Lords of the Treasury, admitting their 'hazardous predicament', in the hope they might step in and rescue the Trustees from the crisis they were facing.[28]

In contrast Lewis Dillwyn was inclined to abandon the New Cut altogether and construct instead a wet dock on Corporation land.[29] Other Trustees were keen to go to yet another Jury in the hope they would review the award given against them the previous July. 'The Cambrian' of November 24 1838 reported that the Trustees had applied to the Court of the Queen's Bench for a *certiorari* to overturn the decision of the first Jury and Mr Justice Littledale had granted their plea.[30] Already, however, on November 23 Mr Benson had applied to the Court of Bail for support of his award and this had been granted by Mr Justice Follett.[31]

The folly of further litigation had been pointed out to the Trustees by Charles Tennant in a special meeting called in the Town Hall the following December. He reminded them that it was the Trust who had opted for a Jury. Were they to assume, he asked, 'because they had a very good natured gentleman to deal with,

27 C July 21 1838, p 3
28 C July 28 1838, p 3
29 C Dec 15 1838, p 3
30 C Nov 24 1838, p 3
31 C Dec 1 1838, p 3

that, after they had cried out war and been beaten, they could cry *"peccavi"* ' and so, presumably get away unscathed?' If they now went to a second Jury, they might find themselves having to pay even more, perhaps up to £20,000, a figure significantly close to Mr Beaumont's calculations. His advice was to let their Solicitor investigate Mr Benson's claim to title and then pay him. He moved accordingly.

This drew fire from Mr Dillwyn who was quick to remind Mr Tennant that, had he attended meetings more frequently, he would have known the Trustees were most anxious to do what was right, querying only claims that reminded him, 'perhaps erroneously', of Shylock's pound of flesh. He personally had never approved of a floating harbour but had gone ahead out of deference to others. Here he got in his jab by reminding the Trust that the elder Benson had not attended their meetings prior to the jury award, leaving his son to answer any queries. As a result, Starling would ask for time to consult his father, thus giving him a month to prepare his answers with the help of skilful advisers. One of these was, undoubtedly, young Florance, now a student at Lincoln's Inn, although Mr Dillwyn did not mention him by name!

Unfortunately, on the day Mr Tennant chose to put forward his resolution in favour of paying Mr Benson, there were only eleven out of the forty Trustees present. This gave Mr Dillwyn an opportunity to ask for an adjournment of the meeting until January 20 1839, by which time seats on the Borough Council would have been filled. Whatever his motive, it appeared that he was holding out for a more representative body to be available to discuss the issue.[32]

In the adjourned meeting Mr Tennant again moved the resolution for the investigation of Mr Benson's title and the completion of the purchase. This was seconded by Colonel Nathaniel Cameron, although he admitted to having reservations on certain aspects of the case. Mr Dillwyn, however, persisted in his objections, and Mr Tennant's motion was defeated by fifteen votes to six.[33]

In a meeting of the Trustees open to the public, which was held on February 11 1839, they were warned that Mr Benson could well call for the production of the Harbour Board accounts, and, should they still refuse to settle, he would be in a position to apply for the appointment of a Receiver to their estate or else agree to take Harbour Bonds to the full amount of the purchase money.[34]

A new sense of urgency was lent to the situation by the loss of six lives in a ferry boat accident on the Tawe. The Duke of Beaufort's agent, Francis Hooper, sought to deflect accusations levelled against the Duke as Lord of the Seigniory by pointing the finger at the Trustees, who had been among his keenest critics. He reminded them that, had it not been for their 'senseless squabbles', a good bridge would long since have been substituted for an inconvenient ferry with its all too inadequate boat.[35]

In the meantime, a letter from Mr Vivian at Singleton, dated February 1 1839, had reminded the Trust that the original plan had envisaged the Cut as being navigable. Had they acted on this in the beginning, the heavy payment to Mr

32   C Dec 15 1838, p 3
33   C Feb 2 1839, p 3
34   C Feb 16 1839, p 3
35   C Feb 23 1839, p 3

Benson could have been avoided. At the same time, he felt Mr Benson should have taken into consideration the arrangement existing between the Trustees and Mr Pocklington at the time of his purchase of Tyrllandwr. Now, in the event of the New Cut project's falling through, he personally was beginning to consider the idea of a dock in Burrows Square.[36]

Letters continued to pour into 'The Cambrian', with W H Smith still among the most vocal of the Trust's critics. He saw the Board dominated by a majority of Proprietary Trustees with coal and copper interests.[37] These had most to gain from the negotiations, unlike the ordinary residents of Swansea who could only lose out from the financial *débâcle* of the New Cut.[38] According to Henry Tennant in January 1839, W H Smith had implied in a letter as far back as July 21 1838 that the development authorised by the 1836 Act would adversely affect the trade of Swansea to the advantage of Port Tennant. This Mr Tennant sought to show was quite untrue. W H Smith, on the other hand rejected Mr Tennant's interpretation of his letter. Both, however, were united in their criticism of the conduct of the Trust.[39]

The Minute Book of the Trustees' Meetings 1835-45 records that on April 1 1839 the Trustees agreed to pay £2864 for the land and £7346 'for severance to be effected by making a waste-water cut'. However, Mr Benson was to be asked to return some should a navigable cut be made and also to renounce his shipping rights. At the next meeting it was reported that Mr Benson had declined the offer, whereupon it was resolved that an account be opened in Mr Benson's name and £1000 be credited to the same. By April 11 it was being denied that there were funds for even £1000. Fortunately there was a swift change of heart and on May 13 it was ordered that £1000 be entered in the account.[40]

Meanwhile this dithering led to a further acrimonious exchange of views. One letter, under the *nom-de-plume* 'An Absent Trustee', written on April 13, sharply criticized the proceedings of the Trustees. The address, '5 New Sq, Lincoln's Inn', plainly pointed to Henry Tennant as the writer. He reminded his readers that, the previous year, in May 1838, the Trust had been granted permission to borrow £99,000 on the strength of their harbour tolls. While claiming to be unable to pay Mr Benson, they had not borrowed a single shilling of that £99,000, nor had they collected the extra income of between £3-£4000 pa which they could have levied under the last Harbour Act.[41]

A reply was printed in 'The Cambrian' of April 27 under the *nom-de-plume* of 'A Tenant in the Town', suggesting that 'Absent Trustee' was 'better qualified to be a tenant of a L _ _ _c Asylum than a member of the Harbour Trust'. This correspondent revealed that the summoning of the Jury had 'devolved on the Deputy Sheriff who was (unfortunately) Mr Benson's solicitor'. Although he claimed to have attended the Harbour Trust meetings, 'apart from the brawling and bawling', he had heard nothing about where the £99,000 would come from. He went on to query whether it was true that two gentlemen had 'leased from a

36 J H Vivian, February 1 1839, Harbour and Dock Reports, SM
37 C Oct 5, 12, 19, 26, 1839, all on p 3
38 C Oct 26 1839, p 3
39 C Jan 11 1840, p 3
40 SHT Minute Book, 1835-45, April 1 - May 15 1839, PRO RAIL 877/5
41 C April 13 1839, p 3

noble Duke the sand-bank on the other side, leading directly to the once intended new cut, in order in the first place to crush the interests and well-being of our commerce, and in the second place to aggrandise themselves by monopolizing all the privileges to themselves'.[42]

Henry Tennant, now giving his name in his reply of May 4, censured the use of 'language which no decent person would allow himself to use' and strongly repudiated the innuendo of the last remark. He offered to give the sources of his information to anyone who applied to him 'in language such as ought to be addressed by one respectable person to another'. He had never wished to say or do anything offensive to anyone else, but felt obliged to state his deliberate opinion that the conduct of the body to which he belonged had been 'very inconsistent, very discreditable, very injurious to the interests of Swansea and neighbourhood.'[43]

In due course the Trustees reluctantly paid Mr Benson the remainder of the sum still outstanding.

Possible ways of reducing the cost of the proposed development were now being considered. Lewis Dillwyn's son-in-law, Matthew Moggridge, suggested, for example, the Trust could modify the terms of the Act and cut down the width of the New Cut, but any further legislation would have cost money the Trustees were loth to part with.[44] By the beginning of May 1840, they had decided to proceed with whatever preparation could be made towards the later implementation of the original plan, and excavations were actually started, with over two hundred 'navigators' employed daily.[45]

The general frustration persisted, however, and in a Public Meeting in January 1841 Mr Vivian repeated the views given in his letter of February 1839. He traced the breakdown of relations,[46] describing the terms Mr Benson offered as being 'very exorbitant' in the opinion of 'most practical men', a phrase taken up by T S Benson in a reply sent to 'The Cambrian' a fortnight later. In it he expressed himself as being most anxious to be seen as 'writing in perfectly good temper with all'. He agreed that he did not provide the Trust with all the land Mr Pocklington was prepared to allow them, being less anxious to dispose of his property than his predecessor might have been. He did not feel any one should be coerced into parting with what was his. He queried Mr Vivian's use of the word 'exorbitant', especially as he had found 'practical' men generally sympathetic to his position, and, in self-defence, he outlined the stages in the negotiations we have already traced.[47]

This letter was written from Teddington where the elder Benson was now settling into the life of a country gentleman, enjoying watching the reapers in nearby cornfields, floating down the river in a punt or sitting peacefully under the catalpa tree in the Manor garden. It was Starling who was left in Swansea to face the current of hostility which persisted towards his father. A Lewis Dillwyn or,

---

42 C April 27 1839, p 3
43 C May 4 1839, p 3
44 C Jan 11 1840, p 3
45 C May 2 1840, p 3
46 C Jan 30 1841, p 3
47 C Feb 13 1841, p 4

later, a George Grant Francis might make sly digs but Starling combined good humour with a canny instinct for self-preservation and let much of the criticism flow over him.

A more placatory letter from Mr Vivian sought to reassure Mr Benson; he had not wished to reflect on him personally. He was merely explaining his reasons for now proposing an alternative site for the dock.[48]

Still the affair rumbled on. In a special meeting of the Harbour Trustees on November 23 1842, with Mr Dillwyn in the Chair, W H Smith continued to press for the controversial resolution of October 1837 to be rescinded in favour of making the New Cut navigable throughout. He was not concerned with what Mr Benson should or should not do, only with what was best for the Harbour.[49]

Mr Benson, it had been suggested, might be prepared to return part of the sum awarded him, but he had disposed of this idea in a letter addressed to the Trustees explaining that he was powerless to do so as the money was secured to a third party under settlement (ie the terms of Mrs Meux's will, bequeathing the Tyrllandwr estate to her daughter).[50] He was, however, prepared to co-operate with them in any definite scheme to improve the work being undertaken.

A second letter from Teddington was less affable. He felt he had grounds for complaint in that, while he answered all the queries put to him, his letters were being ignored by the Trust. He now suggested the propriety of appointing a Committee to treat with him, with full powers to settle outstanding differences once and for all.[51]

A former Mayor of Swansea, Mansel Philipps, recalled the occasion in 1838 during his year of office when, before going to the Jury, Colonel Cameron had proposed offering Mr Benson 'some trifling sum', around £2500. He himself had suggested £5000. Eventually, by his casting vote, £3500 was agreed on, although he said at the time 'it would be useless'. He felt, from the letter, that Mr Benson's attitude was still the same. According to Mr Philipps's interpretation of it 'if the Trustees would row in the same boat with him,' (Mr Benson) 'it would save them money - not by his giving them money but advice (ie money's worth). He would concur with them entirely as long as it did not touch his pocket.'

Although Mr Philipps had always been personally in favour of a navigable cut, he still felt the Trustees had only one duty, to preserve inviolate the resolution of October 2 1837, until such time as a navigable cut could be made on terms favourable to the Trustees and the public generally. 'Mr Benson had one course to pursue, they, as conservators of public interests, another', a remark which produced hearty support. Obviously the owner of Tyrllandwr had been over-optimistic in hoping for 'a verdict that would satisfy all parties.'[52]

Starling, patiently listening to the varying degrees of hostility in his fellow Trustees' comments, merely said his father would be most ready to co-operate with the Trust in any way.

48 C Feb 20 1841, p 3
49 C Nov 26 1842, p 3
50 *Vide* p 12
51 C Nov 26 1842, p 3
52 *Ibid*

He was not without sympathisers. Richard Aubrey, one of the most balanced of the Trustees, who had been Mayor from 1841-42, saw the October resolution as hampering proceedings by clogging Mr Benson's movements without producing any advantage to the port. W H Smith used similar language when he accused the Trustees of being prepared 'to clog and harass Mr Benson's operations' in the hope that he would return part of the money. He blamed the Trust for forcing Mr Benson to go to a Jury rather than pay him the £5000 he had originally asked for. Now after a total expenditure of £35,000 they were still prepared to hold up the development of the port as prescribed by the Act of Parliament, out of sheer malice.

After heated discussion, Mr Smith at last managed to prevail on his hearers at least to listen to his plea for 'some practical plan of improvement' which would benefit shippers in the upper part of the river on whom he claimed fraud had been practised. They had accepted extra levies under the impression that 'the Cut would afford them greater facilities and conveniences by being made navigable.' This argument had little effect on the anti-Benson faction, and his motion that the resolution of October 2 1837 be rescinded was lost by eleven votes to thirteen.[53]

If you cannot beat them, join them, and on this principle, W H Smith, bowing to majority opinion, proposed in the next meeting that the October resolution be implemented and that a committee be appointed, consisting of Messrs Vivian, Aubrey, Benson, Essery, Glover, C H Smith and himself, to carry the work into execution. But even this apparent *volte-face* did not get the better of the opposition, and an amendment by Mr D Sanders was carried, adjourning the matter to the next meeting.[54]

A special meeting was called in January 1843, the beginning of the year in which, despite all the resentment toward his father, Starling was elected Mayor of Swansea, a remarkable tribute to his personal credibility. Here several issues of importance, including the rescinding of the offending minute and restricting the width of the Cut by seven yards, were brought up by Mr Joseph Martin. He was anxious, however, not to proceed before the arrival of a Mr 'Rendall' *(sic)* who had been engaged to give his professional advice. Mr Smith also felt they should wait as several Trustees whose interests were especially involved had not yet arrived.

Quick to employ any kind of delaying tactics, Mr Dillwyn, who had been voted to the Chair, now proposed a further adjournment until the following Friday, but on a successful amendment by Mr Smith, it was carried that business should be deferred only until the arrival of the latecomers. When, however, Mr Rendle had still not appeared, it was agreed, this time with the support of Mr Martin, to adjourn the meeting to allow him to attend.[55]

When the meeting eventually took place the following Friday, Mr Vivian presided. He made it quite clear that he would never have supported the waste water cut had he been in the meeting which passed it. He went on to put Mr Martin's resolution that a float should be made where it would be most profitable

53 *Ibid*
54 C Dec 5 1842, p 3
55 C Jan 21 1843, p 3

to the whole town. At this juncture Mr Dillwyn intervened to call for Mr Rendle's report and, in spite of the Chairman's obvious desire to proceed with Mr Martin's resolution, persisted in his point. Little was gained in this way as, when Mr Rendle rose to speak, he was not prepared to commit himself on specific issues although questions had been submitted to him beforehand in writing.

Probably out of sheer frustration, the edge of criticism was now turned against the unfortunate Mr Martin. J C Richardson, whose business interests were intimately bound up with the dock area, pointed out that it was Mr Martin himself who had originally proposed the waste-water cut. Joseph Martin retaliated by reminding him that all twenty-five Trustees who voted for it were equally responsible for the decision.

Whether it was because of Mr Vivian's expressed preference for the navigable cut or the failure of Mr Rendle to supply Lewis Dillwyn with further ammunition, eventually, before the end of that long-drawn-out and hard-fought meeting, a unanimous verdict was reached that the New Cut should be made navigable and a working committee be set up to supervise developments. This should consist of Messrs Vivian, Dillwyn, Grove, Essery, Richardson, Benson, J W James, Martin, Aubrey and the two Smiths, C H and W H.[56]

Lewis Dillwyn's attitude to the affairs of the Harbour Trust had had a certain ambivalence about it from the early days of negotiations. Soon after the verdict in the Quarter Sessions in favour of the Bensons, he had served notice that he intended to propose abandoning the existing Parliamentary plan and to take measures for constructing a Wet Dock on Corporation land. When he put forward his resolution, however, it emerged that he was proposing a dock, not on Corporation land as mentioned in the notice, but on the west side of the river above the Pottery Mill. This discrepancy led to the defeat of the motion,[57] but it was only time before the idea of a dock on Corporation land was to gain ground, with the full support of Mr Vivian.

This scheme came a step nearer reality with the formation of 'The Swansea Dock Company', a group of private individuals prepared to undertake at their own expense the development of what was to become the South Dock. This new venture, together with the acceptance of the principle of the Float, (later to be known as the North Dock), meant there were now two plans afoot for greater shipping accommodation in the area, both of which would undoubtedly be needed with the expected increase in trade through the growth in local industry. Once the controversy over the New Cut had been settled, the Float was obviously going to be the easier and, ironically, the cheaper project to carry out.

By the end of 1843, work on the New Cut had progressed sufficiently for preparations to go ahead for its use as a waterway. Early in 1845, owing to the closure of the river so that work on the dam being constructed at the Pottery could proceed, notice was given that all vessels should travel through the New Cut.

The first vessel to use the channel was the 'Charles Clarke', a barque captained by Henry Edwards.[58] Its passage through the Cut on March 11 1845 was greeted

56 C Jan 28 1843, p. 3: *cf* Swansea Journal, Jan 25 1843, p 9
57 C Aug 11 1838, p 3
58 W H Jones, *op cit*, p 184

with the firing of guns as it sailed through in 'most gallant style, without touching either sides or bottom, or meeting any obstruction to her free navigation'. The contractor, Charles Burrows, who had been living with his family at Tyrllandwr House[59] while the work went on, had ample reason to be satisfied, and Starling might well have heaved a sigh of relief.

The 1836 Act had given the Trustees powers for seven years and upon their expiry a new Act had been obtained early in 1844. As this was for three years only, it became necessary in 1846 to apply to Parliament for a further Act. Accordingly, on July 22 1847, 'An Act to amend the Various Several Acts relating to Swansea Harbour' came into force, allowing the Trustees a further five years to complete the work and additional powers to raise money.[60] Also, an Act had been passed on July 2 1847 called 'The Swansea Dock Act'. This included the plans for what was to become the South Dock.[61]

By 1848 the cut through Tyrllandwr was completed, and after some delay over the Duke of Beaufort's personal project for a private dock, work proceeded on creating the Float. On November 12 1850, the large centre stone of the lock of the Float, with a number of items likely to be of interest to posterity entombed within it, was lowered into position with appropriate ceremony. Passage from the east to the west bank of the Tawe was now possible by means of a temporary bridge replacing the ferry. The following year, on the advice of the Chief Engineer, Mr Abernethy, a hoist bridge was substituted across the New Cut, and on December 17 1851, water was impounded in the new Float for the first time.

When the Float was finally opened on January 1 1852, there was far less public celebration than might have been expected. A few banners on adjacent premises and flags on some of the vessels in the harbour were the main sign that over half a century of speculation and negotiation had at last borne fruit. The first vessel to enter the Float was the 'Lord Beresford' which had had her trial run in Swansea in June 1824 and then seen service in other ports before returning to Swansea at a much later date. The Mayor, Thomas Edward Thomas, with several members of the Harbour Trust, visited the Quay during the day, while many of the ordinary residents came along out of curiosity to see what had taken up so much of their money in the hope of securing the future prosperity of port and town.[62] There is no reference to Starling's being there. The chances are that he was still at Teddington where he usually spent Christmas and the New Year. Family loyalties were high on his list of priorities.

---

59 Census Returns for Swansea, 1851
60 10 & 11 Victoria *cap* cclx 1847
61 11 Victoria, Session 1847
62 W H Jones, *op cit*, p 189

Chapter IV

Putting Down Roots

Fortunately Starling had already established himself in his own right in the social and cultural life of Swansea before the unhappy wrangle over Tyrllandwr.

His first independent home was in Cambrian Place where, from 1833 to 1842, he lived next door to the Assembly Rooms, at that time the centre of a constant round of lively activities. Only someone who could enter whole-heartedly into the high spirits of these occasions, often lasting late into the night, would have chosen such a house. Indeed its very convenience for attendance at the various functions might well have commended it to him and to Florance who spent much of his university vacation with his brother.

One such function, a Fancy Dress Ball, held in the Assembly Rooms on January 18 1836, was attended by a hundred and fifty of 'the principal Gentry of the County', among them Mr F Benson, dressed as a Bolero Dancer and William Logan, as a Contrabandista.[1] Starling was also present but was not in fancy dress, possibly because of his recent accident, of which we shall hear more shortly.

Later that year came the Bachelors' Ball, again at the Assembly Rooms, 'graced by all the beauty and elegance of the neighbourhood'. Dancing commenced at 10 pm, and at 1 am the company sat down to a magnificent 'Picnic Supper' ... 'liberally contributed by the ladies of the neighbourhood'. Dancing then continued until later in the morning.[2]

Although no mention is made of individual guests, it is hard to imagine Starling's not being there, unless he was away from home. Sleep would have been impossible anywhere in the immediate vicinity of the Assembly Rooms.

That same week, on September 20 1836, an important event was taking place in his parents' social calendar. Mr and Mrs Benson were entertaining the new Duke of Beaufort at Sketty Park in the morning and, later the same day, after his visit to Kilvrough and his Gower seigniory, to dinner in the evening.[3] The Duke had only recently succeeded his father and it was of prime importance to T S Benson's future plans to establish a sound relationship with the present holder of the title.

At the time of the late Duke's death in November 1835 Elizabeth Benson, writing to their old family friend and adviser, Alfred Turner, had expressed her admiration for his widow with whose schemes for the extension of education in Swansea she had enthusiastically associated herself.

1 C Jan 30 1836, p 3
2 C Sept 17 1836, p 3
3 C Sept 24 1836, p 3

His excellent Widow - is beautifully supported by divine Grace under her great bereavement, and his Daughters, I suppose you are aware all spiritual Christians - and united to them who are devoted Christian characters. May the Lord endue her Sons also with his heavenly grace to enable them in their high stations to witness a good Confession of Christian doctrine & practice.[4]

There were to be times in the future when Mrs Benson might have justifiably felt that the new Duke was falling short of her high aspirations for him, at least in his relations with those seeking to plan for the future prosperity of Swansea.

Whatever difficulties his father's business interests were to create later for Starling, his stepmother, at least, had built up a fund of goodwill by her exertions on behalf of others. As early as April 1831, she was already involved in the Duchess of Beaufort's project of setting up a school for the younger children of Swansea, as described in 'The Cambrian' of April 9 and 23. She was elected President at a meeting of subscribers, where the thanks of those present were extended to her 'for her universal exertions in establishing this society'. Her two stepdaughters, Sarah Jane and Emma (shortly to be married to Thomas Henry Usborne, the nephew of her father's partner) were put on the Committee, while Starling became a Trustee for the ground in Orchard Field generously granted them by the Duke of Beaufort.[5]

Mrs Benson had been collecting vigorously for the fund. The three elder Benson children, Starling, Sarah Jane and Emma, had donated £1 each, while young Florance gave 10/- and little Henry and Richard, 5/- each.[6] Later Emma's husband also became a subscriber, and Mrs Meux's friend, Miss Salmon, who had accompanied her to Woodlands Castle, contributed 5/-. Mrs Benson increased her annual subscription from £1 to £3, and by the March of the following year was seeking to increase it further, but by that time sums over £1 were being returned, including Mr Vivian's £10.[7] Even the staff at Sketty Park had joined in the effort, their 'voluntary contributions' amounting to 17/-.

Later, in December 1835, Elizabeth was busy promoting the Duchess's scheme for an Infants' School in Morriston, the district closest to the Forest Works, which Starling was about to represent on the Town Council. She was now once more collecting enthusiastically among family and friends, including the Hart Logans in Suffolk and her close personal friend, Mrs Pringle, who was still living in North Cray.[8]

There were plenty of other examples of the family's willingness to be involved in 'good works'; the help given to the distressed Irish clergy,[9] donations made to the work of the Auxiliary Bible Society for Swansea and the Deanery of Gower,[10] and Elizabeth's support of the British and Foreign School for Boys in Goat Street

4 UCS/BC, EMB to Alfred Turner, Christmas 1835
5 C April 9 1831, p 3; *cf* April 23, p 3
6 C April 30 1831, p 3
7 C March 3 1832, p 3
8 C Dec 12 1835, p 2
9 C Jan 9 1836, p 3
10 C July 25 1835, p 3

under the patronage of the Duke of Beaufort.[11] Then there was the Swansea Infirmary to be supported by voluntary donations. Mrs Benson made an annual contribution of a guinea and continued to do so even after leaving Swansea, in addition to the subscription of seven guineas given annually by the firm of Benson, Logan & Co. Starling was elected to the committee.[12] Later, during Mansel Philipps's year of office, he was involved with the Mayor's fund aimed at 'mitigating the sufferings and privations of the poor'.[13]

More personal perhaps was their interest in the case of Charles Tedball, bankrupted through the loss of his ship, the 'New Blessing', on October 31 1835. The Committee set up to aid the unfortunate seaman had undertaken to give 2/6 in the pound as a general release, but there was still room for individual contributions such as Starling's £2 and Mrs Benson's £1, given undoubtedly with the greater sympathy because of Starling's own experience that same week.[14]

On October 26, the Monday before the accident to the 'New Blessing', a sloop called the 'John', carrying a mixed cargo of copper, stone coal and oysters *en route* for Bristol, had been wrecked off the Neath bar with the loss of one life. Starling himself had gone on the following Wednesday evening to supervise the salvaging of the Benson cargo. This expedition undertaken by boat in the dark would have been taxing enough in itself, without what ensued. On reaching the West Pier, then in dire need of repair, he fell and broke his thigh. The journey from the pier to Cambrian Place must have been a painful one and the whole experience made a strong impression on Starling and the family.[15]

Mrs Benson, writing to their friend, Alfred Turner, recalled that they had lately 'had great occasion to bless and praise God's holy name in the deliverance of our dear son Starling from imminent danger when he broke his thigh which misfortune he bore with Christian patience and submission to the Will of God'.[16] Certainly good did come out of evil in that the accident alerted members of the public to the dangerous state of the pier and eventually the necessary repairs were put in hand.

In spite of his misfortune Starling was still present, as we have seen, at the Fancy Dress Ball of January 18 1836. By the time of the Fancy Dress Ball in the Assembly Rooms at the beginning of January 1839, there was no going simply as himself. Both brothers now took up the Spanish theme Florance had adopted three years earlier, the latter going as a Spanish matador, with Starling as a Contrabandista, showing a certain wry humour in his choice of character.[17] There is no mention of William Logan's being there. One wonders indeed whether, on this occasion, Starling was wearing the very costume previously worn by Logan. Even their choice of theme may well have reflected Logan's interest in all things Spanish. During his London years he had been very much drawn to the Spanish community in the Metropolis and had learnt the language, giving him an

11 C Aug 20 1836, p 3
12 C July 16 1836, p 1
13 C Jan 27 1838, p 3
14 C March 26 1836, p 2; *vide* C Oct 24 & 31 1835, p 3
15 C Oct 31 1835, p 3; *cf* Nov 7, 1835, p 3
16 UCS/BC, EMB to Alfred Turner, Christmas 1835
17 C Jan 5 1839, p 3

advantage when he travelled abroad in the interests of his uncle's business.[18]

According to his biographer, by the end of his time in London, Logan had become frustrated by the social round in which his uncle's commitments had involved him. Here in Swansea he may well have opted for a less hectic life in order to concentrate on his researches. Starling, on the other hand, seems, with the passage of time, to have entered even more enthusiastically into the social activities of his peers.

By 1856 the January Ball in the Assembly Rooms had been replaced by the one given by 'The Bachelors' among whom Starling was to play a prominent part. This event was announced as follows:

> Our merry and mirth-loving friends, the Bachelors of Swansea, ever anxious to cater for the innocent amusement and recreation of the fair, purpose giving a ball at the Assembly Rooms on Tuesday evening next on a scale of liberality superior to anything of the kind which has taken place for some time past.[19]

Upwards of a hundred and fifty ladies and gentlemen attended the ball. The setting in the Assembly Rooms had been converted into an 'artificial landscape' with flowers presented by the 'fair ones'. Dancing commenced at 9.30 and continued until 6 am. Although the honour of being Head of Table fell to Dr Thomas Williams, with Mr Padley as Vice Chairman, Starling's name led the list of Bachelors given in 'The Cambrian' report.

By the following year, as we have already seen in the account of the glamorous event where he opened the dancing with Mrs Vivian, he had progressed to Senior Bachelor. Starling was now approaching his fifties and we can well imagine that, from time to time, he needed a break in the course of the twenty-five dances named in the programme, ranging from the opening Paris Quadrille, through the Sultan Polka, the Sebastopol Quadrille (its topical title undoubtedly touching a deeper note in Starling than in many others taking part because of Henry's involvement in the Crimea) and the Lily of the Valley Valse, to the final Sir Roger de Coverley Country Dance.[20]

The vigorous exercise of the evening obviously made for large appetites. The delicacies consumed included four York hams, turkeys, tongues, beef, mutton, brawn, lamb, veal cakes, chickens, pheasants, calves' head pie, woodcock and partridge pie, jellies, sweets, creams, custards, trifles, cheese cake, tartlets, mince pies, plum cakes, tipsy cakes, sponge cakes, plum puddings, sandwiches, Stilton cheese, etc, etc.

Later that same year, in April 1857, the 'Benedicts', those who had succumbed to the allurements of the fair sex, reciprocated by entertaining the Bachelors to a Ball, the last of the season, where the need of a hall capable of housing four hundred rather than the two hundred there present was keenly felt.[21] By now the

18   Bernard J Harrington, Life of Sir William E Logan (Montreal 1883), p 58
19   C Jan 18 1856, p 4
20   C Jan 16 1857, p 4; Sw and Glam Herald, Jan 21, p 2
21   C April 17 1857, p 4

12 Cambrian Place in the 1830s showing the Assembly Rooms and Starling's house on the left
Sketch: DMB

13 Visit of the British Association for the Advancement of Science to the RISW, 1848
SM, Swansea City Council

THE ROYAL INSTITUTION OF SOUTH WALES, FROM A TALBOTYPE.

Assembly Rooms were admittedly in decline, inadequate in accommodation and shabby in appearance. Already, to meet expenses, cheap concerts were being held there, and the pressing need for a new venue for civic functions was being stressed, although no one seemed committed to forge ahead with the proposed scheme for the new Prince's Hall.

This, however, is to look well into the future. Back in the 1830s, Starling had found another interest which led him to play a prominent role in the developing cultural life of the district.

He became with Logan one of the founder members of the newly formed Philosophical and Literary Institution. The ever-energetic G G Francis, with the help of J G Jeffreys and others, had persuaded over fifty gentlemen to become subscribers to this body, and by May 1835, a list of rules had appeared in 'The Cambrian'. On June 1 1835, a General Meeting of these subscribers was held at the Town Hall under the presidency of the Revd Dr William Hewson, Vicar of Swansea. William Logan was elected to a committee of ten, including such notables as W R Grove, the banker J M Voss, Dr Howell and G G Francis himself, while here, at the initial meeting, Mrs Benson of Sketty Park was named among the additional subscribers.[22] A week later a second General Meeting was held, with the Vice-President, Sir John Morris, in the Chair.

Young Logan's reputation as a geologist was already established locally and was to be acknowledged further afield when he exhibited a map of the coal basin between the Vale of Neath and Kidwelly at the British Association Meetings in Liverpool in 1837.[23] Before that, however, he had been elected a Fellow of the Geological Society, sponsored by R J Nevill of Llanelli. Logan's achievements had attracted the attention of no less an expert than Sir Henry de la Beche, father-in-law of Lewis Llewelyn Dillwyn. His colleague's success undoubtedly gave an added impetus to Starling's interest in the subject.

Not surprisingly, in the First Annual Meeting of the Philosophical and Literary Society on June 4 1836, Logan was made its Honorary Secretary. At that same meeting Starling was appointed to the committee.[24] By the following year, 1837, Hart Logan, although living at Kentwell House in Suffolk, had also become a subscriber, as had William's youngest brother, Henry, who was still in London. Thus both the Benson and Logan families were closely involved from the beginning of an important move to enhance the cultural standing of Swansea. In addition, Starling had been put on the Managing Committee of fifteen and retained his position on it even when, in 1838, it was reduced to seven, exclusive of Hon. Curators, Librarians and Secretaries.

The time had now come to establish a permanent home for the Institution and on April 19 1838 a special meeting was convened in the Town Hall to consider the erection of a building to house the society.[25] It was also necessary to appoint Trustees and to form a committee to draw up a code of rules for the approval of subscribers at their next General Meeting. It was a tribute to the good impression he had made on his contemporaries that, as a young man of twenty-nine, Starling

22   C June 6 1835, p 3
23   C Oct 14 1837, p 3
24   C June 8 1836, p 3
25   C April 21 1838, p 3

should become one of the first Trustees of the new Institution, together with Sir John Morris, J H Vivian, the two Dillwyns, W R Grove and T E Thomas. As a Trustee, he automatically served on the Building Committee, which was given extra support by the election to it of such members as the redoubtable C R M Talbot, Matthew Moggridge, G G Francis, Richard Aubrey and W H Smith of Hen Dderwen.[26]

It must have been an exciting time as this body of enthusiasts saw their vision realised in the magnificent Palladian building on the Burrows, fortunately still the home of the Swansea Museum. From March 1839 it was henceforth to be known as the Royal Institution of South Wales. The Burrows was at the time a much sought-after area, its reputation still unsullied by the taint of commerce and its accompanying evils which were later to isolate it from other centres of culture. In our own day the wheel has come full circle, making its location once more a valued part of Swansea's heritage.

At the time the project seemed a promising investment. Like the Logans, Starling had taken out two shares of £10 each, bringing in £3 interest per annum, but neither the shares nor the annual subscriptions were sufficient to meet all the expenses involved in setting up the new venture, and over the years it was the generous donations, such as L W Dillwyn's £25 and Starling's £10 towards the purchase of a geological cabinet and Starling's £5 towards the extension of the library, which helped to provide the extra amenities needed.[27] By 1843 he had become Curator of the Geological Section, and when a new appeal was made in 1849 for show cases, with L W Dillwyn contributing £25 and his son, Lewis Llewelyn Dillwyn, £10, Starling came up with the gift of £100.[28]

It was not only financial support that was needed. Donations of exhibits were also welcome. His excursions into the wilds of Gower in the company of Logan and Colonel Wood of Stouthall, with Florance sometimes accompanying them, had already resulted in the discovery of valuable specimens from the area. These included alluvial fossil bones from the Paviland Caves which had been deposited in the Institution as early as 1837,[29] followed in 1838 by Florance's donation of the vertebrae of the Ichthyosaurus. That same year Starling contributed such exhibits as the Common Gull (*Larus Camus*), a Knot (*Tringa Canutus*) and Fossil Shells, collected from shale at Penclawdd.[30]

Also in 1838 a contribution of personal interest to the Bensons was made by G G Francis. He presented the Museum with a copy of a sermon 'On the Duty of Contending for the Faith', preached on October 4 1835 by the Revd Henry Maude Roxby at St John's, Swansea, to mark the Third Centenary of the publication of the first entire Protestant version of the Bible in English.[31] Did Grant Francis (no lover of the Bensons, especially at that time) realise that the author was Mrs Benson's first cousin on her mother's side who, moreover, was married to her cousin on her father's side, Uncle Thomas's daughter, Jane?

---

26 C March 23 1839, p 3
27 Annual Report of the RISW Council, 1845-46, p 5
28 *Op cit*, 1849-50
29 *Op cit*, 1837-38
30 *Ibid*
31 *Ibid*

Each year one member or other of the family or firm had some aspect of his activities recognised by the Royal Institution. Starling's involvement with the local coal industry was shown in 1839 by his unusual gift of 'a specimen of the canary bird', presumably of the sort used for testing for gas in mines, and also 'a very fine ditto (!) of stalactitic oxide of iron' from an old coal level, Graigola.[32] Logan's contribution was a specimen of 'the scorpion and three ditto of snake'. In the 1839/40 Report reference was made to Benson, Logan & Co.'s use of Nicholas Troughton's 'discovery of a simple and efficacious contrivance to destroy injurious vapours' connected with copper smelting.[33] Yet another link with the Company was provided by William Edmond who had communicated to the Institution a description of the self-regulating anemometer he had invented.[34]

By this time his cousin, William Logan, was well advanced in his plans for his visit to Canada where he was to head the first Geological Survey of the country. His donations to the Museum were coming in thick and fast. These ranged from a Welsh New Testament and a Welsh Grammar Book, from which he had been learning the language so as to be able to converse with the local population, to some of his paintings, including a sketch of Mumbles viewed from Sketty Park.[35] His final paper during 1840/41 session was on a subject near to his heart, a lecture on 'Beds of Clay lying immediately below Coal Seams of South Wales'.

Logan's leaving Swansea entailed his resignation from his various commitments, including his Honorary Curatorship of the Geology Section, his immediate successor being Dr Nicol. The following year, however, Starling was elected to this prestigious position. As a result, he was in office when the British Association visited Swansea in August 1848, an honour for which the town was indebted to its illustrious son, W R Grove, the eminent scientist and lawyer. As a member of the local Committee, Starling was caught up in much of the planning, particularly for the use of material relating to the geology of the area. A copy of a speech bearing his name and delivered at the Annual Meeting on August 11 on the 'Mineral Productions of South Wales' can still be seen in the Royal Institution. So far his pronouncements were mainly to do with the subjects he knew best, copper and coal, as shown in the title of a lecture he gave before the Royal Institution in 1847 on 'Copper, its Ores and Uses'.

For the actual meetings, between August 9 and 16, Starling had two of his brothers staying with him at his home in Gloucester Place where he had moved in 1842. Florance was now practising at the Bar and Richard, having just finished his year as Kennicott Hebrew Scholar at Oxford, was about to enter into holy orders at Surbiton. According to the list of those present at the meetings, members of the Hewson family were also staying in Gloucester Place and might well have been Starling's guests. The former Vicar of Swansea had been a neighbour in Cambrian Place and a friend in a way Dr Hewson's successor, the Revd E B Squire, would never be.

---

32 *Ibid*; *cf* C April 8 1837, p 3
33 Annual Report of the RISW Council, 1839-40, p 32
34 *Op cit*, p 84
35 *Op cit*, pp 51-55, 57

Starling's personal contribution to the programme was obviously much appreciated by Professor John Phillips of York, the Assistant General Secretary of the British Association, who had travelled to Swansea in the June before the meetings to check the arrangements. There had been some opposition to the gathering's being held in a location 'so remote from the Metropolis and the chief seats of English learning, remote also from those great highways of communication ... the highways of steam,' but happily that had been overcome.[36]

J H Vivian was entertaining at his Singleton mansion a house party of nineteen guests, including the president, the Marquis of Northampton, and the former president, Sir Robert Inglis, while other influential visitors were being entertained by Lewis Weston Dillwyn at Sketty Hall, by his son, John Dillwyn Llewelyn at Penllergaer and by Robert Eaton at Brynymor. W R Grove was staying with his family at Danycoed and among the highlights of the meetings was a discussion between him and Dr Michael Faraday as the result of a paper on the effects of carbonic acid on the growth of ferns. Of particular interest to the Geology section was 'a marathon extemporaneous lecture lasting two and a half hours by Sir Henry de la Beche on "The Geology of South Wales, Gloucestershire and Somerset".'

During the course of the meetings Starling had presented some abstracts based on a study of the local coalfields. He was obviously not entirely satisfied with his work and later, he had written to Professor Phillips asking his opinion. The reassuring reply he received from the Professor's home at St Mary's Lodge, York, is of particular interest as little of Starling Benson's private correspondence has been preserved.

> My dear Sir,
> Your abstracts are not too long nor have they any other fault that I can discover. They might be longer if you wished but they are so clear as they stand that I should not desire any change. The subject of the change of the coal to anthracite is so interesting that I think it might have been made a topic for a special enquiry and report.
>
> You will perhaps give any further thought you have about it at Birmingham ... What a most curious subject.
>
> Yours truly,
>
> John Phillips[37]

This was a gratifying response to his query and the encouragement must have fuelled his enthusiasm for his studies; by the end of 1851 Starling had been elected a Fellow of the Geological Society together with Dr John Percy.[38]

In the meantime there had been an exciting development involving his friend, Colonel Wood of Stouthall, to whom exclusive permission had been granted by

36 Margaret Walker, 'The British Association in Swansea is 1848', reprinted by courtesy of the Gower Magazine to celebrate the BA's visit to the city in 1990
37 UCS/BC, John Phillips of York to SB, Aug 30 1848
38 C Dec 5 1851, p 2

the Duke of Beaufort to examine the Bacon Hole Cave. This expensive operation was commenced in April 1850 and was planned to extend over a whole year. In the upper deposits the bones were found to be in a fair condition, although it proved difficult to separate them without breaking them, but those in the lower deposit of dark marl fell apart at the slightest touch. Nevertheless, by drying and preserving them in the manner adopted by experienced collectors, they could be made perfectly sound and useful for examination. Several treated in this way by Starling were capable of being re-formed and these, including specimens of elephant, rhino, cave-bear, wolf and other bones, were deposited in the Royal Institution.[39]

Darwin would not publish his 'Origin of Species' for another eight years but already the investigations of such writers as Sir Charles Lyell had awakened a wide-spread interest in the age of the planet and the nature of its early inhabitants. A paper given by Starling in 1851 on the Bone Cave of Bacon Hole would therefore be of great topical interest. It was later published in the Report for that year with diagrams and section, and has left us some indication of the optimism with which he at least looked forward to future scientific developments which we can well imagine would strike the rest of his family with dismay.

In the main, however, he tended to concentrate on what he knew best, soil and mineral deposits. In 1849 he had spoken on 'The Fossils of the Old Red Sandstone', and the following year on 'The Limestone of the Castle Quarry, Mumbles'. Later, in 1852, came a paper on 'The Varieties of Coal in the South Wales Coal Basin', but by 1853 he was ready to embark once more on a theme related to that of his 1851 paper, with his 'Comparative Anatomy, recent and fossil'.[40]

Already his growing versatility had been proved when, in 1849, in the absence of Lewis Llewelyn Dillwyn through illness, he had filled the gap at a *Soirée* at the Royal Institution with an address on 'The History and Advantages of Literary and Scientific Societies'. Here he paid tribute to the contribution being made to contemporary knowledge by such bodies and congratulated Swansea on having an institution second to none in the provinces. His talk was pithy and to the point, as was his treatment of any subject he might be discussing, a quality which stood him in good stead when he became President. But that came further on in his career and is something to which we must revert at a later stage.

Meanwhile he was finding yet other outlets for his energies, one of which was through his love of music. Soon after settling in Swansea, he had become a Director of the Musical Department of the Swansea Harmonic Society,[41] and in the future his name was frequently to be found among the patrons of major musical events, such as the Grand Amateur Concert held in 1862 in aid of funds for those bereaved by a serious explosion at the Gethin Colliery, Merthyr.[42] He had also apparently had some intention initially of interesting himself in Welsh culture at a time when native traditions were in danger of being swept away by

39   Annual Report of RISW Council, 1849-50
40   Reports of Swansea Literary and Scientific Society, 1846-53
41   C Jan 7 1837, p 3
42   C March 1 1862, p 15

the arrival in South Wales of so many outsiders who either despised or ignored the language. He became a subscriber to the *Cymreigyddion*[43] and among the many family relics preserved in the home of his great-nephew, Colonel J R E Benson, of Dorchester, is a copy of a Nineteenth Century Welsh grammar book, by which Starling had possibly hoped to make some progress in a better understanding of the vernacular, probably during his years in Penclawdd. How far he succeeded we shall never know.

But not all Starling's pastimes were as highbrow as his incursions into the realms of paleontology or his interest in music or Welsh. As early as September 1835, soon after settling in Cambrian Place in the still unspoiled area of the Burrows, he had applied for a game certificate.[44] In Norman Thomas's 'Swansea's Districts and Villages' there is a lively description of a group of local sportsmen, including Starling, hunting the hare from Heathfield through the outlying districts of West Swansea as far as Hill House in Cockett. There Iltid Thomas, its owner, entertained them to cigars and 'cwrw' before they set off again once a scent had been found in a dell at the back of the house, with the dogs dashing 'in and out of brambles and furze bushes.' Those opposed to blood sports will be relieved to hear that at this time the scent was lost and the hare got away although, earlier, two others had been killed by their pursuers.[45]

Among those present on this occasion, apart from Starling and their host, Iltid Thomas, had been John Dillwyn Llewelyn of Penllergaer, his brother-in-law Matthew Moggridge, Captain Lindsay and the ever-vocal W H Smith of Hen Dderwen. It was a good thing that they should have got to know Starling for what he was in himself in an atmosphere of relaxed *camaraderie* before they became too deeply embroiled in the heated debate generated by his father's challenge to Swansea.

43   Collected Reports of *Cymreigyddion* Society (Swansea; Rutter), Jan 27 1837
44   C Sept 19 1835, p 1
45   Norman Thomas, Swansea's Districts and Villages, (Swansea: Qualprint Wales, Ltd, 1965) p 139

Chapter V

The Battle of the South Dock

Not even after the opening of the New Cut in 1845 was Starling able to sit back and let matters take their course. He had been aware from 1839 that the idea of a dock on the Burrows, supported by both J H Vivian and Lewis Dillwyn, posed a threat to the Benson hopes of developing the east bank of the Tawe. He was also concerned about the depreciation of property in the area where he was renting a house in Gloucester Place. This belonged to Timothy Essery who had other houses in the Burrows, all likely to be affected by any commercial changes in the nature of the locality.

A similar development in Fabian's Bay on the east side of the river would have enhanced the value of the Tyrllandwr land, as his critics were quick to point out when he ventured to criticise the South Dock plan. He had therefore to convince them that, in seeking to advance the claims of the east side, he was not acting from ulterior motives. He genuinely believed in the feasibility of having a shipping place where it would be most convenient for the increasing volume of coal being sent down from the South Wales coalfields.

So compelling were these advantages to him that, by November 1846, 'averse' as he claimed to be, 'to any newspaper controversy', he felt bound to go into print in the columns of 'The Cambrian' to bring them to the public notice, while always seeking to treat the subject in 'a fair and courteous manner'.[1]

This phrase was taken up by the irrepressible George Grant Francis, a keen advocate of the proposed dock on the Burrows (later to be called the South Dock) and secretary of the privately promoted Swansea Dock Company. He, writing at first anonymously and then under his own name, sought to prove 'courteously' that not all Mr Benson's arguments were as 'fair' as he would have them believe. 'Self-interest', he wrote, 'is known to warp even strong judgments.' With the second adjective 'courteous' he had no quarrel:

> ...everyone who has the pleasure of Mr Benson's acquaintance knows how eminently he possesses the qualifications of a Gentleman and that nature has blessed him with an amiability really enviable; - but I believe it is equally well known that, as "smooth waters run deep", so few individuals possess a keener sense of their own interest, or know better how to wield even adverse elements to their own advantage.[2]

In September 1846 the Duke of Beaufort visited Swansea and was met by a deputation seeking his patronage of any undertaking on the Burrows where he held the mineral rights. As a result, the distinguished engineer, Isambard

---

1   C Nov 24 1846; later published as a pamphlet, Dec 1 1846
2   C Dec 1 1846; *cf* Swansea Harbour and Docks SM 66/102

Kingdom Brunel, who worked for both the GWR and the SWR, was instructed to prepare a report on the site. This appeared on October 9, and stated that the development of the float or the North Dock (as it was to become) was 'inapplicable'; any dock so formed would be totally inadequate for the needs of the port and militate against the general development of the harbour. His preference was for the new dock on the west side. He insisted, however, that such a dock would be useless without communication by railway through the town. Without that rival docks would spring up on the east side.[3]

Already the South Wales Railway Company, incorporated in 1845, was authorised by a second Act in 1846 to build a line into Swansea via Landore, with two termini, one for passengers in the Pottery Field, where the High Street Station was later built, and the other for minerals at a lower level on the Brewery Wharf adjoining the river. How the railway was to be linked with the new dock had obviously presented the members of the Swansea Dock Company with certain difficulties. These, their secretary, G G Francis, had sought to meet by suggesting to the SWR an alternative rail route into the town. This provided for a branch to come from Landore, under the Graig quarries, then in front of Heathfield, across the Mysydd Fields, on to join the Oystermouth tramroad and so into the dock.[4]

Whichever way it went, such a link between railway and dock would bring inconvenience to the part of the town it crossed, as Starling sought to show. To gain wider publicity for his views, he now published his letter of November 1846 as a pamphlet in which he outlined vigorously his objections to the suggested dock and the railway that would feed it. These were not limited to the threat to property in the Burrows, though in this he whole-heartedly supported his Gloucester Place neighbours who were anxious about the possible depreciation of their houses. His special concern was with 'the alleged diversity of interests in the western and eastern sides of the river' which he saw as a serious stumbling block to any true progress.[5]

The concentration of trade on the western side since 1830 had done nothing to increase the local coal trade, although the population had doubled and the amount of coal to be exported had escalated. Swansea had missed out on the opportunity to benefit from the situation. The growing trade had gone to other ports such as Newport, Cardiff and Llanelly where access to the sea was easier and greater shipping facilities were available.

Wharfs for ships bringing in copper ore had originally been on the western side, but with the development of the larger type of shipping, owners of smelting works had erected their own wharfs on the eastern side of the river. Had it not been for their initiative, the town would have been the poorer. The large amount of money brought into the area by the trade carried on on the eastern side benefited business on the western side. He estimated that in 1844 this had amounted to exactly £50,000.

Facilities existing on the western side had, according to Starling, failed to advance the prosperity of Swansea, while the persisting fear of competition from

3   W H Jones, *op cit*, 178
4   *Ibid*
5   C Nov 24 1846; later published as a pamphlet, Dec 1 1846

14   Isambard Kingdom Brunel.   Illustrated London News

the east had stifled growth which would have proved profitable to the whole
community. For example, had there been support for the earlier idea of a railway
up the Swansea Valley, the shipment of coal would have been easier and
employment prospects improved, thus leading to a general increase in trade. The
idea, however, was dismissed, simply because the railway would terminate on the
eastern side (ie, at Tyrllandwr).

   A survey by George Bush, engineer to the Llanelly and Taff Vale Railways,
initiated by Starling in 1840, had shown it was as expensive to develop three
miles of railroad on the western side as the whole sixteen miles on the east. But

again the project had fallen through because certain of the promoters would not countenance a railway on the eastern side, nor could they afford the high cost of its construction on the west. Now, Starling pointed out, at last the principle of a railway had been accepted. The Swansea Vale Railway would come into being with its terminus exactly where it had been proposed before (at Tyrllandwr). As a result, the lower costs of transporting coal should attract more trade to Swansea, with increased prosperity for the whole area.

Starling had also consulted Rhys W Jones, a civil engineer who, in addition to his work in connection with the Swansea Vale Railway, had worked on Newquay Harbour and assisted Brunel in laying out the Vale of Neath Railway. The result was a plan for a dock on the eastern side, at Fabian's Bay, at an estimated cost of £120,000, which, in addition to being less expensive, would require less tonnage duties. Direct access would already be provided by the SVR, whereas, on the western side, the connection between railway and port would have to be made at a great expense to the residents, possibly as high as £200,000.

All these difficulties would be obviated by a dock to the east of the Tawe. If a bridge were to be built across the river at the Corporation Quay, a dock at Fabian's Bay would be as near the old Town Hall as one on the Burrows. For those interested in promoting trade in general, either site would be acceptable, provided there were an accessible railway, a port with a float for the transport of minerals, and adequate wharfage.

There was a further point to consider. Increase in trade led to an increased demand for residential accommodation, but no one would look for property in an area adjacent to the docks:

> It is well ascertained that while water or Dock frontage is most valuable, the house property adjoining it is far inferior in value to that situated in the cleaner parts of the town; and therefore it is important to have docks not only within reasonable distance, but also at a reasonable distance from, the best parts of the town.[6]

Moreover, unless the property was actually needed for the development, there would be no compensation, a fact of which those involved needed to be made aware.

In addition to making his views known through the Press, Starling, in his capacity of 'a large shipper in the port', appeared before a preliminary enquiry held on Thursday, February 18 1847, to voice concern about the injurious effect on shipping of the proposed entrance to the Harbour. He felt the capital available was inadequate and the scheme, therefore, likely to prove abortive. In support of his arguments he called as witnesses both the Harbour Master, Captain John Edwards, and the Harbour Engineer, James Hall, while himself raising several technical points about the measurements likely to be adopted; these did not, he felt, correspond to the plans.[7]

He was destined to remain a lone voice crying in the wilderness as far as his doubts about the future success of a dock in such a position were concerned,

6   *Ibid*
7   Swansea Docks Pamphlets, Report of preliminary enquiry, Thurs, Feb 18 1847, SM 66/110

doubts which he was to see amply and painfully justified during his years as Chairman of the Swansea Harbour Trust; but on the more immediate issue of his fears for the depreciation of property in the vicinity of the docks, he had the full support of his neighbours.

The application for an Act of Parliament for the provision of a dock on the Burrows came before the House of Commons on May 6 1847. Among the most active promoters of the project were Lewis Llewelyn Dillwyn, Nathaniel Cameron, Nathaniel Pryce Cameron and William Booth Joseph Pryce Cameron, Michael J Michael and Edmund Nash Norcott. Together with 'other persons and corporations', many from outside the Principality, they were putting up a capital of £100,000 and were accordingly the first directors.[8] The local chairman of the new board was Colonel Evan Morgan of St Helen's, whose family claimed descent from Bleddyn ap Maenerch, Lord of Brecknock, while the secretary, as we have seen, was George Grant Francis. Promoters and opponents both appeared before the Committee. Those petitioning against the Bill included Dr Bird, Starling's predecessor as Mayor, Starling himself, his landlord, T B Essery, and Richard Aubrey, together with Thomas Attwood, their solicitor, and Rhys W Jones, the civil engineer already mentioned.[9]

There had been a last minute hitch when there had not been a quorum present in the Committee in the House of Commons to enable proceedings to go ahead, but, fortunately, it had been possible for the Speaker at the last moment to add Mr J H Vivian to those already present, Sir D L Evans, Mr Booth and Mr Sanderson, with Mr Hinde in the Chair.

Those petitioning against the Bill were represented by Florance Benson. In the light of hindsight, one wonders whether representation by someone less closely connected by family ties to one of the petitioners might have carried more weight before those assessing the merits of the case.

Starling's old associate of early days in the Royal Institution, William Grove, appeared for the promoters. He outlined the transactions that had already taken place in connection with the purchase of Tyrllandwr and the creation of the New Cut, leading on to the point that, of all the objectors, only Starling Benson had business interests at stake. The others were concerned merely as occupiers of houses likely to be affected by the dock development. Moreover, Mr Benson had himself projected a scheme for a dock on the east bank of the river which, it was pointed out, would have very much enhanced the value of his father's property had it been adopted.

When Starling's time came to put the case on behalf of the residents of Gloucester and Cambrian Place, he called for support upon the Mayor of Swansea, Mr T B Essery, who held the leases of two houses in Gloucester Place, including Starling's, and two in Cambrian Place. The Gloucester Place houses had eighty years' unexpired lease and were worth between £1100 and £1200; those in Cambrian Place near the Assembly Rooms with seventy years' unexpired lease were valued, one at £900 and the other at £1000. One of these had been an earlier home of Starling's. Now as the occupier under agreement of one of Mr

8   Swansea Dock Act 1847, 11 Victoria; *cf* Swansea Docks Pamphlets, Proceedings and evidence before the Committee of the House of Commons, SM 66/110
9   *Ibid*

Essery's houses in Gloucester Place, he had no doubt that the creation of a half-tide basin of the type envisaged would cause the property on the Burrows to depreciate considerably.

In his evidence, Starling also referred to the damage likely to be done to the Burrows by the shipping of coal. Only three years before, in 1844, the Corporation had spent a large sum of money to level the ballast bank and form a walk along the seafront, with bathing facilities. These would be lost to the public if the proposed development went ahead. Private families would no longer choose to reside in the district, nor would there be anywhere to walk, the promenade in Burrows Square being the only place of its kind on the seafront.

Pointing out on a map the way in which communication between the Docks and the South Wales Railway would have to be made, either along the existing line of the Oystermouth Tramroad or intersecting Wind Street, he gave it as his opinion that an efficient communication to the Dock could not be made without the use of locomotives, and without a good system of communication the Dock would be useless. This issue had come before the House previously when Cameron's Coalbrook Steam Coal and Swansea and Loughor Railway Company had been incorporated by a private Act of Parliament in 1845. In it provision had been made to debar the use of locomotives between Dunvant and the terminus because of threatened damage to residential property in the area of Swansea Bay, a restriction to which both Starling and Florance drew the attention of the Committee. Nor was there any feasible alternative. Unfortunately the Canal could not be extended, and to have to transfer coal from the Canal *en route* for the Docks was not likely to attract trade to any port.[10]

A further objection, foreseen by Starling, to the creation of a Docks on the western side was the absence of any place for the depositing of ballast. These arguments, however, failed to convince the Committee, and on July 2 1847, the Bill was passed as 'An Act for Constructing and Maintaining Docks and other works at or near the South side of the Town of Swansea' or, in short, 'The Swansea Dock Act'.

It was not long before cracks began to show in the affairs of the privately promoted Dock Company as the interests of the local members were felt to clash with those of investors coming from outside Swansea. At an Extraordinary General Meeting at the Guildhall Coffee-House in London, objections were raised to decisions being taken in Swansea rather than by the whole Board. It was suggested the local chairman, Col. Evan Morgan, had taken the minutes of a previous London meeting home with him and altered and added to them.[11] The disparate interests of this mixed bag of promoters thus militated against progress from the start.

As both Town Councillor and Harbour Trustee, Starling found himself with a double commitment to the interests of the Borough. His constant vigilance is shown by an incident at a special meeting held by the Town Council at the end of October 1851. The privately promoted Swansea Dock Act of 1847 had authorised the Dock Company's acquisition of certain lands belonging to the

10   *Ibid*
11   Rutter, Collected Reports, Swansea Dock Company, UCS Library

Corporation. C H Smith had already proposed the transaction, and Lewis Llewelyn Dillwyn was rising to second the proposition, when Starling intervened. He had no wish, he said, to offer opposition to what was being decided by the Corporation, but he was desirous of submitting one question for information. He wanted to know how the promoters of the Dock scheme defined in the plan under consideration the land that belonged to the Duke of Beaufort and that which was the property of the Corporation (a matter, still in dispute between them).[12]

Lewis Llewelyn Dillwyn, whose family had so often crossed swords with the Bensons before this, and George Grant Francis, with his ambivalent attitude towards Starling personally, were obviously nettled by this interruption. On such occasions, Starling's very politeness must have been infuriating to his opponents. Mr Dillwyn had to admit that the matter had not yet been resolved but held that the question did not apply to the Dock Company as they had asked only for land belonging to the Corporation. Grant Francis objected to the dispute's being brought in to prevent discussion of the real issue.

Starling persisted, however, in asking if the Dock Company had defined the land they wanted, to which Mr Francis replied that it was all within the pink lines on the map. The question, he felt, should be referred to such a body as the Property Committee. It was important that the Corporation should not appear in any way hostile, as that could impede progress. A long discussion ensued, at the end of which Mr Dillwyn agreed to refer the matter to a special Committee, made up of Messrs E Richards, Benson, Hallam and Grenfell. Starling had made his point.[13]

One of the issues at stake between the Duke of Beaufort and the Corporation involved reaching a decision on the highwater mark in connection with determining the boundaries of the Burrows. A magnanimous gesture by the Duke made it possible to adopt a straight line between the look-out house on the Burrows and the old gate-house on the sands as the highwater mark, thereby settling the matter of the site of the new Dock. The Corporation were thus enabled to seal the necessary documents in favour of the Dock Company 'who became the purchasers of the land for five shillings'.[14]

The new relationship thus forged with the Beaufort family culminated in the Duke's son, the Marquess of Worcester, being invited to 'cut the first sod' of the proposed dock. He was entertained by Col. Evan Morgan at St Helen's, and on Thursday, February 26 1852, carried out the ceremony on the Burrows in the presence of 'some 70,000 to 80,000 people'. He afterwards perambulated the boundaries of the dock, 'attended by the officers of the Dock Company and a band of stalwart navvies'. The celebrations were concluded with a dinner in honour of the occasion that same evening.[15]

Although begun with such high hopes, work on the South Dock did not proceed as rapidly as the members of the independent Dock Company might have wished. As early as 1848 the Corporation had mooted the question of purchasing the rights of the Dock Company and had gained authorisation by the Swansea

12 C Oct 31 1851, p 2
13 *Ibid*
14 W H Jones, *op cit*, p 193
15 *Ibid*

Corporation Act of 1850 to take up shares in it. This, however, they had neglected to do and the Dock Company found themselves struggling to meet the demand upon their financial resources.[16] Extra time for completing the work originally undertaken under the Swansea Dock Act of 1847 had been granted by the Swansea Dock (Amendment) Acts of 1850 and 1855, but even after some £90,000 had been spent on the project, there seemed little prospect of completing the work within the time allowed. The Company now found itself facing serious difficulties, making it inevitable that the Swansea Harbour Trust would have to take responsibility for continuing and completing the work.[17]

Accordingly in the Preamble to a new Bill brought forward in 1857, it was proposed as desirable that the Dock Company be dissolved, its affairs be wound up and the Trustees be authorised to complete the Docks. All the powers of the Company were to be transferred to them, and the indenture which conveyed Corporation property to the Dock Company should be confirmed. It was considered that the proposed work would be of great advantage to the Borough of Swansea. Recommendation was therefore made that the Trustees be authorised 'to make and maintain a railway to join the South Wales Railway, in the parish of Swansea, the South Wales Railway and the Vale of Neath Railway Companies guaranteeing the interest on the monies so expended.'[18]

In August 1856 Starling had been elected Chairman of the Harbour Trust in succession to Pascoe St Leger Grenfell, and now in his dual role of Chairman and member of the Town Council, he was deeply involved in the negotiations. In his former capacity he was bound to oppose a clause in the Bill authorising the taking away from the Trustees of dues on vessels entering the docks. The Executive Committee which had been examining the Bill had recommended obtaining a *locus standi* to get this clause struck out, and in order to do so, it was necessary to petition against the Swansea Harbour Bill. Apart from this clause, Starling saw no further reason to oppose any other part of the Bill as such; but to oppose any particular clause meant opposing the whole preamble which contained it. Nevertheless, it was essential, according to Starling's predecessor, Mr Grenfell, that such objection should be seen to be made 'not in any spirit of hostility, but in fairness to themselves, the public and their bondholders', words which undoubtedly reflected the Chairman's own attitude.[19]

A strange situation had arisen from the need to reach an agreement with the South Wales Railway and the Vale of Neath over their proposed approaches to the Dock. When it came to appointing representatives of the Trust to treat with the railway companies, E M Richards, who had spoken in such glowing terms of Starling in commending him to the Trustees as their next Chairman, inadvertently cast what seemed to Starling himself a slur on his integrity which he found difficult to overlook.

In suggesting that the composition of the committee to negotiate with the Directors of the two railway companies be limited to Mr Vivian, the Mayor (John Oakshot) and himself, Mr Richards explained that he 'could not ask the

16   W H Jones, *op cit*, p 186
17   *Ibid*
18   20 & 21 Victoria, *cap* cxlii - Preamble, Swansea Harbour Act, 1857
19   C Feb 13 1857, p 8

Chairman of the Trust to give his important services to the Committee' because of his connection 'with another line on the other side of the river', a reference to Starling's chairmanship of the Swansea Vale Railway.[20]

Starling was deeply hurt by the implication of Mr Richards's remarks, fearing that they would be interpreted by the public at large as suggesting his interests were at variance with those of the other Trustees, as though, by being connected with the Swansea Vale Railway, he could not act impartially as Chairman of the Trust or even as a Trust member.

In spite of Mr Richards's protest that no such aspersion was intended and that he had only wished to save Mr Benson possible embarrassment, Starling continued to smart under a sense of implicit criticism. He assured his fellow Trustees that, had he been appointed to the Committee, he would have looked only 'to those things which would promote the trade and prosperity of the place irrespective of any private view', having no wish whatever 'to impede the extension of the South Wales Railway to the Docks on the western side of the river'.[21]

By the following month, December 1856, Starling's words had obviously borne fruit as the sub-committee, appointed to meet the representatives of the South Wales Railway Company, now consisted of himself, Mr H H Vivian and Mr Richards. Fortunately Starling was never one to bear a grudge; he had, in the meantime, gone on working as though nothing had happened, seeing both Mr Talbot, the Chairman of the SWR, and Mr Brunel. Mr Talbot strongly supported the idea of the Trustees negotiating with the Swansea Dock Company for the purchase of the Dock, as this would then make it possible for the railways to apply to Parliament in the next session for the right to purchase their part of the undertaking from the Trust.

The Committee had already received a copy of the resolution of the Directors of the Vale of Neath Railway Company, authorising their Chairman, Mr H A Bruce (later Lord Aberdare), to negotiate on behalf of his Directors with the Harbour Trust and with the South Wales Railway Company on the terms of any co-operation on their part. Mr Vivian, too, had been active in his approach to representatives of both Railway Companies; they would be asked to guarantee the interest on the outlay of some £60,000 needed for the extension envisaged.[22]

By the March (1857) meeting of the Harbour Trust, another sub-committee also consisting of Messrs Benson, Vivian and Richards had been appointed to confer with the Dock Company and the Duke of Beaufort in order to obtain modification of a number of points in the terms of sale proposed by the Dock Company. A meeting with Mr Hooper and the Duke's legal adviser, Mr G H Somerset, on Thursday, March 5, led to the proposal of the terms on which the Duke would join the Dock Company in transferring the Company's undertaking to the Harbour Trust, with the ultimate proviso that if, on and after July 1 1864, the interest on the purchase bonds whereby the Trustees hoped to finance the new undertaking was two years in arrears, the Duke and the holders of these purchase

20   C Nov 14 1856, p 6
21   *Ibid*
22   C Dec 12 1856, p 8

bonds to the amount of £500 should be entitled to enter into possession of the docks with the power of sale, subject to prior encumbrances. To the proposed Dock Railway itself the Duke had no objection.[23]

It was further agreed with Mr Somerset that his Grace would not present a petition to Parliament to obtain a *locus standi*, although nothing at their present meeting should be taken as binding on either party. Should no arrangement be reached between the Trustees and the Duke, the former would agree to withdraw that part of the Bill relating to the purchase of the Docks.

The work upon which the Harbour Trustees were now embarking was obviously not to be undertaken lightly. Their former Chairman, Mr Grenfell, reminded them that, with the £100,000 needed for the Docks, another £100,000 to complete them and the £75,000 for the construction of the railway line, they could end up facing a bill of £275,000 and have to delay work already undertaken, such as the extension of the piers, which was absolutely necessary; but others, like Mr J W James and Mr Richards, felt he was being unnecessarily gloomy, and that the creation of the new dock would guarantee an increased income which would help their general expenditure.

In the meantime the Town Council had also been discussing the proposed Bill, and had come to the conclusion that the line of the railway advocated by Brunel was far from advantageous to the Borough. They further felt 'divers other clauses and provisions in the said Bill' would, if passed into law, prejudicially affect the property, rights and interests of the people of Swansea, particularly its traders, and accordingly arranged for the Town Clerk to bring a petition against it in its existing form.[24]

The Town Clerk's wording came in for strong criticism in a subsequent meeting. It had been understood that the petition should be drawn up in such a mild form as merely to give them a *locus standi* to enable them to watch their interests in Parliament, whereas the present wording could hardly have been stronger had the Committee wished to act in the most hostile manner. The Town Clerk, however, held to the view that such wording was necessary if they were to obtain the required *locus standi*. At the same time, he sought to pacify the dissidents by reassuring them that they would not be bound by the present form of the petition unless they made a personal appearance to support it in the House.

Starling was less dismayed than many by the wording, feeling the Corporation should not be expected to bear the blame for a petition that had been drawn up under the guidance of the Town Clerk, although he accepted that the wording could have been much milder. Nevertheless, he agreed with the view that, unless someone appeared in the House to support it, the petition would merely lie on the table without being considered. For him the main thing to petition about was the provision of a new quay to replace that being taken by the railway.[25]

The issue was clarified by the legal acumen of John Rolley Tripp in analysing the implications of their action. The Bill had two distinct objectives - the transfer

23   C March 13 1857, p 8
24   *Ibid*
25   *Ibid*

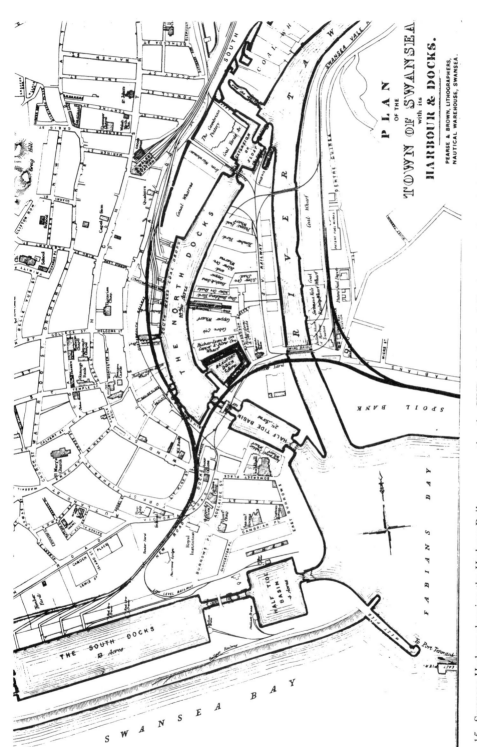

15 Swansea Harbour showing the Harbour Railway connecting the SWR with the South Dock, passing through the Dry Dock. The proposed route of the S&NR (vide Chapter XIII) is shown coming from Fabian Street, over two bridges, and joining the Harbour Railway. The Wind Street station was situated just beyond this junction.

and completion of the Dock and the extension of the railway from the new South Wales station down to the Dock. The arrangement between the Dock Company and the Duke of Beaufort's agent, who no longer intended petitioning against the Bill, made its passing inevitable. All that the Council needed to do was to obtain a *locus standi* against the second objective in order to attain modification of the line. This in its present form would cross the public streets and destroy the public quay, as well as removing the dry dock which was felt to play an important part in the life of shipping in the area.

Mr Tripp accordingly moved an amendment that the portion of the petition relating to the purchase of the Dock be omitted and only that referring to the construction of the railway should be retained, an amendment carried by ten votes to eight, Starling voting in its favour.[26]

A fresh complication was the return of a new Parliament as the result of the General Election in the spring of 1857. In the April meeting of the Harbour Trust, Mr Grenfell asked whether the Docks Transfer Bill would stand in the same position as in the previous Parliament, a point on which he was reassured by Starling from the Chair.[27] It would still be read in its existing form, with the same petitions as had been deposited against it by the Corporation, the South Wales Railway, the Swansea Canal Company and Mr Joseph Pickering, a contractor in the employ of the Swansea Dock Company.

After three successful years between 1852 and 1855, James Abernethy, Engineer-in-Chief to both the Dock Company and the Harbour Trust, had found himself forced to call off work on the Dock as a result of diminishing funds. This made it necessary for Joseph Pickering to sell off at a loss plant he had already obtained. For this loss he was now seeking restitution, and to this end was petitioning against the Bill. In addition, he was a considerable shareholder in the Dock Company. His position, however, was unique in that the shares he held were payment for the work he had already carried out, and in his capacity of a major shareholder, he was objecting, among other things, to the mode of security being offered the shareholders in the Swansea Dock Company in the form of Dock Bonds rather than Harbour Bonds.

Apart from Mr Pickering, the Harbour Trust had been experiencing difficulties on several fronts. At the end of May 1857 Starling was spending much of his time in London, but by the June meeting of the Trust, he was back in Swansea reporting that 'in view of the magnitude of the interests involved', the Duke of Beaufort was again proving awkward. As late as the Saturday night of June 6, one representative of the Trust had felt they could 'go no further down the road of concessions'. An unexpected letter from the Duke had, however, changed the whole situation and the prospect for agreement was much improved.

Nevertheless, there were still problems with the railway companies who were slow in reaching decisions over the details of their agreements with the Harbour Trustees. The need was felt for a firm approach, and a Committee comprising the five men most intimately concerned since the start of negotiations, the Chairman and Vice-Chairman of the Harbour Trust, Messrs H H Vivian, E M Richards and

26 *Ibid*
27 C April 17 1857, p 8

J R Tripp, had been appointed to meet the representatives of the SWR and GWR. The same Committee had also dealt with the Duke of Beaufort.[28]

In the June meeting of the Trust it was revealed that the railway companies had now presented them with an ultimatum. They had to accept or reject an offer very different from what the Committee had understood when they had previously met their Directors. Only the amount of money estimated for the cost of the construction of the works was to be guaranteed by the railway companies, leaving the cost of the land itself to be borne by the Harbour Trust, a burden they felt unable to shoulder alone.[29]

The Trust now turned to the Corporation and other owners of land required for the railway, without whose co-operation they felt the whole project was in danger of collapsing. In the absence of Starling, the approach was made at the beginning of June by E M Richards who explained to the councillors that

> Mr Benson very naturally as Chairman of the Trust felt very great difficulty in involving the Trust in unlimited expenditure but finding this was the ultimatum of the railways, after giving the subject the gravest consideration during the whole of yesterday, came to the determination of asking the Corporation if they were willing to take any share of the risk on themselves.

He had very properly said that there was a certain limit beyond which the Trustees could not possibly go, and unless therefore the Corporation said they were willing to take some share in the responsibility, he did not think the Trustees could go any further and the negotiations would therefore 'fall to the ground'.[30]

Although many of the Councillors were themselves members of the Harbour Trust, there was a distinct atmosphere of suspicion of the latter, with a frequent questioning of the motives of the Trustees. This was voiced particularly by Messrs Hoare and Rutter, who were undoubtedly expressing the feelings of others in stating their unwillingness to commit themselves to any such undertaking without an exact knowledge of the evaluation of the land required. They denounced those who had come there asking them for what was 'unreasonable, childish and unjust', and objected strongly to 'voting away public property' which they believed they held in trust for future generations.[31]

There were, it emerged, two conflicting estimates, one from Mr Rhys Jones, made earlier without details and for a purpose that had nothing to do with the railway, the other from their own surveyor, Mr Hall. The latter, used flexibly, had become the basis for the calculations of those willing to entertain the idea of supporting the Trustees. The Corporation, as Mr J T Jenkin pointed out, had always been anxious to have the docks on the present site and had, in the past, given the Dock Company a lot of property. Why should its interest cease now?[32]

28   C May 15 1857, p 6
29   C June 12 1857, p 6
30   C June 12 1857, p 8
31   *Ibid*
32   *Ibid*

Eventually a proposition from Mr Michael was accepted, to the effect 'That this Corporation being desirous to aid in the projected scheme of the railway to the docks pledged itself to accept £6000 for the ground required for the purposes of the railway, including a portion of the Corporation river frontage known as Cameron's Wharf, subject to such conditions as are contained in the Surveyor's report of March 15.' Nevertheless the debate continued into the meeting of June 15, with the inclusion of Cameron's Wharf in the package raising further heated questions.[33]

As early as the first reading of the Bill in Parliament at the end of May 1857, the Town Council had considered sending a committee to London with a watching brief to safeguard its interests.[34] The Mayor (John Oakshot), Messrs Hoare, Lumley, Michael, Rutter and Stroud were accordingly appointed and in due course despatched to London.

Their aim was ostensibly to 'protect the rights of the public without jeopardising the passage of the Bill'. Unfortunately their stay in London was made more stressful by their inability to make contact with the members of the Harbour Trust Committee in charge of the Bill. They had hoped to get from them a satisfactory explanation of why the line of the proposed railway needed to be constructed through the existing Dry Dock and to gain from them information on other questions of importance to the Council.[35]

The Trustees were now reasonably hopeful of a successful outcome to their endeavours. Agreement had been reached with the Duke of Beaufort and the sanction obtained of both the Board of Trade and the Admiralty. There remained, it seemed, only Mr Joseph Pickering as an obstacle to the acceptance of the Preamble to the Bill, the Swansea Canal Company and the South Wales Railway having failed to appear.[36]

Among those cross-examined in Committee by Mr Pickering's counsel, Mr Quain, was Mr H H Vivian who that year became MP for Glamorgan. He pointed out that, in its present unfinished form, the dock was valueless. It was therefore of prime importance to all concerned that the present Bill should be adopted and, as a private individual, he would do all in his power to promote the present undertaking. The weakness of the previous scheme had been the lack of a railway link with the docks, but now with the creation of such a link and the growing prosperity of the town, the Dock share-holders, of which he was one, should benefit from an increase in the prospective value of their shares.

The Committee was then adjourned until the following day. Having failed to gain further information from the Harbour Trust representatives, the Corporation Committee had engaged Mr Denman as Counsel. He put forward their objection to some four or five of the clauses. Their principal concern was the threat presented by the proposed line of the railway to the existing Dry Dock.[37] Consequently a special clause was introduced to ensure its survival.

33   C June 19 1857 p 6
34   C May 26 1857, p 8
35   C July 17 1857, p 6 (reported in retrospect)
36   C June 19 1857, p 5
37   C June 26 1857, p 8

Unfortunately there was such conflicting evidence given on the value of the Dry Dock to the town that the Council's case was tenuous from the start. The Town Clerk, Mr Mansfield, was anxious to convince the Committee that the ship owners and traders of Swansea were all for preserving the Dry Dock, whereas Mr E M Richards, representing the Harbour Trust, though also a Council member, pointed out that there were two other dry docks and a patent slip in the harbour, while the dry dock in question was small and inconvenient, abandoned by its late tenant who had made himself another on the opposite side of the river.[38]

It was little wonder that 'The Cambrian' had scant praise for the efforts of the Corporation Committee, dismissing their visit to London as a 'fruitless, quixotic journey' … 'an unnecessary, if not a wasteful expenditure of the public money.' It went on to point out that there had been four of the ablest members of the Council in town already, namely Messrs Benson, Tripp, Jenkin and Richards.

> The disinterestedness, the practical knowledge and ability evinced by these gentlemen in the course of the protracted negotiations with the dock and railway authorities ought to be an earnest, we should think, of their readiness and capacity to protect and conserve the interest of the Borough. Why was not the matter entrusted to them?[39]

The answer, of course, was self-evident. The suspicion many of the Councillors felt towards the Trustees had eroded from the start their confidence in any proposition put forward by the latter. It must be admitted, however, in fairness to the Council's representatives in London, that the 'disinterestedness' of those 'ablest members of the Council' - who were also Harbour Trustees - had gone perhaps a trifle too far. It had kept them incommunicado during the vital period when the Swansea petition was being heard.

What the Council representatives were asking for in seeking to preserve the Dry Dock seemed to them little enough but it was sufficient to endanger the very life of the Bill. In rapid succession two letters reached them from members of the Harbour Trust.

On June 22 Starling wrote from Hatchard's Hotel in Piccadilly to the Mayor to the effect that

> Mr Brunel has stated to the Committee of the Harbour Trustees that any deviation from the line of the railway which will altogether avoid any interference with the Dry Dock will create such difficulties in the construction of the railway that he could not advise the Railway Company to acquiesce in accepting such a bill.[40]

He was hopeful that the Corporation Committee would accordingly agree to withdraw the clause and that the Mayor would let him know that same day.

38 *Ibid*
39 C June 26 1857, p 4
40 C July 17 1857, p 6 (Report)

Otherwise he would have to see the South Wales Company to find out how far their engineer's objection to the deviation in the line proposed by the Corporation would affect the proposed agreement made with them. Any refusal by them to co-operate would involve the necessity of withdrawing the Bill.

This was reinforced by a letter to Mr Michael from the Clerk to the Harbour Board, Mr Lewis Thomas, stating that Mr Brunel had informed the Committee of the Harbour Trust that, if the clause relating to the Dry Dock was persisted in, it must prove fatal to the negotiations now pending between the Trustees and the South Wales Company. The solicitors to the Company, Messrs W O and W Hunt, had already informed him that

> if the clause remains in the bill, it is useless to proceed with the agreement between the parties as the Company would not be party to it.[41]

The news of the inevitable failure of the Bill unless the offending clause was removed caused a furore in Swansea. In the absence of the Mayor in London, two of the Councillors, George Grant Francis and Richard Aubrey, took it on themselves to call a public meeting in the Guildhall that same evening, Saturday, June 20, at 5 pm. Although there was no time for any official notice of the meeting, a large attendance of the town's traders was sufficient evidence of widespread concern.[42]

Mr Aubrey's information came from the Vice-Chairman of the Trust, J W James, and Mr Francis's from J R Tripp. The two conveners of the meeting had already telegraphed to the deputation in London to defer proceedings until the result of the meeting was known. Mr Francis had drawn up a memorial asking for the clause which was preventing the successful progress of the Bill to be removed and this was given overwhelming support.

Armed with this memorial bearing 250 signatures, Mr Francis, accompanied by Mr Sydney Hall, left for London. By Monday, the clause had been withdrawn and the Corporation petition abandoned, much to the satisfaction of the Editor of 'The Cambrian' who, on the following Friday, expressed in its leader his relief at the withdrawal of 'the obnoxious clause about the Dry Dock.'[43]

He could not refrain from castigating the shortsightedness of certain members of the Corporation in failing to recognise the magnitude of the Docks question.

> When we see gentlemen animated by such nibbling propensities as we have observed of late, attaching as much importance to the retention of an old, dilapidated dry dock as they do to a broad gauge railway approach to a capacious docks, can we wonder at the feeling of strong dissatisfaction which has existed in the town?[44]

41 *Ibid*
42 C June 26 1857, p 8
43 *Ibid*
44 *Ibid*

South Dock: the cutting of the first sod by the Marquis of Worcester, Feb 26 1852.

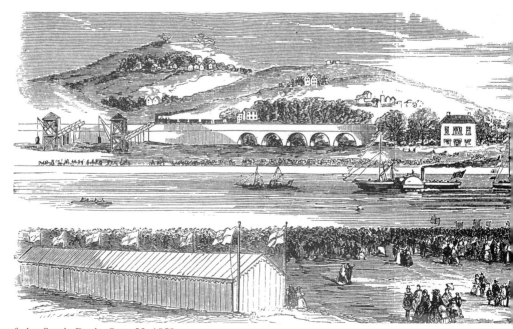

Opening of the South Dock, Sept 23 1859.

Illustrated London News

Illustrated London News

At the time of the London Committee's presentation of its report, couched in somewhat muted tones, to the Town Council, it was at pains to point out that it had thought it was carrying out the wishes of the Council. They attributed their need to engage Counsel to their failure to establish contact with the members of the Harbour Trust in charge of the Bill. This had led to the insertion of the offending clause. They had resolved from the start to do nothing to jeopardise the Bill but had hoped that, if they had to lose the Dry Dock, they might gain something in its place. Even without the memorial, they would have withdrawn the offending clause in the light of Mr Benson's letter to the Mayor. Indeed they still thought that, without it, they might have still salvaged something, whereas with it, there was no alternative to abandoning the petition.[45]

Rather lamely, it may seem, Starling expressed the hope that the Harbour Trustees had not appeared reluctant to meet the Corporation representatives and discuss points with them before the Committee stage of the Bill. He personally had been most anxious to do so but it appears 'certain other gentlemen had pooh-poohed' this approach until suddenly their hand was forced by the threatened breakdown of the whole Bill unless the offending clause was withdrawn.[46]

Rumours continued to circulate. At the end of a meeting of the Swansea Board of Health, reported in 'The Cambrian' of July 3, the Mayor sought to scotch one rumour (not, it appeared, from anyone of much influence, although none the less it could do harm) that the clause in connection with the Dry Dock would cost £1200. There was no report from the London deputation as this was not a meeting of the Town Council as such, but he could reassure them that it would not cost even 1200 farthings.

Mr Jenkin promised that all details would be forthcoming before the proper meeting. He personally thought it would cost rather more than 1200 farthings, but the Mayor persisted in his view that the clause itself had not cost anything. The only expense entailed was that of sending the deputation to London - a bit of casuistry which failed to fool the Editor of 'The Cambrian'.[47]

In the last resort the Town Clerk was an obvious scapegoat for much of the blame, as his insistence before the Parliamentary Committee that the ship owners and traders of the port were anxious to retain the Dry Dock at all costs had helped to create an impression of inflexibility which, fortunately, the memorial had dispelled.[48] This obstacle overcome, there remained no major hindrance to the passing of the Bill. 'An Act for the Transfer of the Docks of the Swansea Dock Company to the Swansea Harbour Trustees and for authorizing those Trustees to make further Works and raise further Moneys and for other Purposes' or, more briefly, 'The Swansea Harbour Act', became law on August 10 1857.

The South Dock was eventually opened on September 23 1859 by Miss Emily Talbot, the eldest daughter of C R M Talbot, the Lord Lieutenant of the County as well as Chairman of the SWR. Proceedings were in a somewhat lower tone than when the first sod had been cut on February 26 1852, by the Duke of Beaufort's heir, the Marquess of Worcester, at a time when the Swansea Dock

45   C July 17 1857, p 6 (Report)
46   *Ibid*
47   C July 3 1857, p 8
48   C July 17 1857, p 6

Company held high hopes of carrying through the proposed scheme. Nevertheless there were still many thousands of applauding spectators assembled around the dock while Starling, as Chairman of the Harbour Trust, delivered 'an interesting speech', in which he mentioned the rise in the income of the Trust from £3000 a year in 1856 to over £26,000 in 1859.

Then, he, with his fellow Trustees and their friends, embarked on the steam tug, 'The Beaufort', lying alongside the quay in the half-tide basin. Meanwhile Mr and Miss Talbot and their party had proceeded to the lock gate. As 'The Beaufort' steamed into the lock, Miss Talbot pressed a lever, thereby opening the gates into the Dock. To the repeated firing of cannon and the strains of 'Rule Britannia', played by bands on either side of the water, 'The Beaufort' led other boats in a trip around the quays and out into the harbour, returning to the half-tide basin to deposit its passengers.[49]

Afterwards, with Starling presiding, the guests breakfasted in a building on the north side of the half-tide basin, later used as a warehouse—not the most spectacular of settings for so momentous an event. For Starling, personally, one of the most gratifying aspects of this event must have been the presence of Henry, recently returned from India. At the breakfast, the toast 'To the Army and Navy' was coupled with the names of Colonel Benson and Admiral Warde, while the honour of responding fell to Henry.[50] This probably meant far more to Starling than any amount of ostentatious ceremony — though one cannot help allowing the imagination to conjure up a vision of the pomp and panoply with which the original Swansea Dock Company of July 1847 would have celebrated the occasion had it survived.

49   W H Jones, *op cit*, pp 178*ff*
50   *Ibid*

Chapter VI

Uncertain Times

One of the reasons for Swansea's need of additional harbour accommodation was its growing reputation as the focal point of the international copper trade, but that in turn brought its problems to the area, largely as the result of fluctuations in copper prices. One of the most dramatic incidents in this connection was the copper strike of 1843, the year during which Starling became Mayor. This was the more disturbing as it coincided with the threat of Chartism in the industrial valleys to the east and the Rebecca Riots in the agricultural west.

Relations between employers and employed were generally stable in the Swansea area but unrest surfaced when, in late July, the coppermen were given notice of a 12½% reduction in their pay. 'The wages proposed were, for slagmen, a reduction from 30/- to 22/6; metal smelters, 30s to 26/3; ore smelters, 26s to 22/6; roasters, 31/6 to 27/6; middle calciners, 2/4 to 2/2 per watch, and ore calciners, 2/4 to 2/- per watch.' The implementing of the new rates led to a strike which lasted five weeks.[1]

At a special meeting of the Town Council, assembled to consider a potentially inflammatory situation, it was suggested that some of the coppermen might be induced to join in the Rebecca Riots. There was a further fear of a link with Chartism, fanned by the rumour that the Irish agitator, Fergus O'Connor, had been seen on the hills. 'The Cambrian' of February 16 1855 in a review of events of the earlier decade recalled that the manager of the Swansea branch of the Bank of England was terrified it was about to be attacked, and so nearly four hundred of the military, including troops of the 4th Light Dragoons from Carmarthen and of the 75th Regiment of Foot, newly returned from Llanelly, were under arms at the Barracks.[2]

The presence of additional troops in the town led to a request for increased barrack accommodation from their Commander, Colonel James Frederick Love, who was strongly opposed to his men being billeted in local public houses. A special meeting of the Town Council, chaired by the Mayor, Dr Bird, was called to consider the question. Although the cost of adapting the existing barracks to house a hundred men was not likely to be more than £150, several councillors felt the expense was not justified as the situation was already quieting down.

When Starling moved 'that a sum of money not exceeding £200 be placed in the hands of the Mayor for the erection of temporary barracks', he was opposed by Mr Glover. He was surprised that such a proposition should emanate from Mr Benson 'who was usually so tenacious of the expenditure of public money'.[3] Starling had good reason for wanting to ensure that army personnel were

1   C Aug 2 1843, p 3
2   C Feb 16 1855, recalled C Oct 4 1907
3   C Aug 26 1843, p 3

adequately housed; the experiences of his brothers, Henry and, before him, Thomas, would obviously mellow his usual caution. His proposition, however, was left on the table 'for the time being'. Even Colonel Love's reputation - he had fought under Wellington from Corunna to Waterloo and had been involved in suppressing both the Bristol riots and John Frost's march on Newport - had little effect on local parsimony.

'The Swansea Journal' of August 2 1843 had sought to restore a sense of proportion by pointing out that the reinforcement of troops was not so much a necessary precaution against their 'agricultural neighbours' - a reference to the Rebeccaites - 'nor against the men employed in the copper industry as against the fears engendered in people's own heated imaginations.'[4]

In view of the havoc being wrought by the Rebeccaites on local toll gates, it was not surprising that imaginations had become overheated. The copper strikers' revolt at the end of July came only a week after the vicious assault at Felindre on Captain Charles Frederick Napier, Chief Constable of the recently formed Glamorgan Police Force, as he and his Inspector tried to arrest one of the men accused of carrying out the attack on the Bolgoed gate near Pontardulais.[5]

In just over a month after the calming words of 'The Swansea Journal', there was launched on September 6 an even more violent attack, this time on the Pontardulais toll-house on the Glamorgan side of the river Loughor. Here Captain Napier and his small group of police accompanied by the Swansea magistrates, J D Llewelyn, L L Dillwyn and Matthew Moggridge, overcame fierce resistance to capture the ringleader, John Hughes of Tŷ Isha Farm near Tumble.[6] He, together with David Jones and John Hugh, was taken with an escort of Dragoons to Swansea where their imprisonment led to angry scenes.[7]

It was not surprising that, amid such tensions, news of unrest among the copper workers had caused alarm. On the evening of Thursday, July 31, after pay had been received, the men employed by Messrs Vivian, Messrs Williams, Foster & Co., the Middle Bank Works, the White Rock Works, the Upper Bank, the Crown Copper Works, Neath and the Red Jacket Copper Works, Neath, stopped work. They met the following day, by which time the men of the Forest Works had joined them. It was decided to form a procession and march through Swansea on the Saturday. It had been arranged by the Council that if such a march should take place, Mr J H Vivian and Starling, accompanied by the Mayor and Mr Attwood, the Benson solicitor, should meet the strikers.

Once news of the approach of the marchers reached the authorities, the four set out on horseback, undoubtedly with some trepidation, since they were unarmed and unaccompanied by the militia. By one o'clock the marchers, over a thousand strong, were reported to have reached the town and were proceeding down High Street.

The two parties met at the Glamorganshire Bank. The Mayor managed to quieten the disgruntled workers and then addressed them. He told them that the

---

4 Swansea Journal, Aug 2 1843, p 4
5 Pat Molloy, And They Blessed Rebecca (Llandysul; J D Lewis & Sons Ltd, 1994) pp 127-29
6 *Op cit*, pp 225, 231-32; David Painting, Amy Dillwyn (Swansea; Graham Harcourt, Printers, Ltd 1987) pp 16, 73
7 Pat Molloy, *op cit*, p 130; *cf* p 237

magistrates had received orders from the Government to prevent large numbers of men from entering the town in procession and causing a breach of the peace. He advised them to return home quietly. As they could see, he and his colleagues had so much confidence in their cooperation that they had come without any protection.

Mr Vivian spoke next, reiterating the advice to the men to leave the town. He promised that, if the men would quietly return to a field above Hafod Works, he would listen to their grievances. The men acquiesced and followed the four on horseback to the field where they made a circle around them.

Mr Vivian then asked for a spokesman to step forward. A minute or so passed, then one man came to the front. No doubt finding difficulty in expressing himself in English, he simply and bluntly stated in one sentence, 'We want our price, as we had it before'. There followed a long reply, attributed to Mr Vivian, first comparing the depressed state of the copper trade with other similar trades and then stating the reasons for the proposed reduction in wages. The coppermen's reduced wages would still give them an average wage of 23s per week, a higher wage than any other industry was providing. The works owners would not reduce wages if they were not compelled by the trade; they had always tried to keep their works running, even in bad times.

In turn, Starling confirmed what Mr Vivian had said and, appealing to the common sense and better nature of the majority, he sought to explain the economic problems facing their employers. It was useless to stand out and resist when the copper industry was in a state of such depression. When conditions improved so would wages. His workers, so he believed, had not come out of their own accord, but had been provoked by a few malcontents.

> I always praise you for your orderly conduct... no men can be more orderly than the coppermen. I address my own men more especially, and say that if any of them feel inclined to return to their work, if they will give notice to Mr Edmonds ... the furnaces will be ready for them.[8]

He added that he was confident that they would only make their position worse by sacrificing all their wages. He then appealed to them to give the Mayor a hearing and, somewhat incongruously to modern ears, requested them to show their loyalty by giving three cheers for the Queen and afterwards to go home quietly.

It would appear he succeeded in defusing, at least temporarily, a potentially explosive situation, making it possible, by his usual unflappability, for the Mayor in turn to receive a fair hearing. The gathering broke up without incident on this particular occasion.[9]

Some of the Hafod men had a meeting that evening with a Mr W P Evans of Morriston. They explained that they had difficulty in expressing their grievances in English and asked for help. Mr Evans duly drew up a list of their complaints

8 C Aug 9 1843, p 3
9 *Ibid*

for the men to present to Mr Vivian. Further meetings were held, each level of workmen putting forward its own particular complaints, but without any solution being found.[10]

Unfortunately the prolonged disagreement led to ugly relations developing between those who wanted to continue the strike and those who were prepared to return to work. 'The Cambrian' of August 16 reported that a crowd of several hundred, assembled in the Hafod, had threatened a small group of men who were continuing to work. Later hundreds of men gathered in a menacing mood outside the Grenfells' Middle Bank Works where the workers were being blamed for persuading some of the Hafod men to return to work.

Once this was known, 'Mr Berrington (a County Magistrate), the Mayor, Mr Grenfell, who was at the Works, Mr C H Smith, Captain Napier and a party of policemen immediately proceeded to the spot' where they expostulated with the men in both Welsh and English on the 'illegality of their conduct'. The strikers withdrew, but only to return, whereupon the Magistrates 'deemed it necessary to read the Riot Act'. The crowd then broke up without violence, although it was understood some of them went on to travel the countryside collecting contributions from sympathisers.[11]

The strike dragged on and it was not until September that the men finally accepted the employers' terms.[12] Before the settlement, however, Rebecca's bid for the removal of the hated toll-gates had taken an ugly turn with the death at Hendy of Sarah Williams, the elderly gate-keeper. As well as betraying a new ruthlessness in Rebecca's treatment of her victims, this event revealed the deeply-entrenched reluctance among local juries to convict those patently responsible for such crimes.[13]

The rest of Britain was made aware of the disturbances in West Wales by the graphic on-the-spot reports sent by William Campbell Foster to 'The Times'.[14] We can imagine the apprehension in Teddington when, later in the autumn of that fateful year, Starling became Mayor of Swansea. This was certainly a time when he needed to the full his natural equanimity to carry him through the upheavals facing him both in public and private affairs.

We have hinted in a previous chapter that, like their contemporaries, the Bensons were experiencing financial problems in their dealings in copper and coal.[15] The time has now come to look more closely at these difficulties.

Keeping abreast of developments in the copper industry required a constant flow of new capital, and fortunately, as it seemed at the time, the Logans had access to the financial high-fliers of the day. W E Logan's sister was married to Abel Lewes Gower whose uncle, Abel Anthony Gower, had founded the large trading company known as A A Gower, Nephews & Co. In 1835 A L Gower introduced 'Mr Logan' at the Bank of England.[16] It was natural that, for the

10 C Feb 16 1855, p 5
11 C Aug 16 1843, p 3
12 C Sept 6 1843, p3
13 Pat Molloy, *op cit*, pp 241-44
14 *Op cit, passim*
15 *Vide* pp 28, 29
16 R O Roberts, 'The Bank of England, the Company of Copper Miners and the Cwmavon Works 1847-52', Welsh History Review, 1968-69 p 224; *Vide* pp 192-4 for Gower family involvement in the SVR

advancement of their interests in the precarious business climate of the 1830s, the firm of Benson & Logan should depend on these valuable connections for support in the Forest Copper Works' struggle to safeguard their business ventures.

In 1835 when the newly formed Benson & Logan Company was re-building the Forest Works and developing its interests in Penclawdd, it had become indebted to the Gowers for £50,000. By the end of 1838 the Gowers were calling for payment of the debt.[17]

In the Logan family there had been an upheaval in the April of that year when both Hart and his nephew Henry had died, leaving their shares in Benson, Logan & Co. vested in William. The financial affairs of the Logans were far from healthy. It emerged that Hart Logan had a personal debt to the company of £3000 and the London firm of Hart and Henry Logan owed a further £5000. In addition, since the Logans' share of the business was 21/48, they owed a proportion of the debt accordingly - a matter of £11,000. The Bensons share was 27/48 and their repayment proportionately was £14,000. The total sum that could be raised from the partners was £33,000. The remainder of the debt - £17,000 - had to be provided by further mortgages of property.[18]

The outcome was that, on 2 February 1839, A A Gower, Nephews & Co. (the three Gowers, Robert Frederick, Abel Lewes and Edwin, together with Gregory Scale Walters) released Benson, Logan & Co. from their debt.[19] On the same date, Articles of Partnership were signed by Starling and William E Logan, Starling by this time having taken over his father's share.[20] Their financial problems were, however, far from over; in ten years' time they were to face even greater trials and Starling must have come to regard their initial involvement with the Gowers with some regret.

While Benson, Logan & Co. were experiencing these difficulties there had been a noticeable fall in the price of ores as a result of the lack of demand. By the end of 1839, three or four large firms accounted for two-thirds of the purchases, Benson & Logan by now being part of the remaining anonymous one third. By February 1 1840, contrasted with the £495,355 spent by Williams, Foster & Co., and the £307,425 by Vivian & Sons, Benson, Logan & Co.'s expenditure at the Cornwall and Swansea ticketings was a mere £694, signalling the end of the Forest Works as an independent concern.[21] The finances of the company were in such a precarious state that their only option was to combine with others similarly situated in the larger English Copper Company which, by the end of May, was emerging as a major buyer.[22]

By 1841 the English Copper Company and the Miners Smelting Company had combined to form the Governor and Company of Copper Miners in England.[23] The Governor was Abel Lewes Gower and his Assistants included Starling, Louis Vigurs and Gregory S Walters. The Company's prospectus issued that same year

17 D/D SB 12/12. The source for all documents in this collection is WGRO
18 *Ibid*
19 *Ibid*
20 D/D SB 12/11
21 C Feb 1 1840, p 3
22 C May 30 1840, p 4
23 Martin Phillips, The Copper Industry in the Port Talbot District, (1935) p 48

gave the capital as £1,000,000 in 10,000 shares of £100 each with Benson, Logan & Co. among its shareholders. Among the various properties which the Company took over as securities were the Cwmavon Works, the Port Talbot Harbour, both formerly belonging to Vigurs & Co., the Forest Works and the Graigola Colliery in the Tawe Valley formerly belonging to Benson, Logan & Co., as well as the Cambrian Copper Works and Mill at Llanelly.[24] In addition, in 1843, Starling and William Logan transferred to the Copper Miners the extensive coal seams of Cwm Cyrnach and Llwyn Erch Edwal which they had originally obtained from John Parsons in 1831.[25]

Before long Gower himself was feeling the strain of the current economic crisis. A full account of the decline in the interconnected fortunes of Gower, Nephews & Co. and the Company of Copper Miners can be found in R O Roberts's article in The Welsh History Review.[26] Here, we are merely concerned with the effects of this on Benson, Logan & Co.

1847 had proved a disastrous year for a large number of firms and Gower, Nephews & Co. was one of these. Before September 11 when its collapse was announced there had been uncertainty about its financial position but the profits made by some of the partners involved in successful railway ventures had served to mask its difficulties. The immediate cause of their failure was the collapse of Gemmell Bros and Co. of Glasgow, one of the leading companies of bill brokers, and then of Alison, Cumberlege & Co.

'The Cambrian' of September 17 1847, which reported the downfall of Gower, Nephews & Co., referred also to the difficulties faced by the Bensons' former partner, Henry Usborne, though with more sympathy than it evinced in mentioning the Gowers. It gave his liabilities as 'somewhat under £100,0000 (*sic*) and although the fallacy of such a statement is now unfortunately a matter of notoriety, a strong belief is entertained by those who have inspected the accounts that the assets will be sufficient, or nearly so, to pay 20s in the pound.'

The columnist went on to say that the firm had been involved in no speculation of any sort. Its present position arose entirely from the failure of others, and it was foreseen that the circumstances connected with the stoppage would 'maintain rather than diminish the honourable character which Mr Usborne has hitherto borne.'

The same edition of 'The Cambrian' mentioned a report that the Gower liabilities amounted to a million sterling, adding, 'Perhaps this is mere conjecture but it serves to show public opinion upon the matter.'[27] It was elsewhere disclosed that Gower Nephews & Co. owed the Company of Copper Miners alone the 'sum of almost £20,000'. When they were forced to suspend payment their precarious position seriously affected in turn the fortunes of Bruce, Buxton & Co., the firm who discounted their bills as well as those of the Company of Copper Miners.[28] This placed Abel Lewes Gower, as Governor of that Company, in a particularly invidious position.

24 *Ibid*; *cf* R O Roberts, *op cit*, p 223
25 D/D SB 12/16
26 R O Roberts, *op cit*, pp 223-234
27 C Sept 17 1847, p 4
28 R O Roberts, *op cit*, p 226

'An extraordinary loan' of £150,000 from the Bank of England to Bruce, Buxton & Co. did little to relieve the affairs of the Company of Copper Miners. A loan of £120,000 to the Company of Copper Miners itself, made at the instance of influential parties in the City of London on the guarantee of approved names, had no greater success. Gower inevitably came under suspicion as the Governor of the Company as well as a Director of the Bank of England. Consequently in October 1847 he was forced to 'retire' from both positions.

At the same time the Bank of England took a mortgage on the Company's property for £270,000 to cover, in addition to the loan, the £150,000 previously advanced to the bill brokers.[29] Among the properties mortgaged was the Vigurs' Cwmavon Works which was put up for sale in July 1849 but withdrawn.[30] This proposed sale became the centre of a long and complicated wrangle.

The Bank had undertaken to operate the works itself through its agent, John Biddulph, but before long it was being accused by local iron-masters of 'underselling in the iron markets' and infringing its Charter by becoming itself a trading company in that commodity.[31]

The involvement of the Bank of England in the affairs of the Company of Copper Miners had been challenged by one of its shareholders, W H Lord, who held preferential shares worth £10,000. He sought a ruling from the Vice-Chancellor that the Company of Copper Miners' Court of Assistants had no authority to give loan notes to Bruce, Buxton & Co. against the Company's assets and that the Bank of England's mortgage on the Company had been improperly obtained.[32] In a further action impeaching the Bank's title, Lord's charge against the Bank was one of collusion with the Company's Assistants and concealment of their suspect financial dealings.[33]

Eventually this second suit was withdrawn, but with the Company of Copper Miners meeting the plaintiff's costs and Lord himself satisfied that he had saved Cwmavon from being sold at a derisory price.[34] Finding its own position an embarrassment, the Bank was now glad to make arrangements for the works to be repossessed by the Copper Miners. On July 24 1851, 'An Act for facilitating the settlement of the affairs of the Governor & Company of Copper Miners in England and for the better management of the said Company' received Royal Assent, thereby clearing the way for the restoration of the properties under threat. The Cwmavon works were finally reopened under their former management amid general rejoicing in May 1852.[35]

The Forest Works, from its takeover by the Copper Miners in 1841, had continued to operate with Starling as manager rather than proprietor[36] but on July 26 1850 it was put up for sale. 'The Swansea and Glamorgan Herald' of July 24 announced the forthcoming sale 'by Messrs Shuttleworth at mart on July 26, by

29   *Op cit*, pp 225-26 & D/D SB 12/22
30   Martin Phillips, *op cit*, pp 55-58; Sw and Glam Herald, July 24 1850, p 4
31   R O Roberts, *op cit*, p 233
32   *Op cit*, p 229
33   *Op cit*, p 231
34   *Op cit*, p 232
35   C May 13 1852, p 3
36   Evidence in support of the South Wales Railway Bill before the Committee of the House of Lords, June 1845

order of trustees under a mortgage deed'. Included in this advertisement was 'the Graigola Colliery in the parish of Cadoxton, situate about 4 miles from the works.'

> The works contain 6 calciners, 11 furnaces adequate to smelting of 350 tons of ore, or 40 tons of copper per wk. 4 metal furnaces, 8 metal calciners, 5 furnaces for reducing calcined metal, 3 roasters & 2 refinery furnaces, together with the necessary warehouses, lime sheds, 2 lime kilns, & a detached suit of offices, part of the buildings being held under a lease of 63 years, commencing 25.3.1843, at a rent of £73.10.0 p.a.
>
> The colliery comprises the coal under the Cwm Cyrnach & Llanerch Edwall farms, & contains 237 acres 2 roods & 8 perches, held under a lease from Messrs Benson & Logan for a term of 50 years, subject to a rent of 6d per ton for small coal & 8d per ton for large coal, & 1s additional for every wey of coal of 13 tons, & a sleeping rent of £300 p a, together with a small piece of land, with stabling for 9 horses, a water-wheel, chaff-machine & ostlers' dwelling houses, held on lease for 60 years from 25.3.1841 at rental of £2.2.0 p a, & all machinery, tools, etc. comprising the inventory etc, together with the bottoms, slags, & copper in process of manufacture to be taken at a valuation.[37]

With the bidding starting at £5000, the Forest Works was finally 'bought in' for £7900, although the deed giving the eventual purchasers as J H Vivian and Michael Williams was dated August 4 1851.[38] There were no buyers for the Graigola Colliery or the 237 acres of coal seams. These were, however, returned to Benson, Logan & Co. A Document of Surrender, signed also on August 4 1851, states that 'it shall be lawful for Starling Benson and William Edmond Logan peaceably and quietly to enter into, occupy and enjoy the said premises without any lawful eviction.'[39]

Whatever their reason, the Company of Copper Miners had also taken over, in 1842, an acre of land, part of the Glais farm.[40] The Benson family had purchased the farm when the Neath Abbey lands had come up for sale in 1838 with an eye to the future development of the SVR.[41] This acre was restored to the Bensons on the same date.

In Penclawdd, since the settlement of the debt in 1839, Benson, Logan & Co. had continued to operate their Penlan colliery and also to develop the Copperworks. The Gowers by now had a strong hold on the company and had entered into partnership. When, by 1847, Benson, Logan & Co were again in difficulties, the only course open to them was further borrowing.

37   Sw and Glam Herald, July 31 1850, p 3
38   Vivian Properties, Yorkshire Imperial Metals, B2 - Title Deeds, p 339, UCS Archives
39   D/D SB 12/22
40   *Ibid*
41   *Vide* p 181

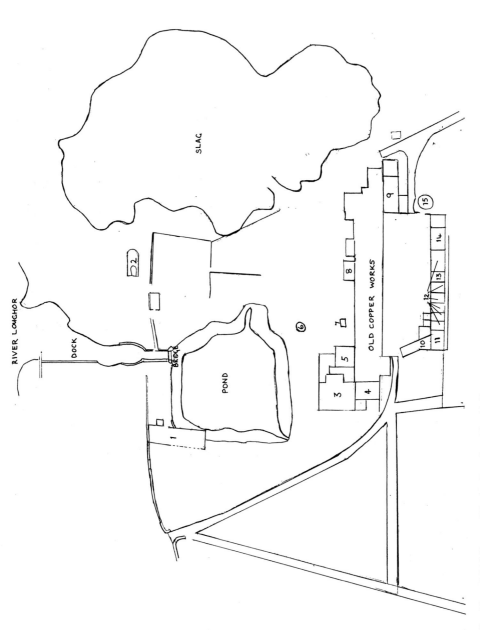

1   Lead works
2   Lime kiln
3   Refinery
4   Calciner
5   Horse mill
6   Coke kiln
7   Clock tower
8   Furnace
9   Old Kent House
10 Pot Room
11 Smithy
12 Cottages
13 Stable
14 Brick House
15 Brick Kiln

Based on D/D P 858, WGRO

18   Site of Old Copper Works, Penclawdd *c*1840s

They drew bills on a number of banks, including Barnett, Hoare & Co., Glyn, Halifax, Mills & Co. and the Bank of England. These bills were accepted by A A Gower, Nephews and Co., with the Penclawdd property as security. By September 1847, however, the Gower Company had failed and were unable to honour their pledge. It consequently fell to the firm of Benson, Logan & Co. to clear the debt which now totalled £16,922 10s. As partners the Gowers were committed to paying a proportionate share of the debt which amounted to £1269 3s. In June 1849 A L Gower had died leaving his wife, Elizabeth, as his sole executrix.[42]

The remainder of the debt, £15,653, had to be met by Starling. It seems that William Logan was taking no part in the negotiations and, in fact, the partnership was dissolved in December 1850. Once again, as in the case of Graigola, the Banks took a lenient view. The parties involved agreed that the minerals of the company had 'not been profitably worked and by reason thereof and of the liability to rents and covenants contained in the Leases the property and effects … have no marketable value'.[43] Consequently they arranged that, if Starling could 'find a purchaser(s) willing to take over the Colliery and Works … premises and effects for the price of £9572 17s 6d', this amount would satisfy the creditors and Starling would be released from all further claims upon him by the other partners in the firm of Benson, Logan & Co., although he would hold himself responsible for the payment of all other debts belonging to the Company.

Starling was successful in finding a buyer but the sale was a family affair, the buyers being his brothers, Henry Roxby and 'Thomas' John. The latter name was clearly a mistake in copying 'Florance John'. The indenture stated that the property remaining to Starling after the settlement comprised two freehold houses in Brighton (which, in all probability, had originally belonged to John Hodgson), ten shares in the Swansea and Liverpool Steam Packet Company and £2250 in the Preference Stock of the Governor & Company of Copper Miners in England now standing in the name of Starling Benson.[44] This seems little enough after all the energy Starling had expended in the family interests.

It was characteristic of Starling that such setbacks in business were not allowed to undermine his confidence. He had learned much since the heady days of the 1820s when the family had invested in a diverse array of industrial enterprises from Ynysygerwn to Penclawdd. Experience had made him more cautious in his future involvement in the two areas of Penclawdd and Glais.

First of all, in Glais in 1852, Starling and C H Smith leased from John Parsons the Ynysymond Colliery and the Graigola vein under Tyr Eynon, Noyadd Wen and Glais farms.[45] In exchange for a mortgage for £5000 provided by John Parsons, a Swansea Vale Railway Company Bond for that amount was transferred to him.[46] After John Parsons's death in 1855, a new agreement was made with his heirs, and by March 8 1858 the debt was cleared.[47]

42 D/D SB 12/20
43 *Ibid*
44 *Ibid*
45 D/D SB 12/25
46 D/D SB 12/27
47 D/D SB 12/31

On Mrs Benson's death in 1859 the Glais farm, originally bought with Mrs Meux's money, was inherited by Henry Roxby Benson and Richard Meux Benson. They, in turn, sold it to Starling in 1860 although, according to Henry's will of November 7 1890, it had later been restored to him 'by my late brother, Starling Benson'.[48] It remained in the family till 1917 when a large portion was sold for £4300.[49]

Secondly, in Penclawdd, Starling was also seeking to re-establish himself. On March 16 1850[50] he had leased veins of coal under Cefn Bychan for twenty-two years from John Nicholas Lucas. Later, on February 23 1856, an agreement was made with the executors of the late Joseph Martin for over forty-two acres of coal seams under Blaenkedy *(sic)*. This was for sixty years.[51] The following year he contracted with Philip Evans of Brynhir to lease veins under the farm and lands called Brynhir and also under Cold Harbour and Saint Walls.[52]

On August 24 1858, he leased to the Penclawdd Colliery Company the surface land including the buildings, spoil bank, incline and quay of the original Penlan Colliery.[53] On the same date he leased to the Company mines and veins under Aberkedy, Caeworth and Penyrheol. This lease also covered veins under Cornel Bach and Kent Meadows and under the side of the old dwelling house and garden formerly occupied by Starling, Hart Logan and others. It further allowed the Company to work any coal seams under the Benson land which formerly belonged to Paul Bevan.[54]

The Penclawdd Colliery Company mortgaged the property to Thomas Stringer for the sum of £5000.[55] When in July 1861 James Whitehead and William Lambert took over the mortgage, the Colliery Company had still not repaid the money so the new investors cleared the £5000 plus interest due to Thomas Stringer.[56]

After the death of James Whitehead on July 7 1865 at Valparaiso, his executors sought to dispose of the portion of his estate remaining after bequests had been made. They accordingly transferred to William Lambert 'for a consideration' his late partner's share. Whatever happened to the affairs of William Lambert is not known but on September 27 1870 he and Starling Benson signed Articles of Agreement whereby Lambert sold back to Starling the Penclawdd colliery and all its appurtenances for the sum of £306 5s.[57] An Assignment of all the leases entered into followed on December 19 with Starling indemnifying Lambert against any future claims.[58]

Later documents are evidence of the continuing Benson involvement with the Penclawdd Colliery, referred to in future negotiations as the property of the

48 Will of Henry Roxby Benson, Nov 7 1890 Office Copy issued by Somerset House
49 D/D SB 12/123
50 D/D SB 12/19
51 D/D SB 12/29
52 D/D SB 12/30
53 D/D SB 12/32
54 D/D SB 12/33
55 D/D SB 12/35
56 D/D SB 12/41
57 D/D SB 12/47
58 D/D SB 12/48

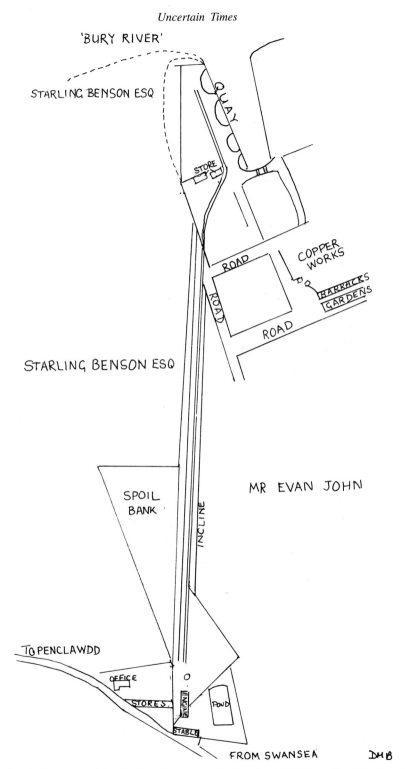

19   Penlan Colliery leased by Starling Benson to the Penclawdd Colliery Co. Ltd, Aug 8 1858
Based on plan accompanying document D/D SB 12/32, WGRO

Penlan Colliery Company of Wind Street.[59] In March 1922 the lease was transferred to the Brynlais Colliery Company by agreement with the family.[60]

Similar changes in occupancy had occurred in connection with the site of the Penclawdd Copper Works. During the Bensons' financial difficulties of the 1840s the Works had been taken over by the Low Patent Copper Company with Charles Low as manager. By 1859 the property was advertised for sale as leasehold, the lease being for 60 years from 1847,[61] the date of Low's occupation.

There appears to have been no buyer but a further lease was taken on January 13 1860 by Charles Low, now joined by Jesse Hall and Stephen Neal in a partnership known as the London Smelting Works. The area leased consisted of 8 acres of land, roughly half of which on the east was slag ground, and the remainder, the site of the old Copper Works. The Works and buildings were included, together with the use of the east side of the dock which adjoined the site.[62] From that date the firm operated as the Penclawdd Copper Works. The partnership does not appear to have lasted long, however, since an Indenture of Assignment was made between Jesse Hall and the other two partners in the August. From that date Hall, on his own, made further arrangements; in August 1861 with Eli Stock who was responsible for the construction of the shipping stage for the Lead Works now on the southern part of the Copper Works site and in November 1864 with a Francis Prior.

The name of Jesse Hall disappears from documents from this date and another becomes prominent, that of Townsend Kirkwood.[63] It was reported that the Kirkwoods were shipping 120 tons of coal per day at Penclawdd from local collieries in 1861[64] and it is clear that Townsend Kirkwood was anxious to establish himself in the area. He was involved in the agreement with Hall and Eli Stock in 1861, another with Stock in September 1868 and a third with Francis Prior in 1869.[65] These gave him control over the whole 8 acres originally leased by the Bensons to Low. To this he added, by a further lease from Starling in January 1872, land, marsh and slag ground north of the area he had already acquired.[66] The buildings were included and the rent for this site was £93 15s for 4 years and from then on £100. Starling, as was his practice, reserved to himself all mineral rights in veins of coal etc under the premises. The leases granted to Kirkwood were further secured in 1876 by an extension of the term originally agreed.

Kirkwood in turn had begun to lease out the premises acquired. In April 1872 he leased a portion of the 8-acre site on the north of the Lead Works to a group of businessmen, Herbert Llewellyn Morris of Pontamman, Gent, John Thomas of Llangennech, Gent, William Morris of Pontamman, Gent, and Robert Smith of Ffrwdgrech, Esq, the firm known as H Ll Morris & Co. The lease was of land

59   D/D SB 12/124
60   D/D SB 12/125
61   C April 29 1859
62   D/D SB 12/36
63   D/D SB 12/50
64   BR MS
65   D/D SB 12/50
66   D/D SB 12/49

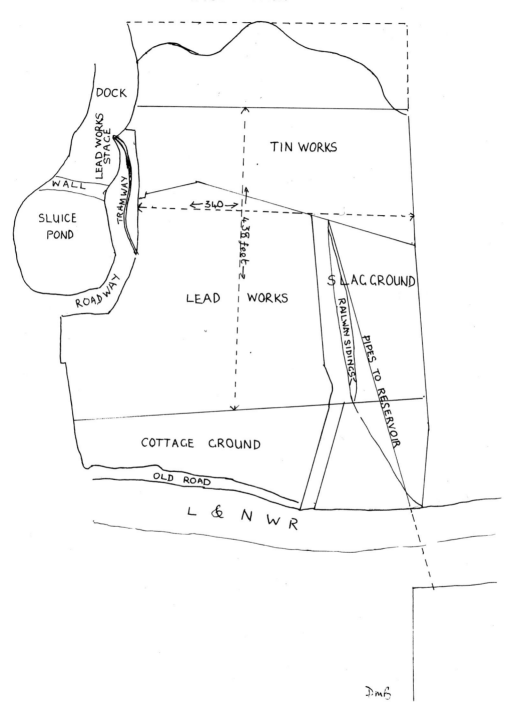

RIVER LOUGHOR

DOCK

LEAD WORKS STAGE

WALL

SLUICE POND

TRAMWAY

ROADWAY

TIN WORKS

←340→

438 feet

LEAD   WORKS

SLAG GROUND

RAILWAY SIDINGS

PIPES TO RESERVOIR

COTTAGE GROUND

OLD ROAD

L & N W R

20   Lease of land and slag ground to H Ll Morris & Co., 1876
      Based on plan accompanying document D/D SB 12/58, WGRO

and slag ground with the use of the east side of the dock adjoining the premises, the term was 36 years and a peppercorn rent for the first 9 months, £375 pa for the next 3 years and £400 pa for the remainder.[67] It was on this site that the Gower Tinplate Works was set up.

By August 1876 a fifth partner had joined the Tin Plate firm, Edward Sumner Morris of the Vernon Tin Plate Works, Briton Ferry. A further lease of land was granted to the company by Kirkwood for the area to the north of the existing Tin Plate Works acquired from Starling in January 1872. In 1876 Starling was dealing directly with the Gower Iron and Tin Plate Works, to give it its full title, leasing to them the Reservoir or Sluice Pond including the sluice gates and fixtures.[68] It was soon after, on September 6 1876, that the firm mortgaged their Works for £10,000 to Susanna Strick,[69] widow of John Joce Strick and daughter of Joseph Martin.

On November 1 1882 John (Glyn) Thomas having retired from the firm, a Deed of Dissolution was drawn up[70] and on July 18 1883 the Works were offered for sale by the mortgagees by public auction at the Mackworth Arms Hotel.[71] It is possible that no sale was effected because on April 16 1884 the remaining partner, Edward Sumner Morris, now joined by Robert Garnaut (sic) Cawker, was assigning the leases for part of the Works with machinery and chattels to John Player, Tin Plate manufacturer of Clydach, for £500.[72] By this time Starling was dead and his nephew, William Denman Benson, was dealing with the affairs of the Copper Works site.

Another company which leased land from Starling Benson was the Amman Iron Company. They held a site on the west of the Copper Works, two fields on the west of the Penlan Colliery and the connecting incline. On November 10 1874 Starling was writing to the company suggesting changes in their lease and rents which were necessary to meet the requirements of the London & North Western Railway Company.

> You will have to divert and fence off the 20 foot road to the Station and to make the road at A so as to connect the various roads there meeting on the Level of the road at the entrance to the Tinplate Works, leaving sufficient head for loaded wagons when you make the proposed railway bridge over this road also to have a footpath from the private road C to road D.

His main concern was the dilatoriness of the Amman Iron Company in making decisions regarding the plans of the LNWR.[73] A railway link between Penclawdd and the Swansea-Pontardulais line had been opened in the late 1860s. The line

67 D/D SB 12/50
68 D/D SB 12/60
69 D/D SB 12/61
70 D/D SB 12/92
71 D/D SB 12/96
72 D/D SB 12/99
73 D/D SB 12/53

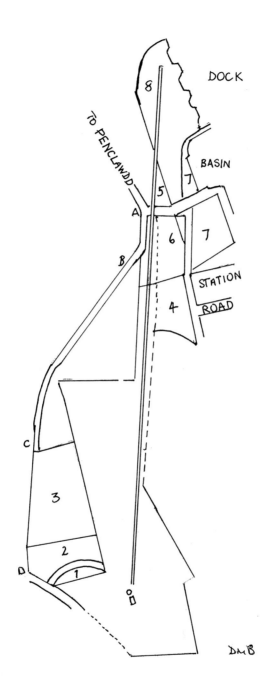

21 Land (1-8) leased to the Amman Iron Co., 1874
    Based on plan accompanying document D/D SB 12/53/2, WGRO

was originally built by the Llanelly Railway & Dock Company (of which Townsend Kirkwood was a director) and offered a far more efficient outlet for coal and manufactured goods than was provided by the existing dock with its dependence on the River Loughor.

By 1876 the LNWR Co. had taken over and, by virtue of its Act of 1874, were making plans for an extension of the Penclawdd line. This involved the purchase of Benson land. A Memorandum of Agreement of March 31 1876 between Starling and Frederick Wood, the LNWR land agent, states that the area to be sold was 1 acre 1 rood and 8½ perches, freehold, together with buildings but subject to several leases. Included in the agreement was a schedule of tenants, one of whom was the Amman Iron Company. The price given was £504 5s 3d which covered compensation for damage or loss caused by severance, construction of the railway and works etc.[74] Some of the buildings would have to be demolished and although the railway with its station had become an important part in the life of the small community, the tenants would not have welcomed the upheaval involved.

Starling leased land, however, not only to industrial or railway companies but also to local families. Many of these he would have known personally from his connections with the area over a period of fifty years. Many would have been employed in his works; some even educated at the school he had started in Penclawdd.[75] The Jenkins family could have been one of these.

Anne Jenkins, a widow, was granted a lease of land in March 1863 for 60 years.[76] The lease was for three lives, Mary Ann Walters aged 19, Joseph Jenkins aged 17 and William Richards also aged 17. Mrs Jenkins was the licensee of the Oddfellows Arms which stood on this site. No doubt it was a busy and prosperous concern situated so near the various works, the railway station and the road from the station to the village of Penclawdd.

In March 1876 the agreement was made by Starling with the LNWR to sell land for the further development of the railway and a small part of Mrs Jenkins's land was included in this. It was stated in the schedule that buildings on the land would have to be demolished[77] and the Oddfellows Arms was one of these. In January 1877 a new lease of land with power to build 'a messuage or dwelling house' was granted to Anne Jenkins by Starling for 99 years at the same rent of £3 pa.[78] The position of the site was described as being bounded on the north by Benson land, on the south east by the old incline from Penclawdd Colliery (ie the old tramway from the Benson pit at Penlan), and on the west and south west by the road leading from Penclawdd Station to Penclawdd. This was the site of the new Oddfellows Arms.

The following November Mrs Jenkins was granted a licence by Starling to assign the premises together with the Oddfellows Arms to Edward Strick[79] and a few days later, on the 20th, Mrs Jenkins mortgaged the property to Edward

74   D/D SB 12/57
75   *Vide* p 265
76   D/D SB 12/57
77   *Ibid*
78   D/D SB 12/62
79   D/D SB 12/71

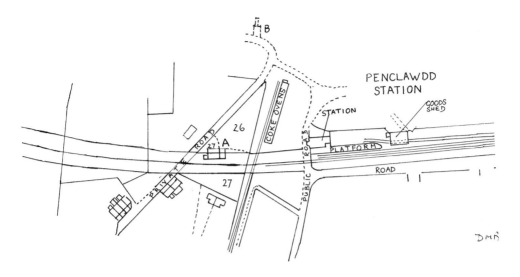

22 Plan for the extension of the LNWR
Plots 26 & 27 leased to Anne Jenkins by Starling Benson
A Oddfellows Arms
B Site of new Oddfellows Arms (later the Railway Inn)
Based on plan accompanying document D/D SB 12/57, WGRO

23 View from the track of the tramway looking towards the Railway Inn. Benson Road lies
horizontally across the photograph. The station was on the right, out of view

Photo: D M Bayliffe

Strick for £190 and a further amount if needed up to £500.[80] In the following May, Edward Strick and Anne Jenkins, now 'late of the Oddfellows Arms', assigned the lease to a Swansea brewer, Henry William Crowhurst. This time the site is described as having an added dwelling house and a road on the south leading to the Tin Plate Works.[81] Starling ratified this agreement, raising the rent to £8 pa and at the same time giving power to Crowhurst to build houses, stables or coach-houses.[82] A document drawn up in 1885 was to establish Crowhurst's title to the property and showed that he had now changed the name of the inn to the Railway Hotel.[83] The Railway Inn now stands on this site.

There were many other instances of Starling's involvement with members of the Penclawdd community; for example, with David Williams shopkeeper of Manchester House, David Williams engine driver, John Thomas mason, and many others. Capt Thomas Lewis, Master Mariner from Llanmadoc, needed 2 roods, 8 perches of land with a licence to build, the lease to cover three lives, those of Ann Lewis aged 6, Edward William Dunkin also aged 6, the son of Edward William Dunkin of Loughor, and Ann Richards aged 3 months.[84]

The family name of Fry stands out in contrast to the commoner surnames, recurring frequently from 1863 on. In that year John Fry, pitman, leased land from Starling Benson for three lives, those of his young sons, Richard (6), John (4) and Thomas (2).[85] In 1876, now a colliery overman, he sought to renew the lease for the same property[86] but also for property already leased in 1873 to another John Fry,[87] described as a licensed victualler, probably his father. After Starling's death, when William Benson was dealing with his uncle's affairs, there were further transactions with the Fry family. According to a draft lease of August 1879 John Fry, still a colliery overman, was living at 1 Benson Terrace but proposed moving into the house previously occupied by the manager of the Penlan colliery.[88] There are later references to John Fry the victualler in 1883 when his address is given as the Ship and Castle Inn.[89]

Thus in one family alone we find at least three generations involved with Benson property transactions in the growing community of nineteenth century Penclawdd.

With the passing of Starling's interest to William Denman Benson in 1879, the date of his death, three generations of Bensons had similarly been associated with the development of the area. Starling's will, made on January 2 1879, only a fortnight before his death, does not specify the actual location of his property, apart from the mention of 'freehold Messuages tenements Lands and hereditaments situate in the higher division of the Parish of Llanrhidian'.[90] The

80 D/D SB 12/73
81 D/D SB 12/77
82 D/D SB 12/78
83 D/D SB 12/107
84 D/D SB 12/43
85 D/D SB 12/42
86 D/D SB 12/55
87 D/D SB 12/52
88 D/D SB 12/85
89 D/D SB 12/94 & 95
90 Will of Starling Benson, made January 2 1879, proved Carmarthen, March 10 1879, Office Copy issued by Somerset House

24   Benson Street looking up towards the site of Penlan Pit (on the left), 1995

25   The Railway Inn, 1995

Photos: D M Bayliffe

Inland Revenue inventory of real property, however, gives full details of Starling's possessions.

The freehold consisted of more than 60 acres and included 15½ acres at Penlan, land at Abercedy and the Copperworks site on which now stood the Lead Works and the Iron and Tin Plate Works. In addition, Starling had as recently as July 1878 purchased for £300 the land and dock at Morfa Cwm which he had previously held under lease for 999 years. He had also bought, in 1873, a portion of the foreshore from the Duke of Beaufort.

The greater part of this property was leased to various tenants. The Copper Works site, for instance, was let to Townsend Kirkwood at an annual rent of £215. Ten cottages and land were still held on lease by Jesse Hall for 60 years from March 25 1860, when he had first taken over the Copper Works.[91]

The inventory also gives details of leasehold property. This had all been leased from William Eaton and had a further 53 years to run. This comprised Kent Meadows consisting of 3½ acres and an old dwelling house and garden (probably the one previously occupied by Starling), a cottage occupied by a Mrs Pugh, and Cornel Bach, sublet to John Fry. The total rents for these properties was £11 6s. The rest of the Eaton land consisted of a quarry, rough land, veins and seams of coal which were at that time not worked and consequently of no value.[92]

Thus Starling, by cautious investment and careful management, had secured a sound financial basis for the rest of his family in the future. He had certainly proved the truth of the Benson motto: 'Opes Parit Industria'. His concern for the next generation was not, however, purely for their material well-being. He had gradually become the central figure in the family, providing care, companionship and advice.

We now have to go back in time to look at the various and varied situations where 'Uncle Starling' was on hand to offer help whenever it was needed.

---

91   D/D SB 12/87
92   D/D SB 12/88

Chapter VII

Uncle Starling

The passing of the 1847 Swansea Harbour Act and the decline of the family involvement in their Forest and Penclawdd copper interests coincided with the arrival of a new generation at the Manor House in Teddington where the elder Bensons had been settled since their departure from Swansea.

Thomas Starling Benson, in spite of variable health, had been still alert and comparatively active for his sixty-three years when, in 1838, he bought what was to be his last home, leaving his eldest son to fight his battles in South Wales. City born, he became quickly acclimatised to the then rural surroundings of his new estate in Middlesex, and grew old contentedly, enjoying the leisurely life afforded by gardens, fields and river, punctuated by the occasional visit to London to attend meetings at the Drapers' Hall. Even when, in the 1850s, his health was showing signs of deterioration, he was still interested in watching the hay making, or, comfortably propped up on cushions, taking the air in a boat on the Thames. At other times he was happy to ride around the garden in his pony cart or simply to sit among the roses and rhododendrons, surrounded by his grandchildren at play.

His wife, some twenty years his junior and always of a comparatively frail physique in the way so many high class ladies were in her day, was still as concerned with good works as she and her mother had been in Swansea. Her activities in the service of the local Church had now to be combined with the responsibility of being a grandmother, starting in 1846 with her son Henry's first born, Starling Meux.

Henry had married Mary Henrietta, the second daughter of the High Court Judge, Sir William Wightman, and his wife, Charlotte Mary (née Baird). Whenever possible, Tiny, as she was known, accompanied her husband on his military postings. This meant leaving little Star, as he became known to distinguish him from his Uncle, with his grandparents at Teddington. Soon after his birth Tiny joined her husband in Ireland. The first parting was recorded by Elizabeth Benson in one of her sentimental 'lays':

> A soldier he, faithful and kind.
> To meet him on the following day
> Was she to brave the sea and wind,[1]

leaving her treasured child behind in their safe-keeping.

Eighteen months later, a second baby arrived. He was christened William after his maternal grandfather, and Denman after Sir William's judicial colleague of

1   E M and R M Benson, Lays of Memory, Sacred and Social, (Teddington) Sept 21 1846

that name. At first he remained with his parents in Dublin where they had quarters in Usher's Island. A letter from Henry to his mother in April 1848 when the baby was just over a month old refers to 'Willy making noises, probably wishes to send love and kisses', and ends with 'Kiss to Star', who was still in Teddington.[2]

The family increased rapidly, two daughters, Alice Elizabeth Frazer and Mary Florance, following each other in swift succession. Both were born at Teddington, which had the advantage of being close to their maternal grandparents' home at St Alban's Bank in Richmond. In February 1853, Star, now six and a half, wrote to his Uncle Richard to say,

> Willy is poorly but if he is better Papa, Mama, Alice, Mary, and I are going to St. Alban's Bank on Saturday & stay till they go to Swansea.[3]

Henry's troop of the 17th Lancers was expected to move from Christchurch, Hants, either to Dorchester or to Hampton Court. In the meantime, he and Tiny had hoped to take advantage of his leave to visit Starling, but the plan was disrupted by Willy's serious attack of croup, requiring the application of leeches as well as mustard poultices.

> The illness seems to render the journey to Swansea improbable as Henry and Tiny will not want to leave Willy and he will if he recovers be quite unable to travel in March. It is a mercy that they had not set off and we are all under one roof so that we can comfort each other.[4]

The precariousness of a child's life in days before the use of antibiotics is underlined by Mrs Benson's ominous words, 'if he recovers', reminding us that even a common childish complaint could be a killer.

Fortunately Willy did recover and by April 5, he was able to travel with his parents and the other children to St Alban's Bank where Henry and Tiny left them, returning the following evening to dine with Starling who was expected to arrive from Swansea. The following day, his brother Florance was expected, although poor Mrs Benson was never quite sure what her step-sons were doing.

> All their movements are so uncertain I never know whether they are coming or going. I suppose it is the Railway that brings Starling up.[5]

In fairness to Starling, be it said, his visits were as frequent as he could make them in view of the heavy demands upon his time. On July 4, Mrs Benson wrote

2 HRB to EMB, April 1848. Family letters unless otherwise stated, are from UCS/BC
3 Starling Meux Benson to RMB, Feb 17 1853
4 EMB (Teddington) to RMB, Feb 19 1853
5 EMB to RMB, April 5 1853

to Richard that Starling had arrived that afternoon. While he was with them, she and his father had taken Star and Willy to Chobham where the Queen was visiting the troops at Virginia Water. There the boys saw their Father in his rather Spartan tent and were able to have lunch with him in the Mess. Starling had gone into town, but was expected back to dinner by 6 o'clock with Tiny. The letter ends with:

> The Children send you best love & kisses - and I am sure Uncle Starling, Tiny and Henry would all send you every good wish in which many others unite![6]

This is the first time for Starling to be referred to as 'Uncle Starling', an epithet he was never again to lose completely within the family. International events were conspiring to give him an even more important role in the lives of his nieces and nephews, whose father was shortly to leave for the Crimean War and after that, for India in the aftermath of the Mutiny.

In the course of her letter Mrs Benson made it clear to Richard how much she would like both him and Starling to follow the example of a certain Mr Barker and each take a good wife. There was a poignant reason behind Mrs Benson's desire to see Richard and Starling married. The middle of the summer of 1853 was in many ways a watershed for the family. Florance John had died suddenly on June 6.

Only a short time before his fatal illness, as 'The Swansea & Glamorgan Herald' pointed out, he had been engaged in his professional capacity before a Committee of the House of Commons. He was, it added, 'esteemed by all classes for the goodness of his heart and the uniform urbanity of his manner.'[7] Much of his work had been done in South Wales, where he had acted as Revising Counsel as well as representing his family's interests in the negotiations concerning the development of the South Dock and of the Swansea Vale Railway. The year before his death, he had taken a leading role in examining witnesses when a Bill to improve the water supply of the area had been before the Committee of the House of Lords. All in all he had undertaken a gruelling schedule which may well have contributed to his early death.

Earlier in 1853, he had been unwell at the time of Willy's severe attack of croup, about which he had been very anxious, but he seemed to have recovered, and on the evening of May 13, was in excellent form. With Lady Wightman and other guests at Teddington, he took part in a game of planchette, sitting with his hands outstretched on his stepmother's rosewood table until it began to move. It then 'continued a rotary motion, causing them to rise and follow it.'

Their involvement with the occult did not appear to have harmed them as, that night, they all had a good night's sleep, which Florance attributed to the activities of the evening. 'I suppose,' commented Mrs Benson with an unusual touch of humour, 'it electrified the people as well as the table.'[8] In just over a month, Florance was dead.

6 EMB to RMB, July 4 & 6 1853
7 Sw and Glam Herald, June 15 1853
8 EMB to RMB, May 14 1853

His death affected his father deeply, and was probably one reason for Starling's frequent visits in the ensuing weeks. There had been other problems too of a distressing nature, dating from earlier phases in the family fortunes.

The Benson involvement with the Usborne family had not ended when, in 1834, Henry Usborne left his business partnership with T S Benson and Hart Logan. In 1831 Henry's nephew, Thomas Henry, had married Emma Benson, the younger daughter of Thomas Starling and his second wife, Hannah Newberry. After Emma's death in 1836, Tom Usborne and his motherless children had continued to enjoy a close relationship with the Benson family, especially with Starling who kept in constant touch with his nephew and nieces.

Tom Usborne remarried in 1843, and thereafter his father, also Thomas, had taken the main responsibility in financial arrangements on behalf of his grandchildren until his death in 1845. Afterwards their affairs had been administered by their two uncles, Starling and the Revd Henry Breedon of Pangbourne, who was married to T H Usborne's sister.[9]

The young Usbornes spent much of their time with their father's mother but continued to come on frequent visits to their Benson relatives. In 1852, however, nineteen-year-old Emma Rebecca Usborne, named after her mother and paternal grandmother, was about to marry a young soldier in the Indian Army, William Louis Mosheim Bishop.[10] With her brother and sister, also minors, she brought, through a 'next friend', a suit in Chancery to sort out their position under an indenture originally made in 1803 at the time of T S Benson's marriage to Hannah Newbury and revised in 1831 at the time of Emma Benson's marriage to Tom Usborne. The purpose in both cases had been to safeguard the financial interests of the children of the respective marriages.

Unfortunately the original money secured under the indenture had been invested in the family firm of Newberry & Co., in which T S Benson was a partner, and was lost when the firm failed. The need to make good this loss at a time when the general economic depression had adversely affected the family fortunes had been yet another cause of concern for Starling as one of the original Trustees, and undoubtedly for Florance too. Both were naturally anxious to protect their ageing father as well as to secure justice for their dead sister's children, and they must have breathed a sigh of relief when a satisfactory compromise was reached, with the appointment of new Trustees.[11]

Relationships in many families would have been embittered by the strain of legal action, yet in the few letters of Mrs Benson's preserved from this period, the references to Emma and Bessie Usborne and to their father and brother remain as warm as ever. Mrs Benson wrote about them as any affectionate grandmother would do. She was as concerned about Emma leaving for foreign parts as she was ready to welcome Bessie when she chose to visit them at Teddington.

Unfortunately Emma's happiness, like her mother's, was doomed to be short-lived. She had gone to live with her husband in the Punjab where her three children were born. There William Bishop died in 1857[12] shortly after the death

9   JREB, Document of Release, Oct 5 1878
10 *Ibid*
11 *Ibid*
12 EMB to RMS, May 6 & Nov 12/13 1857

of their third baby, Florance Louis. Emma, in poor health herself, returned to England later in the year with her two surviving children and was surrounded by the loving concern of all the family, especially Elizabeth Benson who was foremost in seeking to secure the young widow's financial future. Starling again became one of the Trustees replacing those appointed in 1852, who had all meanwhile sought to be relieved of their responsibility.

Emma subsequently remarried but died a comparatively young woman. Starling, however, continued to exercise his trust, now caring for the interests of her two children until they came of age. Only in the October of 1878, three months before Starling's death, did they sign a document of release, freeing their great uncle from all future responsibility for their affairs.[13]

Thomas Starling Benson had in general enjoyed the reputation of being an astute businessman. That he had now shown himself to be so inept in his handling of family finances must have come as a devastating shock to Starling and Florance, revealing all too clearly the brittle condition of so many of his transactions. Both men must have felt their own integrity sadly compromised by the muddle surrounding the money due to their dead sister's children, and undoubtedly agonised about finding a just solution to this delicate and potentially dangerous situation. Starling had the resilience to ride the storm, but for Florance, during the period immediately leading up to his death in 1853, the tension must have been a contributory factor in undermining his health, already strained by the unduly heavy work-load he was carrying at the time.

That same year Starling left Gloucester Place. With the growing commercialisation of the Burrows as a result of the South Dock development, the changes he had foreseen had had their undesirable effect on the area, and in 1853 Starling was obviously glad to move to the more agreeable prospect of Russell House in Russell Place. Was he, one wonders, seeking to shed his ghosts? Gloucester Place must have been full of memories of Florance.

His years there had not been without their excitement. On the night of Tuesday, January 29 1847, the alarm had been given that fire had broken out in Starling's house, but in spite of the loud knocking on the door and the violent ringing of the bell, there had been no response from within. Eventually the door had been burst open while the fire brigade waited to go into action. It was then discovered that all was well inside. A very high wind had drowned all the noise outside and what had been taken for flames was only the vivid glow cast on walls and windows by a very brisk fire burning in one of the bedrooms.[14] Such alarums and excursions were, however, well in the past by the time Starling moved to his new home in Russell Place.

Be that as it may, that same summer Starling and Richard went off together to the Continent. Lady Wightman, Tiny's mother, was staying at Schwergerhoff, and in a letter home to her husband on August 21 1853, she mentioned that the Benson brothers were at Vevay, while their sister, Sarah Jane, had gone to Aix-les-Bains, presumably for her health which had never been robust.[15] The

13 JREB, *op cit*
14 C Jan 29 1847, p 3
15 Lady Wightman to Sir William Wightman, Aug 21 1853

Wightmans were still abroad in October continuing their journey from Genoa to Nice, but by that time the call of duty had taken the Benson brothers back to Britain.[16]

Within a year of Florance's death Starling lost his remaining sibling. Sarah Jane died on March 5 1854 at Suna in the district of Pallanza in Piedmont. Only the day before she had made, in Italian, a 'Secret Testament', in which she described herself as 'possessing a sound body and mind altho' at this time suffering from accidental illness'. She had become 'a member of the Holy Catholic Church', a conversion which may well have caused the religious rift still referred to within the family. Nevertheless, she named her 'dear brother', Starling Benson, as her heir and residuary legatee, subject to the value of two thirds of her property (mainly in Southwark) being bequeathed 'to the dear child Jean Petrouville Uffrouville commonly known under the name of Gaufridy'. As her 'executor and universal legatee', Starling was to transmit Jean's legacy to François Gaufridy (or de Gaufridy) to administer for him until the boy came of age 'in what way shall seem best to his own judgment and without anyone having the right at any time to call him to account for it.' The annual sum of £100 was to be paid to Mons. Gaufridy during his life 'unless he should persist as at present in refusing this'.[17]

François Gaufridy not only refused the money but also renounced the role of Testamentary Legatee conferred on him under the terms of the will. Probate was subsequently granted to Starling and the will eventually proved on December 1 1854 in London. In it the deceased was described as Sarah Jane Benson Spinster.[18] Her exact relationship - whether natural or adoptive - to the 'dear child' remains unclear. Mrs Benson's existing letters make no mention of Sarah after July 1853 when she reminded Richard that the following Saturday was her forty-first birthday.[19] Jean Gaufridy, however, kept in touch with the family, considering both Richard and Henry as uncles and referring in later correspondence to the latter's children as his cousins who he hoped would visit him in his new home outside Turin.[20]

By this time, however, Starling had died and it had been left to Henry to settle the final payments of his legacy. That Starling had fulfilled meticulously his duties as executor there can be no doubt but there is no evidence that he was directly involved in any way with 'the dear child'. From now on he was mainly concerned with Henry's increasing brood.

Tiny's third daughter, Margaret Elizabeth, known in the family as Madge, had been born on September 11 1853 in Teddington. Henry and Tiny were obviously curious about Starling's new house in Russell Place which, happily, offered ample accommodation for the extended family. As Henry was on leave until the end of the year, they decided to take Willy, the three girls and their nurse to Swansea in October, while young Star was at Brighton with his grandmother.

16 Lady Wightman and Georgina Wightman to Sir William, Oct 6 1853
17 D/D SB 12/28, WGRO
18 *Ibid*
19 EMB to RMB, July 6 1853
20 Jean Gaufridy to HRB, Nov 8 1880

Already Uncle Starling and Swansea were playing a major part in the lives of his nephews and nieces, and this was enhanced by Henry's absences abroad. On November 30 1854 Henry, setting out on his journey to join his regiment in the Crimea, was accompanied to London Bridge Station by a party of family and friends including Starling and the two Tom Usbornes, his late sister Emma's husband and her son. Mrs Benson, writing to Richard, describes the leave-taking: Some of them

> accompanied them to Gravesend where they found the Vessell all ready - and went on board, where as you may suppose there was much confusion! Starling soon left having business in London - and advised the ladies to go with him - but naturally Tiny preferred to remain with darling Henry to the last - so - they remained and accompanied him to Queenshithe whither the Vessell had to go - to have the compasses adjusted. At Queenshithe they landed and had a scrambling dinner at a little Inn - which being quite unused to so large a company was quite taken by storm! - The Major dined with them and all THIRTY followed in so there was a regular scramble for mutton chops and beefsteaks, in which Tom Usborne and Parsons proved very useful *Aid de Camps!*[21]

Henry's ship, the 'Alma', set sail two days later, only to be delayed by adverse weather conditions and various other factors.[22] Eventually, after a number of unexpected returns home, Henry decided to travel overland to Marseilles and thence by sea to Constantinople where he joined the 'Alma' for the rest of his journey to Balaklava.

Early in the New Year of 1855, Starling was in Teddington and another visit was expected at the end of February, when the older Bensons would be returning home from Brighton. During his February visit to London he chaired the Committee to select a new Member of Parliament for Swansea to replace J H Vivian who had recently died. A letter from his step-mother to Richard, written on February 28, while they were still at Brighton, informed him that it was Starling who had proposed 'Louis' *(sic)* Dillwyn who was duly elected.[23]

Starling was next due in Teddington on April 9. Mrs Benson hoped Richard would come over while he was there. Lady Wightman, with whom Tiny and four of the children were staying, had asked if they might rent the Manor for a couple of months while the Bensons were away, and so there were plans to be made for visits to both Oxford and Swansea.[24] His mother had asked Richard to find them suitable accommodation in Oxford with possibly an extra bedroom as they would probably have visits from Starling. In addition she suggested Richard should accompany them to Swansea as she felt he needed a change.[25] There is nothing to suggest that Richard followed his mother's advice, but, by July, the

21   EMB to RMB, Nov 30 1854
22   EMB to RMB, Dec 10 1854
23   EMB to RMB, Feb 28 1855
24   EMB to RMB, March 31 1855
25   EMB to RMB, March (no date) 1855

grandparents were in Swansea with Star and Willy, now aged nine and seven respectively.

They visited Oystermouth Castle together, and the boys, in the care of Mrs Benson's companion, Miss Bailey, attended by the ever faithful Parsons, explored the ruins. On the Tuesday they visited Sketty and the new Church built by Henry Hussey Vivian in memory of his young wife, Jessie. This had been dedicated only in September 1850, long after the Bensons had left Swansea for Teddington. Mrs Benson was very impressed by it, considering it equalled 'Clifden Hampden'. From there they went on to Sketty Park, their old home, but were unable to go into the house, 'the Welsh woman who had charge of the house having orders to admit no one'. It was being prepared for the new Sir John and Lady Morris who were expected in two to three weeks' time and who, apparently unknown even to his family, had been married many years.

The following day, Mr and Mrs Benson took the boys to see Tyrllandwr, and afterwards the old people drove over to Mumbles - 'so much altered with marine residences and lodgings. It looked very pretty in the evening tide of the setting sun' *(sic)*. In the meantime the boys had been with Uncle Starling on the sands, and were picked up by the carriage on its return journey, Mr and Mrs Benson having met several old acquaintances on their way home to tea, including Pendarvis Vivian and his sister out riding, and Dr Bird and others in their carriages.[26]

Mrs Benson was full of praise for Starling's house, 'perfectly convenient, well arranged and the garden a wonderful advantage. There is a verandah so we can sit under it of a morning or evening and enjoy the air without fatigue.' Later in the day it became too hot to be exposed to the sun, so they normally dined at 4 o'clock, 'which pleases us all.'[27]

A more succinct account of the visit was given by Star to his Uncle Richard in a letter conveying birthday greetings for July 6:

> On Monday we went to Oystermouth Castle & climbed all over it & brought home some pieces. Yesterday we all had a drive to Tyrlandor *(sic)* and then G'Mama and G'Papa set Uncle Starling, Willy and I *(sic)* down at the Sands while they drove on to the Mumbles and then picked us up, on their return.[28]

Willy, twenty months Star's junior, was obviously the brighter, (as was shown later when he was sent to Eton while, after much heart-searching, Star was sent to Radley). Twelve months later, in July 1856, Willy's birthday letter to Uncle Richard, written from Teddington, contained a very full and graphic account of their activities in which Uncle Starling was again the central figure.

> On Wednesday Uncle Starling took us to see the Zoological gardens, first we saw the bears, and then the birds, the white Polar bear, and the camel, the Monkey, the Lion, the Tiger, etc, etc. Then we went to

26 EMB (Swansea) to RMB, possibly July 1 1855
27 *Ibid*
28 Starling Meux Benson to RMB, July 6 1855

27 'Willie' Benson with his grandmother   UCS/BC, Courtesy of JREB

26 'Star' Benson with his grandfather   UCS/BC, Courtesy of JREB

Cremorne and walked about the gardens and then we had some lunch which consisted of mutton cutlets, salad, and bread and cheese, and beer. Then we went to hear the band play and then to see the tumblers, and we walked about till 6 o'clock, and saw a picture as large as two of these houses with the Lake of Geneva and the cows going down to water and the snowy mountains. We heard a concert and one of the men who were singing said he had a ton of coals thrown down upon his head, and when they would not let him in at the door he climbed in at the window and there was a tub of water under him and he fell into it and cried for help and a man ... and cried "fire, fire", and after this was over there was a grand rush to the theatre. We went into the gallery and saw a play acted and some dogs rolled a roller up and down a ladder. When we arrived at the Vauxhall station the train had just left, so Uncle took us to Vauxhall gardens as there was more than an hour to wait for the next train, we walked about the gardens and saw some brilliant illuminations. We had some supper there and then came home. It was past eleven o'clock when we arrived at the Manor. On Thursday we all went to the Flower Show at Hampton-Wick.[29]

What their grandmother thought about such hours we shall never know. She may well have considered it was time for their father to come home to check up on their movements, but then she knew they were in Uncle Starling's capable hands, so she could safely allow a little latitude.

As it happened, Henry was on the point of returning from the Crimea where his service had brought its rewards. Early that year he had become a Lieutenant Colonel, thanks in part to the effort made by Starling on his behalf, for which he wrote to thank him in a letter from the Crimea, dated May 11 1855. He had been hoping his senior officer Lawrenson would retire on full pay; this would certainly have been to Henry's financial advantage as he was the one most likely to succeed him. Lawrenson, however, decided to return, making the possibility of quick promotion more remote.[30] Nevertheless, matters did sort themselves out, and his mother's letter to Richard on November 9 1856, proudly began with, 'Our dear Colonel and his wife arrived last night'.[31]

An earlier letter from his father to Starling, dated April 4, 1855, reveals something of the manipulation that had gone on behind the scenes to achieve the desired promotion. Encouraged by the opinion of her father who considered the present opening 'an advantageous offer', Tiny had come over to Teddington especially to discuss the matter. It seemed that £1000 would be required from the Bensons and the old gentleman was not sure how that could best be managed. He outlined to Starling the position as he understood it. The 16th Lancers were to join the 17th,

> that is a large part of them and they come under a Major. This Major
> is a few months sen. to Henry - consequently would be Senior Major

29 William Denman Benson to RMB, July 5 1856
30 HRB to SB, May 11 1855
31 EMB to RMB, Nov 9 1856

- Now to meet this Lawrenson tells Morris He *(sic)* will sell out and He will take 3000. However this Morris who is now Major is willing to give valn. prin, by abt 13 or 14 for the Majority. This is to fr in ara of the 3000 to Laurenson - Thus Henry would be Coln of the 17th ... The Col. of the 16th is not to go out - but Remains with His Reg ... how can you advise the best way of having the 1000? perhaps the Judge would (if He can) adve it - but then what secry can he give, but Tiny thinks he would not adv. beyond his life or I judge Sir H. Meux would advance it if We ask Him, or do you know a better plan.'[32]

As we have already seen, the family fortunes were in none too healthy a state. In any case, the older Bensons were never loth to profit from their more prestigious family connections. When Richard was about to leave Oxford in 1849, Mrs Benson had written to Lord Brougham, her father's cousin, seeking a suitable settlement for her son. Henry's comment was: 'I read your letter to Lord Brougham & his answer and thought it could not have been better. I hope he will get Dick a good living.'[33]

How far it was now necessary to enlist Sir Henry Meux's help for Henry we do not know. About this time Starling saw him in Town looking very unwell and within a short time he suffered the stroke which seriously incapacitated him.[34] Presumably Starling and the Judge between them were able to effect all that was necessary.

With the arrival of Tiny's third son, Henry Wightman (Harry), born on July 22 1855, there was a christening to be arranged. Their old friend and family solicitor, Alfred Turner, had agreed to be one of the godfathers, the other being Tiny's brother-in-law, Matthew Arnold. Unfortunately the Arnolds were away at Fox How where Arnold's mother and his unmarried sister Fanny were still living. As Arnold would not be back till September 18, the very day Alfred Turner was going away, Uncle Starling had once more to step into the breach and act as proxy.[35]

The date was eventually fixed for Saturday, September 15, Elizabeth Benson's sixty-second birthday. Before that, Starling had managed to fit in a holiday for himself, apparently by yacht. He had a pleasant visit to Boulogne, and had been able to see 'all the proceedings of the Queen's departure, when the Queen's Yacht was almost too large for the harbour so when she swung the tide took her and made clear the quay of all the vessells *(sic)* lying against it.' They would obviously 'have to pay for a few spars, etc crushed in the melee by her stern'.[36]

Starling's yacht did not suffer, being higher up.

He returned via Land's End and reached Swansea by September 6, so as to be available to travel to Teddington shortly after the 10th, soon enough for there to be no last minute panic. There were times, of course, when even he could not

32   TSB to SB, April 4 1855
33   HRB to EMB, May 20 1849
34   EMB to RMB, April 1855
35   EMB to RMB, Aug 1855
36   *Ibid*

arrive at the drop of a hat. The triumphal return of the 'Colonel' the following year should have coincided with a visit of Starling's, but unfortunately on November 9 1856, he was 'delayed by municipal business'.[37] He was, however, up by the end of the following week for a short stay.

The morning they left, the two brothers travelled to London together. Starling was returning to Swansea, while Henry intended to visit the Drapers' Company and then to order the book of poems recently published as a joint venture by his mother and Richard.[38] For the moment, 'the Colonel' was less under pressure than Starling whose appearances had always to fit in with 'municipal business' or the concerns of harbour and railway. The interests of Swansea were ever present with him, even in Teddington.

The following year was to be a gruelling one for Starling. As the newly elected chairman of Swansea Corporation's Cemetery Committee he found himself involved in controversy with the Bishop of St David's. The Burial Board of the local Town Council and the Vicar of Swansea, supported by the Bishop, were at variance over the question of transport to the new municipal cemetery. This led to a long-drawn-out battle of wills which will be considered in detail later. Here it suffices to say that both his father and step-mother, devout Anglicans as they were, took quite a pride in the long and heated correspondence which resulted, although Mrs Benson, writing to her son, Richard, in Oxford, commented on the irony that one 'who so much dreads notoriety' should be brought into public controversy of this kind.[39]

T S Benson also wrote to Richard, 'You may have noticed Starling is at war with the Bishops'. He promised to send on to him Starling's reply to the Bishop's recriminations, due to appear in the following Saturday's paper.[40] 'The Record' had also taken up the matter, and there was a short note in 'The Glamorgan', recommending the sale of the present Vicarage to buy a house for the same purpose nearer the Cemetery![41]

Starling, however, had other things to do beside brooding over Burial Board affairs. There was much to do in connection with the Swansea Vale Railway, and this kept him from visiting London at the end of the month, but by mid-February, he managed a visit to Teddington, hoping to stay, if possible, over May's birthday on February 20.[42] May had always been particularly close to her uncle, and the following year we find him back in Teddington for the same event, when he took Star, Willy and Margaret to Eaton Place to stay over May's sixth birthday which was being celebrated, in her parents' absence, at the Wightmans' London home.[43]

Henry and Tiny had left for Ireland at the beginning of the month, with the understanding that once they were settled in a house, the four younger children would join them. Star and Willy were living permanently with their Benson grandparents, being educated at this time by various tutors. Engaging the right

37   EMB to RMB, Nov 9 1856
38   EMB to RMB, Nov 15 1856
39   EMB to RMB, Jan 19 1857
40   TSB to RMB, Jan 21 1857
41   EMB to RMB, Jan 22 1857
42   EMB to RMB, Feb 17 1857
43   EMB to HRB, Feb 20 1858,

men was a matter of great concern to Mrs Benson, although, in advance of many of her contemporaries, she showed equal concern about the girls' education. She would have liked May and Alice to remain at Teddington as they were getting on so well with Miss Bailey, but she appreciated their parents' natural desire to have the children with them.[44]

As it happened, their departure was delayed by a period of illness, but eventually they were able to leave the second week in April, Uncle Starling having been up to see them before they left. They travelled with their nurses to Liverpool where they were met by their Uncle Matthew's brother-in-law, Wakefield Cropper, who saw them to the steamer. They arrived safely despite a very rough crossing, during which they were all seasick.

> Master Harry was not a little angry, however by Gods *(sic)* help they reached their dear Parents safely at Montpelier & were very soon busy running all about the house … I am most thankful they are all now with their dear Papa & Mama but we miss them very much and the servants here are quite dolorous.[45]

In the previous March, Starling had been ill with the worst cold he could ever remember, possibly the outcome of the stress at the beginning of the year when he was caught up in the Burial Board controversy.[46]

With the absence of Henry's children in Ireland, Starling now busied himself with other members of the family, notably his niece Bessie, her father Tom Usborne, and the Youngs, connections on the Newberry side. Bessie that year celebrated her twenty-first birthday on May 11,[47] a sad reminder of her mother's death at the time of her birth in 1836. Uncle Starling was at the Usborne home in London for the occasion, and from there he came on to Teddington with his niece and her father for a further celebration. Bessie remained with Mrs Benson after the two men had left, sharing their mutual grief over the latest news of her elder sister, now Emma Bishop, who had lost her baby boy, Florance Louis, on March 7.[48] Later that year, Emma also lost her husband,[49] necessitating her return from India with her children. Here again the family rallied round, led by Mrs Benson, to secure, by a concerted effort, some financial security for their future.[50]

Towards the end of May Starling returned to Teddington,[51] hoping to see Henry who was in London for a regimental dinner, but unfortunately the latter did not arrive before Starling had once again to be on his travels.[52] The time for the hearing of the Swansea Dock Transfer and Harbour Railway Bill was getting painfully near and much as he must have wished to see his brother, this was no time to be cooling his heels at Teddington.

44 EMB to RMB, March 26, possibly 29 1857
45 EMB to RMB, April 11 1857
46 Starling Meux Benson to RMB, March 25 1857
47 EMB to RMB, May 6 1857
48 *Ibid*
49 EMB to HRB, Feb 20 1858
50 EMB to RMB, Dec 22 1857
51 EMB to RMB, May 19 1857
52 EMB to RMB, June 6 1857

Henry had to go back to Ireland, but his parents found consolation in the prospect of a visit there in the summer.[53] They hoped to take a house near Henry and Tiny, even though their visit would coincide with that of the Wightmans.[54] In any case, Henry and Tiny expected to be back in London in October or November 'as an increase in the family was expected in December'. By the September, however, Henry's regiment had been ordered out to India as a result of the Indian Mutiny.

At the time, Uncle Starling had arranged to go to Tenby with C H Smith, leaving his niece Bessie in Swansea in the care of Mrs Smith. On his return, the four 'Irish' children were to take up their abode with him in Russell Place. Starling accordingly went to collect them, and their grandmother was able to report by October 7 that they had 'gone off in high spirits in their uncle's chaise', Tiny remaining with her parents to await the birth of her baby.[55]

Starling wrote promptly to say that he had arrived safely in Swansea with his young charges. Soon afterwards, Henry, whom his mother saw looking 'much fagged', was on his way over land to Alexandria, and thence to India. She was, Mrs Benson wrote to Richard, very anxious about him and the dear children.[56] Presumably it was left to the Wightmans to be anxious about Tiny!

She need have had no fears about the children. Before long she was wishing that they could have stayed with Starling in Wales until after Christmas. But Tiny who expected to be confined early in December at her mother's home in Eaton Place wanted the children back with her before the birth of the new baby. Her wishes naturally prevailed, and the young quartet arrived in Eaton Place on December 1, 'looking extremely well - a great credit to Uncle Starling's care of them'.[57] After the birth of little Charlotte Leonora on December 3, at the end of a labour of thirty-two hours, the other children went off to Teddington Manor, although Tiny and the new baby were not to follow until March.

Uncle Starling joined them there for the holiday, arriving on Christmas Eve and accompanying the elderly couple to Church on Christmas morning. Although his father, for all his frailty, remained for Communion, Starling did not. After lunch he took the children for a walk while his step-mother went to afternoon service and his father to bed.[58] One cannot help wondering whether the testing time he had experienced in the struggle with the Bishop of St David's had somewhat jaundiced his feelings towards the Anglican Church. Nevertheless, the following day, after visiting both Tiny and Emma in London, he returned in time to meet the Trinders, the new Vicar of Teddington and his wife, at dinner. In spite of some of the heterodox views he had expressed in connection with the claims of the Vicar of Swansea to preferential treatment, he found himself getting on well with this representative of the cloth. With Mrs Trinder especially he found he had much in common, as, before her marriage, she had stayed in Gower for three months with her uncle, Dr Hutton.[59]

53   *Ibid*
54   EMB to RMB, July 27 1857
55   EMB to RMB, Oct 7 1857
56   EMB to RMB, Oct 9 1857
57   EMB to RMB, Dec 2 1857,
58   EMB to RMB, Dec 26 1857
59   EMB to RMB, Dec 28 1857

Starling was thinking by this time of a possible move to Gower. When, as a young man, he had lived in Cambrian Place, one of his neighbours had been Catherine Lucas, the widow of John Lucas of Stouthall, near Reynoldston in Gower. As a young bride of sixteen, she had gone to live in a neighbouring mansion, then called 'Pear Tree', within easy access of the ancestral home where she and her husband later moved upon the death of his father.

Catherine's background had been marked by an unusual degree of intrigue and violence, her mother's lover having been suspected of involvement in her father's gruesome murder. Life at 'Pear Tree' must have come as a welcome relief from the tensions of her girlhood, and her new home took on such a magical quality that she and her husband changed the name to 'Fairy Hill'.[60] She might well have regaled her young neighbour with tales of her beloved home so that when the house came on the market in 1858, Starling secured it for himself.

From 1814 to 1823 the house had been the home of Lady Barham who had pioneered several Nonconformist causes in Gower. Lady Barham's daughter, Juliana Noel, later became the second wife of a well-known clergyman, the Revd Samuel Phillips, who succeeded Lady Barham at Fairy Hill, moving in on the occasion of his first marriage.

News of Starling's projected move reached Henry in India early in the New Year, reviving memories of his visit there as a young boy when the first Mrs Phillips had been alive.

> I suppose Starling will have left you ere this - I was quite astounded to hear he was thinking of moving into Gower - and taking a house at Fairy Hill - as I do not remember any house but the one Mrs Phillips used to live in - where you and I stayed one night.[61]

The first Mrs Phillips, née Anne Shaftesbury Horsley, the niece of the then Bishop of St David's, was a distant connection through marriage of Tiny Benson's grand-mother, Mary Baird, although obviously, at the time of his visit, Henry's future involvement with the Wightman family was a long way off.

Starling was undoubtedly aware of the great possibilities of Fairy Hill as a congenial setting for his large brood of nephews and nieces. Memories of the family's years in Sketty Park may well have evoked in him a desire for a more spacious home in the country. He naturally had in mind too the dangers to which Henry was exposed and also his father's deteriorating health which might necessitate leaving Teddington.

The move eventually took place, in fine weather, as Richard noted in a letter to his mother on July 22,[62] and coincided with Harry's third birthday. The family, gathered together on the lawn in Teddington, were very much aware of their missing uncle and the reason for his absence.

For Starling, the change gave him an opportunity to sort out his options. It made feasible his resignation from the Town Council, although he was still near enough to Swansea for him to retain his Chairmanship of the Harbour Trust and

60 Robert Lucas, A Gower Family, (Lewes; The Book Guild Ltd, 1986) pp 18-27
61 *Cf* p 3, n 6
62 RMB to EMB, July 22 1858

28 Madge, Alice and May   UCS/BC, Courtesy of JREB

29   Father R M Benson   UCS/BC, Courtesy of JREB

the Swansea Vale Railway and to continue in one of the roles he most enjoyed, as a steward for the annual Regatta.

With this move there came the close of more than one chapter in his life. The following October, his father died, after a long period of increasing weakness,[63] and by June 1859, his step-mother was dead too. Henry, advised to rest by the doctors attending the troops in India, arrived home in the August, knowing nothing of this second loss,[64] and having to face, with Starling, the complicated business problems which the two family deaths in close succession had left for those surviving.

For the moment, however, it is the responsibilities which Starling was now laying down on his retirement from the Town Council that we need to review in order to appreciate the substantial part he had played in the life of Swansea during his years as a resident in that fast developing town.

63   EMB to RMB, June 25, 1858; *cf* RMB to TSB, July 3 1858
64   HRB to EMB, June 6 1859

Chapter VIII

Municipal Affairs

Mayor in the Making

When, in 1835, the year of the Municipal Corporations Act, Elizabeth Benson sent a copy of 'The Cambrian' to Alfred Turner, she commented:

> I thought it might be interesting as an evidence of the progress which is taking place in the cultivation of knowledge in this part of the world, which is I think likely to make a rapid growth - judging by the change in the last 20 years. - A great struggle is just now making for the election of the Council of the Town - some of the lists are in the same Paper - but - you can form no judgment from them as they are the result only of the lowest polling - and the Radicals have the upper hand so far - but - a change is taking place - and it is hoped and expected before the decision more respectable lists will be supported.[1]

It was only three years since the 1832 Reform Act had radically altered the face of national government. Now local government was being drastically overhauled by the Municipal Corporations Act, 1835 (5 & 6 William 1V, *cap* 76), and to the Bensons the election of Swansea's new Town Council was of particular interest because of Starling's personal involvement. Nine people were to be nominated for the poll to represent the Upper Ward in Morriston, and in the first round, young Starling, then aged 27, came joint third with 49 votes, with only Sir John Morris (51 votes) and William Martin (50) ahead of him, and well in advance of such notable figures as Lewis Weston Dillwyn and C H Smith who both had 35 votes.[2]

In the final poll, four Upper Ward councillors were chosen, L W Dillwyn, Starling, Sir John Morris and William Martin, Starling becoming one of the councillors responsible for preparing schedules of Goods Exported and Imported and liable for Quay Dues, an excellent preparation for his later role as Chairman of the Swansea Harbour Trust. He was also made an alderman.[3]

For reasons of his own, presumably connected with the Tyrllandwr controversy, Starling did not seek re-election in 1838, but in 1841 he yielded to the pressure of local supporters and was returned to the Council in November of that year.[4]

---

1 EMB to Alfred Turner, Nov 28 1835
2 C Dec 19 1835, p 2
3 Swansea Council Minute Book, 1835, UCS
4 C Nov 13 1841, p 3; *cf* letter of thanks to Burgesses of the Upper Ward, C Nov 20 1841, p 2

It must have been an acute embarrassment to him, therefore, to find himself, that same week, being nominated for Mayor by none other than Lewis Weston Dillwyn who referred to him as 'a gentlemen well qualified in every respect for this high office'. There was already one nominee, Richard Aubrey, with whom Starling had always enjoyed an excellent relationship. He had been proposed by Starling's neighbour, Dr Bird, making the situation all the more delicate for the newly returned councillor.

L W Dillwyn's proposition had been received with loud cheers. Starling, however, made it quite clear he could not accept the nomination. He said he was fully aware of the onerous duties attached to the office of Mayor, and so would not like 'to undertake that office without being able to devote sufficient time to its duties, which I could not conveniently do during the ensuing year'. Moreover, there had already been nominated an 'eminently qualified gentleman' whom he intended to support with his vote. He added, however, that he hoped at some future period to be better prepared to fulfil the duties of the honourable office for which he was being proposed.

Mr Dillwyn, rather ill-humouredly, retorted that Mr Benson should have thought of these excuses before consenting to contend the Upper Ward, claiming that he would not have much more to do as Mayor than as an ordinary councillor, remarks which were warmly endorsed by numerous shouts of 'Hear! Hear!'

Lewis Dillwyn had obviously touched a tender nerve in Starling. While repeating his reluctance to be nominated when there was 'so suitable a gentleman able and willing to fill the office', he expressed his surprise that, if Mr Dillwyn thought so highly of him, he had not supported his candidature at the local election. Although he also thought highly of Mr Dillwyn, he now suspected that his nomination was a ploy 'to exclude another', someone whom he personally hoped to see elected.[5]

In spite of Starling's resistance, his nomination was seconded by Owen Gething Williams who, while admitting that he knew very little of Starling personally, considered him 'to be a very estimable man, and as well qualified to fill this office as any gentleman in the room'. He then added the amazing statement, 'Indeed I consider him the only fit person in this Council to fill that Chair'. This remark drew a gasp of disbelief from the Chamber and led to a heated debate between Mr Williams and Dr Bird who was astonished by Mr Williams's 'remarkable change of heart' in now giving such enthusiastic support to Mr Benson. Opinion was generally divided, although Mr Aubrey had, admittedly, an advantage in his longstanding family associations with the town which made him, in Mr John Grove's eyes, 'PARTICULARLY well qualified.'

Starling continued to protest that he had been nominated expressly against his own wishes and that he wanted Mr Aubrey to be elected without opposition, but still the debate continued. Eventually Colonel Cameron summed up the situation by pointing out that, although he considered the appointment of Mr Starling Benson would be the more likely to be beneficial to the town (cheers) as he was

5 C Nov 13 1841, p 3

the best *(sic)* qualified (more cheers), in the present case of one willing and one unwilling horse, he would vote for the willing person (cheers) as he would probably exert himself more than one who had had office forced upon him contrary to his inclination.[6] Mr Aubrey had made it quite clear that he had come prepared to vote for himself, in accordance with precedent, and when voting took place, there were nine votes for Starling and twelve for Richard Aubrey, including those of both Starling and Richard Aubrey himself.

The following year, Dr Bird became Mayor, but in the autumn of 1843, Richard Aubrey redressed the balance by proposing 'his friend, Mr Benson, as Mayor for the next year'. He thought the gentleman 'in every way eligible' and he would content himself by merely stating that he felt happy in proposing him. The proposition was 'carried by acclamation'. The bells of St Mary's were rung and continued 'to send out merry peals throughout the afternoon'. In accordance with precedent, the following Sunday, the Mayor elect walked in procession with Dr Bird, his predecessor, and other members of the Town Council from the Town Hall to St. Mary's Church where they attended a service conducted by the Vicar.[7]

As the representative of the Morriston area where so many of his work people lived, Starling was naturally involved with matters of special significance for his constituents, such as extending the police services to the whole of the borough. For purposes of watching and lighting, he wanted Landore and Morriston, the hamlet of St Thomas and the western side of the town included among those parts of Swansea defined as 'the Borough', and he was anxious to see improvements brought in quickly as winter was coming on. Unfortunately for Starling, his fellow councillors did not share his sense of urgency; his suggestions were passed over in favour of an amendment by Thomas Glover that a Committee be set up to report on the funds applicable for paying a police force to watch the whole borough.[8]

There was certainly a reason for the Council's caution. Immediately after the passing of the Municipal Corporations Act in 1835, it had been decided during the mayoralty of Colonel Cameron to suspend payment of the long-established dues of moorage and keelage, payable to the Water-bailiff and the Layer-keeper, two officers appointed by the Duke of Beaufort. When an action was later brought against the Corporation by the Duke for the payment of six or seven years' arrears of these dues, judgment was given against the defendants.

Public funds were in a parlous state, and the prospect of prosecution by Mr Hall, the Borough Surveyor, in 1842, left the councillors, in their capacity of Paving Commissioners, facing the threat of distraint upon their property.[9] Their failure to collect conscientiously the rate chargeable under the Municipal Corporations Act meant that, over three years, they had raised less than the gross amount of £1800 payable in a single year. Lots of Corporation property were already, with the permission of the Lords of the Treasury, being valued by Adam

6 *Ibid*
7 C Nov 11 1843, p 3
8 C Oct 21 1843, p 3
9 C Dec 17 1842, p 4; for role of Paving Commissioners, *vide* J R Alban, 'Local Government and Politics 1700 to 1830s', from Swansea, An Illustrated History ed. Glanmor Williams (Swansea: Christopher Davies, 1990)

Murray with a view to their being sold. This situation obviously could not be allowed to continue and so, in August 1842, when Mr Hall submitted his list of 'Corporation Rent defaulters', Starling moved and Dr Bird seconded that 'Mr Hall be directed to call upon the tenants of the Corporation for an immediate payment of arrears due up to March 24 1842'.[10] This did little to improve the financial *impasse* and so Starling, during his year as Mayor, found himself presiding over a Council hamstrung by lack of the resources for the improvements he saw as essential to the development of the Borough.

The most immediate way out of their dilemma was to apply to Parliament for a new Paving and Lighting Act, a course which proved a veritable hornet's nest for Starling and the more progressive members of the Council. W H Smith, whom we have already met in connection with the Tyrllandwr controversy, had himself, some four years earlier in 1840, proposed raising funds 'by subscription' in order to improve the town. A veteran of Waterloo, he had come to Swansea about 1831 and had quickly involved himself in local affairs. Public opinion of him ranged from his being a brave officer and a gentleman to the less flattering description of an inveterate dabbler. Not surprisingly, his proposal had been turned down, largely through fear that it would entail the expense of a New Act, combined with the suspicion in some quarters that Smith was being used as a scape-goat for the Paving Commissioners.[11]

These feelings had obviously not gone away. Nevertheless, by January 1844, a Committee consisting of the Mayor, Messrs Vivian, Aubrey, Glover and Michael had been appointed to meet W H Smith, together with William Walters who represented several of the Council's creditors pressing for immediate payment. As a result of this meeting it had been proposed that legal action against the Commissioners should be stayed, with Mr Walters himself lending them £1000 to settle their debts, and that an application be made for a New Act to effect the necessary services. It was further recommended that Mr Walters should become the Solicitor to the proposed Bill, with instructions to W H Smith, who was himself a barrister, to draw it up.[12]

Accordingly, Starling convened a meeting of 'all Inhabitants assessed for Paving and Lighting Rates' in the Town Hall on Friday, January 26, 1844. Here he explained to those present that, in view of the critical position facing the Commissioners, the Council had asked Mr Smith to draft a Bill for the provision of paving and lighting and generally improving the town.

Mr John Grove revealed his suspicions of Messrs Smith and Walters' motives in putting themselves in positions of 'special advantage'. He accordingly moved a resolution that, in the opinion of the present meeting, it was unnecessary to incur the expense of the proposed Bill. With judicious management, the present rate should be sufficient to defray current expenses and to pay the existing liabilities of the Commissioners.

Such opposition from within the Council itself served to fan the growing resentment at the prospect of increased rates. One vociferous critic, John Bevan, an ironmonger, insisting the existing powers of the Commissioners were

10   C Aug 20 1842, p 4; *cf* Jan 21 1843, p 4
11   C Oct 31 1840, p 3
12   C Feb 3, p 4 and Feb 10, p 3; both 1844

sufficient for them to frame the necessary bye-laws, challenged the Mayor to examine the present Act.

> Whoever is in the Chair is the individual whose duty it is to do that. You are put in the Chair, Sir, by the whole constituency of Swansea, and if you do not perform your duty, you shall be indicted.

However this remark was meant, the audience greeted it with shouts of 'Bravo, Bevan' and loud laughter, in which the Mayor himself joined. Obviously Starling was not taking the threat too seriously. It soon became evident, however, that Mr Bevan was serious. He urged the Council to give Mr Walters his £1000 back; 'Lawyers would only fleece them'. He was convinced the inhabitants of Swansea would oppose the new Bill, and he was prepared to divide the town on the subject.

Here Mr Smith, who had not intended to speak, intervened. He felt bound to defend Mr Walters and refute the accusations against himself. He blamed the original Commissioners, going back to Mr Dillwyn's days on the Council, for mismanagement; in any case, Mr Vaughan Williams, the Counsel they had consulted, considered the clauses of the existing Act to be so loosely framed that it was impossible to know how far their powers went.

Not all the objections came from the Bevans of the town. Lewis Weston Dillwyn, supported by his son, John Dillwyn Llewelyn, and his son-in-law, Matthew Moggridge, was clearly against the Bill. He was nettled, however, by the implication that he was opposed to it through self-interest, although to the satirical Mr Planche, a self-styled 'working man', it seemed strange that anyone could object to such a charge, since self-interest seemed to him to be 'the first law of nature,' particularly apparent in both Houses of Parliament!

Eventually there were two propositions before the meeting, Mr Grove's original resolution and an amendment, moved by Mr Aubrey, calling for discussion of the proposed terms of the Bill, the purpose for which he understood the meeting to have been called. The Mayor invited Mr Grove to reply to what had been said. On his declining, Mr Aubrey's amendment was put to the meeting. Only a few hands went up, whereas a whole forest of hands shot up in support of Mr Grove's resolution.

Unwilling to admit defeat, Mr Aubrey now demanded a poll. Wisely or unwisely, Starling agreed, fixing the following Wednesday as polling day. This evoked strong opposition. David Sanders, always a sharp critic of Starling, suggested that, had the amendment been carried, the poll would have been taken on the spot, an imputation of deviousness Starling particularly resented. Up until now he had maintained his usual calm, but in the face of what he saw as a personal attack, he challenged Mr Sanders's right to make such a statement.

> Have you ever known any act of my life which would warrant your coming to such a conclusion?

He got up and, amid general confusion, promptly vacated the Chair.

Mr Grove was invited to preside but refused on the grounds that the meeting had already decided against the Bill by a large majority, a view shared by Mr Dillwyn and others who, believing the issue had already been settled, declared themselves unwilling to take part in a poll.[13]

A further Public Meeting was held the following Tuesday by the ratepayers, of whom only Mr Planche was prepared to admit any responsibility for calling it. Here, opinion was more equally divided. Mr Rutter, the *enfant térrible* of the Town Council, had suspected that Mr Planche had been 'tampered with'. He was glad to hear the meeting had not been convened to overturn the decision of the ratepayers the previous Friday. When a Mr Moore moved a resolution that, in view of the defectiveness of the existing Paving and Lighting Act, it was expedient to apply for a New Act, Mr Rutter was ready with an amendment, that the idea of a new Bill be rejected.

In seconding Mr Moore's resolution, Mr Rogers had warned that, unless something was done to extricate the Commissioners from their predicament, the ratepayers might find themselves paying 5/- in the £. Nevertheless, on a subsequent show of hands, the amendment, calling for the rejection of a new Bill, was successful.[14]

The following day the poll went ahead.

Only those who paid paving and lighting rates were allowed to vote. In case of doubt, the would-be voter had to produce his last receipt. Even so, there was a great deal of confusion; the names of some ratepayers who did produce receipts were not on the lists, and the payment of their accounts was not recorded in the rates book.[15]

In spite of a result of 56 in favour of a new Bill and 197 against, steps were still taken to proceed. In the next Commissioners' meeting, where a hastily drawn up abstract of their finances was given, Richard Aubrey spoke at length, contending that the public had been misled about what was entailed. He therefore moved that it was desirable to obtain a new Act of Parliament for better paving, repairing and cleansing of the town of Swansea and for other purposes connected therewith. This was seconded by O G Williams.

The fact that the views of the majority of voters in the poll seemed now to be in danger of being overridden led Mr Sanders to direct his criticism against the Mayor for allowing a poll at all. It would have been better not to have consulted the ratepayers if their wishes were now to be ignored. Used aright, the Commissioners' powers under the existing Act gave them ample scope to secure the figure assessed by Mr Grove, as indeed Mr Sanders had good reason to know, having had personal experience of the force of their authority when he had tried to avoid paying his rates. Apparently, W H Smith had done the same over a period of three years.

Although prepared to act on behalf of the promoters of the new Bill in Parliament, Mr Vivian, as their MP, would still have preferred to see the matter

---

13   C Feb 3 1844, p 4
14   C Feb 3 1844, p 3
15   *Ibid*

dropped rather than force it upon the ratepayers, a comment greeted with cheers. He felt the Committee appointed by the Council had not had sufficient time to study the situation before the first public meeting and so had appeared ill-prepared. A new committee was now proposed by Mr Glover to consist of the Mayor, his predecessor Dr Bird, Mr Grove and Mr Glover himself, with a view to investigating the whole situation, including the publication of the previous year's accounts.[16]

After a series of meetings of the Town Councillors in their capacity of Commissioners, the proposed Bill was eventually printed and presented to the House of Commons by Mr Vivian on the last Friday of February 1844. A proposition by Mr Aubrey at the next meeting of the Council that copies of the Bill should be circularised among residents and another public meeting subsequently called to receive suggestions for improving the Bill was not seconded. Most of the Council obviously agreed with Dr Bird that it was better to let the residents call their own meeting rather than leave the Mayor to face the inevitable flak.[17]

That there was powerful opposition was clear from the objections of L W Dillwyn, J Gwyn Jeffreys and J T Jenkin, pointing out important deviations from the printed Bill being proposed in the Commons.[18] At a special meeting of the Council on April 27 to receive communications in writing from those who had petitioned against the Swansea Improvement Bill, one of its opponents was the local Gas Company. Mr Glover, speaking both as a Councillor and as a Gas proprietor, was ready to resist any clause purporting to give the Commissioners the right to trade in gas. The Mayor suggested negotiation over such a clause; in any case, Lord Shaftesbury as Chairman of the Lords' Committee had already chosen to limit Councils' powers to the provision of lighting for the streets only.

The 'Ownership Clause' stipulating that only members of the Corporation could serve as Commissioners also aroused dissension. Those petitioning against this wanted anything from twelve to twenty other qualified Commissioners to be added. It was ultimately resolved that the Mayor should meet Mr Dillwyn to prepare, for the approval of the Council, the necessary clauses for the addition of twelve commissioners, qualifying on possession of rateable property of £300 pa. These were to be elected annually. Provision was also made for rates on all cottages with an annual rent of £10 and under to be chargeable on the landlord, while houses with annual rents above £10 should continue to be the responsibility of the occupiers, as under the present Act.[19]

At their May meeting the Paving Commissioners passed that the Mayor and any member of the Town Council in London when the Bill came before the Committee of the House of Commons should be empowered to consent to alterations proposed in that Committee, with the exception of the above clause.[20]

16 C Feb 10 1844, p 3
17 C March 2 1844, p 3
18 C April 20 1844, p 3
19 C April 27 1844, p 3
20 C May 4 1844, p 3

An Editorial in 'The Cambrian' of May 25 reported the passage of the Bill through the Commons Committee the previous Friday when, in spite of an exceptionally able speech of two and a half hours by Mr Sergeant Jones for the opposition, the Preamble was proved. Starling, John Brenton, a rate collector, and a builder named William Richards gave evidence in defence of the Bill. The revised Gas clauses were later carried but the Ownership Clause remained under discussion. It was eventually agreed that twelve proprietary Commissioners from among those with £20 pa of rateable income were to be chosen for life, in addition to members of the Town Council. Whenever a Proprietary Commissioner died, his successor was to be appointed by the survivors.[21]

A new difficulty arose with a change in the wording defining the scope of the Bill. The substitution of 'within the limits of the borough' for 'the town and franchise' could involve the rating of copper works within the area. Mr Vivian was anxious to return to the original wording, a move which might entail extra expense. Even though Starling dismissed the likely cost as 'very trifling', there was still a feeling of resentment that Mr Vivian, who had been one of the Committee appointed to extricate the Commissioners from their difficulties, should now be putting obstacles in the way of the smooth passage of the Bill through Parliament.

Starling was at pains to defend Mr Vivian who had given the Committee active support and had offered to come to Swansea to discuss this particular issue. The impression persisted, however, that, because he was rich and owned the copper works at Hafod, he was taking an unfair advantage to safeguard his own interests for fear of action being brought against him under the 'nuisance clause'. Small traders, on the other hand, had no such power to appeal though the damage to their business might be even greater.[22]

'The Cambrian' showed little enthusiasm for the measures being taken. It had come out strongly in defence of the opposition, the more so as critics of the Bill had been soundly trounced by its rival publication, 'The Swansea Journal', of which W H Smith was 'the reputed editor'. 'The Cambrian' sought to counter 'the torrent of abuse and mis-statement' directed against Mr Dillwyn and his party, who had acted all along in a 'straight forward and manly fashion'. This view, it claimed, was supported by a large number of highly respected individuals, including both County and Borough Magistrates, who feared the Bill would injure the interests of many of the poorer landlords of Swansea and Llansamlet who had invested their savings in buying cottages in the area.[23]

A last minute opportunity had been given witnesses against the Bill to proceed to London. For this, the Mayor had sought from their Solicitor the names of his clients. The only one specifically named had been Lewis Llewelyn Dillwyn, who had replied in answer to Starling's letter asking him to withdraw his opposition, that he was not answerable for the others.[24] In spite of this prestigious opposition, the Swansea Improvement Bill passed through the Lords with merely verbal amendments and received Royal Assent, a fact briefly noted in 'The Cambrian'

21   C May 25 1844, p 3
22   C June 8 1844, p 3; *cf* June 22 1844, p 4
23   C July 20 1844, Editorial, p 2
24   C Aug 17 1844, p 4

of August 10 1844, the Editor dismissing its success as just another part of 'the legislative scramble which usually takes place at the close of the session'.[25]

Starling's year of office as Mayor had not been an easy one in many ways. Nevertheless, the year ended on a happy note. Dr Bird, in proposing John Richardson as Starling's successor, begged leave to express the Councillors' gratitude 'to the gentleman to whom their thanks were so eminently due for the manner in which he had during the last year performed the functions of the office ... Looking at the whole tenour of his conduct during the period of his mayoralty - taking into consideration the zeal, assiduity, punctuality and business-like habits always displayed by him, whether in the discharge of his duties at the Council board or in the performance of his magisterial functions, he thought they were all greatly obliged to him for the able and efficient manner in which the office had been conducted.' Seconding, T E Thomas added that 'it was impossible that the office of mayor could be filled with greater efficiency than it had been during the past year.'[26]

One wonders how Starling reacted inwardly to such fulsome praise, especially as the course of action he had followed might well have led to his being charged with the one 'offence' the Corporation, still in its infancy, was most afraid of committing, that of acting *'ultra vires'*. He obviously felt his policy had been justified by its results. In responding to Dr Bird's eulogy, he admitted that he had not accepted the office at his own desire, fearing the duties of office might divert his attention from other business to which he should have been applying himself, but now, looking retrospectively over the year, he was most grateful to find his neighbourhood in so uniformly flourishing a state. No serious breach of the peace had taken place, while the commercial and manufacturing interests of the town had progressed most satisfactorily.

He referred to the 'temporary trouble and difficulty' caused him by the passing of the Paving and Lighting Bill, which had led to division among his most intimate friends. Nevertheless, once the Council had decided to proceed with the Bill, he had thought it his duty to 'lend his best assistance in carrying such determination into effect'. As a result of gaining the permission of the Lords of the Treasury for this new expenditure, it might now be possible to clear their existing debts and even retain a surplus in hand.[27]

All was well that ended well.

Post-Mayoral Years

Although by the autumn of 1844 Starling had served only part of a term as an alderman, he came up for re-selection. His position on the retirement rota had been determined by that of his predecessor, R Mansel Philipps, one of the first aldermen to be elected under the provisions of the 1835 Municipal Act, as indeed Starling himself had originally been. Mr Philipps's death had created a vacancy

25 C Aug 10 1844, p 2
26 C Nov 16 1844, p 3
27 *Ibid*

for the Upper Ward which Starling was now nominated to fill. In proposing him, Mr Essery referred to the distinguished position held by Mr Benson and his extensive knowledge of all local matters. 'Above all, considering that his interests are identified with the prosperity of the place he would be representing', Mr Essery considered him 'eminently qualified for the office.'

He was comfortably returned, together with M J Michael and Richard Aubrey, only to find the result called into question when it was discovered that a part of the Act calling for voting papers to be openly produced and read had not been complied with. Consequently, the spoiled voting paper of one of the councillors who had voted for Messrs Benson, Bird and Walker had not been detected immediately. Dr Bird had, in any case, been defeated but Mr Walker had not even been standing. This *gaffe* was seized upon as evidence of the need to read the voting papers as the Act directed in order to give members a chance to correct any such errors.[28]

The meeting was adjourned to the following Monday when the erring councillor queried the proposed need for a new election, contending that the voting papers had been openly produced. The councillor sitting next to Dr Bird had been able to tell the gentleman at fault the number of votes cast even before the Mayor announced the result. At this point it emerged that the Town Council was powerless to set the result aside, even though it was considered altogether void. Being entirely outside the jurisdiction of the Council, it could be nullified only by law. As it was, no major wrong had been done to anyone, so the matter was allowed to drop.[29]

One needed to be adaptable to survive on the Town Council of the day. In general, Starling possessed that quality to a high degree. There were times, however, when even Homer nodded. During his mayoral year he may well have appeared to us to be almost autocratic in his determination to force through the procedure leading to the Swansea Improvement Act in spite of the wide-spread opposition. There his tenacity was justified. Now we have to consider a chapter in his career where his better judgment was sadly misplaced in his support of that maverick operator, W H Smith.

For some time the overdue provision of a safe and adequate water supply had given rise to prolonged and heated negotiations. In the opening decades of the century the town's water still came from local canals and wells. One such well at St Helen's was renowned for the medical efficacy of its waters which were recommended for the treatment of boils and ulcers. This had attracted a large crowd of 'bathers', but so immodest had been their behaviour that Colonel Morgan, its owner, had had a wall built around it to spare the blushes of the more sensitive passers-by.[30]

Such uses of a well obviously did nothing to preserve the purity of its water; but without proper sewerage any supply of water was liable to be polluted by the disposal of waste matter which found its way from the unmade roads into nearby streams. Subsequent upon the setting up of the 1844 Royal Commission on the

28 *Ibid*
29 C Nov 23 1844, p 3
30 Alderman E Harris, Swansea (Cardiff; Western Mail and Echo Ltd, 1935), p 180*ff*

Health of Towns, Sir Henry de la Beche had issued his report on conditions in Bristol and other towns in the west of Britain. This showed Swansea to be one of the most notorious areas he had inspected.[31]

There had already been one outbreak of cholera in 1832 affecting the Wind Street area. A second outbreak in 1847, responsible for deaths in the upper part of the town, finally brought home to those in office the need for action, although so far the link between sewage and polluted water had not been generally perceived. It was now clear that something had to be done to improve the situation. As a result, in 1849, a local doctor, William H Michael, was approached by the College of Physicians to draw up a report on the state of hygiene in Swansea. The town already owed a debt of gratitude to the Michael family. In 1847, Dr Michael's uncle, Michael J Michael, also a doctor, had been Mayor. So assiduous had been his care for the victims of cholera during his year of office that, at the end of the epidemic, he was presented with an award of plate for his services.[32]

William H Michael's report was completed in 1854 but meanwhile the Public Health Act of 1848 had empowered a General Board of Health to support the action of Local Boards of Health in providing the necessary water supplies for the communities they served. Swansea had, in 1850, been one of the first towns in the country to set up such a Board. Much of the credit for this must go to the ever resilient W H Smith who, in the face of the opposition of many members of the Town Council, had collected a large number of signatures in support of his campaign. We have already met the instigator of this reform in connection with the Tyrllandwr controversy and the problems of the Paving Commissioners.

In 1845 he had faced financial ruin when he was gaoled for bankruptcy. This disaster some attributed to his overreaching himself as promoter of the progressive 'Swansea Journal',[33] founded in 1843, while others put it down to heavy gambling combined with a flamboyant life style.[34] His release in 1848 coincided with the passing of the Public Health Act. As a result of his initiative the area was inspected by G T Clark who produced a damning report on the prevailing lack of public hygiene which made the need for a local Board of Health irrefutable. Its first minutes were taken on September 4 1850 and the following November Starling was appointed to its Committee of Works with M J Michael, Lewis Dillwyn, George Grant Francis, J W James, J J Strick, E M Richards and Robert Eaton.[35]

W H Smith had already been instrumental in an attempt to provide an improved water supply to the Borough by the setting up of the privately owned Swansea Water Works Company as early as 1837. Beside W H Smith who acted as Manager, this included such well known local figures as C H Smith, Matthew Moggridge, Dr Bird, Thomas Glover, H H Price, W E Logan, John Edmonds and M J Michael. They had obtained Parliamentary powers to construct a reservoir at

31   J F Wright, The Development of Public Water Supplies in the Swansea Area, 1837 - 1989 (Thesis,1991, Miners' Library, Hendrefoilan) p 19
32   *Ibid*
33   Sw and Glam Herald, March 12 1851, p 5
34   W H Jones, History of the Indefatigable Lodge No. 237 (SM) p 38
35   Minutes of Swansea Local Board of Health from Sept 4 1840 (Swansea City Archives)

Brynmill, served mainly by a local stream which had previously driven two water-powered corn mills. Unfortunately they had grossly underestimated the volume of water required. They had also overlooked the fact that the reservoir was too low-lying to be able to supply the upper part of the town.[36]

Realising these deficiencies, the ubiquitous Smith, although still Manager of the Water Works Company, had, by the beginning of the 50s, begun work on a reservoir of his own in the higher region of Cwmdonkin with a view to forming a second company to supply the upper reaches of Swansea with water. He had applied to Parliament for powers to proceed with his plans by promoting the 'Upper Swansea Water Works Bill'.[37] He was, therefore, not a little put out to find that the Local Board of Health Committee, of which Starling was a member, was advertising in the press its intention of also applying to Parliament for a Bill in the next session to enable it to secure for the Borough an extended water supply. To this end, it was seeking to borrow £60,000 in order to build the necessary works.[38]

On November 13 1851 the Board had engaged the London-based civil engineer, Michael Scott, and by the end of the month was considering his suggestion that it should build its own waterworks. His initial idea was to construct a reservoir at Cwmgelly *(sic)* and adopt five separate local schemes based on brooks at Ffynone, Mount Pleasant, Penfilia, Nant Vellin *(sic)* and Foxhole. The Bill which allowed the Local Board of Health a certain latitude in selecting potential sources of supply was deposited on January 5 1852.[39] Seeing this action of the Board as a possible threat both to the original Company and to his own latest enterprise at Cwmdonkin, W H Smith now set about selling the latter to the Board.

While W H Smith was thus intent on his independent schemes, other members of the Swansea Water Works Company had already entered into protracted negotiations with the local Board. On their behalf, C H Smith had agreed to sell the Company at a price to be assessed by Mr Stroud of the Glamorganshire Banking Company. Starling was deputed to bring this resolution to the full Board with the unanimous support of his Committee. He expressed his personal relief that agreement had been reached so that any future confusion of private and public interests would be avoided.

The local solicitor, J T Jenkin, who served on the Committee of the Board with Starling, felt that this agreement subsumed the need for a Bill, but it was eventually decided to go ahead with the application to Parliament lest wider powers should be required at some future date.[40] W H Smith's Bill had already been lost through failure to comply with Parliamentary Standing Orders, 'not withdrawn,' in the words of 'The Cambrian', 'as fictitiously represented in the small print which has just appeared'. 'The Cambrian' could not resist getting in a jab at its old opponent![41]

36   E Harris, *op cit*, p 180*ff*
37   E Harris, *op cit*, p 188*ff*; *cf* C Jan 9 1852, p 3
38   Sw and Glam Herald, Dec 3 1851
39   J F Wright, *op cit*, p 25
40   E Harris, *op cit*, p 188*ff*; *cf* C March 5 1862, p 3
41   C Feb 20 1852, p 3

At Starling's instigation the Board met on March 15 1852, so that the Clerk, Edward Strick, could read the draft agreement between the Board and the Water Company and the Mayor be authorised to affix the Corporate Seal to the deed when prepared. This proved a lengthy and tense meeting with W H Smith engaged in an impassioned debate on the wording with regard to the exact length of time allowed for the completion of the deal.

Eventually, just as an acceptable compromise was being reached through the mediation of C H Smith, Richard Aubrey and Starling, L L Dillwyn noticed that the Cwmdonkin stream was omitted from the list of properties under consideration. W H Smith himself, whose relations with the Committee arranging the purchase had been strained, to say the least, now sought to explain this away by claiming that the stream in question was not necessary for the volume of water needed by the Board. It could not reach Brynmill and was therefore useful only to his own new reservoir. If, however, they wished to persevere with acquiring it, he was ready to give up all claim to it, leaving the Board to negotiate with Mr Eaton from whose premises it flowed.

Unfortunately, at this point, Starling's usual caution seems to have deserted him. He played right into the hands of W H Smith by suggesting that the Board should consider buying, as a sound business investment, the still unfinished reservoir at Cwmdonkin in addition to the property of the Swansea Water Works Company at Brynmill. Smith was quick to respond; Mr Benson had forestalled his intention of offering the Board his own water works at the next meeting so that the Brynmill and Cwmdonkin schemes might be combined. He stressed the financial advantage of such a transaction which would, for an outlay of only £6000, apart from the purchase money of the works, give the whole town an adequate water supply throughout the year. He felt, however, that the Brynmill and Cwmdonkin transactions should be conducted separately.[42]

By the next meeting of the Board at the end of March, a favourable report on the Cwmdonkin reservoir was presented by Mr Samuel Jones at W H Smith's instance. Fortunately, Mr Grenfell, although personally impressed by the report, had the foresight to suggest that the municipal engineers, Mr Abernethy and Mr Scott, should be asked to look over Mr Smith's figures.[43]

A special meeting was called in April to receive the Scott report,[44] but this was not ready for presentation either at that or at a subsequent meeting called for the beginning of May. The Bill before Parliament was due to reach the Committee stage by May 14, and Mr Dillwyn's readiness to go on waiting for Mr Scott incensed W H Smith who felt time was running out, a concern with which Starling felt some sympathy.[45]

When the voluminous Scott report eventually came, it showed the limitations of the Brynmill system. These could, however, be overcome at a price. Much more severe was his criticism of the Cwmdonkin project on account of the inadequacy of both water supply and storage conditions. The quality of the water, too, according to the official analyst, Professor Brande, was inferior to that in the

---

42 E Harris, *op cit*, p 188*ff*; *cf* C March 19 1852, p 3
43 C March 26 1852, p 4
44 C April 23 1852; *cf* April 30 and May 7 1852, all p 3
45 C May 7 1852, p 3

Brynmill reservoir. Far better, and also cheaper, facilities were likely to be offered by building two reservoirs at Cwmgelli in the Treboeth area. These could provide sufficient resources for the whole town, with ample storage space available at a reasonable cost.

Because of the pressure of time, W H Smith now again proposed that the Local Board of Health should withdraw its Bill. This suggestion Starling felt bound to oppose, both in view of the amount of work so 'assiduously' done by other members of the Board of Health Committee, although he had to admit to his own failure to attend as regularly as he had done previously. Moreover, there was their arrangement with the Swansea Water Works Company - in whose interests, incidentally, Florance was due to appear before the Parliamentary Committee. Initially Starling had had doubts about Cwmgelli, but now he admitted he had been won over to the idea. What was important to him, however, was to obtain the powers to proceed with whichever option was financially the more feasible.

Mr Dillwyn had been asked to supervise the passage of the Bill through Parliament. This he was loth to do at first, feeling the Mayor, T E Thomas, with two or three other representatives, was better placed to undertake the task.[46] He was, however, present at an interview with the General Board of Health confirming the Local Board's efforts to have the Bill passed. Other members of the deputation were the Mayor and E M Richards, supported by the clerk (Mr Edward Strick) and the engineer (Mr Scott), together with W H Smith, now popularly dubbed 'Water Works Bill', present in his Swansea Water Works Company capacity.[47]

Even now the question of purchasing the Cwmdonkin reservoir independently of the Bill had not been settled. Mr Dillwyn felt bound to oppose its purchase out of deference to Mr Scott's opinion. Starling, however, was still attracted by the property which he saw as a sound investment, in spite of Mr Scott's reservations. So persuasive was he that his proposal that it should be purchased by the Local Board was carried, although L L Dillwyn was joined by E M Richards, Thomas Owen and J T Jenkin in publicly dissociating themselves from this decision.[48]

The public reaction was that W H Smith, to attain his own ends, was playing a double game. As Manager of the Water Works Company, he wanted Morriston included within the operation of the proposed Act, thereby offering a stronger guarantee to the Water Works Company that the sum proposed by Mr Stroud for the purchase of the works would be forthcoming. On the other hand, as owner of the Cwmdonkin reservoir, he was playing on the fears of property owners in the outlying areas covered by the Act in order to sabotage it. When, however, in order to allay these fears, J T Jenkin had suggested the substitution of 'occupiers' for 'owners' or 'owners and occupiers' in the controversial Clause 20 of the Bill, Smith had reversed his position and opposed the amendment.[49]

46   C May 14 1852, p 4
47   C May 21 1852, p 2; *cf* Sw and Glam Herald, May 19, p 3
48   C May 21 1852, p 2
49   C May 28 1852, p 3; *cf* Sw and Glam Herald, June 2, p 3

'Is it not,' wrote Fair Play, 'a fact that, until Mr Benson, in a hasty and, I think, unjustifiable manner, proposed to buy the upper water works, W H Smith was a most virulent opponent of this very clause?'[50]

It is difficult to conceive of Starling acting in a hasty manner. There was, nevertheless, a not unnatural resentment of his support for W H Smith in what was seen as the latter's exploitation of the people of Swansea. That he was not aware of the full implications of his own proposal would suggest that, at the time, he was preoccupied by the family problems we looked at in an earlier chapter as well as by negotiations concerning the SVR. Both of these would have explained his absence from vital meetings of the Local Board of Health Committee at earlier stages of its deliberations and his failure to grasp the full import of the Scott recommendations.

There was still widespread opposition to the Bill. Memorials had been received from owners of property and ratepayers in Foxhole and St Thomas, Landore and parts of Llangyfelach, the latter represented by such influential figures as Byng Morris, Edward Brown and James Pooley.[51] Nevertheless, the Bill was passed by the House of Commons.

On L L Dillwyn's recommendation, it was seen through the House of Lords by the same Committee as had supervised its earlier stages, T E Thomas (the Mayor), L L Dillwyn, E M Richards, Grant Francis, J W James and Starling. There the Committee had been chaired by Lord de Manley, and among those taking part in the cross examination of such key witnesses as Dr W H Michael and Mr Abernethy, on June 18, 21 and 22, had been Florance Benson[52] who, as we shall see, was concerned at this time with several other bills, involving a strain which may well have shortened his life.

The Swansea Local Board of Health Waterworks Bill finally received its Royal Assent on July 2 1852.[53]

Ironically the works authorised by 'The Swansea Board of Health Waterworks Act 1852' were still not even commenced by 1860 when a new Bill had to be introduced, with future planners looking elsewhere for new sites.[54] By that time Starling was no longer serving on the Town Council.

Swansea faced other demands as well as those of supplying the basic amenities for its escalating population. Its development as a commercial centre brought growing pains as it faced rapid change, often forced upon it from outside. In the summer of 1850 George Grant Francis drew the Council's attention to a modification in the London Mail route to South Wales. The new route via Bristol was likely to prove more hazardous and subject to delays than the existing route via Gloucester. As the change would mean a financial gain of £436 per annum, he concluded that the GPO's main interest was simply in pounds, shillings and

---

50 C May 28 1852, p 3
51 C June 4 1852, p 3
52 Swansea Journal, July 2 1852, p 1
53 C July 2 1852, p 3; 23 & 24 Victoria, July 23 1860; An Act for Enabling the Local Board of Health for the Town and District of Swansea to Construct and Maintain an Improved System of Waterworks and for Other Purposes
54 J F Wright, *op cit*, p 37*ff*; *cf* J R Alban, 'Municipal Administration and Politics from 1830s to 1974' from Swansea; An Illustrated History, ed. Glanmor Williams (Swansea; Christopher Davies 1990) p 299

30   Brynmill Park 1995 - Site of Reservoir   Photo: D M Bayliffe

31   The Head Post Office   Courtesy of W C Rogers

pence rather than in safety. He therefore proposed that a Committee consisting of Starling, Pascoe St Leger Grenfell and himself should be set up to memorialise the Post Office, advocating the transmission of London and Western mails via Gloucester rather than Bristol. It would be wise to communicate with the other towns of South Wales and Monmouthshire on the subject, a course supported by Mr Grenfell.[55]

The growing interest in the Postal system led to a movement for a new Post Office in the town. Ease and speed of communication with the outside world were of prime importance to those representing Swansea's industrial and commercial interests. During Starling's mayoral year he had been disappointed in the poor attendance at a meeting he had convened in the Town Hall to consider a national testimonial to Rowland Hill, the founder of the modern postal system. At that meeting Starling had declared himself 'ready to forward the object of the requisitionists by every means in his power' but with little response.[56]

By 1851, however, the public attitude towards the postal system had changed. A Committee was set up to consider the building of a new Post Office on the site of the old Town Hall. This consisted of the then Mayor E M Richards, J H and H H Vivian, Starling, Sydney Hall, J R Tripp, Thomas Glover, John Oakshot and G G Francis. Although over the next few years the Committee dwindled to six, their hard work was rewarded in January 1856 when the plans for the new building were approved by the Town Council, the Treasury and the Post Office authorities.[57] George Grant Francis had asked for full powers for the Committee to carry the whole project through independently within the limit of £1500 for total expenditure set by the Council. This was granted without opposition. Grant Francis had a way of reassuring even the more suspicious of his fellow councillors!

There were, however, two unforeseen difficulties. J H Vivian had undertaken to pay for extra ornamentation to be introduced into the plans. With his death, this had to be modified to fit in with the original sum authorised. In addition, the Duke of Beaufort was claiming the right of his agent to occupy a room in the new building as he had done in the old Town Hall. Mr Francis now moved that the Post Office Committee be authorised to appoint a sub-committee with full powers to deal with this question of the Duke's claim, even if it meant litigation.

The wisdom of this course was emphasised by Mr Michael: discussion of their proposals before the full Council would alert their opponents to their moves and undermine any further action they might wish to take. He had met the Duke's agent and thought they had reached agreement, only for Mr Hooper to change his mind, so that any progress was nullified. According to the Mayor, E M Richards, what had to be decided was whether the Council 'considered the Committee was composed of gentlemen of sufficient ability and experience that they could entrust the details to them.' That trust was evident when the Council voted in favour of delegating power to the Committee by sixteen to two, only Mr Rutter and Mr Lumley being against.[58]

55   Sw and Glam Herald, July 17 1850, p 2
56   C June 29 1844, p 3
57   C Jan 18 1856, p 6
58   *Ibid*

A further embarrassment was caused by Mr Vivian's having offered to advance money to furnish the Council Chamber. The furniture had already been procured but not paid for. It now emerged that money was also owing to Mr Richardson and the estate of the late Mr Stroud, while the Council was in debt to Mr Francis for book-binding. Likewise the salary of the former Mayor, Mr J T Jenkin, was still unpaid.

These debts came to light when the Councillors were considering their offer of £500 towards the cost of the new Grammar School on Mount Pleasant. A cheque for that amount had already been handed in to the Glamorganshire Bank, to be paid as soon as the Council had a balance in hand.[59] On the strength of the Council's commitment, Starling and his fellow feoffees of the Grammar School had proceeded to build on a scale they would not otherwise have envisaged.

In the meeting of February 1856, Mr Tripp contended that, legally, this payment could be made only out of surplus income. Mr Michael, on the other hand, felt they were pledged to something they must honour at the first possible opportunity, a view shared by Starling. To him, once the resolution had been passed and the cheque given to the Bank, they were morally bound by their commitment, whether such payment was strictly regular or not. He reminded them archly that this would not be the first time for the Council to do what was not precisely legal as such. He might well have been remembering the confusion over the election of the three Aldermen when he had come up for re-selection in the autumn of 1844.

The present Mayor felt, however, that there was an urgent case for settling their more immediate debts, especially that to Mr Francis. Eventually, after much discussion on the uses to which a large sum of money due from the County could be put, it was resolved, on an amendment by Mr Tripp, that the section referring to the payment of the cheque intended for the Grammar School be dropped from the Treasurer's report. Starling, M J Michael, Richard Aubrey, T E Thomas, J T Jenkin and John Oakshot, no light-weight opponents, voted against the amendment.[60]

Starling was to retain his interest in the Grammar School for many years. As late as May 28 1875, he was present at the Annual Prize Giving at 11 am on the Tuesday morning after what must have been an early start from Fairy Hill. On behalf of his fellow feoffees, he expressed their satisfaction with the school's progress under the Revd Mr Heartley. It would always be their endeavour to make Swansea Grammar School useful to the town and neighbourhood, and equal to any Grammar school in the Principality.[61]

Starling's interest included too, as we shall see later, less academic forms of education.[62] At the same time as he was fighting the cause of the Grammar School's delayed cheque, he was also serving on a Committee connected with the Iron and Coal Masters' Association for the awarding of prizes in Elementary

59   C Feb 15 1856, p 6
60   *Ibid*
61   C May 28 1875, p 8
62   *Vide* p 265*ff*

Schools for the Working Classes, to which he and C H Smith each donated £5.[63]

Benevolence was, however, touched with caution. In the October of 1858 the question of Reformatory Schools for the County was raised. If, as Borough Magistrates, they took the initiative, Starling wanted to be certain that the County Magistrates would not expect them to bear the financial burden. Only after Richard Aubrey had assured him that the costs entailed would be a mere 7/- per head per week, (of which only about 4s 6d would be needed for each child, leaving 2s 6d for the expenses of the establishment) did he agree to join his fellow councillors in asking the Mayor to sign the Memorial proposed by G G Francis and seconded by Richard Aubrey.[64]

His vigilance showed itself in other ways. The Council had received a recommendation from the Property Committee that the Assembly Rooms, now too small for many of the functions previously held there, should be let for a Custom House at a rent of £120 per annum. Starling, however, like the Mayor, E M Richards, did not believe they should dispose of the premises before they had comparable accommodation to put in their place. He reminded the Council of the origins of the Assembly Rooms, bought with the £2000 subscribed by private individuals, to which the Council had added a further £2000. He did not believe the Corporation would have the power to use money out of its own funds for the erection of new Assembly Rooms. In any case, it seemed a private individual had offered his property to the Custom House and they did not want to jeopardise this transaction. The proposition was therefore withdrawn.[65]

The problem of a fast growing population also affected the planning of special celebrations for the general holiday given to mark the close of the Crimean War. It was suggested that the Council should provide a free dinner for the poorer classes in the market place, with illuminations by night. To Starling it was simply not feasible to seat three or four thousand people comfortably in the open air, nor did he think the idea of public illuminations would serve, even if it could be set up. The Mayor had pointed out that there could be practical difficulties as they were not very well blessed with gas, while candles were very dirty. They were also, Starling added, very dear. Instead, he proposed amusement for the people during the day and a display of fireworks during the evening.[66]

There was a need for something more than either bread or circuses for those doomed to life in the densely populated courts which had sprung up to accommodate the influx of workers into the town. Although the means were now available to provide uncontaminated water for at least part of the population, there was still the question of sewerage, with gutters polluted by deposits of human and household waste, creating a breeding ground for disease. Even in the better planned terraces occupied by the work-people of the more socially conscious employers like the Vivians and Grenfells, the problem of inadequate sewerage and drainage remained.[67]

63   C Dec 26 1856, p 4
64   C Oct 17 1856, p 5
65   C April 17 1856, p 4
66   C May 16 1856, p 4
67   J R Alban, *op cit*, p 295

The Local Board of Health, since its inception in 1850, had struggled to overcome resistance from those loth to pay the rates necessary if services were to be improved. In December 1856, it was proposed at a meeting of the Board of Health that a special district, to be called the Town District (consisting of the town and franchise of Swansea, the hamlet of St Thomas and the parish of St John-juxta-Swansea) should be declared. This would be responsible for meeting from their rates the expenses involved in providing sewerage and drainage in such a district.[68]

Such improvements had not extended to Morriston, nor, as yet, to St John's and St Thomas. Early in the New Year, Starling, in the interests of the district he represented, sought legal advice as to whether the same rates should be paid in these outlying areas as in the centre of the town, since their residents enjoyed fewer advantages. Was it fair, he asked, on the existing basis of rating, that people of the outer districts should pay for draining from which they would not benefit? Under Section 84 of the Public Health Act (11 & 12 Victoria, *cap* lxiii), the Board had no power to enforce payment of rates for sewerage except from the immediate district benefited.

Starling proposed that, for the purpose of rating, the Borough be divided into two parts, as determined by the Board of Health under resolutions of September 6 and December 6 1854. Mr J T Jenkin, in seconding, pointed out that a Bill had already been projected in Parliament with a view to achieving the objective Mr Benson was now proposing. Starling was strongly opposed to an amendment by Mr Evan Evans that Morriston only should be excluded; even if he represented the people of Morriston, he wanted to safeguard equally the interests of St John's and, especially, St Thomas. Eventually it was resolved that the charges and expenses chargeable on a general district rate should be for that part of Swansea which was rateable under the Swansea Improvement Act of 1844 - such part to be called the town of Swansea district. This excluded, at least for the time being, Morriston, St John's and St Thomas. Starling had again won his point.[69]

There still remained the question of adequate lighting. In his 'Swansea' Alderman Edward Harris remarked that the Paving Commissioners for the Borough should have done the same for gas as was later done for water by the Local Board of Health which took over their powers.[70] This had been very much in Starling's mind from 1852 on. In March of that year J T Jenkin had proposed and H K Eaton seconded that the authority of the Local Board of Health should be given the 'New Gas Light Co.', once it was fully registered, to open up all roads and other thoroughfares within the Borough to the maintaining of an appropriate supply of gas.[71]

The following month Starling brought forward the resolution:

That in order to ensure the future supply of Gas to the Borough of Swansea at the least possible rate, and at the same time to avoid the

---

68   C Dec 19 1856, p 8
69   C Feb 13 1857, p 8
70   E Harris, *op cit*, p 188*ff*
71   Minutes of Local Board of Health, March 22 1852, p 97

constant alteration and repairs of streets, which would arise from the operation of competing Gas Companies, it is in the opinion of this meeting desirable that the Local Board of Health should take the supply of Gas under their control.

He went on to nominate a Committee of nine to consider and report fully on the question and to ascertain whether 'any arrangement beneficial to the Town can be entered into with the existing Gas Company.' In spite of Mr H K Eaton's concern that the Board would be taking on too much if they assumed this responsibility in addition to the water works and cemetery, the motion was carried unanimously.[72]

Nothing came of it, however, and by January 1858 the Board was facing a crisis. Notice had been received from the Gas Company that all supplies of gas for public lighting would be cut off at the end of a month unless the Board met its revised terms. There had been discussion with the Company and in view of the extra expenditure involved in lighting outlying areas, an increased rate had been verbally agreed. The Company, however, did not find itself in a position to enter into a contract, and when the Board had written to ask what the new rate would be, there had been no official reply. The Company had, however, contacted the Mayor personally, an action which, to E M Richards, reflected 'signal discourtesy' towards the Board. To Starling the Company had a moral, if not a legal, obligation to abide by the terms previously proposed which the Board had recently considered in full. He did not feel they should allow themselves to be intimidated by the Company's threat. If the Board could not obtain satisfactory terms, they should supply themselves with gas by some other means, a view fully supported by E M Richards.

J T Jenkin considered it pointless to talk of a moral obligation if there was no contract to enforce the legal obligation.[73] He attributed the delay to serious consideration on the part of the Company whose peculiar organisation took time to function. His optimism was justified. At the next meeting on February 19 1858 a letter was read from Mr Thornton Andrews, the Manager of the Swansea Gas Light Company, giving terms for the supply of gas to 231 street lamps and to all future lamps in the present area of the Gas Company's mains for a period of five years. Tenders for repairs from Mr William Davies and Mr Alfred Aston were submitted to a sub-committee comprising the mayor (T E Thomas), J T Jenkin and Starling who would report on them and on the gas question in general.[74]

Thus the gas crisis was averted, but by now Starling was coping with yet another crisis which would engage all his energies until his resignation from the Council in the summer of 1858 upon his removal to Fairy Hill.

---

72 *Op cit*, April 16 1852, p 99
73 C Jan 29 1858, p 6
74 C Feb 19 1858, p 6

Chapter IX

Starling and the Bishops

'Strange he who dreads notoriety should have controversy with the Bishop of St David's', wrote Mrs Benson to her son, Richard, in January 1857.[1]

It had been Richard who had had to face notoriety when, in the February of the previous year, he had been summoned before the County magistrates in Oxford at the instance of the superintendent-registrar. He was accused of marrying a couple without calling the banns or having a licence, an offence which could carry the penalty of deportation. The couple had originally been married in a registry office but after the birth of their third child, the wife had asked to be churched, a rite Richard, as incumbent at Cowley, was not prepared to administer unless she and her husband were remarried in church. As they were already legally married, he saw no need to call banns or obtain a licence before performing the ceremony.

Richard deferred his defence until the Summer Assizes. There he was completely exonerated by the Jury on the advice of Mr Justice Alderson who made it clear that the religious ceremony in no way affected the couple's marital status as they were already married in the eyes of the law. Nevertheless the six months between the hearing before the Magistrates and his eventual acquittal must have been agony for his devoted parents.[2] Now here was Starling involved in yet further 'notoriety'.

In December 1856 he had been elected Chairman of the Cemetery Committee, the section of the Corporation Burial Board responsible for the new municipal cemetery to be provided in accordance with the Burial Acts of 1852 and 1853. This was required urgently to replace both the churchyard and the so-called 'New Burial Ground' at St Mary's which were now full,[3] largely as a result of recent outbreaks of cholera.

Initially the setting up of new public cemeteries financed by local rates had been intended for the interment of workhouse inmates. In the fast growing urban areas the large numbers of paupers had quickly exhausted the available space in their parish churchyards. This in turn made it necessary to include provision elsewhere for the burial of other residents, both members of the Church of England and Dissenters. As a result, under the legislation of the recent Burial Acts, such cemeteries would contain portions of consecrated ground for members of the Established Church and of unconsecrated for Dissenters.

In his new role Starling found himself in the forefront of the prolonged argument that developed with the Bishop of St David's over the new municipal

---

1   *Vide* p 108, n 39
2   C July 18 1856, p 7; *cf* Feb 29 1856, p 7
3   C Dec 19 1956, p 6

cemetery for Swansea. Various sites had been considered, but choice in the centre of the town was restricted by the sea on the one side and the spread of industry on the other. One site had been considered at the Rhyddings, near the former home of the celebrated Dr Thomas Bowdler, and another at neighbouring Brynymor, but the prices were too high. The Council eventually settled on a piece of land at Danygraig which could be obtained from the Earl of Jersey on terms acceptable to the Corporation. It was admittedly well to the east of the town, across the bridge over the now diverted Tawe, but in Starling's description of it to the Bishop it was 'the most eligible, nearer to the Guildhall and more approachable than previous land selected at Penygraig'.[4] It was very little further from the Guildhall than was the Vicar's new residence at the top of Walter Road and 'certainly as near as cemeteries should be to a rapidly increasing town'.

The initial application for the consecration of the ground had been made by the then Mayor, John Trevilian Jenkin, on September 1 1855.[5] An acknowledgement was received two days later from the Bishop who asked for time to consider its implications.[6] In just over a week, however, he felt in a position to reply, setting out four conditions requisite to his agreeing to consecrate the site.[7]

(1) There must be an abolition of tolls for funerals crossing the bridge

(2) A permanent arrangement must be made for the conveyance of the official clergyman

(3) There must be an undertaking given that no prospector should be allowed to come within 100 feet of the surface in a search for minerals

(4) The consecrated ground was to be effectually secured to the use of all the inhabitants of Swansea.

Connop Thirlwall had become Bishop of St David's in July 1840. He was acknowledged as one of the leading scholars among the Churchmen of his day, a classicist and a philosopher. At the time of his appointment, the Venerable Archdeacon Richard Davies of Brecon had sent a request to Queen Victoria for a Welsh-speaking successor to Bishop John Banks Jenkinson but his letter arrived too late. The appointment had already been made. In his earlier days the new Bishop had been recognised as a man of an energetic and liberal mind. The energy he seems to have retained, but life in the Bishop's Palace in Abergwili may well have dulled the edge of his liberalism. Nevertheless Connop Thirlwall

4 C Jan 9 1857, p 2
5 C Sept 1 1855, (part of the complete correspondence between the Bishop of St David's and the Town Clerk between Sept 1 1855 and Nov 20 1856, as given in 'The Cambrian' of Jan 23 1857)
6 *Op cit*, Sept 3 1855
7 *Op cit*, Sept 12 1855

32 Connop Thirlwall, the Right Revd Bishop of St David's   J Vyrnwy Morgan,
            Welsh Political and Educational Leaders in the Victorian Era, UCS

33 The Revd Edward Squire, Vicar of Swansea, 1846-76
                                    Oxford St Senior School Brochure, SCL

34 Danygraig Cemetery, 1995   Photo: D M Bayliffe

appears to have occupied his see quite equably until a handful of Swansea councillors saw fit to defy him over something that he considered the most reasonable of requests.

All the correspondence relating to the new public cemetery was laid before the Cemetery Committee by the Mayor, still J T Jenkin, on September 15 1855.[8] At that time, yet another attempt was being made to find a more central location. This failed and eventually, on December 4, preliminary arrangements were entered into with the Earl of Jersey to finalise the Danygraig transaction. The same month, the plan for the chapel in the consecrated part of the cemetery was forwarded to the Bishop and returned with his approval.

So far, so good, but after this, there was virtually no movement during the earlier part of the following year. E M Richards, now Mayor, had offered to meet the Bishop but his offer had been declined. The main subject for discussion by the Board had, in the meantime, been the table of burial fees set by the Legislature.

Apart from the initial letter by the Mayor, all the correspondence on behalf of the Board had been conducted by the Clerk to the Council, C B Mansfield, who was not given to being over-hasty in the execution of his duties. It was November 20 1856 before he took up the four points in the Bishop's letter of September 12 1855, a lapse of fourteen months,[9] as the Bishop obviously took pleasure in reminding the Board when he referred sarcastically to the 'speed' with which his letter had been considered.

The Board had no hesitation in meeting three of the four conditions laid down by his Lordship; only the conveyance for the officiating clergyman offered any difficulty. Here the Committee had agreed unanimously that the Board had no power under the Act of Parliament to provide such a conveyance and that, even if it had such power, it ought not to exercise it. The fund which would have to be used for such provision was contributed to equally by Anglicans and Nonconformists, and it would be unfair to the latter to utilise it to transport Anglican clergy while leaving Dissenting ministers to make their own arrangements.

In the less sectarian climate of our day the Burial Board's objection may seem petty or even churlish, but in the 1850s, hard-won concessions to Dissenters were jealously guarded against any encroachment by the Established Church. That only Anglican communicants and their children were entitled to burial in consecrated ground remained an inflammatory issue. As long as the graveyard was attached to a parish church there was a logical connection. Now with the introduction of the new corporation cemeteries, the question of dividing them into consecrated and unconsecrated sections gave rise to frequent controversy.

Few local politicians would risk alienating the strong body of sectarian feeling in a stronghold of Nonconformity like Swansea. Even Anglican members of the Town Council had a stake in retaining the goodwill of the Nonconformist electorate. Consequently, on the receipt of a letter from the Bishop on December 1 insisting that his remaining condition was complied with before he agreed to

8   *Op cit*, Sept 15 1855
9   *Op cit*, Nov 20 1856

consecrate the ground, the Board replied immediately, still declining to provide transport.

The next communication from the Bishop was written on Christmas Eve, 1856. with special reference to the newspaper report of the Burial Board proceedings of December 5. In it Mr Benson - 'the chairman I believe of the Committee' - was represented as observing with regard to the conveyance 'that the Committee were of the opinion that no distinction between ministers should be made', not an easy sentiment for Mrs Benson to accept at her Teddington home, surrounded by her close circle of clerical relatives and friends! But when Starling believed in something, he held to it without fear or favour.

To the Bishop such language was 'mockery' when used as an argument for refusing to provide transport for the Vicar of Swansea, the Revd E B Squire, who had succeeded Dr Hewson. For him, there existed a fundamental distinction between the Anglican clergyman and his Dissenting counterpart: 'whereas the latter's attendance is optional, the former's upon the consecration of the Cemetery is compulsory'. Personally he would be quite happy for the Board to provide transport for Dissenting ministers as well, providing it met with his requirements regarding the clergy.

The Bishop took further exception to Starling's comment that it was not fair to burden the funds of the Burial Board with this expense. Without this concession, it would be the Vicar's own salary, a pittance of something short of £90 a year, that would be burdened. This, to the Bishop, was neither 'fair' nor right. It was 'repugnant' to him that the Vicar should be burdened with an expense so heavy that the Board itself shrank from incurring it. In addition there would be 'the drudgery' of getting to the Cemetery, which would consume both time and strength, and 'disable' the Vicar from fulfilling other duties. For him to comply with their request for consecration under these circumstances would be 'a flagrant act of injustice and cruel oppression to one whose legitimate interests' the Bishop was bound to protect as far as lay in his power. He could not believe Mr Benson and the Board could feel justified in such a stance.[10]

This letter awaited Starling on his return to Swansea from Teddington after Christmas. He took up the points made by the Bishop in a reply published in 'The Cambrian' of January 9 1857, the letter praised by Mrs Benson when writing to Richard. In it he assured the Bishop that it had been his earnest endeavour in his capacity of Chairman of the Cemetery Committee 'to provide a sufficient and convenient Cemetery for the borough of Swansea, with as much consideration for the feelings of all parties as the interests of the Borough would permit.'[11] Assured that the Board under the terms of the Burial Act was not required to provide transport, he had voted accordingly. Otherwise he would have felt that he was acting wrongly in incurring unnecessary expense for something that was not legally required. He hoped that his Lordship would not withhold consecration if it was found that the Cemetery Committee had been correctly advised.

The issue of 'The Cambrian' which published Starling's letter also reported the Order in Council confirming the expiry date for the use of the churchyard and 'New Burial Ground' of St Mary's. Originally burials had been directed to finish

10 C Jan 9 1857, p 4
11 C Jan 9 1857, p 2

on and after July 1 1855, but an extension had been granted to January 1 1857.[12] As the new cemetery was not yet available, an urgent appeal had been sent by the Vicar and Church Wardens on the previous Christmas Day to the Home Secretary, Sir George Gray, for permission to continue burying in the existing graveyards, but no concession was made. Burials had now to be discontinued forthwith, except for those in existing vaults and walled grounds. This made a settlement on the issue of consecrating the new cemetery all the more vital.

In his next letter published in 'The Cambrian' of January 16 the Bishop sought to explain the appearance of his previous letter in the press. Although only a handful of people in Swansea would have known the contents of his letter to the Burial Board, the editor of the 'Swansea Journal' (whom he believed to be a member of that Board) had taken it upon himself to discuss it on December 31 in a leader in his paper. For that reason, a copy of the whole letter had, unknown to the Bishop, been forwarded for insertion in the 'Swansea Journal' of January 3 1857.[13]

Starling replied on January 19. His answer of the 7th instant had been a purely personal response to the references made to him in the Bishop's letter. It had certainly not been written with a view to biassing the people of Swansea in favour of the action of the Board, as had been suggested by the Bishop. He accepted that the Vicar's attendance at funerals was compulsory, but it seemed to him that the moral obligation to attend would be felt equally strongly by ministers of other denominations. The Vicar was at least compensated by fees for his services; the others were not. He could only say as before that he had assumed 'the Legislature, in enacting the Burial Act, had provided adequate remuneration'.

The Bishop must have been taken aback to find an Established Churchman identifying to such an extent with his Nonconformist brethren, but Starling had a word too to say in relation to other Anglicans. Not only was it unfair to provide a conveyance for the Vicar out of the Borough Fund to which all denominations contributed; that fund was sustained by the contributions of those living in parishes other than Swansea. They had their own burial grounds and therefore would not benefit from the new Cemetery.

Starling now repeated the reason for the delay in taking up the suggestions in the Bishop's letter of September 12 1855, long before he became Chairman of the Cemetery Committee. They had been looking for a more central site, but that would have doubled the cost of the Cemetery. If any disrespect had been shown the Bishop by this delay, he was prepared to offer any proper apology, and in this, every member of the Board would concur. He allowed that the Bishop's insistence on a conveyance arose from his concern for the interests of another, but he hoped that, on closer consideration of the location of the Cemetery, he would come to see a conveyance was not so necessary. Indeed, from its position, the parochial duties and attendances there might equally well have been supplied by the incumbent of another parish, but the Vicar of St Mary's had objected to this, reserving these services for himself.

12. C Jan 9 1357, p 4
13 C Jan 16 1857, p 5

If, as Starling believed, the granting of legal power to clergy to perform burial services depended upon the rite of consecration, the delay in performing this was naturally causing concern to parishioners as their ministers were being denied a legal right. If that was so, he felt his appeal to the Bishop to perform that ceremony was not 'curious and original', as the Bishop had called it, but fair and reasonable.[14]

A further exchange of letters between the Bishop and Starling appeared in 'The Cambrian' of January 30, showing the problem was no nearer a solution.[15] A new turn in events was taken, however, when, in answer to popular demand, a public meeting was convened on Wednesday, February 13 by the Mayor, John Oakshot. As churchman, Church Warden and member of the Burial Board, he wished more Anglicans had signed the requisition, though personally he would have preferred to see the issue resolved without such a meeting.[16]

The question of fees caused as much discussion as that of conveyance. Here, Mr Michael explained, the Bishop had no control as the fees were sanctioned by the Secretary for State. Information about them had been sent to the Bishop merely out of courtesy. On the question of transport, there was general sympathy with the Vicar's dilemma even among the Nonconformists present, one wag even suggesting that the Vicar might share his conveyance with his Dissenting counterpart.

It emerged, however, that the purpose of the meeting was not to sway the Board but to influence the Bishop through Parliament. It was moved that a petition should be presented in the House of Commons, and 'that the attention of L L Dillwyn, Esq, M P, be drawn to the existing situation and that he be requested to take such steps as must appear to him desirable in order to obtain such an amendment of the Burial Act as shall prevent the recurrence in the future of such disputes as are now pending between the Bishop and the Burial Board.'

No mention was made of Starling Benson's presence at the public meeting. About this time his nephew, young Star, had written of his uncle's having the worst cold he could ever remember. The following week, however, he was again presiding over the Cemetery Committee when the Clerk read his report on various aspects of the work in progress.[17]

In spite of such views as those expressed in 'The Parish' by a Mr Toulmin-Smith, Barrister at Law, who denounced the Bishop's position as 'a striking example of modern ecclesiastical usurpation ... an attempt by means of superstitious usages to extort fees; the taking of which fees is in itself an act of simony, even were consecration itself lawful',[18] there were those hopeful of effecting some kind of reconciliation. At a special meeting of the Town Council on May 29, Messrs Grenfell, Grant Francis, R W Beor and Dr Howell, representing the lay members of the Church of England in Swansea, presented a memorial towards a final settlement of the dispute. They had communicated with

14   C Jan 23 1857, p 4
15   C Jan 30 1857, p 5
16   C Feb 13 1857, p 3
17   C Feb 20 1857, p 4
18   C May 22 1857, p 5

Bishop Thirlwall who was agreeable to the same solution as in the Church of Ireland, that a fixed sum be paid the Vicar annually in lieu of fees.[19] The Board would then receive all fees paid on burials in the consecrated part of the cemetery. To this the Vicar had agreed, proposing a fee of £120. He wished, however, to restrict funerals to certain days of the week, *viz* Mondays, Wednesdays and Fridays (except in cases of epidemics) as this would reduce the inconvenience of the distance from the town to the Cemetery. The question of conveyance would then be dropped.

In the ensuing discussion, Mr Michael felt that more than one year's receipts should be considered before settling on an amount. There were likely to be fewer interments in Church of England cemeteries now that Nonconformists had their own burial grounds. This could offset the general increase in population. He proposed a Committee consisting of Starling Benson, E M Richards and Richard Lumley be set up to confer with the Vicar. Mr Richards objected that they might seem to be prejudging the case by appearing to accept the principle of commutation, but the proposal was carried.

In spite of this conscientious effort being made to meet difficulties raised, the Vicar had by this time come to feel himself a figure of general opprobrium. In the June meeting of the Burial Board, a letter from him was read, complaining about the many false and foolish statements in its last report.[20] Starling was away in London for the Swansea Dock Transfer and Harbour Railway Bill. Nor was he at the July meeting when the Special Committee recommended £100 per annum for the Vicar's fees as this happened to coincide with the Second Reading of the Harbour Bill. Mr Edward Thomas therefore requested an adjournment. This was strongly opposed by Mr Hoare who, although he had the greatest respect for Mr Benson, did not consider it 'right that matters of public interest should be adjourned to suit private individuals'. The resolution to adjourn was carried, however,[21] absence in London because of the Dock Transfer Bill hardly ranking as a 'private' choice.

There were now two approaches to the cemetery problem, one pressing for legislation, the other advising reconciliation. As a member of the Committee nominated to wait upon the Bishop, Starling's sympathies were with the latter. But by now the initiative had passed to the legislators. The Burial Act Amendment Bill was already before Parliament, giving an opportunity for Mr Dillwyn to draw attention to the unhappy situation existing in Swansea, paralleled only by the *impasse* between the Bishop of Exeter and his local Burial Board over the wall dividing consecrated from unconsecrated ground.

Already in the House of Lords Lord Wensleydale had shown that the terms of Canon Law on which the two recalcitrant bishops had taken their stand applied to parish churchyards but not to the new public cemeteries.[22] Later, in the Commons, in order to break the existing deadlock, Mr Massey, the member for Salford, proposed a clause be inserted in the Burial Act Amendment Bill, providing that, where the Secretary of State had approved of a burial ground, the

---

19 C May 29 1857, p 3
20 C June 19 1857, p 6
21 C July 24 1857, p 5
22 C June 5 1857, p 9

incumbent of the parish or his curate might bury in it before consecration without incurring spiritual censure.[23]

In the ensuing debate Mr Gladstone objected strongly to establishing a universal principle in order to deal with two merely local cases. That a particular bishop, and here Mr Gladstone was clearly referring to the Bishop of St David's, had refused to do his duty and had made a demand which was unreasonable and absurd did not justify so grave an innovation in ecclesiastical law. He still believed that, if a little time were given for consideration, the dispute would be brought to an amicable settlement.

Mr Dillwyn, as the member for the constituency affected, held out little hope of its being amicably resolved, and so, in spite of Mr Gladstone's intervention, it was decided to give Mr Massey's clause a second reading. Mr Dillwyn himself then moved a further clause, restricting the payment of fees for services connected with interment in public cemeteries.[24] After the Bill had passed through Committee, however, it was announced that Mr Massey had withdrawn his clause, leaving matters in Swansea no further forward than before.[25]

Meanwhile, the Bishop had been smarting under the public censure directed against him. In a letter to 'The Times', he gave vent to his annoyance with Mr Massey, Mr Gladstone, Mr Dillwyn, the House of Commons and the world in general. His arrangement with the Swansea Burial Board to substitute a monetary payment for conveyance had been delayed only by the absence of some members in London on Town Council business. Agreement had been already in sight when Mr Massey had introduced his clause which the Bishop described as both 'gratuitous and unnecessary'. Being ignorant of the true circumstances, the House had passed it, under the false impression that 'an interminable quarrel between the Bishop and the Town Council interposed between the burial ground and its consecration'.[26]

He was prepared to make allowances for Mr Massey's 'vulgar sectarian animosity' in the light of Mr Dillwyn's own confirmation that there was no immediate prospect of the resolution of the dispute, but the comments of Mr Gladstone, himself a staunch Churchman, he particularly resented as 'a calumnious insult to an absent man'.

Nevertheless the main cause of the trouble was obviously the local MP. In a letter to 'The Times' Mr Dillwyn claimed that he had been misreported. He had meant to say, not that there was no prospect of an amicable settlement but that, up to the present, no settlement of the question had, to the best of his belief, been effected. If, as the Bishop's letter suggested, the question was virtually settled, why had he not taken immediate steps to consecrate the cemetery and relieve the residents of Swansea of the ongoing inconvenience consequent upon the closure of the old parish burial ground the previous January?[27]

The Burial Acts Amendment Bill came before the House of Lords on Thursday, August 19. Feeling himself to have been maligned in the Commons by

---

23   C July 24 1857, p 8
24   C Aug 7 1857, p 6
25   C Aug 7 1857, p 5
26   *Ibid*
27   C Aug 21 1857, p 3

one of Her Majesty's Secretaries of State, the Bishop rose to ask the customary indulgence afforded to those whose character and conduct had been called in question. If he had infringed the law in any way, it had been done in innocence. His only aim was to establish that he was acting in this case, not as an individual but in a pastoral capacity, using what discretionary power he might have so as not to hurt anyone whom he was bound to protect. He felt it hard to be accused of violating the law when he had thought he was acting in accordance with its spirit and intention,

He had been accused of shifting his ground on finding his original request for transport to be untenable and of then imposing another condition upon the Burial Board in the form of financial compensation. It was the Board, however, that had suggested compensation. Being approached on the matter by some of the gentlemen who had consulted Counsel, he had undertaken to reach an arrangement with the Vicar. The latter had agreed, as a reasonable compromise, to a payment of £100 a year, £20 less than had been originally suggested. The Bishop had thought negotiations were now at an end. If, however, the reasonable proposition recommended to the Board by its own Committee on the advice of Counsel was rejected, he would consider its rejection entirely due to the Secretary of State.[28]

Mr Dillwyn, in turn, accused the Bishop, in a letter to 'The Times', of being less than ingenuous in estimating the Vicar's salary as a mere £95 pa, apart from occasional fees. A local paper had, the previous January, given an estimate of his total receipts, including various extras, as £596.10. This had not been contradicted.[29]

The Swansea MP was not the only one to use the columns of 'The Times' to point out discrepancies. Another correspondent, this time on the Bishop's side, criticised its Editor for being biassed in favour of the Burial Board. He had published the statement that the Committee had recommended an extra £100 be paid the Vicar whereas the £100 represented the total payment. A further error had been made in the calculation of the distance from the Vicar's home to Danygraig as two miles instead of two and five-eighths. This would amount to a walk of five and a quarter miles there and back.[30]

Apart from the original interchange of letters, Starling had held aloof from the verbal battle that had developed, obviously anxious not to aggravate the situation by a further heightening of the tension. In the May meeting of the Burial Board he had moved the reception of the report on the Vicar's fees. Now, in the August meeting, he proposed it be adopted. He had, as we have seen, been unavoidably absent in London in connection with the Swansea Dock Transfer Bill at the time of the June and July meetings but now he was most anxious for something definite to be decided.

He explained that, at the time of going into Committee, he fully believed it was the Burial Board's intention to make a payment in lieu of transport, and under that impression the Committee had unanimously passed a resolution in favour of such commutation. Now it appeared it was not so. The £100 suggested might not

28 C Aug 21 1857, p 5
29 *Ibid*
30 C Aug 21 1857, p 6

be exactly the average of the Vicar's fees for the past three years but he felt it to be a reasonable sum, and the Vicar had agreed to it. It was now appeared that the Board had still to accept the principle of commutation. He hoped they would do so and also concentrate on finding a just sum without reference to anything happening elsewhere. If they could not reach agreement themselves, they should refer the subject to other parties for them to say what was a fair and just sum.

If Starling expected plain sailing from now on, he was to be sorely disappointed. Mr Michael objected to commutation as a devious way of side-stepping the differences existing between the Bishop and the Board. He felt £75 was enough to give the Vicar until they knew how much the Board had received in payments. John Tripp, who had been absent during earlier discussions, considered that, by freeing himself of the responsibility of collecting fees, the Vicar had passed on to the Board a responsibility which in some cases might involve legal action. As they had no exact data on which to calculate future receipts now that Dissenters had a burying place of their own, he proposed commutation be deferred until the Board had a clearer picture of the probable average of fees per annum.

Mr Rutter, as a Dissenter, did not think they could expect much help from the Bishop in the revision of fees. He was strongly opposed to making up any shortfall out of public money, thus imposing a rate on Dissenters as well as the Church of England. He would prefer the old system whereby the Vicar collected his own fees.

Whatever progress the Committee believed it had made was now in shreds. One can imagine the effect of all this to-ing and fro-ing on a man of Starling Benson's direct and decisive nature, especially when a fellow member of the Committee, E M Richards, claimed that, when the proposal in favour of commutation had been moved the previous May, it had been referred to the Committee without the Board's avowing its acceptance of the principle. As a result the Committee had been in error in assuming it had merely to fix the amount to be paid to the Vicar.

Starling could only point out that, if it was considered the Committee was at fault, it would have been better to come out with it at once rather than allow its members to proceed under a false impression. Further deferment would be unfair to the members of Committee; they had been requested to report on the situation and were now being criticised for their efforts.

Eventually an amendment by J T Jenkin: 'that this Board considers it inexpedient to enter into any arrangement with the incumbent or clerk of any parish wholly or in part within this borough for the substitution of any fixed annual sum for the fees payable to such incumbent or clerk' was carried by 11 votes to 7. It was seen by Mr Rutter as 'the only honest, consistent, straightforward course' and, disappointing though it was for the Committee after all their endeavours, in the existing climate of opinion the Chairman could only agree.[31]

They were back to square one.

31 *Ibid*

Bitterness continued to escalate with charge and counter-charge, mainly between the Vicar and the local MP, though J R Tripp did not escape his share of criticism for his statement at the Burial Board Meeting about the discontent felt in the Vicar's own parish on account of changes in the system of fees he had recently introduced.[32] 'The Times' eventually refused to print any further correspondence, so the Vicar had to rely on 'The Cambrian' in order to vent his anger against Mr Dillwyn who, he felt, had exhibited throughout the issue 'more misguided zeal at the dictum of a party than of the sound judgment, discretion and equity which we have a right to expect from one placed in his position.'[33]

Nevertheless, by September 18, the tide was beginning to turn. The Bishop's 'manly and courageous stand in defence of parochial clergy's rights against the inconsiderate - not to say aggressive - spirit manifested by Swansea Burial Board' had won the overwhelming support of local clergymen. Perhaps he could now afford to be magnanimous.[34]

Shortly afterwards, John Oakshot, Mayor and, as such, Chairman of the Burial Board, received a letter from him indicating his willingness to consecrate 'that portion of their cemetery designed for interments according to the rites of the Church of England at any convenient time after the necessary instruments shall have been prepared.' He was obviously anxious to dispel in the minds of the people of Swansea any suspicion that he had been 'wilfully obstructive' in trying to exact from the Burial Board something the law did not require of them: he had only been anxious 'not to exercise his discretionary power in a way that would hurt one he was bound to protect'.[35]

The reading of this letter coincided with the proposal of a resolution by Starling, introduced in his absence by Mr Hoare, the Council having resolved itself into a meeting of the Burial Board. In moving the resolution, Mr Hoare apologised for not being himself a member of that Board and then went on to propose: 'That for ordinary afternoon funerals, it is desirable that certain days should be fixed; it is therefore resolved that Mondays, Wednesdays and Fridays be appointed, on which days the attendance of the clergy and ministers should be expected.'

This certainly went a long way towards meeting the wishes of the Vicar, but unfortunately it was seen as making a sharp distinction between the well-to-do and the poorer classes, on whose funerals only small fees would be collected. Their funerals were generally in the afternoon and so would be limited to certain days. There would be no such restriction for the funerals of the better-off whose family or friends could afford to pay for transport for officiating clergy. Such funerals would be mainly in the morning.

While allowing that, in proposing the motion, Starling Benson had in mind the convenience of vicars and ministers in general as well as the public, Mr Michael feared it would be seen as introducing such a distinction between rich and poor.

32 C Sept 4 1857, p 6
33 C Sept 11 1857, p 8
34 C Sept 4 1857, p 6
35 C Sept 18 1857, p 5

He accordingly introduced an amendment: 'That it be a recommendation from this Board that so far as it may prove practicable, funerals should be conducted at the Cemetery on Mondays, Wednesdays and Fridays, except in cases of emergency; and that afternoon funerals take place from Michaelmas to Lady Day at 3.30 pm and from Lady Day to Michaelmas at 4 pm.' This was felt to avoid the suggestion of one rule for the rich and another for the poor and was passed unanimously.[36]

New problems surfaced even after the licence for the Danygraig Cemetery was issued, with the promise of consecration at a later date convenient to the Bishop and the Vicar. The first burial, that of a child, gave rise to further criticism of the Burial Board. The Vicar, in a censorious correspondence, blamed the Board for 'a sad lack of service books, surplices, etc', referring bitterly to difficulties deliberately thrown in his way by 'contentious men'.[37]

In moving the adoption of the Cemetery Committee's report at its next meeting, the Chairman explained that they had considered the furnishing of books to mean two copies of the services for the consecrated chapel and whatever books were needed for the chapel of the unconsecrated part of the cemetery. These, as they understood it, were all that had to be supplied by the Board. He deplored the tone of the Vicar's letter which would not have been justified even if the Board had refused to supply anything - but suggested, with his usual equanimity, that it was best ignored. As the required items would cost not more than 15/-, Mr Tripp saw no objection to their meeting the cost. This seemed only fair to the Mayor as the consecrated ground would be used by seven or eight different parishes, and it would not be right to expect the parish of Swansea to bear the whole burden alone.[38]

Even so, the Board did not escape the censure of 'Nathan' who accused its members of 'foisting the Burial Act upon the town', thereby wasting upwards of £4000 in order to comply with the arbitrary conditions of the Act. Having overspent in order to provide a cemetery sufficient to bury the dead of Swansea for ever, they now sought to bolster up their waning popularity by maintaining a perpetual quarrel with the Vicar over such trifles as prayer books, etc.[39]

Such sniping could not, however, go on indefinitely. By December 18 the Mayor announced that every preliminary had been completed and the Bishop could be expected to perform the ceremony before the end of the month.[40] It was, however, January 7 1858 before the Consecration eventually took place. The Bishop was met at the entrance to the Cemetery by the Vicar and numerous other clergy. The Mayor, his predecessor John Oakshot (there also in his capacity of church warden), the Town Clerk and a large number of Councillors, including Starling, were in attendance. Also present were H H Vivian and Pascoe St Leger Grenfell accompanied by his family whose home, Maesteg, was in the Danygraig neighbourhood. Not surprisingly, the local MP, Lewis Llewelyn Dillwyn, was engaged elsewhere.

36 *Ibid*
37 C Oct 23 1857, p 5
38 C Nov 13 1857, p 5
39 C Nov 13 1857, p 8
40 C Dec 18 1857, p 6

The Consecration ceremony in the burial ground was followed by a service in the Church where the Bishop spoke about the issue that had caused so much trouble. He was at pains to explain that the consecration of the ground was required as much by civil as by ecclesiastical authority. He also sought to clarify the issue of the division of the ground into consecrated and unconsecrated parts. 'This in no way reflected upon the future destiny of those buried in different parts of the graveyard.' If he could have broken down the separation between denominations by removing the visible division, he would have been the first to take up spade and pick axe, but as long as the breach existed, it was deceitful to try to hide it. It could only be healed by overcoming prejudice against those of a different persuasion, and if the day's assembling together achieved that, it would be well worthwhile.

In the ensuing 'collation', members of the clergy, headed by the Bishop and Vicar, mingled with Dissenting ministers, councillors and pressmen. The Mayor presided, flanked by the Bishop on his right and Mr H H Vivian on his left. Mr Dillwyn was again absent. He might have found it difficult to subscribe to the eulogistic terms in which the Mayor, in proposing the Bishop's health, thanked him for the act he had performed and 'the Christian-like address he had delivered.'[41]

How much did the wrangling of the past eighteen months affect Starling's decision to move out of the parish of Swansea away to Gower? The issue of 'The Cambrian' which reported the consecration of the cemetery gave details of a New Year's gift to the Revd E B Squire, Vicar of Swansea. The Vivians, Pascoe St Leger Grenfell, the Richardsons, Struvés, Stricks, Esserys and the Bishop of St David's had all subscribed to it but not Starling Benson. It looked as though he no longer felt himself part of the parish and was taking the Bishop's words at their face value: it was no good trying to hide a breach as long as it existed.[42]

Before the end of 1858 there was a new *contre-temps*, this time not with one bishop but two. An advertisement in 'The Times' of November 18 1858 had clearly stated that a knowledge of Welsh was not needed by applicants for the posts of chaplain in Cardiff prison and in the Swansea House of Correction. In spite of an upsurge of public indignation, the Glamorgan magistrates went ahead and drew up a short list of seven out of the original seventy-eight applicants. Not a single Welsh speaker was included.[43]

In response to popular demand, the Mayor of Swansea, J T Jenkin, convened a public meeting which decided to memorialise the County Magistrates, asking them to reconsider their decision. Copies of the day's proceedings were sent to the Home Secretary, the Lord Lieutenant and MPs for the County, the Chairman and Vice Chairman of the Quarter Sessions and to the Bishops of Llandaff and St David's, who had to license the successful candidates.[44]

The Cardiff magistrates felt the need for Welsh was minimal. In Swansea, however, even the non-Welsh speakers, like H H Vivian, P St Leger Grenfell and

41 C Jan 8 1858, p 5
42 C Jan 8 1858, p 4
43 C Jan 7 1859, p 8
44 C Jan 28 1859, p 6

Matthew Moggridge, had come to realise that, whereas prisoners might be able to use English for business matters, those used to worshipping in Welsh found it hard to discuss spiritual problems in a second language. Again, those in solitary confinement had only the chaplain, apart from the prison officials, to talk to, so it was essential they should be able to communicate in their native language. The previous chaplain, none other than our old friend, the Revd E B Squire, had been assisted in his duties by a Welsh-speaking curate, the Revd George Edmund Williams.

The latter had applied for the post but had been ignored. Similarly the Swansea magistrates' opposition was brushed aside, and at the next meeting, at the instigation of the Chairman, the Cardiff Stipendiary Magistrate, R Oliver Jones of Fonmon Castle, the election went ahead. The Revd John Dreaper of Wakefield was appointed to Cardiff and the Revd James Elger of the Isle of Wight to Swansea.[45]

Loud rumbles of discontent persisted. It was rumoured that a Welsh curate was being offered £30 pa to work among the Welsh prisoners, whereas each chaplain was being paid £250 for working among the English, suggesting a Welshman's soul was worth less than an eighth of an Englishman's.[46]

At the Swansea Quarter Sessions on April 5 1859 it was discovered that the two Bishops were refusing to license the chaplains on the grounds of non-competency to carry out duties in Welsh. As Mr Dreaper had now been offered a rise of £30 at Wakefield, it was hoped he might withdraw from his new appointment so that Mr Elger could be transferred to Cardiff and a Welsh-speaker be appointed to Swansea. This solution had one drawback which Mr Justice Falconer pointed out. The Welsh speakers sent to Cardiff Prison for debt were usually law-abiding Church-goers who had been made insolvent by the depression resulting from the coal-strike. They needed the consolation of religion in a language they could respond to, but would be quite out of place in the Swansea House of Correction with its strong criminal element.[47]

Mr Dreaper did not withdraw and the Magistrates seemed to have reached a stalemate.[48] It was suggested he be asked to resign so that Mr Elger could take up the Cardiff chaplaincy, leaving the Swansea post vacant for a Welsh-speaker. Here Starling came up with a solution, albeit rather a drastic one. He proposed both men be asked to resign and a completely new list be drawn up, consisting of Welsh-speakers only, but as the field of candidates would be considerably narrowed, the salary should be dropped to £150 pa.[49]

The next meeting was held in Cardiff in July. It emerged that, quite naturally, the rejected candidates felt aggrieved. James Elger had already spent time and money on lessons in Welsh; John Dreaper wanted a written explanation of the circumstances surrounding his withdrawal to present, should he apply for another post, lest his disqualification might suggest some sort of misconduct. Some financial recognition of their situation had also to be forthcoming. Mr Bruce's

45   C Jan 28 1859, p 5
46   C March 18 1859, p 8
47   C April 8 1859, p 8
48   C May 6 1859, p 6
49   *Ibid*

proposal to award both men half the annual salary was accepted. In vindication of their own position, the East Glamorgan Magistrates wished it to be made known that, at the time of appointing the two chaplains, they had no idea their decision could be vetoed by the Bishops.

There was a delay in proceedings while the Court waited for the arrival of the Swansea contingent. Eventually the meeting had to go on without them. Mr Bruce regretted their absence as it had been Mr Benson who had suggested reconsidering salaries. It had, moreover, been the situation in Swansea that had led to the difficulty in reaching a decision. He personally felt that the original salary should be retained in order to attract Welshmen of weight and ability. Although £250 was high in comparison with clergymen's salaries in general, it was hopeless to expect men of talent to apply if a lower stipend was offered, especially as it had to cover residence.

Starling's point of view was put in his absence by Mr Richard Franklen who pointed out that the field of candidates would be considerably narrowed by the exclusion of monoglot Englishmen. Hard though it was for a layman to set a figure on spiritual duties, in view of the fact that the salary for curates was between £80 to £100 a year, £150 seemed an adequate stipend since the new chaplains would still be learners in matters relating to their prison duties.[50] (As things worked out eventually, this was certainly not the case in Swansea!).

The amendment to this effect was now seconded by the Chairman, Mr Henry Thomas, followed by a suggestion of £200 from Mr R O Jones. When, however, the original proposition of £250 was put, it was carried comfortably. A suggestion that the final appointments be left to the Bishops was greeted with laughter. Instead, the Court of Quarter Sessions would still be responsible, but the six candidates short-listed were to have a certificate of proficiency in Welsh from the Bishops before being interviewed.

The Editor of 'The Cambrian', in the issue reporting this meeting, took the Chairman to task for pejorative remarks about Bishop Thirlwall's knowledge of the Welsh vernacular, claiming he was as much master of it as he was of classical Welsh.[51] A year had done much to improve the Bishop's public image in the eyes of the Swansea press!

This long-drawn-out affair was finally rounded off in Bridgend the following November at an adjourned meeting of the Court of the Quarter Sessions under Mr Bruce's presidency. Here the Revd Joshua Evans and the Revd Edmund George Williams were appointed. Mr Williams had experience of Swansea House of Correction as assistant to the Revd E B Squire, so he continued there, while Mr Evans went to Cardiff.[52] Justice had at last been done, thanks to the wisdom and insight of the Bishops.

Although neither Bishop Thirlwall nor Bishop Ollivant was himself a Welshman, both in this instance showed a gratifying awareness of the importance of the Welsh language to those in trouble with the law, something which many of the magistrates had failed to understand. As a result, the East Glamorgan Justices in particular had shown themselves to be, at the best, insensitive, at the

50   C July 1 1859, p 8
51   C July 1, 1859, p 5
52   C Nov 11 1859, p 5

35   Alfred Ollivant, the Rt Revd Bishop of Llandaff   J Vyrnwy Morgan, *op cit*

36 Henry Austin Bruce
 - later Lord Aberdare
 J Vyrnwy Morgan, *op cit*

worst, indifferent, to the needs of those in their charge. Starling, at least, had dared to suggest a bold way out of the tangle created by their initial mistake but unfortunately spoiled the effect by linking it with what some would see as an all-too-typical desire to save money. Luckily Henry Bruce was at hand to make sure there was no cut-rate salary for the cure of souls, especially Welsh ones!

Chapter X

Starling in Court

No, not the Court of her Majesty, Queen Victoria, though undoubtedly his step-
mother would have been overjoyed if it had been, but the weekly Police Court
in Swansea during the term of his service on the Town Council and frequently
the County Court for the hearing of cases from further afield. Later, as a
Magistrate for the County, he was on the Jury both for the Glamorganshire
Quarter Sessions and the Assizes which alternated between Swansea and
Cardiff.

We have already seen that Starling's privileged family background in no way
shielded him from the vicissitudes of private life, while his participation in public
affairs exposed him, sometimes ruthlessly, to the follies and foibles of his fellow
townsmen. There was, however, a yet darker side to life in the fast growing
community for whose law and order he and his peers had made themselves
responsible. For a magistrate there was no way of ignoring the ugly realities
which others, less privileged than they, were having to face in their daily
lives.

What these realities were is graphically brought home to us in the columns of
'The Cambrian' of the day. A typical cross-section of the cases heard in the local
courts in one selected period, between 1856 and 1858, gives the reader a
significant reflection of the life of contemporary Swansea.

The area was being rapidly transformed from its rural stolidity to a bustling
seaport. This was in turn closely impinged upon by the escalating industries
which were bringing in a vastly expanded population, both from other Welsh
districts and from various areas further afield, especially Ireland and the North
and West of England. But although the details of the cases may be peculiar to
their particular locality and epoch, the underlying nature of the offences was little
different from the perennial problems which recur in every generation: theft,
drunkenness, immorality and violence, amounting in its worst manifestations to
homicide and murder. Some of the cases had a special relationship to the
seafaring character of the district, in one case smacking of smuggling. Several
were the forerunners of our modern traffic offences where, even before the days
of the combustion engine, the contemporary form of transport presented a
danger.

Contemporary novelists like Dickens tend to give us a picture of an
overbearing magistracy meting out harsh justice to the offender with little
concern for the individual transgressor. If 'The Cambrian' reporter is to be
believed, the attitude of the group of magistrates with whom Starling most
frequently acted, was unmistakably firm but rarely, if ever, bullying or vindictive.
In Wales the situation could easily be aggravated by the fact that the proceedings

in the courts were in English while many of those appearing before them spoke only Welsh. No reference to that difficulty is mentioned in any of the cases tried by Starling. One can only hope the comparatively few Welsh-speaking magistrates were assigned specially to such cases. Indeed the majority of those appearing before Starling had English, Irish or even Jewish surnames, while many of the Joneses, Evanses and Bowens he met in court seemed to be natives of the English-speaking district of Gower.

Much of the petty crime in Swansea, as elsewhere, stemmed from drunkenness, particularly in the area of the Docks and the central part of the town. It may seem surprising, therefore, to find that, in the main, drunken offences were treated with a surprising degree of leniency. Joseph Williams and George Abraham, found drunk and fighting in High Street in January 1856, were discharged on payment of costs.[1] The following year, Mary Rees was charged by PC Brooks with drunken and disorderly conduct in Temple Street, but as nothing serious had occurred during her 'drunken fracas', Starling and his fellow magistrate, the Mayor, John Oakshot, dismissed the case on payment of 1/- costs.[2] Similarly in the same court, Thomas Dullivan, found stupidly drunk by PC No.33, who stumbled over him as he lay on the ground in Caer Street, was discharged on payment of costs.[3]

A rather sterner view of drunken behaviour was taken by the Revd Samuel Davies, sitting in the County Court the following week with Starling and Matthew Moggridge. There had been a disturbance at a local public house on the Good Friday evening when one, John Rogers, had 'drunkenly assaulted' PC John Nation who had been called to quell it. Mr Davies 'felt a stop should be put to the disgraceful scenes at Mumbles on a Good Friday when many of the most abandoned characters visited the area'. He had written to the Mayor asking him to send down some of the borough police, a step which he believed had served to prevent even worse disturbances. Should he be spared to see another Good Friday, he was resolved to act in order to prevent a recurrence.[4] However, as the policeman in question did not press the charge of assault, Rogers got off with a fine of 5/- and 3/6 costs.

A similar fine was given an anonymous woman found drunk in the public streets the following July, and also to John Bird charged by PC Brown with creating a disturbance in Regent Court. The Magistrates, John Oakshot, Matthew Moggridge and Starling, were told he was very drunk and insolent to the officer who, Bird claimed, had struck him several times across the shoulders, an accusation Mr Brown vigorously denied, claiming he had never even drawn his staff. When the accused was examined by Sergeant Bennett, the latter found only a small mark on one shoulder, probably caused by a fall on the way to the police station.[5]

A 5/- fine plus costs seems to have been the standard. A John Williams of Merthyr had, by his drunken behaviour, attracted the attention of several girls of

1   C Jan 25 1856, p 8.
2   C April 10 1857, p 8.
3   *Ibid.*
4   C April 24 1857, p 6.
5   C July 3 1857, p 6.

loose character in the Strand. He then turned into a shop kept by Mr Clinton who had to get the police to remove him. After a severe reprimand from the Bench, the prisoner was given the usual fine.[6]

Under the caption 'A Hard Antagonist', 'The Cambrian' reported the antics of Richard Davies, a copper man, who had been drunk and disorderly in High Street on a Sunday night. By the time PC Davies arrived, a crowd had gathered and Richard Davies was hard at it, fighting with the lamp-post. He got off rather more lightly than the previous prisoners, the case being dismissed on payment of the cost of a summons, 4/-.[7]

The heaviest charge made for costs was in the County Court in the case of Edward George, a master painter, described as 'a respectably attired man', who had pleaded guilty to being drunk. He was reprimanded and discharged but only on the payment of the unusually heavy costs of 7/-. Presumably in the eyes of the three Magistrates, the Revd Samuel Davies, Matthew Moggridge and Starling, his respectable appearance went against him. He was one who should have known better.[8]

At the same time Mary Williams, landlady of the Lamb and Flag in Greenhill, was charged with opening at illegal hours. The case was proved, the fine of 5/- being 'mulcted in expenses'.[9]

Apparently not all the police were considered reliable witnesses. One officer claimed to have seen men drinking after hours in the Glebe beer house in Loughor. The case against the landlord, Daniel Morris, was dismissed after two of his lodgers testified that they were the last up at the beer house, and they were in bed well before 11.20, the time at which the officer claimed to have seen men drinking there. Further, they denied that the officer had been anywhere near the Glebe that night. The case was dismissed.[10]

A stronger line was usually adopted where there was violence involved as a result of excessive drinking, though other causes of disagreement could also lead to blows. In April 1857, just before an Election, two women, Elizabeth Lewis and Elizabeth Davies, were found fighting in Waterloo Street. The one was trying to rip the other's bonnet and each was intent on scratching her opponent's eyes. When it was explained that they were fighting over politics because of the forthcoming Election, the Mayor and Starling took a lenient view of their quarrel, dismissing them with a reprimand.[11]

Mary Jones, a vagrant, driven to violence by her destitution, had resorted to smashing the relieving officer's windows. As a result, she was sent to the workhouse, possibly the end she was trying to achieve.[12] In general, however, those in need of parish relief would do anything to avoid the so-called 'House of Industry' which, from 1817 on, had been housed in part of the Bathing House on the Burrows, until increased numbers led to the building of a separate workhouse in Tawe Lodge.

6 C Jan 15 1858, p 5.
7 C March 12 1858, p 6.
8 C March 13 1857, p 6.
9 *Ibid.*
10 C Aug 14 1857, p 8.
11 C April 10 1857, p 8.
12 *Ibid.*

Sometimes there seemed to be no reason for the violence. Charles Coleman, 'a respectably dressed young man', had set upon John Jones on the Oystermouth tramroad in the Strand early one evening. The complainant shook him off and went home, but his assailant followed him into the house where he insulted Jones's mother. When John Jones threw him out of the house, Coleman tried to fight him. The Mayor and Starling considered the charge of assault had been substantiated and gave the defendant the choice of either fourteen days in prison or a fine of ten shillings, to include costs. He chose the prison sentence, but with the threat, 'When I come out, look out - that's all'. As a result he was ordered to give sureties to keep the peace.[13]

The close proximity of dwelling houses to each other in the squalid, overcrowded courts off the main streets frequently led to friction between neighbours. In the County Court Margaret Thomas was given the unusually high fine of 14/6 (including costs) or fourteen days in prison for assaulting Tabor Griffiths. The latter had accused the defendant's daughter of throwing stones into her house. When Tabor had gone to complain, Margaret Thomas struck her three times on her shoulder with a stick. The defendant's story was that she had only struck Mrs Griffiths after first being pushed against a chest of drawers. She added that the complainant had come to her door armed with a pitchfork, but after hearing the case, the magistrates (Matthew Moggridge, Dr Bird, the Revd Samuel Davies and Starling) were convinced that it was Margaret Thomas who had taken the initiative in violence.[14]

One might have expected a slightly less tense atmosphere in an area where houses had hedges between them, but it was, in fact, the dividing hedge, claimed by both families, which led to the dispute between William and Mary Jones and Mary Evans. The latter accused her neighbours of using threatening language and was afraid of their doing her serious bodily harm. They, on the other hand, claimed that all they wanted was to be left alone by the complainant. They were all bound over by the Mayor and Starling to keep the peace for six months in sums of £10 each.[15]

Another case which had a relatively peaceful outcome was that of John Tierney who had been charged with an assault on Thomas Carpenter, a lodger in Tierney's house. There was a quarrel over the lodger's wearing his landlord's jacket. Tierney, it was claimed, had thrown a black tea pot full of boiling water at Carpenter, thereby scalding him. This, Tierney explained, was done in self defence when Carpenter put up his fist in his face. The same magistrates as had heard the case of Margaret Thomas v Tabor Griffiths advised the two men to settle their differences amicably, and as a result, Tierney agreed to pay Carpenter 20/- and costs.[16]

In view of the cramped conditions in which families lived it was not surprising that many cases were domestic in origin. Benjamin Richards appeared before the same court on a charge of violent assault on his wife, Ann, who was also attacked by her step-daughter. Relations between the two women were frequently strained

13 C April 24 1857, p 8.
14 C May 8 1857, p 8.
15 C Dec 24 1857, p 5.
16 C May 8 1857, p 8.

as Ann's husband encouraged his children to be impudent to their step-mother. In addition, he squandered his money, a view endorsed by the Revd Samuel Davies who knew Richards's conduct had been so unreliable that he had been turned away from his work on the Singleton estate.[17] Although they had no power to enforce it, the Bench strongly advised the unhappy couple to separate. The complainant, it appeared, did not want to punish her husband, only for him to keep the peace. The latter agreed to give her a separate maintenance allowance of 2/- a week and was bound over in the sum of £20 to keep the peace towards her for six months, as well as being ordered to pay 19/- costs.[18]

On another occasion, the Revd Samuel Davies and Starling gave the opposite advice. The couple had been married only fifteen months when David Lewis of Oxwich was charged with the neglect of his wife whom he was also supposed to have beaten. He, on the other hand, claimed that he gave her all his wages but she still managed to get into debt. The overseer of the parish said there was fault on both sides. As a result of the Bench's advice, the young people agreed to try again, 'and thus the matter was settled amicably.'[19]

There were far more unpleasant cases. A navvy named Aaron Stock had attacked his wife so violently that she was found by PC Lewis badly covered with blood in the bedroom. Her 'inhuman husband' had dragged the hair from her head. Unfortunately the wife's non-appearance in the police court before John Oakshot, Starling and Matthew Moggridge meant her husband had to be discharged, obviously much to the regret of the Magistrates who warned him that he could otherwise have been sent to the House of Correction for six months.[20]

Jealousy frequently played a part in the outbursts of anger leading to violence. Jane Keath applied to the Court for sureties of the peace to protect her against Mary Ann Austin who had threatened to do her bodily harm. Jane Keath had accused her husband of being too intimate with the other woman who had given Keath her ring, telling him to take it to his wife. She had threatened to split his hand open with a flat iron if he didn't and was apparently the more aggressive. In view, however, of the fact that the two women had come to blows, the summons was held over for the future good conduct of both, with each paying her own costs.[21]

In another case, two sisters living next door to each other in Back Street had quarrelled over a house left them by their mother. Jane Bowen accused her sister, Catherine Walters, of throwing half a brick which hit her in the back. Catherine Walters, on the other hand, claimed it was her sister who had thrown the brick. With the wisdom of a Solomon, the usual trio of John Oakshot, Matthew Moggridge and Starling divided the costs, although they did fine the defendant the princely sum of 6d.[22]

Not all the violence was confined to the back streets and crowded houses of the poorer parts of Swansea. There was a rowdy element even in deepest Gower.

17 *Ibid.*
18 *Ibid.*
19 C Aug 7 1857, p 6.
20 C July 3 1857, p 6.
21 *Ibid.*
22 *Ibid.*

Two lusty country lads, Evans and Gwynn, had assaulted PC Evan Bowen at Parkmill. The officer had gone into the New Inn to tell the landlord to close. On his way out of the inn, Evans claimed to have seen the officer fire at two or three boys who were going into the woods. He approached him to say there was no need to do that, but he did not touch the policeman. PC Bowen, on the other hand, said he had been hit on the head by stones aimed at him out of the wood. He had then gone about thirty yards into the wood. When he returned to the road, Gwynn and others jumped out and threw him to the ground where they went on kicking him. It was then he fired his revolver, only to have it forced from him. He managed to retrieve it but the youths again forced him to the ground and continued to kick him. Starling, speaking for his fellow magistrates, said the Bench took a serious view of the assault. Had the policeman been on duty, they would have inflicted on the culprits the full penalty of the law, fining them £20. As it was, they were fined £5 each or two months in prison.[23]

A more amusing incident from the countryside led to the appearance before the same Justices of Thomas Lewis accused of a violent attack on Elizabeth Williams who had found his donkey in her garden between 6 and 7 am. She had thought to put it in the pound but then told her son to turn it into the road. The defendant came on the scene, obviously in a fury. He swore at her, hit her on the head with his fist and then struck out at her with his meat basket. As he pushed her into the hedge, the gate fell on her leg. Lewis's version was that he merely took her by the arm after she had thrown stones at him. The case, however, was proved against him, and Lewis was given the option of a 5/- fine and 10/6 costs or fourteen days' imprisonment.[24]

Breakdowns in family relationships leading to violence were not confined to the poor and uneducated in the town. One of the most painful cases concerned Elizabeth Kent of Bishopston, the daughter of the master of the National School there. She had applied to the County Court for sureties of the peace against her mother. As Mrs Kent failed to appear at the first hearing, a warrant was issued against her.[25]

When she eventually appeared the following week, it was reported that she had used threatening language and had taken up a knife to stab her daughter, whose evidence was corroborated by her father. Mrs Kent's behaviour in court, according to 'The Cambrian', was 'anything but respectful and lady-like'. The case ended with her opting to go to gaol rather than agree to keep the peace for three months.[26]

Some cases had a direct connection with Swansea's maritime character. An assistant to a local druggist named Harris had walked, in pursuit of orders, into the state room of Captain Lecomte of the brig 'Borland' while the Captain was dressing. The latter was so incensed that he set about the man, William H Reynolds, and then turned him ashore. The case was heard by the Mayor, Starling and John Richardson. While not condoning Reynolds's conduct, they felt the

---

23   C Feb 12 1858, p 6.
24   *Ibid.*
25   C March 12 1858, p 6.
26   C March 19 1858, p 5.

Captain should not have assaulted him and he was accordingly fined 6d, with 9/6 costs, which were promptly paid.[27]

A more complicated case connected with the port of Swansea was heard by Starling, John Richardson, Matthew Moggridge and the Revd Samuel Davies. Thomas Matthews, bosun of the 'Vulcan', was charged with unlawfully concealing thirteen pounds of cigars in sixteen packages in the sleeping berth of the state-room, hidden between the deck beams. The chief officer of the vessel was already in prison for the same offence.

Captain John Brown deposed on oath that he had taken out a warrant against Matthews for deserting ship, although he had previously had confidence in him and had taken him frequently with him in the boat going into Gibraltar where the Captain made various purchases. These Matthews had taken back to the 'Vulcan', while the Captain returned separately by the shore boat.

It was suggested by Mr Tripp, acting for the defendant, that the cigars could have been placed there with the full knowledge of the captain. He suspected Brown of conniving with Matthews over his desertion. The captain had then taken part in the search for him to put the police off the trail, intending later to reinstate him as bosun as a reward for his taking the blame if the cigars happened to be discovered.

In spite of the circumstantial case built up against the captain by Mr Tripp, the Bench was not impressed. A suggestion that the defendant should be cross-examined by his solicitor was turned down by Mr Benson on behalf of the Bench who rejected such evidence as inadmissible. Mr Tripp could call on his client to make a statement but this could not be taken down as evidence.

Eventually the Bench considered the case had been proved against Matthews who was fined £100. Mr Tripp considered that, in some cases, all the passengers on a ship could be found guilty under the relevant Act of Parliament, but Mr Pitman, prosecuting, pointed out in reply that the authorities only prosecuted individuals with a guilty knowledge of smuggling when they were convinced an offence had taken place. In addition to the heavy fine, the defendant was ordered to pay costs.[28] The magistrates were obviously determined to suppress any action suggestive of smuggling which might give the port a bad name.

Another case associated with travel was that of Abraham Hopkins who had been found in a First Class compartment with a Second Class railway ticket. He had failed to produce his ticket when challenged to do so. It emerged that this was not his first offence of the kind. He was accordingly fined 40/-, with 46/- costs.[29] In contrast, two women, Ann Morgan and Ann Evans, charged with stealing half a hundred weight of coal, were discharged with a reprimand by John Oakshot, George Grant Francis and Starling, the same three magistrates as had come down heavily on Abraham Hopkins.[30] Contrary to the impression frequently given of one law for the rich and another for the poor, operating in Victorian times to the disadvantage of the latter, it would seem the exact opposite

27 C Jan 25 1856, p 8.
28 C May 15 1857, p 8.
29 C Feb 13 1857, p 6.
30 *Ibid.*

prevailed from time to time with several of the Swansea magistrates, the poor being treated with noticeably greater leniency.

The following month, March 1857, the Mayor and Starling faced an unusual case when 'two daring young imps of 14 years', Thomas Jones and John Gammon, were charged with stealing about a pound of sausages from John Price, butcher, of Cross Street. 'The Cambrian' report, headed 'Artful Dodge', recounted how the one threw his accomplice's cap over the dish of sausages. The other then picked it up with the sausages underneath it. The whole episode had been witnessed by the butcher's wife from the back room. She was therefore able to identify the boy. The offence was reported to PC Davies who, that same evening, had apprehended Jones and found two of the sausages in his house. His excuse was that Gammon had given them to him, while Gammon in turn blamed Jones. As evidence given by them against each other could not be accepted, the case was dismissed with a severe reprimand to the two culprits who were reminded that they had had a narrow escape.[31]

From time to time the absence of the prosecutor led to the discharge of a prisoner, as in the case of a defendant named Peacock who was charged with stealing a duck![32]

The pawn shop was often the last resort of those in need. Maria White, 'an apparently respectable young woman', was charged with stealing an apron from Mrs Phillips of Quarry Street who had put it on her garden hedge to dry after washing it. Mrs Phillips missed it the next morning and found it in Mr Moses's pawn shop in College Street. Moses recalled it had first been offered as a pledge by a small child who said she had been sent by Sarah White. He had refused to take it from so young a child, but he later took it from a young woman to whom he gave 2/- and an ounce of tea. The prisoner was remanded until the following Monday.[33]

Mr Moses was to figure in another case later the same year. He had missed three guernsey frocks worth 20/- which had been hanging outside his shop. They had had no identifiable marks but he was still able to recognise them as the items in a bundle dropped by a man whom he chased up the street. Although he could not himself say that Samuel Davies, who had been arrested on the charge, was the man, he believed what he had been told by John Kilner of James Street. The latter claimed to have seen Davies unhitch the frocks, and later pointed out the prisoner to Mr Moses.

Kilner had himself been in trouble with the law although he had been acquitted on the most recent charge of receiving stolen carriage lamps. He testified that the man in question was wearing dark clothes. Another witness described the man who stole the garments as wearing a 'beautiful black coat' but light trousers and as having long, 'lankey' (*sic*) hair, which he said at the same time was 'well oiled'. He was sure the man was not Davies, whom he knew.

Mr Moses had delivered the bundle of clothes he had picked up to PC Jones who had then gone to arrest Davies at his own house. He stated that the prisoner,

31 C March 13 1857, p 6.
32 C May 1 1857, p 6.
33 C May 8 1857, p 8.

while affirming his innocence, had agreed to accompany him to the police station at once.

The strongest evidence in Davies's favour came from his next door neighbour, David Morgan, who had seen him lying in his doorway, playing with his child, at 5.10 pm. The first time for Davies to go past Morgan's window was when he was taken by the two constables. He had never seen him wear a dress-coat; usually it was a monkey jacket.

Not surprisingly, the prisoner was discharged.[34]

The Mayor, Matthew Moggridge and Starling, the three magistrates who discharged Samuel Davies, had another encounter with a pawnbroker early the next year. A boy of ten, William (or John, as reported in the following week's paper) Stapleton, was charged with stealing his sister's 'mantle' and other garments and pawning them with Mr Jacob of Oxford Street whom the magistrates reprimanded for accepting articles from a child obviously under twelve years of age. The pawnbroker claimed the boy had said he was thirteen. He had charged him 7d for two ounces of tea and given him 3/4 in cash. The boy, according to him, had asked for the tea.

The previous week's paper had made it quite clear that pawnbrokers were licensed to advance money, not tea, and the Bench was determined to act upon this. The police officer had a specimen of the tea which, valued by the best grocers, would sell from 3/- to 3/4 a pound whereas, at Jacob's rate, it would cost 4/8 a pound. Jacob protested that he never forced anyone to take tea, but Starling saw the practice as virtually compelling people into taking what he would give them.

The sister put forward a strong plea on behalf of her young brother. He had been ill-treated by their father who she felt was to blame for the neglect of his family. The Bench dismissed the case, expressing the hope that the father would in future try to keep the family from evil companions. The boy himself was to be sent for a week to the House of Correction, not as a punishment, but 'for his own good', and from there to be transferred to a school 'to be taught to read and write, to make him a respectable member of the community'. One hopes their aim was realised. It would be interesting to know how John - or William Stapleton turned out.[35]

Taken in the context of their day, the Justices were not too hard on little children like Richard Edwards and Sarah Thomas, charged with stealing coal from a barge on the canal. They again were discharged with a caution.[36] John Bowen, however, did not escape so lightly. A lad of twelve, he was convicted of stealing a flannel petticoat belonging to a Mrs Samuel Hopgood from a line and was sentenced by Starling and Matthew Moggridge to a day's imprisonment and to be once whipped severely.[37]

There was petty crime in the countryside as well as the town. A charge of poaching was brought against Samuel Eaton who was said to have killed and pocketed a hare while on Fairwood Common, the property of Mr Thomas

34 C July 3 1857, p 6.
35 C Jan 29 1858, p 5.
36 C Feb 12 1858, p 6.
37 C Feb 19 1858, p 3.

Penrice. He and another man had been coursing with a brace of greyhounds and other dogs. The defendant's version of events was that he was on the Common looking for cattle when the dogs chased a rabbit. He denied beating for game or setting the dogs on a hare. The magistrates, Starling and the Revd Samuel Davies, at the instance of Mr Penrice, gave him a nominal penalty of 1/-, with costs.[38]

Sterner judgment was meted out to Rees Evans and William Clement of Llandilo-Talybont for trespassing on Henry Harris's lands in pursuit of game. The boys had started and coursed a hare but did not kill it. They pleaded guilty to the charge, and were fined 10/- with 9/9½ costs each, or fourteen days' imprisonment.[39]

In addition to dealing with drunkenness, violence and theft, the Police Court had frequently to decide in paternity cases, both in town and country. A forty year old widower had paid court to a Margaret Howells of Reynoldston and was accepted by her parents as her future husband, having promised on 'repeated' occasions to marry her. When she became pregnant, he at first agreed to support the child, but afterwards deserted her 'in the most disgraceful manner and without apparent reason'.

Brought before Mr Moggridge, Starling and the Revd Samuel Davies in the County Court, Clement claimed he could not pay. When the Bench told him he would be made to do so, he said he already had to pay 5/- a week for two other children. This was greeted by loud laughter from those present at the hearing. He went on to explain that these were 'not bastard ones'; they were his dead wife's children.

On being told he would be expected to pay 2/- a week for the support of the child, he retorted he could only do so if they docked something off from the other two, adding that he could not go naked. The order, however, was enforced by the magistrates who advised him to marry the complainant, thereby making '*amendi honorabile*'.[40]

The next month the same three magistrates were joined in the County Court by Dr Bird when they heard another paternity case, this time against John Davies of St Thomas, brought by Ruth Davies who was living at her brother-in-law's in Port Tennant. She claimed to have been seduced during the courtship which went back over the past twelve months. The defendant, who was apprenticed to Mr Meager, a shipwright, denied the charge '*in toto*', saying he had never been in the applicant's house in his life. Nevertheless, an order was made for 1/6 a week although, in view of the fact that the girl was twenty-two, while the defendant was only seventeen, the Bench found she had chiefly herself to blame.[41]

An even less successful affiliation case from the applicant's point of view was that of Sarah Austin who had summoned Leyshon Davies, son of the licensee of the Malster's Arms, Reynoldston, where Austin was a servant. Davies admitted courting her but denied he had ever promised marriage. As the offence had taken

38 C Nov 13 1857, p 8.
39 C Jan 22 1858, p 8.
40 C April 24 1857, p 6.
41 C May 8 1857, p 8.

place 'a very long time ago', the case was dismissed by the Bench which, on this occasion, consisted of the Mayor, Starling and G G Francis.[42]

Illegitimacy was all too common in Gower of that day. Starling and the Revd Samuel Davies together heard an affiliation case brought by Elizabeth Badcock of Llangennith against John Grove, Jnr, of Llanddewi, who had been courting the complainant for three years. The case had to be conducted in the defendant's absence, the claim being supported by a number of witnesses. An order was made for 1/6 a week.[43]

In the unavoidable absence of Mr Tripp, acting for the defence, and also in view of the failure of the claimant to appear, the case against Henry Burgess as the putative father of Elizabeth Hughes's child was adjourned from January 28 1858 to February 12th. At the later hearing the defendant produced a document in which Elizabeth Hughes agreed to release him of all further claims on payment of one sum of £6/10/0. As a result, no order was made.[44]

A distressing case was that of Edward Evans aged about forty and of weak intellect. He was ordered to pay 2/- a week towards the illegitimate child of Ann Jenkins. He had already been in prison three times on the same charge and was quite prepared to go there again rather than pay. Starling and the Revd Samuel Davies, sitting in the County Court, tried to find some arrangement to avoid having to commit him again, but Evans refused to comply. There was, therefore, no alternative to his being sent to the House of Correction for three months, with the warning that he would be sent there yet again if he refused to support his child.[45]

More straightforward was the case of Griffith Thomas of Llandilo-Talybont, summonsed by Mary Evans of the same district, in respect of her third child. He had already admitted paternity of her two older children. Thomas had been courting her for eleven years and had promised to marry her. Now, after a long investigation, he was ordered to pay 2/- a week for the support of the third child.[46]

It was not only in respect of jilted sweethearts that orders for payment had to be made. Richard Hopkins was summoned to show cause why he should not contribute towards the support of an aged and infirm father who was now on the parish. Hopkins normally earned 30/- a week but now, through illness, he had, for the past few months, been getting only 10/- a week. He was ordered to pay 2/- a week. This would be in addition to payment for the lodgings which the Bench would find for his father but for which he would be financially responsible.[47]

The growth in population had brought new problems in transport. Thomas Bowen, a haulier at the Forest Tin Works, was discharged on the payment of 5/- costs after being charged with leaving a horse and cart unattended in the street.[48] In the same court, a driver in the employ of the Swansea Brewery, belonging to

42   C August 14 1857, p 8.
43   C Nov 13 1857, p 8.
44   C Jan 29 1858, p 3 & Feb 12, p 6.
45   C Jan 22 1858, p 8.
46   C March 12 1858, p.6.
47   *Ibid.*
48   C Feb 19 1858, p 3.

John Hoare, appeared before Starling and John Oakshot. He was accused of riding on a dray drawn by two horses without a guide, either on foot or on horseback, 'the same not being a carriage normally driven by reins'. The Superintendent of police withdrew the summons on hearing the horses had been frightened. Both Mr Hoare and the Bench wanted a verdict on the situation, but as the case had been withdrawn by the Superintendent, they would have to wait for a decision in some other case of the same kind, which would undoubtedly occur before long.[49]

Present-day motoring offences had a precedent in events in the last century, long before the creation of the modern automobile. Thomas Elliott Morgan was summoned for running a stage-carriage without a licence to do so and also without a number affixed as required by Act of Parliament. The prisoner pleaded guilty. Evidence was given by one, Thomas Rees, that he had travelled on November 9 1858 from Swansea to Parkmill in the carriage for 2/- at a pace of more than four miles an hour. The journey had taken one hour twenty-nine minutes. There had been no number plates.

Mr Ivey, the Supervisor of Excise, said the defendant carried the mail between Swansea and Parkmill. As mail carrier, he was permitted to travel at four miles an hour, but that speed had been exceeded. The defendant explained he had not actually been driving himself on the day the offence took place, adding that he had warned his drivers against going any faster than the speed stipulated. The Bench fined him £5 and costs in each case, the minimum amount for such offences. They obviously sympathised with the prisoner's predicament as they expressed the hope that the Supervisor would petition the Board for still further reductions; the maximum penalty at the time was £20.[50]

Another case of exceeding the speed limit was brought against Evan Jones who was summoned for driving a certain cart in High-Street 'at a faster rate than a common walk'. After pleading guilty, he was discharged by W H Michael, John Oakshot and Starling on payment of costs. The case was reported in 'The Cambrian' under the heading 'Furious Driving'.[51]

Even more incongruous was the charge brought against a butcher boy of driving a bull 'furiously' through High-Street. The boy denied going through High-Street. He had driven the bull quietly through a back street to the slaughter house. The charge was dismissed.[52]

Shopkeepers had their problems too. Mr Thomas Rees of the Porter Stores was charged with obstruction in Waterloo Street by leaving casks on the pavement. On hearing the premises were being extended so that, in future, there would be ample storage space, the Mayor and Starling decided to dismiss the case on payment of costs.[53]

The importance of the oyster industry in the Mumbles area made it a source of income not only for the oyster-gatherers themselves but also for the local Church or its representatives. In the same court as heard the case of Thomas

49 *Ibid.*
50 *Ibid.*
51 C March 12 1858, p 6.
52 C May 21 1858, p 6.
53 C Dec 25 1857, p 5.

Bowen leaving his horse and cart unattended in the street and John Hoare's brewery dray being without a guide, five oyster-gatherers were summoned for arrears of their oyster tithes by Jenkin Berrington who owned the rectorial rights to the tithes.

Of the five only one, John Bevan, was present. The defendant undertook to pay arrears and costs. The case was adjourned until the following week when it was heard by Starling and Matthew Moggridge. Mr Berrington's previous agent, Jacob Rees, had received tithes for many years from John and Thomas Michael, two of the defendants, and from the late husbands of the two other defendants, John Morgan and William Hullin. Their widows, however, had paid nothing since their deaths. Mr Evans, the present agent, had served notice on them without response. Judgment was given against all four in their absence; they were to pay the full amount owing plus costs.[54]

Presumably there was no complaint about the quality of the oysters but a growing concern with hygiene was slowly emerging. The Market Inspector, P C Lodwick, brought a case against David Rees, a butcher, for bringing unwholesome meat into the market and exposing it for sale. The meat was burnt by direction of the Inspector of Nuisances on the evidence of four competent judges.[55]

A case that must have held special interest for Starling was that against Thomas Davies, the proprietor of the Kilvey Mount Colliery, for infringing the provisions of the recent Act of Parliament for the Inspection of Mines. There had not been fitted an adequate brake on each machine worked by steam or water-power which was used for lowering or raising people in the said colliery. In addition, Davies had failed to display the general rules, nor had he provided a steam boiler with a proper gauge. Moreover he had not provided every working pit or shaft with the means of signalling from the surface to the bottom of the colliery.

Mr Tripp, for the defendant, admitted the infringement of five out of the seven provisions under the new Act, and also referred to the death of a boy or man which had not been reported to the Government Inspector. The Inspector, however, was prepared to accept a nominal fine if the defendant undertook to put these matters right, safety rather than punishment being the object of bringing the case.

In reply to the Bench, it was stated that the boy in question had been killed on the spot. The Coroner had been notified but had not considered an inquest necessary. Previously the defendant had proposed writing to the Government Inspector himself but had not done so as the Coroner had undertaken to contact the Government Inspector on his behalf. The life of one young boy seems to have been regarded with a certain callous indifference by officialdom. The frequency of such accidents had obviously hardened even the Coroner who, on surface appearances, would seem to have forgotten the incident as, according to the Inspector, he had received the information only indirectly through a friend. The Revd Samuel Davies intervened to say he believed that any Inquest would have returned a verdict of 'Manslaughter'.

54 C Feb 12 1858, p 6 & Feb 19, p 3.
55 C May 8 1857, p 8.

165

As the defendant had promised to rectify matters in accordance with the view expressed by the Government Inspector, a nominal fine of 1/- was imposed on each charge, with costs, and the warning that, if there was a recurrence of the various forms of negligence, the full penalty empowered by the Act would be exacted. It apparently took a full-blown disaster or possibly a mine-owner who was outside the Old Boy network to move those exercising the law of the day to exact a penalty reflecting the grim responsibility each owner had for his men.[56] It would have been interesting to know what action had been taken by Starling and William Logan when, as reported in 'The Cambrian' of January 20 1844, an accident had occurred at their Penclawdd Colliery in which 'Edward Hughes, a collier in Messrs Benson and Logan's employ, fell to the bottom of the pit and was killed. He left a wife and four children unprovided for.'[57]

We can only hope the two owners met their obligation to relieve the obvious distress in this case. That some mine owners did take their responsibilities very seriously is shown by the action of Mrs C H Smith when, some years later, an explosion occurred at her husband's Llansamlet Colliery. She had straightaway collected £90 in the Llansamlet, Swansea and Tenby districts as well as distributing gifts of food and clothing to the widows and 5/- to each boy suffering the effects of the explosion. This was in addition to the public fund, to which Starling made a donation of £10.[58]

That, however, was in 1870, By that time Starling was less involved in municipal affairs, having moved to Fairy Hill in the summer of 1858. His subsequent resignation from the Town Council had involved the relinquishing of his duties as Borough Magistrate. From now on, his administration of the law was to be as a County Magistrate, sitting in the Glamorganshire Quarter Sessions and the Assizes, bringing his store of experience in municipal, maritime and industrial affairs to bear on a wider orbit. It had become vital to make a firm stand on behalf of the interests of the West as the go-ahead representatives of East Glamorgan sought more and more to shift county business away from the town that had previously been acknowledged as the capital of South Wales.

56 C Nov 6 1857, p 8.
57 C Jan 20 1844, p 3.
58 C Aug 12 & 19 1870 both on p 5.

Chapter XI

County Business

The spring of 1857 witnessed the usual fever associated with a General Election which, as we have seen from the antics of Elizabeth Lewis and Elizabeth Davies, was not confined to the gentry.[1] Starling himself was a member of the Swansea District Committee which met at the Liberal Committee Rooms in Fisher Street to promote the return of Mr Talbot and Mr Vivian as members for the County. There was a strong rival candidate in Nash Vaughan Edwards Vaughan who was seeking to succeed the retiring Conservative candidate, Sir George Tyler.[2]

It was just two years since Lewis Llewelyn Dillwyn had become Liberal MP for Swansea on the death of J H Vivian, and although he was now returned unopposed, he obviously still felt the need of gathering round him a loyal band of supporters. Starling had been one of those involved in the original nomination[3] and he was now present at a public dinner given by the Swansea MP at the Assembly Rooms to a number of his constituents early in April. Among these were other such Swansea notables as the Town Clerk (C B Mansfield), the Clerk to the Harbour Trust (Lewis Thomas), George Grant Francis, John Richardson, Richard Aubrey, W H Michael, Dr Bird, R A Essery, J T Jenkin and W P Struvé.[4]

Far greater excitement naturally surrounded the election of the County members, the result of which was to be declared by the High Sheriff from the steps of the Town Hall in Bridgend, then considered to be virtually the 'County' Town. Mr Talbot, accompanied by a hundred and thirty-two tenants and supporters, arrived on horseback, followed by a local band, amid a display of flags and banners and the firing of cannons. The party then went on to the station to meet the special train from Swansea bringing Mr and Mrs Vivian and their supporters, with two more bands. At the Town Hall the candidates took their stand on the Town Hall steps while the High Sheriff announced a sweeping victory for the two Liberal candidates. This Mr Grenfell attributed to keen canvassing in all weathers, 'even in remotest Gower', resulting in an 80% poll.[5]

A 'magnificent dinner' given in honour of the elected Members for Borough and County at the Mackworth Arms Hotel followed later in April. The price of the tickets at £1/1/0 a head caused some consternation, but it was pointed out that six pineapples cost £7, twenty-four small apples 5/-, strawberries 10/- a pound.

---

1 *Vide* p 155, n 11
2 C March 20 1857, p 4
3 *Vide* p 103, n 23
4 C April 3 1857, p 6
5 C April 10 1857, p 6

Pea-hens were 15/- each and Galena fowls 7/6, while cucumbers of about two foot long were 8/-. In view of this, as well as the fact that Mr John Viner of the Mackworth Arms Hotel had employed four professional chefs and expressly engaged fifteen or more waiters, the cost for three courses, plus dessert and ices and wine, was really quite reasonable.

Among the toasts proposed in the course of the evening was one by Starling to 'The Iron Trade', coupled with the name of James Palmer Budd. Mr Budd, he said, was one of those who had brought the power and strength of the manufacturing industries to ensure a Liberal victory, a need that Mr Budd himself had pointed out in 'a strong rallying speech' made at the time of the announcement of the result of the poll at Bridgend.[6]

1858 started with junketings to mark the marriage of the Princess Royal to the nephew of the King of Prussia. Swansea, 'as principal borough in Wales', was determined not to be outdone by any other town in the United Kingdom. Buns and oranges were distributed to some three thousand children through the kindness of the Mayor, W H Michael, while the new Post Office was illuminated in the evening by courtesy of the Gas Company. The leading figures of the town gathered at a dinner in the Mackworth Arms, presided over by the Mayor, with Mr Vivian on his right, and on his left, John Oakshot and Starling who acted as Vice-Chairmen. The Mayor proposed the health of the Prince Consort, the Prince of Wales and the rest of the Royal Family. This was followed by a toast to the Lord Bishop of the Diocese, about whom at this time, Starling at least must have had very mixed feelings.[7]

It then fell to Starling to propose the toast to the County Members, C R M Talbot and H H Vivian. He reminded his audience of the recent political contest which had produced so gratifying a result for Swansea. He pointed out that one of its happiest aspects was that party rivalry could be so soon forgotten once the event was over, lost in the general respect felt for the two gentlemen elected, not only in their individual capacities but as members representing the whole of the county.

In addition Starling had to respond to the toast to 'The Harbour Trust and Port of Swansea', linked with his own name. In proposing the toast, G T Stroud had paid tribute to the able body of public-spirited men responsible for its affairs, including the provision of extensive floating accommodation and the forthcoming completion of the new western docks (the South Dock). In replying, Starling had to admit that he had had reservations about the siting of the docks, but once they were commenced, he had done everything in his power to see the scheme was carried through successfully in the hope that the increased facilities for goods would lead to an increase in trade generally.[8]

With Bridgend being described as the 'County Town' and Swansea claiming to be 'the principal borough in Wales', the growing polarisation of Glamorgan into East and West was going on apace. This became particularly apparent during the Quarter Sessions of April 1861. 'The Swansea Herald' had been one of two local papers carrying notices of county business until it was decided to limit such

6 C May 1 1857, p 8
7 C Jan 29 1858, p 5
8 *Ibid*

notices to 'The Cambrian' in order to bring Swansea into line with Cardiff which had only 'The Cardiff Guardian', alternatively referred to as 'The Cardiff and Merthyr Guardian'. When Mr Talbot proposed re-instating 'The Swansea Herald', the prompt response was that Cardiff also should have a second paper.[9] Fear that this would trigger off demands by other towns such as Merthyr led to the loss of the motion, but the matter re-surfaced two years later when a choice was called for between 'The Cardiff and Merthyr Guardian' and 'The Cardiff Times' to represent the east of the County.

Although the latter had the larger circulation, especially in the Valleys, Mr R Oliver Jones advocated keeping 'The Guardian' as the older paper with more regular and cultivated readers. Mr Grenfell, on the other hand, considered the ordinary working man needed a newspaper for its notices far more than the professional reader. He particularly deprecated the polarisation of the County into east and west, a division reinforced by the erection of two county prisons. He proposed the amendment that 'The Cardiff Times' be substituted for 'The Guardian', while George Clark of Dowlais proposed, as a solution, advertising in more than two papers. In the event, both amendments were lost, the second undoubtedly helped on its way to defeat by Starling's characteristic query how much they would have to pay for the advertisements. R O Jones informed him the cost would be £45 per paper![10]

At the Sheriff's Ordinary at the 1864 Quarter Sessions in Swansea, it was George Clark who proposed the toast to 'The Town and Trade of Swansea'. As a representative of the interests of the north of the County, he paid special tribute to 'General Joshua Williams' of the Vale of Neath Railway, and to the Harbour Trust, coupling with this the name of the Mayor of Swansea, Charles Bath. In replying, the Mayor admitted that he felt somewhat out of place in the presence 'of a gentleman ... the Chairman of the Harbour Trust, who was always most active and foremost in promoting any and every measure which had a tendency to improve the trade of the port.'[11]

Two years later, Starling had a chance to answer for himself.

George Clark again proposed the toast to 'The Town and Trade of Swansea' when the Spring Assizes of March 1866 visited the town. He playfully pointed out his own resemblance to the majority of prisoners about to appear in court as 'not being from Wales but an importation'. As an outsider he was perhaps better able to appreciate the merits of the town. Among these was the advantage of being able to 'boast of more able and practical men of business' than Cardiff and Newport, the other centres of commerce with which, as a resident of Dowlais, he was involved. With the toast, he coupled the name of one of its most able men, Mr Starling Benson, the Chairman of the Harbour Trust.

Starling's reply was typically brief and unassuming. All connected with the port must be very satisfied with the unanimity which had lately characterised the various local authorities, leading to the flourishing condition of the trade of the town. He could only say on behalf of the Harbour Trustees that they would

9   C April 12 1861, p 8
10   C April 10 1863, p 8
11   C March 18 1864, p 6

endeavour to accommodate all the trade which Mr Clark or any other merchant would send them.[12]

The acuteness which, as we shall see, Starling displayed in the business of the Harbour Trust was equally directed to other questions affecting the affairs of his adopted town. As a member of the County Finance Committee which met before each Quarter Sessions, he kept his usual watchful eye on expenditure. The question of tolls was one in which he felt a personal involvement. He was curious to know why the £1800 to be contributed by Swansea in turnpike tolls had been increased to £2500.[13]

The following year, 1865, at the corresponding meeting, he again queried the amount required by the County Roads Board, viz £2406 2s 3d. Referring to the £1000 included in this as provision for the erection of new toll-houses, he suggested it might be better to rent these at first rather than build houses that might later have to be altered or removed. There were varying opinions about the viability of such an idea. The Clerk argued they had no power to adopt this course. Indeed there was some uncertainty whether payment of tolls could be exacted in the Swansea district and in view of this, T E Thomas, who had been present at the County Board meeting, advocated leaving the matter for further clarification. Eventually the matter was left in the hands of the officials.[14]

Some situations would seem to cast their shadows before them, revealing even then problems that still bedevil local politics. In 1867, in the Finance Meeting before the Easter Quarter Sessions, Starling was again anxious to discover how the County rate was evaluated for the various parishes. He knew there was great dissatisfaction in some of them over discrepancies in the rate fixed. The Clerk of the Peace explained that this was assessed by valuers who were paid by percentage. The Chairman added that he believed that this was 2% on the rate of valuation. Starling was obviously not satisfied. He wanted to know if there was any right of appeal if it was felt an overcharge had been made.[15] Two years later Starling was back in the same arena, proposing, in the Finance Committee of the October Quarter Sessions for 1869, a motion that, in connection with the County rate, various assessment committees of the County be directed to revise their assessments in several parishes and report to the Court of the Quarter Sessions, a necessary measure because of the large number of discrepancies.[16]

Starling was equally energetic in the struggle against the rigorous restrictions imposed under the Cattle Diseases Act on the movement of cattle in rural areas as a result of the serious outbreak of Foot and Mouth Disease in the summer of 1866. This, as he now knew well from first hand acquaintance with the plight of agriculture in Gower, had serious consequences for the small farmer who had no means of advertising what animals he had for sale and who therefore depended almost entirely on the local market or fair for their disposal.

By the time of the October Quarter Sessions, the danger of infection had receded as far as Glamorgan was concerned, and Starling begged the magistrates

---

12   C March 9 1866, p 5
13   C April 8 1864, p 8
14   C April 7 1865, p 8
15   C April 12 1867, p 3
16   C Oct 22 1869, p 3?

to relax the restrictions on markets and fairs which, in Swansea at least, might be safely held for the sale of cattle belonging to the County, though not for animals imported from outside. He had strong support from Mr Vivian. Mr Penrice and Mr Grenfell also felt that present restrictions were discriminating unfairly against the farmers of South Wales, and, in spite of a strongly worded letter of opposition from Mr Talbot, the Court decided, by a majority of 17 to 7, to apply to the Privy Council for exemption from the general order, as the most westerly counties of England, Monmouth, Hereford and Gloucestershire, had already done.[17]

The following spring the situation regarding the free movement of cattle had still not been resolved completely. A memorial had been received from the inhabitants of Cowbridge seeking the resumption of the customary fair. The Chairman held out little hope of the Government allowing the free movement of cattle while cases of the disease remained anywhere in the country for fear of infected animals being smuggled in. Mr Vivian, however, felt the Court should emphasise the freedom of the County from any infection, making it clear their application referred only to movement of animals within Glamorgan. He accordingly moved that a memorial be sent to the Home Secretary, asking for the customary country fair to be restored. This was seconded by Theodore Talbot who obviously did not share his father's fear that, without the continuing restriction, the disease might still spread into South Wales.[18]

His ongoing concern with the administration of the Contagious Diseases (Animals) Act was again evident when, in the Finance Committee of the October Quarter Sessions of 1869, Starling proposed a Committee be appointed to look over the Act and advise generally at the next session. As the Committee's report might take some little time, he advised that those who were magistrates for the Petty Sessional Division should be appointed, in conjunction with the police superintendents, as Acting Committees with full powers to operate as Inspectors under the Act until the next session. By this time, he was himself involved in the Gower Petty Sessions which he could attend near home. This proposition was duly approved.[19]

It was not only Starling, however, who was taking an interest in local affairs. In the list of new magistrates for the County in February 1867 there had appeared the name of Colonel Henry Roxby Benson.[20] Now retired on half-pay from the Army, Henry was spending much of his time with his half-brother at Fairy Hill, though his address was given in 'The Cambrian' of the following week as 'Tyrlandwr'.[21]

The ensuing Spring Assizes were held in Swansea before Sir Henry Keating. For some reason, the High Sheriff's Ordinary, held at the ever popular Mackworth Arms, had been less widely advertised and, as a result, was less well attended than usual. Starling was there, however, as was Henry whose son, William, would within ten years, marry the daughter of the High Sheriff for that

17 C Oct 19 1866, p 3
18 C April 12 1867, p 3
19 C Oct 22 1869, p 6.
20 C Feb 15 1867, p 4
21 C Feb 22 1867, pp 4-5 (Edltorial)

37 Starling Benson in later life
Courtesy of JREB

38 Henry Roxby
Benson and Family,
including William
Denman Benson
UCS/BC Courtesy
of JREB

year, Thomas Penrice of Kilvrough. When the High Sheriff proposed the toast to the Armed Services, it was, very appropriately, Henry who responded, while Starling responded to the toast in honour of the Harbour Trustees.[22]

Travelling from one end of the County to the other was not always easy. The meeting of the Magistracy in Bridgend later in March to elect a Chief Constable of the County Police was held up on account of the difficulty experienced by the Swansea contingent in reaching their destination. The 'Swansea Express' was snowed in on the Margam Moors, but in the end they managed to get through so that eighty-one County Justices, including Starling, were present to appoint Lieutenant Colonel Lindsay to the post.[23]

When next the Assizes were held in Swansea in the Spring of 1868, the High Sheriff was George Clark. He had been given a rousing farewell at Merthyr by a large deputation of local tradesmen, many of whom had then travelled all the way to Swansea. Both Starling and Henry were among the general company at the High Sheriff's Ordinary. In the toast to the Army, the Navy, Militia and Volunteers, the High Sheriff had referred to Welshmen in Her Majesty's services, associating with it the name of Colonel Benson. In responding, Henry assured the company that, next to the good will of Her Majesty, there was nothing the Army more appreciated and valued than the good opinion of their fellow countrymen. It takes rather a stretch of the imagination to see Henry Benson as a Welshman, but he apparently accepted his new nationality without comment![24]

The calendar for the Assizes covered a large number of crimes, including a case against a suspected Fenian, named Doran who, with nine others, was charged with treason-felony under provisions of the Act of the 11th and 12th Vic *cap* 62. A 'cell' of Fenianism, with its members administering the oath to each other and swearing allegiance to the Irish Republic, had now virtually been established, declaring itself ready to take up arms in the defence of the Republic.[25]

Starling was once more serving on the Grand Jury. He might well have recalled the experiences of Tiny's grandmother, Mary Baird, who was the wife of a serving soldier in Ireland at the time of the threatened Napoleonic invasion. She had described graphically the unrest of the native population in a series of letters preserved in the Wightman family archives and ultimately passed on to Mrs Baird's Benson descendants,[26] Henry too, with Tiny, had spent much of his Army career in Ireland and had reason to be keenly aware of the tension between the Nationalists and their British rulers.

Of more local interest was the case of the Duke of Beaufort v George Byng Morris, brother of Sir John Morris from whom T S Benson had leased Sketty Park in the 1830s and a keen opponent, as we have seen, of the 1852 Swansea Waterworks Bill.[27] The present dispute was over a strip of land, claimed by the Duke as Lord of the Manor and by Byng Morris as owner of the railway from

22   C March 8 1867, p 8
23   C March 22 1867, p 8
24   C March 6 1868, p 5
25   C March 13 1808, p 8
26   UCS/BC, Mary Baird to her cousin Elizabeth Morris
27   *Vide* p 128, n 51

Swansea to Oystermouth. Judgment was given in favour of the Plaintiff, with the derisory sum of 1/- damages.[28]

In spite of the large number of cases dealt with by the Assizes, there still remained a considerable number of prisoners to appear before the ensuing Quarter Sessions in April, the result of the rapid growth in Glamorganshire of an increasingly heterogeneous population. Previously prisoners from the west of the County had been tried in Swansea at the one Quarter Sessions while those from the east had appeared in Cardiff at the next. Under a new system, all cases were now being heard at alternating venues.

The Grand Jury had been dismissed as recently as March 8, and by April 7 there were thirty new cases for trial. It was obvious that the County needed two judges to deal with this workload and it was hoped the Court of the Quarter Sessions would make that need known in strong terms.[29] Mr Vivian accordingly saw the Secretary of State on their behalf but the only satisfaction he had received by the next Quarter Sessions was that extra judges were about to be appointed and the case of Glamorgan would be reviewed accordingly.[30]

'The Cambrian' had drawn attention to the significant discrepancy between the number of prisoners tried and of those found guilty. Of the thirty-four prisoners charged, only seventeen were convicted. These came mainly from Merthyr and other densely populated areas. As there had to be a fair amount of incriminating evidence presented to the local magistrates before they committed a prisoner for trial, it was surprising that there were so few convictions. 'The Cambrian' queried the efficiency of the police and the tendency of some magistrates 'to pass the buck' by handing on the accused to a higher court. It also considered the reluctance of witnesses to give evidence in Court and of juries to reach an unbiassed verdict. If, in the end, the prisoner was proved innocent, a preliminary committal nevertheless involved a slur. It also meant a loss of earnings to the jurymen who had to miss work to attend, as well as extra expense for the ratepayers.[31]

The concern voiced in 'The Cambrian' Editorial was justified by the outcome of the case of Henry Evans who appeared before the Spring Assizes of 1869, charged with the murder of John Morgan, aged 71, of Henglawdd. So disgusted was the visiting Judge, Chief Baron Sir Fitzroy Kelly - 'one of the ablest and most careful Judges that adorn the Bench' - with the conduct of the common jury who had returned a verdict of 'not guilty' that he refused to try three remaining cases of perjury with any of the juries empowered throughout the Assizes. The impression being given to criminals was that common juries in the county (his strictures did not apply to the Special Juries) could be so manipulated that the guilty party would, in the last resort, be saved by their verdict.[32]

He had previously told the Grand Jury that he regretted not being able, on his first visit to the County, to congratulate them, as he had the adjoining counties. The calendar included a foul murder, where the evidence was mainly

28 C March 20 1868, p 8
29 C April 10 1868, p 8
30 C July 3 1668, p 6
31 C Oct 30 1868, p 5 (Editorial).
32 C March 26 1869, p 5

circumstantial, and several cases of manslaughter, either accidental or through a miscarriage of treatment, such as the death of a woman treated by a farrier for a disease of the breast. He stressed particularly the need for educating the lower orders, as well as introducing stronger measures for repressing excessive drinking.[33]

Far less critical was the Rt Hon Sir John Mellor at the Glamorgan Spring Assizes in 1871 when Starling was again on the Grand Jury. The Judge praised the public spirit of so many gentlemen who were 'ready to share in the administration of criminal justice.' Although he could not congratulate them on the small number of cases to be tried, at least there was not as much violence as he had expected in view of the size of the population.[34]

The following year the Spring Assizes gave Starling a chance to meet an old acquaintance. The Hon Sir William Grove had been a colleague in the early days of the Royal Institution and had more recently been involved in the same law suits as Florance. Now he was paying his first visit as Judge to his native town, an occasion marked by the reading of a special address by the Town Clerk, R A Essery, who had succeeded Mansfield.[35]

There was some dissatisfaction that the Assizes Service should, that year of all years, have been moved from the parish church of St Mary's to the more distant Trinity Church. A somewhat xenophobic correspondent to 'The Cambrian' felt it wrong that a Swansea man, visiting his home for the first time as a judge, should have to proceed with his retinue to a Church out of the centre of the town because the pulpit at St Mary's had been previously engaged for a German Jew to deliver a sermon few could understand because of his foreign accent.[36]

Mr Justice Grove's next visit to the Glamorgan Assizes in the summer of 1873 was even less auspicious.[37] There were very few from Swansea at the High Sheriff's Ordinary at the Royal Hotel in Cardiff, and in the actual Court, F E Stacey, the High Sheriff, was himself excused further attendance on condition that the Under-Sheriff was present. Unfortunately the Under-Sheriff, L V Sherley, was late in arriving at the Court and earned a severe rebuke from the Judge. The noise from the adjacent Assembly Room where a presentation party to the Mayor was in progress had drowned the speakers, and on learning the Under-Sheriff was not yet in Court, Sir William Grove had considered adjourning proceedings, but instead 'he animadverted strongly' on the disrespect shown to the Court and, on the Under-Sheriff's arrival, promptly fined him twenty pounds.[38]

At the beginning of the previous year there had also been trouble with those responsible for law and order. The Governor of Cardiff Gaol and his wife who served as Matron had been suspended from their duties and later appeared at the 1872 Epiphany Quarter Sessions in Cardiff on a charge of claiming for and travelling in second class railway carriages while paying only third class fare.[39] As a result, a special committee was formed to report on the management of the

33   C March 19 1869, p 6
34   C March 10 1871, p 8,
35   C March 15 1872, p 6; *cf* Editorial, p 2
36   C March 15 1872, p 8
37   Western Mail, July 12 1873, pp 2 & 3
38   C July 18 1873, p 6
39   C Jan 5 1872, p 8

County Prisons. This consisted of Starling, J Coke Fowler (the Deputy Chairman of the Court, who the following July was appointed Stipendiary Magistrate for Swansea), H H Vivian, John Dillwyn Llewelyn, C W David and the Revd C R Knight. It later emerged that the Swansea Prison Governor had also been cheating on train fares. He, however, was only censured and asked to repay any sums received in excess of the amount spent, but the Cardiff Governor and his wife were sacked.[40]

A special meeting of the Court of the Quarter Sessions was held in Neath on March 21 to draw up a short list for the appointment of a new Governor at Cardiff. Here, with the wisdom of hindsight, it was decided that in future the Governor and Matron should not be related and, in view of the ex-Governor's claim that he had taken his wife with him on his travels because her health was affected by the unhealthy position of their house within the prison walls, it was recommended that they should reside outside.

Starling's favoured candidate, Captain Knight, was eventually outvoted in favour of a Captain Knox. The latter's qualifications were such that no one could have questioned his suitability, certainly not Starling Benson. As a Captain in the 4th Battalion of the Rifle Brigade, Knox had gained a Crimean medal with four bars. He also held the Légion d'Honneur and Turkish medals and the Victoria Cross, while among his testimonials was one from General Sir William Knollys, KCB, Comptroller to HRH, the Prince of Wales.[41]

In spite of the reprimand, the Governor of Swansea Prison continued to enjoy the confidence of the Magistrates, and his sudden death, in the summer of 1873, after escorting prisoners to Broadmoor, came as a shock to those who had known him.[42] The vacancy thus caused was soon filled by the appointment of Captain Knight, so in the end Starling got his man.[43]

Glamorgan's application for the services of two judges was shortly granted, but even so, the Assizes still lasted twelve or thirteen days. It was, therefore essential that the judges should be made comfortable during that time.[44] Almost twenty years earlier, as a Swansea Town Councillor, Starling had served on a Committee appointed to look into the question of judges' lodgings![45] This was a question into which he would have had a special insight from his knowledge of some of the problems encountered by Henry's father-in-law, Sir William Wightman, as he travelled the circuit, accompanied very often by his other son-in-law, the writer, Matthew Arnold, who acted as his marshal. It was therefore natural that he should now be the one to propose that 'the Court agree to provide half the expense of the judges' lodgings at Cardiff and Swansea'.

The present house in Swansea which belonged to the Corporation on a sixty-year lease was let out during most of the year on the understanding that the tenants moved out when the judges came into residence. Mr Justice Bovill had apparently been delighted with the accommodation provided. Another house next door to the present lodging was now available and might be used for a second

40   C Jan 19 1872, p 5
41   C April 12 1872, p 3
42   C July 4 1873, p 8
43   C July 18 1873, p 5
44   C Oct 23 1874, p 6
45   C Dec 19 1856, p 5

judge. On Starling's proposition, seconded by Mr Rhys Rhys, it was left to the Chairman, with Mr Vivian and the Revd C R Knight, to arrange concerted action between the two towns.[46]

Swansea was thus able to provide residences for two judges whereas Cardiff had failed to find accommodation for the second judge. It was accordingly decided in the summer of 1875 that only the Spring Assizes should be held in Cardiff while the two other Assizes would be in Swansea.[47] The previous Spring Assizes had, however, been held in Swansea and was the first time for two judges to visit the town. These were Baron Cleasby and Mr Justice Mellor, and on this occasion Starling was foreman of the Grand Jury.[48]

The Midsummer Assizes of 1876 also held a special interest for Starling, for two reasons. First, in proposing the Toast of the Mayor and Corporation at the Sheriff's Ordinary, he was able to pay tribute to James Livingston, one of the most energetic new members of the Harbour Trust. No one, he said, had performed the office of Mayor more efficiently than Mr Livingston.[49]

Secondly the appearance in court of his nephew William provided Starling with a personal interest in the current proceedings. According to his Oxford mentor, the distinguished Dr Jowett, William Denman Benson had sacrificed his degree at Balliol to his rowing prowess. He had later, however, justified his name ('William' after his maternal grandfather, Judge Wightman, and 'Denman' after Sir William's colleague, the Lord Chief Justice, Thomas Denman) by becoming on June 6 1874 a barrister of the Inner Temple, and subsequently, like his uncle Florance, appearing frequently on the South Wales circuit.

In the 1876 Assizes his fortunes as an advocate were mixed.[50] His impassioned defence of thirty-five year old Hannah Wilks, accused of killing her illegitimate child by prolonged neglect, failed to convince the jury of her innocence. He fared no better when he appeared for the prosecution in the case of Mary Calman, a married woman with a child in her arms, who was accused of unlawfully wounding Maria Lewis. On the other hand, his prosecution of an Italian seaman named Martino Severo for stealing a bag of bedclothes and four pairs of boots from Evan Davies as the result of an incident on the railway led to a conviction. Similarly, his defence of Edward Harries, a lodging-house keeper, charged with wounding one of his lodgers who had returned home drunk, succeeded in securing a 'Not Guilty' verdict.[51]

Starling may have lacked the 'impassioned' oratory of his nephew,[52] but he was still very much in demand when toasts were to be proposed or responded to. Whether he was invited to speak because he was known to be attending or whether he attended because he had been asked to speak, whenever Starling was present at a public function, his name was sure to be on the list of speakers. When, for example, in the Parliamentary election of 1865, his old colleague, E M Richards, failed to be elected Liberal member for Honiton, his fellow Liberals

46 C Oct 23 1874, p 6
47 C Aug 6 1875, p 5 & Aug 13, p 5
48 C March 5 1875, p 6
49 C Aug 4 1876, p 3
50 *Ibid*
51 *Vide* C Oct 20 1876, p 7; July 6 1877, p 8; Aug 3 1877, p 5
52 C Aug 4 1876, p 3

in his home town, partly out of sympathy for the disappointment but also as a tribute to his public services to Swansea, arranged a dinner in his honour. Here Starling proposed the toast 'To the Staples of the District'.[53]

Though never a voluble speaker, he always had something relevant to say. The one occasion where he apparently excelled himself was the banquet in honour of F A Yeo as Mayor, on the night of Wednesday, December 9 1874. Proposing 'The Members for the County and Borough', he jocularly pointed out that, seated as he was between Mr Dillwyn and Mr Charles Bath, Mr Dillwyn's Conservative rival in a recent election, he could not very well enter the arena of politics in his speech. Even so, one of his pleasantest reminiscences was that, although they fought political battles during the election, once the election was over, these were forgotten and the successful candidate was forthwith received as the representative, not just of the party electing him, but of the whole constituency. The toast, we are told, was drunk with great warmth. The remarks had obviously struck a sympathetic note with his audience, particularly Mr Dillwyn who, on this occasion at least, was pleased to refer to Starling as 'my old friend'.[54]

Equally well received were his remarks at the Mayor's Banquet of March 1876 when Sir Daniel Gooch, representing the Railway Companies, proposed 'The Prosperity of the Harbour Trust', coupled with the names of Starling Benson and F A Yeo. Sir Daniel referred to the good offices of Mr Vivian and one or two other Trustees in approaching the GWR Directors in connection with the new dock at Fabian's Bay which, as we shall see, was so much exercising Starling's mind at the time. Realising that a large part of local produce would have to be shipped at Swansea, the GWR had sought to meet the requirements of the Harbour Trust as far as possible.

Loudly cheered as he responded on a subject so near to his heart, Starling said his remembrance of harbour affairs went back further than most of his audience's. Then, their revenue had been £4000 per annum, and a 400-ton vessel was rarely seen. To him the port was the backbone of the town whose prosperity was due to its rail and port accommodation. In order to complete the new east dock so that they might receive revenue from it, the Trustees had approached the great railway companies and, with their cooperation, had been able to obtain the Bill which was before the House of Commons during the current Parliamentary session. Rather than let wharfs to individual applicants, they had preferred that the Corporation should help guarantee the money needed and then make their own letting arrangements. The Trustees had zealously endeavoured to do their best for the town, a view endorsed by Frank Yeo.[55]

One important toast to the Swansea Harbour Trust was proposed on the occasion of the Lord Mayor of London's visit to the town on August 2 1877, the day before he travelled to Pontypridd to present awards to those involved in the heroic rescue work carried out after the terrible explosion at the Tynewydd Pit in the Rhondda Valley. At the banquet given in the Lord Mayor's honour by the Mayor of Swansea, the toast to the Harbour Trust was given by E M Richards

53 C Aug 4 1865, p 5
54 C Dec 17 1874, p 8
55 C March 10 1876, p 8

178

who followed the now established pattern of associating with it the name of its Chairman. To this Starling duly responded.[56]

He had already made it clear to his fellow Trustees that he considered the time had come for him to retire from many of his commitments. When, the day after the Lord Mayor of London's visit, Starling proposed the Toast to the Army, Navy and Reserve Forces at the Sheriff's Ordinary at the Mackworth Arms Hotel, the toast was, according to 'The Cambrian', 'drunk heartily'. In proposing 'The Town and Trade of Swansea', the High Sheriff, Herbert Lloyd, linked with it the name of the Chairman of the Harbour Trust. He expressed the hope that Mr Benson would be induced to continue in that post, or at any rate, that he would live for many years to come. Even if he did not hold the post of chairman, he hoped that he would consent to direct the affairs of the Harbour Trust in the future.

In his reply Starling gave it as his opinion that, when a person reached a certain age, he should retire, a view strongly disputed by his audience. No one, he claimed, was irreplaceable. Though current trade was in a depressed state, he was 'confident it would increase in ratio to the past,' and he was happy to recall the vast increase in harbour receipts during his time in office, from £5000 to £50,000.[57]

A glance back over his forty-five years of public service reveals Starling Benson's steady, unostentatious approach to the problems of his day, his earnestness tempered by an equitable weighing of the pro's and con's of each issue. Free from any vindictiveness or undue social bias, he had throughout his public life held in check any extremes of euphoria or despair. Not a man to set the Thames on fire, he at least helped to fan a steady flame of faith in the future of the port on the Tawe. This he had done without betraying any trace of resentment or envy of the progress being made in other parts of the County during those testing years when Swansea was struggling for recognition in the tough nineteenth century world of industry and commerce.

56   C Aug 3 1877, p 7
57   *Ibid*

Chapter XII

The Swansea Vale Railway

Starling's involvement in his own business interests as well as in the municipal life of his adopted town cannot be separated from his activities in two other sectors, the development of the Swansea Vale Railway and the work of the Swansea Harbour Trust. If a more detailed study of these two aspects of his career has been left to this late point in our story, it is so that they can be explored in greater depth without holding up too much the overall picture of the man responsible for much of the spade-work in both fields.

The Swansea Canal, stretching from Brewery Bank in the borough of Swansea to Hen Noyadd in the parish of Ystradgynlais had been completed in 1798. This was a welcome alternative to transport by pack-horse and a great incentive to the industrial development of the area. Wharfs were built on the canal with connecting tramways to industrial concerns of the valley. At Gurnos, for example, railroads had been constructed to carry coal from Cwmllynfell and Cwmtwrch to be loaded into canal boats, while there were wharfs at Clydach and Pontardawe. The linking up of industrial railroads by a track over which steam locomotives could be run would obviously revolutionise the traffic of the area.

Most of the trade on the canal came from the upper part of the valley and among those paying tolls on the goods being conveyed to the coast were John and William Parsons of Pontardawe, James Palmer Budd of Ystalyfera and George Crane of Ynyscedwyn.[1] The Parsons family had been mining in the area since 1829, and in March 1831, as we have seen, John Parsons transferred coal seams at Cwm Cyrnach and Llwyn Erch Edwal, in Glais, to Usborne, Benson & Hart Logan. From June 8 to 11 1831, William Kirkhouse was involved in taking stock of the Graigola Colliery for the company and estimating the value of a tramroad to the Swansea Canal at £1534 2s 6d.[2] Like others involved in industry in the Swansea Valley, the Bensons soon realised that a direct railway line to the port was essential if the coal was to be moved efficiently and economically. His father's vision of such a railway, undoubtedly one of his incentives in buying Tyrllandwr, was to be eventually fulfilled in Starling's creation of the SVR.

On the east side of the river, a waggonway built by Chauncey Townsend, the owner of pits in the Llansamlet area, had been superseded in 1785 by a private canal made by his son-in-law, John Smith. A tramroad of three and a half miles from Gwernllwynchwyth to the White Rock Wharf was built in 1817-19 by John Scott, a London attorney. He had taken over mineral leases from Charles and

---

1 John Henry Davies, History of Pontardawe and District, (Llandybie; Christopher Davies 1967) pp 40-1
2 Kirkhouse Correspondence, Jordan Collection, MS 466 WGRO

Henry Smith, the grandsons of Chauncey Townsend, and had sunk a pit in the vicinity. Scott's venture, however, failed and by 1828 he had sold the pit and the tramroad to Charles Henry Smith, the son of Charles. C H Smith continued to work Scott's pit and his other pits which were served by his tramroad.[3] He also was to play an important part in developing what was to become the Swansea Vale Railway.

In 1835, the idea of extending Scott's Tramroad was being mooted. William Kirkhouse, in a reply dated January 13 to a letter from Charles Tennant, reported that he had had a conversation with Mr Smith on the subject:

> He told me that it was intended to extend it as far as Graigola Colliery which is worked by Messrs Benson & Logan and Parsons and Price which are working annually about 4500 weys of coal, the principal part of which is shipped for Steam Packets abroad; there are other collieries which would all come to this Railroad it being more convenient than to go to the Swansea Canal and they are all on the Eastern side of the Tawe.[4]

One survey had been carried out in 1830.[5] Another was made by Kirkhouse in 1836. He referred to this during the July Quarter Sessions of 1838 at which the value of the part of the Tyrllandwr Estate needed by the Harbour Trust for the New Cut was being assessed.[6]

> I was employed about two years ago to survey a line of railway on the east side of Swansea river. The line was to begin at Gwain-y-coed up the vale of Tawe, about nine miles, and to terminate at Tyrllandwr. The reason it did not go on was that they heard the Neath Abbey Estate was to be sold, and they were waiting till that took place.

This sale was also referred to by Mr Meyrick, the solicitor involved in the Tyrllandwr assessment:

> About two years ago a plan was set out to make a railway down the Vale of Tawe and to terminate at Tyrllandwr. We considered it prudent to wait until the Neath Abbey Estate was sold. The Neath Abbey lands have since been purchased by Mr Price and Mr Benson, and thus every difficulty of carrying on the railway has been removed. After the purchase I went with Mr Price to Mr Benson and we agreed with him for a frontage of 300 feet on Tyrllandwr at £40 for every 100 feet making £120 a year.

We already know that the Bensons were fully aware of the potential of the Tyrllandwr estate which they had purchased on behalf of Mrs Meux in 1834.

3 P R Reynolds, Scott's Tramroad, Llansamlet, Journal of the Railway & Canal Historical Society 1980, Vol xxvi, p 85*ff*
4 Kirkhouse, *op cit*, WGRO
5 D/D SB 12/7 WGRO; *vide* p 22
6 C July 21 1838, p 3

Firstly it was to become of major importance in the development of Swansea as a harbour and by 1836 it could also play a valuable part, if the proposed railroad were constructed, as an outlet for their Graigola coal.

In a survey of the Vale of Swansea which the Bensons had made in 1840 Mr G Bush, engineer to the Taff Vale Railway, pointed out that 'three miles on the western side was equal to the cost of ... sixteen miles on the eastern side'.[7] From this time on, there was a continued advance in the purchase or lease of the land required for the project and in negotiations with the Earl of Jersey.

On December 15 1843 an agreement was made between John Nicholas Lucas of Stouthall and Starling Benson, who by now had been joined by another interested party, Joseph Martin of Glyncollen. This leased them a right of way for the construction of any 'Railway Road or Canal' on the 'farm and lands called respectively Garthen and Cefnygarth ... situate in the parish of Llansamlet' for 999 years.[8]

The partners, Starling Benson, Joseph Martin and others, who were intending to form the Swansea Vale Railway Company, made a much more important and complicated agreement on April 27 1844 with C H Smith.[9] Smith had held a lease of the residue of 99 years from 1833 of Smith's Canal and Scott's Railway partly on the lands of the Earl of Jersey and partly on the lands of Mrs Lucy Bowen in Llansamlet. His use of the railway was, however, limited to carrying the mineral produce of the lands of the Earl and Mrs Bowen. At this point he had applied for the waiving of the restriction; in consideration of this he would pay a toll of 1d a ton on produce other than the Earl's. Provided this concession was made, Smith agreed to repair Scott's Railway and to extend it from White Rock to the boundary of the lands of T S Benson at Pentreguinea (viz Tyrllandwr). This was to be done within nine months of notice being given by the partners. They, for their part, had to lay down a line from Pentreguinea to the proposed terminus and a line from the boundary of Lucy Bowen's land to the tramroad leading to the lower level of the Graigola Colliery.

The agreement also stated that S Benson and J Martin would act as provisional Directors of the Company and proceed with the allotment of shares and preparation of a Deed of Settlement.

Further progress was made by an agreement[10] of September 25, in which J Martin granted rights of way and leases of land in the Glyn y Gorse, Drumma and Birchgrove Estates. The necessary agreement between C H Smith and the Earl of Jersey was signed on December 30 giving the former the right to extend his tramway over the lands of the latter.[11]

On February 20 Lucy Bowen was involved in yet another agreement, together with Arthur Francis Gregory, by which lands in Gwernllwynchwyth, Cwm and Glyn y Gorse were leased to Starling and Joseph Martin. It is interesting to note that the agreement refers to land required for making a station and that a plan of the SVR indicates a station at Cwm.[12]

7   C Nov 24 1846, later published as pamphlet, Dec 1 1846
8   BR MS
9   BR MS
10   BR MS
11   BR MS
12   BR MS

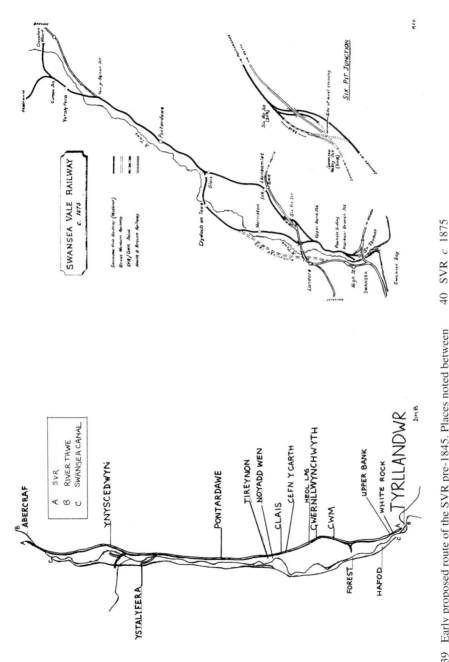

39 Early proposed route of the SVR pre-1845. Places noted between
Forest and Pontardawe are those where the Company acquired land or
rights of way

40 SVR *c* 1875

There followed on March 22 1845 the purchase of parts of Tyr Evan Llwyd Farm, Llansamlet.[13] The agreement was between Starling and Joseph Martin of Glyncollen and a local farmer, Benjamin Evans, for the 'sale and purchase of Leasehold Lands part of the Tyr Evan Llwyd farm situate in the parish of Llansamlet, Glamorganshire.' The sum paid was 'one hundred and thirty four pounds and three shillings of lawful English money.'

A most interesting agreement was made on March 25 1845.[14] That was the lease of land at Glais farm for 99 years by T S Benson to S Benson and J Martin. The circumstances relating to the family's possession of this farm are discussed elsewhere.[15] Amongst the other portions of land leased in this agreement was a tract of land in Tyrllandwr from Pentreguinea to the land purchased by the Swansea Harbour Trust, of sufficient width for the proposed railway, with branches to communicate with the wharfs along the banks of the New Cut, and for a terminus.

Work on the project was clearly advancing as may be seen from an advertisement in 'The Cambrian' of April 26 1845, for tenders to extend Scott's Railway. Further information is given in a letter[16] written by Starling to the Welsh Midland Railway Company on May 2 1845. This company proposed a railway to link the Midlands with Swansea and other ports and was supported by many notable South Wales figures such as J P Budd and, indeed, Joseph Martin. The WMR had asked for information regarding the use of the SVR to reach a possible terminus to their railway at Swansea. Starling described the line as follows:

1 The Railway is formed, by agreement with the Earl of Jersey and Mr Smith, in connexion with Mr Smith's road made in 1816, and the line now in course of Execution and relaying, which can be completed without Act of Parliament, will extend about $6\frac{1}{2}$ miles, commencing at the lower end of the Harbour, and Terminating at the Graigola Collieries. It was further our intention to Extend the main line under Act of Parliament, to Gwainclawdd at the head of the Swansea Valley, with a branch from Ynysymond to the Cwm Avon Valley, the whole of which was surveyed for us by Mr George Bush of the Llanelly & Taff Vale railways in 1840, when the plans were deposited and Parliamentary Notices given; but which notices we have postponed until the present year, in consequence of opposing interests, which would have entailed much expense and risk in forming a way to the terminus, but are now entirely removed.

2 The land between the terminus and Graigola is held by us under Agreements for terms of 99, or 999 years, in most cases with the power to purchase; and where the landowner had not the power to sell, it is proposed to do so under future parliamentary powers. The control of Mr Smith's road is held for 999 years on the payment of 1d per ton per mile.

3 At the terminus we have in our own hands merely a wharf of 250 feet frontage and about an acre of ground adjoining the road for a station. At the

13   BR MS
14   BR MS
15   Will of Henry Roxby Benson dated November 7 1890. Office Copy issued by Somerset House
16   SVR Letter Book PRO RAIL 679/12

Neath turnpike road we have also about 8 acres for engines and station. It has been deemed more advisable that each trader should take of the landowner such extent of wharfage as he individually requires, but the line of river frontage east of the navigable cut and river, at present almost entirely unoccupied and approachable only by the railway, is about 5000 feet, whilst a communication over the swivel bridge would connect the railway with wharfage to the extent of 4000 feet additional making together 9000 feet in the best part of the river.

4 The line was fenced this Spring, the Contracts for relaying parts of the road are now in Execution, and the whole of the Contracts will probably be settled this week.

In accordance with the Act for the Registration of Joint Stock Companies, 1844, the SVR had to draw up a Deed of Settlement.[17] This was an agreement of July 26 1845 between Starling Benson, Joseph Martin, William Meyrick and C H Smith of the first part, William Stroud of the second part and other parties of the third part and stated that the first object of the Company should be to make a railway from a terminus at Tyrllandwr to a point of junction with Scott's Railway at Pentreguinea; the second object should be to make a railway from the junction with Scott's Railway on the Old Neath Road to the point at which the line of the proposed railway intersects the tramroad leading to the Lower Level of the Graigola Collieries; and the third object should be to extend the railway up the Swansea valley and make branches as determined by the shareholders.

The Company had a capital of £20,000 in 400 shares of £50 each. The directors were Starling Benson, Joseph Martin, William Meyrick and C H Smith; Starling Benson and Joseph Martin being the managers, William Stroud the auditor and Thomas Attwood the solicitor.

Another document of July 26[18] transferred to the SVR all the agreements that Starling Benson and Joseph Martin had made on behalf of the Company. £1000 was allotted to each of them in 50 shares on which £20 was considered to be paid. The complete list of shareholders[19] when the Company was registered on August 5 was as follows:

Starling Benson	50	William Meyrick	40
Joseph Martin	174	Adam Murray	20
Richard Meux Benson	30	Henry Reynolds	25
Florance Benson	40	C H Smith	1
A L Gower	10		
R F Gower	10		

It was essential now to consider the development of the railway up the Swansea Valley. To this end a 'Licence to purchase and hold land' was granted to the Company on October 17 1845.[20] The licence allowed the purchase of the

17　BR MS
18　BR MS
19　SVR Minute Book PRO RAIL 679/2
20　BR MS

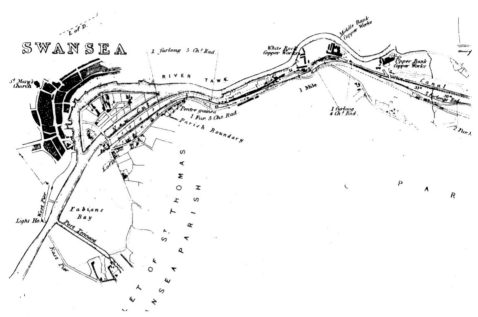

41   Deposited plans of the SVR, 1845, used also by the Swansea Valley Railway, 1847

BR MS

42   Detailed Section of above

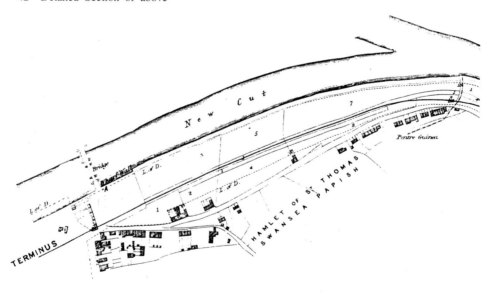

land required for the railway from Tyrllandwr to Pontardawe, land for wharfs, warehouses and a station at Tyrllandwr, and land for a station on the north side of the Old Neath Road in Llansamlet.

Two extraordinary meetings of the SVR were held on November 19 and 24 at which it was decided to apply for an Act of Parliament.[21] In preparation for this a Subscription Contract was drawn up on January 14 1846.[22] Among the fourteen signatories were:

> Robert Baxter, a Solicitor, of Westminster
> Henry Roxby Benson, a Captain in the 17th Lancers, then stationed at
>   Brighton
> Richard Meux Benson of Christ Church, Oxford
> Starling Benson, Merchant
> James Palmer Budd, Iron Master, of Ystalyfera
> Joseph Martin of Glyncollen
> Anthony Mervyn Story Maskelyne of Swindon
> William Meyrick of Merthyr
> Charles Henry Smith, Colliery Proprietor of Swansea

The areas of land required for the railway were now mentioned specifically: firstly, from Abercrave Farm, Ystradgynlais, to Tyrllandwr; secondly, land for five branch railways, Pwll Mawr to the Old Rolling Mill on the Lower Forest Farm, Llansamlet; Ynisgeinon Farm, Cilybebyll, passing near to Ystalyfera to the Cwmtwrch Railway Wharf on the north side of the Swansea canal; the junction of the Rivers Twrch and Tawe to the Cwmtwrch Railway Wharf; Ynysyci Farm, Cilybebyll, to Yniscedwin Iron Works, Ystradgynlais; and an extension of the Main Line near Abercrave Farm to Pentre Cribath, Ystradgynlais. Finally the Subscribers agreed to finance the obtaining of an Act of Parliament to enable the works to be embarked upon.

An agreement of February 2 1846 with Joseph Tregelles Price and his partners of the Neath Abbey Coal Company gave the SVR the right to make a railway over Tyr Eynon and Noyadd Wen farms. This was the last portion of land required to give them access to the Graigola Colliery.[23]

At two Extraordinary General Meetings of the Company on March 6 and 7 1846[24] it was decided to purchase the interest of the Earl of Jersey in Scott's Railway for £10,000 to be payable on January 1 1847, and the interest of C H Smith and his lease from the White Rock Company for £20,000 to be represented as 333 shares, £60 of which should be considered paid up. A Supplementary Deed of Settlement followed on April 18 incorporating all the decisions made at the November and March meetings.[25]

By the beginning of 1846 the SVR were holding separate negotiations with both the WMR and the South Wales Railway companies to lease or sell to them their railway and so make a connection with the Midlands either via Brecon and

21 SVR Minute Book PRO RAIL 679/2
22 BR MS
23 BR MS
24 SVR Minute Book PRO RAIL 679/2
25 BR MS

Hereford or via the proposed railway to Gloucester. This would have saved them the expense of further development and provided a great boost to the trade and industry of the valley. The company had indeed been approached by the Welsh Midland Railway in May 1845 for information (see above). In the meantime, on January 14 1846, Florance Benson had been appointed to negotiate with the WMR and the Swansea Canal Navigations to ensure that there would be no opposition to the proposed SVR Bill.[26]

The proposed railway to Gloucester was part of the plan of the South Wales Railway - a company closely associated with the Great Western Railway. Meetings had been held in the more important towns of South Wales in September 1844 at which Charles Russell, the chairman of the GWR, and I K Brunel, the engineer, gave details of a proposed line through South Wales from Newport to Fishguard passing on the north side of Swansea. The meeting at Swansea was chaired by the Mayor who at that time was, indeed, Starling Benson.[27] He, together with Joseph Martin, was a member of the Provisional Committee for the development of the railway and both subscribed for shares in the proposed company.

Later that year the promoters presented a Bill to Parliament. At a meeting of the House of Lords Committee considering the Bill in 1845, Starling gave evidence in support. He first described himself as manager of the Swansea Copper Works and Collieries of the Governor and Company of Copper Miners. He went on to outline the advantages the railway would bring to the trade and industry of Swansea. Further he mentioned the benefit to passenger travel, 'a great portion of it being at present by long tedious and uncertain sea voyages.'[28]

The SWR was incorporated by an Act of August 4 1845, which authorised a line from Fishguard and Pembroke Dock to Chepstow, leaving the rest of the route to Gloucester to be dealt with later.[29] The line was to pass to the north of the town of Swansea and at Llansamlet it was to cross Scott's Railway on the level; this was to be a cause of serious friction between the SWR and the SVR in later years.

As negotiator for the SVR Starling's brother, Florance, met the Directors of the SWR to consider a lease of the SVR to the SWR but when the Directors discovered that the SVR was contemplating an amalgamation with the WMR the discussions were terminated.[30] However, the WMR Bill was rejected by Parliament on March 3 1846. When the scheme was abandoned many angry shareholders lost a great deal of their investment.[31]

On July 7 1846 the SVR Bill was read for the third time in the House of Commons and passed to the House of Lords. At this stage the Select Committee on Standing Orders pointed out that notice had not been given to the Duke of

26 SVR Minute Book PRO RAIL 679/2
27 Railway Chronicle, Sept 28 1844
28 BR MS
29 8 & 9 Victoria *cap* cxc
30 SWR Minute Book PRO RAIL 640/3
31 Railway Times, Aug 22 1846

Beaufort that the line of the SVR was to cross three water courses, the Glais, Brain and Tawe, of which he claimed ownership. The SVR Parliamentary agents argued that since the Duke of Beaufort did not own the land on either side, the wording 'Duke of Beaufort' should be changed to 'landowner'. All this delay meant that the Bill was not presented by July 20 which was the final day allowed by the House of Lords for a second reading in that Session. Thus the Bill failed on a trivial technical point.[32]

On July 27 the SWR obtained a second Act authorising a deviation of their line to bring it nearer to Swansea with a branch from Landore to High Street and to link up with the Oystermouth Railway at Brewery Bank. The Act also authorised an extension from Chepstow to link up with a line from Gloucester.[33]

In August SVR negotiations with the SWR were resumed and on August 17 the former agreed to sell their undertaking for £74,516. Florance was authorised to make the offer and 'to finally conclude any arrangement on their behalf'.[34] On August 19 he forwarded copies of the SVR resolutions and balance sheet, together with details of the terminus at St Thomas, to Louis Vigurs, the SWR deputy chairman. He also suggested that the £74,516 could be paid in SWR shares.[35]

On August 20 the SWR resolved to pay £70,000 in shares subject to the approval of I K Brunel on his return from the Continent and an agreement to that effect was signed by Louis Vigurs. This stipulated that the SVR proprietors were not to support any rival line up the valley.[36]

In October the SWR Board, under the impression that Brunel had approved the transaction, decided to introduce a Bill in Parliament for the purchase and extension of the SVR.[37] For this purpose they were to promote a separate company called the Swansea Valley Railway. All the documents received from the SVR were forwarded to the Company solicitors, Messrs W O & W Hunt, and further details, such as a plan of the line, title deeds and assets and liabilities, were requested. It would appear that Louis Vigurs' agreement to the sale was decidedly premature and on November 18 Brunel informed the Board that he could not approve the terms of the purchase. He wrote, 'There appears to have been some material error in the accounts on which the bargain was founded or at least a mode of stating the accounts which has led to a very considerable error on our part.'[38]

On December 3 1846, Charles Russell, the chairman of the SWR, wrote[39] to Starling

> Dear Sir
> At the meeting of the SW Board yesterday Mr L Vigurs, Mr Brunel
> and I stated to the Directors all that had passed when we met yourself

32   BR MS
33   9 & 10 Vic *cap* ccxxxix
34   BR MS
35   BR MS
36   BR MS
37   SWR Minute Book PRO RAIL 640/3
38   BR MS
39   BR MS

and your brother at 449 in the Strand and when Mr Brunel met you at his own house on the following morning. Under the circumstances which were urged on you at both those meetings the directors did not feel that they could justify it to their proprietors to confirm the provisional Agreement which had been entered into by Mr L Vigurs and Mr Benson, and I was unanimously requested to suggest to you that the whole question should be referred to some competent and impartial Gentleman of high standing to be jointly chosen who should determine on reviewing all the facts of the case what should be done between us.

Yours very faithfully

C Russell

Starling replied[40] from Swansea on December 7:

Dear Sir

I have to acknowledge the receipt of your letter of the 3rd instant - the Swansea Vale Railway Company never intended nor are they now, under the present depressed value of the Railway property, willing to sell their interest for less than £70,000 as specified in their agreement of 20th August. If the Directors of the South Wales Company desire to cancel this Agreement and will refer to any Barrister or Gentleman of high standing to say what should be done under all the circumstances to compensate for the loss and delay which the Swansea Vale Company will have incurred by having entered into this Agreement I shall be happy to lay such proposal before our shareholders for their consideration.

Yours very faithfully

S Benson

In further correspondence the differences between the two companies became clearer. Charles Russell considered the value of the SVR as the amount spent on its development; while Starling was adamant that they would not accept anything less than the £70,000 agreed.

In reply to the letter of December 20 from Charles Russell, Starling sent a full and lengthy account of his point of view. The letter[41] was dated December 26 which meant that he and Florance must have spent most of their Christmas in discussion to decide on its content. Starling sought to show they had provided all the information required of them and had endeavoured to accommodate the SWR Board in every way.

40 BR MS
41 BR MS

He concluded:

In consequence of Mr Brunel's absence from England the agreement of 20th August was made subject to his approval on his return. We consented to this condition on the understanding that his confirmation of an agreement deliberately entered into by your Directors was a mere form. I however thought it right to come to London on the 21st October for the express purpose of affording information if required, and of ascertaining whether this matter was to be considered as finally arranged in such form as would render it unnecessary for us to proceed with our Parliamentary notices with which we were fully prepared. Whether Mr Brunel has confirmed the agreement is a question of law, on which I have no desire to enter, but from what passed on that occasion, I left Town under the impression that the matter was finally settled. Had it been otherwise, we should at least have taken the precaution of giving our notices in November. The Swansea Vale Co. can only consider that this agreement had been arrived at and acted on in a manner that renders it final and conclusive.

If however any circumstances have since occurred to render the purchase less material to the South Wales Co., I am willing to suggest to our proprietors that it should revert to them but inasmuch as the agreement of 20th August and the proceedings taken under it have delayed the opening of the line to the lower collieries and have prevented them from going to Parliament this year in accordance with their original scheme, I must claim that it must be left to a referee to decide what loss they have sustained by this delay and what ought in Justice to be done to reinstate them in the position which they would have occupied had no such agreement been entered into. If this reference should subject the South Wales Co. to a penalty I think we can give you some consideration for it by the formation of an additional broad gauge line from the junction to our terminus and I shall be ready at any time to meet you in London for the purpose of carrying out this suggestion or acting on the original agreement.

Yours very faithfully

S Benson

Starling was writing again [42] to Charles Russell on January 15 1847, this time from Florance's Chambers, 2 Paper Buildings, Temple:

Dear Sir
Our shareholders are pressing me for some definite information as to their position under the agreement for the sale of the Swansea Vale Railway. There were certain suggestions in my letter of the 26th

42   BR MS

December last, with respect to which it might be desirable that we should meet if your objections to the arrangement are still unsatisfied. I leave town tomorrow night, but I shall be ready to attend any appointment that you may make previous thereto.

Yours very faithfully

S Benson

On January 20 1847, Messrs Russell, Brunel and Hunt stated to the SWR directors 'their opinion that unless the South Wales Company abided by the Agreement entered into with the S V Company, the former might be subject to an imputation of bad faith'.[43] It was decided to carry out the Agreement subject to the approval of the South Wales Proprietors and sanction of Parliament. It was also decided to communicate with Mr Gower and Mr Benson.

One difficulty in proceeding with the purchase of the SVR was that no South Wales shares were available as they had all been subscribed for. Mr R F Gower, one of the South Wales directors, had been approached and had agreed to lend 5000 shares to be put in trust to carry out the purchase. Two Trustees were to be named by the South Wales Company and two by the Swansea Vale Company. The deposit of £2 10s per share which Mr Gower had paid was to remain with the South Wales Company who would refund to Mr Gower the calls of £7 10s per share, (£37,500 in total). When the Act authorising the purchase of the Swansea Vale Railway was obtained, Mr Gower was to take up 5000 shares and pay back the money refunded by the Company.[44]

In a letter [45] of February 11 to W O Hunt, Charles Russell was beginning to show definite signs of impatience with the slowness of the proceedings:

My Dear Sir

Pray do what you can to hasten the arrangement we have made with Mr Gower. I am very anxious to get the covenants signed, the money paid and the whole of this disagreeable matter finally disposed of. In opening the discussion with Mr Benson, pray state that we do not admit the accuracy of the facts alleged in his later communications to me, and that you proceed to consider the arrangements, without prejudice, in the event of any obstacle being thrown in the way of a final adjustment.

Yours very truly

C Russell

Consequently a draft agreement was drawn up between the SWR, the SVR, the Swansea Valley Railway, the Trustees and T S Benson. A copy was sent to

43 SWR Minute Book PRO RAIL 640/3
44 BR MS
45 BR MS

Florance which he then returned with his comments.[46] Also, according to the instructions in Russell's letter, an agreement[47] covering the loan of the 5000 shares was drawn up and approved by R F Gower on March 2.

On July 2 1847 the Swansea Valley Railway Company finally had its Bill passed. The content was almost exactly the same as that of the SVR Bill, the new company using the same deposited plans. Starling gave evidence in support of the Bill, stressing the need for the railway as a means of transporting the Graigola coal to Swansea and encouraging development of collieries further up the valley.

The Act authorised 'a railway from Abercrave Farm in the parish of Ystradgunlais (sic) ... to Swansea'. There were to be three branches, 1) to the Old Rolling Mill on the Lower Forest Farm, 2) to terminate near the Cwmtwrch Railway Wharf and 3) to the Ynyscedwyn Iron Works. One difference was that the Railway was to be constructed on a gauge of 7 feet to allow it to be worked continuously with the South Wales Railway. Whereas the line followed the course of a certain existing private railway or tramway known as the Swansea Vale Railway, power was given to alter the levels and improve the line of that railway and to purchase 'so much of the said SVR and the lands connected therewith as may be necessary and as may be or may have been agreed on with the Proprietors of the said Railway'.[48]

The GWR had previously adopted a practice of promoting a nominally independent company with a separate share capital and GWR directors on the Board. The Act of such a company would contain powers enabling it to sell the undertaking to the GWR subject to the approval of both sets of proprietors.

However, the Swansea Valley Act contained a clause, based on a resolution passed in that session by the House of Commons,[49] which obstructed the original plans of the SWR to purchase the railway. Although powers to sell to the SWR or the GWR were given, the clause stated that the Swansea Valley Company could not exercise those powers until half its authorised capital had been raised and spent on constructing the railway.

By this time money was in short supply as a result of the current financial crisis in which hundreds of firms went bankrupt. One of these was A A Gower, Nephews & Co. which ceased trading[50] on September 11, rendering it unlikely that R F Gower would be in a position to keep his agreement to repay the £37,500 in calls on his shares which had been refunded to him by the SWR. On September 22, the SWR Board resolved to request Mr Gower to transfer the required 5000 shares into the names of the Trustees.[51] The transfer was duly executed and the document sent to Starling, as one of the four Trustees, for his signature.[52]

---

46 BR MS
47 BR MS
48 10 & 11 Vic *cap* ci
49 BR MS
50 C Sept 17 1847, p 4
51 SWR Minute Book PRO RAIL 640/4
52 BR MS

On November 3 the SWR Board instructed their solicitor to proceed in giving effect to the agreement for the purchase of the SVR.[53] There were still difficulties in that the SWR company did not have the powers and the Swansea Valley company did not have the capital. The solution suggested by the SWR was that the Swansea Valley Company should pay £70,000 in shares of £15 each paid up in the SWR Company. The 5000 shares held by the Trustees were to be transferred to the Swansea Valley Company for that purpose.[54]

Accordingly, on December 15 1847, the Board of the SWR passed a resolution authorising the Swansea Valley Directors, all nominees of the SWR, to complete the purchase of the SVR on behalf of the SWR although in the name of the Swansea Valley Company.[55]

Florance, however, raised objections to the solution suggested by the SWR on the grounds that the marketable value of the shares had fallen considerably. He stated[56] that 'on the 1st of January next, the South Wales share with Calls of £15 paid and £3 due upon it, will probably be worth £4 and the consideration for the Swansea Vale property agreed to be worth £70,000 in August 1846, will be under £19,000 in January 1848.'

Further correspondence and meetings on the subject followed without a satisfactory conclusion. The Parliamentary expenses of £9267 for the incorporation of the Swansea Valley Company were paid by the SWR, appearing in the capital account as a payment on a transaction not properly known to the shareholders. Together with the £37,500 refunded to R F Gower, the attempt to purchase the SVR had cost the SWR to date a total of £46,767 with nothing to show for it.[57]

Meanwhile the SVR had remained, as before, a Joint Stock Company, using their line from Tyrllandwr to Llansamlet, which was basically a slightly extended and improved version of Scott's Railway. Traffic was being worked by C H Smith. Messrs Davey & Pegg were other potential users and, together with the Patent Fuel Company, made a request for permission to extend the line to Graigola and use it as a temporary horse railway. They pointed out that the line could easily be adapted for locomotives when required, with no impediment.

Their proposals were made to Joseph Martin and were forwarded by the SVR Engineer, Rhys W Jones, to the SWR solicitors in May 1848. The reply[58] from the SWR directors was that 'the line not being the property of this company (they) were not in a position to give their sanction to the arrangement proposed by Messrs Davey & Pegg.' Nevertheless Davey & Pegg worked their traffic over the existing line for a few years, paying tolls to the SVR.[59]

More light is thrown on the situation at this time by a letter[60] from Charles Russell to W O Hunt dated October 1 1848. The text also gives an insight into

53   SWR Minute Book PRO RAIL 640/4
54   SWR Minute Book PRO RAIL 640/4
55   SWR Minute Book PRO RAIL 640/4
56   BR MS
57   Bradshaw's Manual, 1854
58   BR MS
59   SVR Minute Book PRO RAIL 679/2
60   BR MS

the thoughts and characters of Russell and Florance:

My Dear Sir,

Just before I left London, Mr Benson, the barrister, called on me. The ostensible object of his visit was to suggest that the South Wales Railway should pass down the eastern instead of the western side of the river, into Swansea, and to speak about some colliery, the owners of which were desirous of using the Swansea Vale line and to pay tolls for it. About the direction of the line, I told him that it had long ago been decided, that all the notices had been given and the works begun, that I had never heard of any disposition to alter it; but that Mr Brunel was the proper person to speak to on the subject. On the other subject, I begged to decline entering, in the present position of the agreement. This led to some little conversation on the subject, which I have no doubt was the real object of the visit. I told him I had an imperfect recollection of the facts, but, as far as I remembered, the agreement had been suspended in consequence of the demands which he had made for interest and some other minor questions; and that subsequently the resolutions of the legislature, about the purchase of lines, had interposed an obstacle. I observed that he endeavoured to make light of the question of interest, and to ascribe the rupture mainly to the resolutions of Parliament. I told him that it was a great inconvenience to us, and a great hardship to other proprietors to have 5000 shares, locked up in trust, on which we were receiving no payment of calls. He was pursuing the matter; but I said that I really remembered the facts very imperfectly, that I stood on unequal ground in discussing such a question with a barrister, and that upon it I must refer him to you. The conversation assumed rather a dissatisfied tone on both sides; and ended by my saying that they had endeavoured to drive too hard a bargain with us, and that they had themselves to thank for their present position. He said he was going to Swansea immediately; and as it is possible he may speak to you or Mr Elsdale before he goes, I think it as well to lose no time in placing you in possession of what passed between us.

I return to town on Tuesday.

Yours very sincerely,

C Russell

On December 13, Starling and Florance met a group of SWR directors to discuss the previous negotiations, and expressed their intention of consulting the traders and other interested parties as to the means most likely to effect the completion of their line. At a SWR Board meeting held on the same day, C R M Talbot of Margam was elected a director, a move which later proved to be most significant.[61]

61 SWR Minute Book PRO RAIL 640/4

Relations between the GWR and SWR Companies were not always harmonious and Charles Russell, being Chairman of both Boards, decided that he might be embarrassed by a conflict of interests. In May 1849, he resigned as Chairman of the SWR Board, and C R M Talbot was elected in his place.[62]

Meanwhile, construction of the SWR was progressing so that by March 1850 work was being carried out at Llansamlet where the line crossed the SVR. On March 12 a formal notice not to trespass on or interfere with the land and property of the SWR, signed by Starling and Thomas Attwood the solicitor, was sent to the SWR.[63] In a letter dated March 18 Starling outlined to C R M Talbot (with whom he had a far happier relationship on the political platform!) the history of the SVR and the previous negotiations.[64] He followed this on March 20:

> I can only assure you that upon accidentally walking up the Swansea Vale road, I found a gang of workmen, who informed me that they were employed by the South Wales to raise the Swansea Vale road for 3 or 400 yards, so as to make it about two feet higher, where it would be crossed by the South Wales.
>
> The men were gradually raising the blocks and rails so as to interfere as little as possible with the Coal Waggons (sic) passing over, and had already altered the level for about 100 yards. Mr S Jones, the South Wales Surveyor, upon my calling at his Office, acknowledged that he had employed the Men & at my request gave me the enclosed Memorandum.[65]

The SWR sought legal advice on the matter and on March 22 instructed Mr J H Lloyd to prepare a notice to be served on the SVR of the intention of the SWR to carry their line across that of SVR on the level and requiring them to send in a claim.[66]

Mr Lloyd replied:[67]
I do not think it necessary to serve any notice, for the S W Ry Co have a right to cross the Swansea Vale Ry's tramroad, leaving it to the latter Co to make their claim for compensation - but it will probably be better to make the offer, and I have therefore prepared a form of notice.

> The notice shd be served on Mr Benson as one of the directors and Mr Attwood the Solr of the Company.

J H Lloyd
I K B Walk   March 25 1850

62 SWR Minute Book PRO RAIL 640/4
63 BR MS
64 SVR Letter Book PRO RAIL 679/12
65 SVR Letter Book PRO RAIL 679/12
66 BR MS
67 BR MS

There was indeed a clause in the SWR Act of 1845 which gave the company the right 'to enter upon, take, and use such of the said lands as shall be necessary for such purpose', but it would have been more courteous of the SWR to have notified the SVR of their intention.

The South Wales Railway from Chepstow to Swansea was opened on June 18 1850 with great celebration.[68] Unfortunately when the line was continued westward from Landore, Swansea found itself at the terminus of a branch line. This was to cause much dissatisfaction in the future.

In August 1850 the SVR was still unclear about the intentions of the SWR. At a meeting[69] on the 25th it was resolved 'that a formal application be made by the Chairman of this meeting to the South Wales Railway Company as to their intention of carrying out the Agreement of August 1846 and as to the nature of the powers by which they purpose to effect that object'.

Eventually, in May 1851 the SWR secretary replied[70] saying:

> I am instructed by the Board to say that the Swansea Vale Co. appear to be under an entire misapprehension of the nature and effect of the Memorandum of August 1846 and to deny that there exists or ever existed any undertaking on the part of the South Wales Railway Co. to obtain the necessary powers for giving effect to any agreement to be founded on that Memorandum.

The SVR Proprietors had been hoping that there was still a chance that the SWR would, through the Swansea Valley Company, complete the line, but that communication made them realise that negotiations were at an end. The Swansea Valley Company's powers of purchase had originally been granted for three years. The time expired in 1850 but had been extended[71] by one year to 1851. Thus by August 1851 the SVR was free to continue its line to Graigola and apply for an Act of Parliament to give it power to complete the line to Abercrave according to their initial plans. Now the company could operate independently which it did for the next twenty-five years, with Starling Benson as Chairman.

An Extraordinary General Meeting on October 13 1851 approved details of an agreement with C H Smith for working the line. It was also resolved that arrangements be made for relaying the permanent way between Birchgrove and the terminus at Tyrllandwr in order to render it fitted for locomotive traffic, and for laying the permanent way between Birchgrove and the Graigola colliery at Glais.[72]

With the use of locomotives on the SVR the risk of a collision at Llansamlet was greatly increased. It was therefore essential that rules and regulations were agreed between the companies, (but the execution of these would seem to cause

---

68   C June 21 1850, p 3; Sw and Glam Herald, pp 2 & 3
69   BR MS
70   BR MS
71   BR MS
72   SVR Minute Book PRO RAIL 679/2

more risk than existed before - see Appendix B for list). These were agreed on July 28 1852 by Starling Benson and C H Smith for the SVR and Frederick Clarke, Superintendent of the SWR.[73]

The extension of the SVR line to Graigola was brought into use in December 1852, and worked by C H Smith.[74] Although he may have owned locomotives before that time, it is known[75] that he purchased one in September, a former Liverpool & Manchester Railway 0-4-2 named 'Bat'.

Thus the SVR now had about 6½ miles of single-track railway in use, and in July of the following year, Starling was able to inform the proprietors that the line was carrying 500 tons per day. He also had to give them the bad news that their Bill had failed in Parliament.[76]

In the summer of 1853, three companies were promoting Bills for lines along the Swansea Valley to the rapidly developing port. The SVR, of course, wanted powers to extend its line to Abercrave. The Swansea Valley Company was seeking to revive its powers to build what was virtually the same line, but on the broad gauge. A newcomer to the scene, the Newport, Abergavenny & Hereford Railway, already had powers to build a line from Pontypool to Quakers Yard, and wished to extend that to Aberdare, then run via Hirwaun down the west side of the valley to Swansea. This was called the 'Swansea Extension', and was to terminate at the dock then under construction, later known as the South Dock.[77]

The SVR petitioned against the other two Bills and, as usual, was legally represented before the Parliamentary Committees by Florance, who was therefore involved in three Bills at the same time. The news of his sudden death[78] on June 6 1853, at the age of 38, came as a severe blow to Starling who depended so much on Florance's knowledge of legal matters and his presence in London to attend to them. At this period Starling was himself undergoing the ordeal of giving evidence to the Committees and the failure of the SVR Bill must have brought yet another cause for distress. The only consolation was that Parliament rejected the two other Bills at the same time.

During 1853 the SVR obtained its first two locomotives, a very definite step forward in its service to its clients.[79] It also purchased the land needed to extend the railway from Graigola to Pontardawe which it was able to do by agreement.[80]

By April 1854, telegraphic bell signals had been installed at the Llansamlet level crossing which gave the crossing keeper advance warning of the approach of a South Wales train.[81] Nevertheless, arguments between the two companies over the working of the crossing and the question of compensation continued for some time.

---

73 BR MS
74 BR MS
75 Baxter, British Locomotive Catalogue (Moorland Publishing Co.)
76 SVR MInute Book PRO RAIL 679/2
77 BR MS
78 *Vide* p 128: n 52
79 Baxter, *op cit*
80 SVR Minute Book *loc cit*
81 BR MS

In 1854, the SVR once more had a Bill in Parliament. This failed yet again. At last on June 15 1855 the Company obtained 'An Act to enable the Swansea Vale Railway Company to extend their Railway and work the same as a Passenger Railway, and for other purposes connected therewith'.[82] This was mainly concerned with the creation of a new statutory company to replace the old Joint-stock undertaking, though with the same directors and capital. It must have given the Proprietors and Starling in particular a tremendous feeling of relief to be able now to make progress after the hard struggle of the last nine years.

This Act sanctioned an extension from the terminus to a point near the commencement of the New Cut in Fabian's Bay, and a branch from Pentreguinea across the New Cut to the Company's wharf on the east side of the Town Float. The Act also authorised the laying down of additional rails on the broad gauge between the terminus and the Llansamlet crossing.

Scheduled to the Act was an agreement dated December 23 1854 between the SWR and SVR that the latter should lay the broad gauge from Llansamlet to the terminus within a period of eighteen months. In return for this the SWR should construct a station and sidings for the interchange of goods and mineral traffic at Llansamlet. The agreement also included new regulations about the working of the crossing until it was abolished. It was agreed that the SWR should obtain an Act authorising the layout to be altered so that the SWR line passed over that of the SVR, in a manner which was to be approved by the latter company. This Act[83] was obtained on June 26 1855 and the work was carried out by February 1857.

In 1856, Starling indicated in his Chairman's report[84] that the Company had applied to Parliament for permission to extend the line to Ystradgynlais, 'an extension much required and approved of by landowners and proprietors of works'. It would 'materially help the trade of a populous district and being only five miles in extent would be cheaply and speedily constructed'.

The mention of cheapness was in typical Starling vein, but that was qualified by an even more typical caution as he went on to remind those listening that it was the directors' object to complete and open the remaining portions of the line 'as soon as is compatible with due economy and consideration for the present state of the money market', words more suggestive of our modern mood of economic sobriety than of the heady optimism we so often associate with the heyday of Victorian expansion.

The Act[85] referred to was obtained in 1856. It authorised an extension from Pontardawe to Claypon's Wharf at the end of his tramroad at Ystradgynlais, with three branch railways, one to the Ystalyfera Ironworks, another to the Palleg or Cwmtwrch Railway and a third to the north of the terminus of the Ynyscedwyn Branch Canal.

---

82 18 Vic *cap* lx
83 18 & 19 Vic *cap* xcviii
84 C Chairman's Report, Jan 18 1856, p 5
85 19 & 20 Vic *cap* xcv

On December 24 1859, a further 2½ miles was opened, taking the line beyond Pontardawe as far as Waun Coed Colliery.[86] By this time the Company was ready to begin a passenger service, and the line between Swansea and Pontardawe was inspected and passed[87] by Captain Ross on behalf of the Board of Trade on February 15 1860. Now the SVR could offer the public the opportunity to travel by rail from its terminus, conveniently placed at St Thomas near the mouth of the Tawe, as far as the new station at Pontardawe. The formal opening of the route took place on February 20 1860, when a special train with a select number of passengers made the journey. On their arrival at Pontardawe they were treated by William Parsons, the owner of the local works, to a glass of champagne. The following day the line was opened to the public, with the train calling at Llansamlet and Glais stations. A large crowd had gathered at Pontardawe, coming mainly from the works, where the day had been declared a general holiday to mark the event.[88]

'The Cambrian' summed up the general reaction at the time when it said that the opening of the Swansea Vale Railway met a greatly felt need and would prove to be 'as advantageous to the public as to the enterprising proprietors'.

Nevertheless all was not sweetness and light. On October 26 1860 'Amicus', writing to 'The Cambrian', demanded to know how the Swansea Vale Directors could justify depriving shareholders by failing to supply the narrow gauge system to the point where it could secure the bulk of the Aberdare steam coal trade, a view also held by 'Aminadab'. Another correspondent, 'Commissary', complained about alterations in the winter timetable which would be highly inconvenient to people travelling to Swansea on business.

Additional stretches of the line were opened for goods and mineral traffic in the following months, and on January 12 1861, the line from Pontardawe to Ynysygeinon was inspected and passed by Colonel Yolland.[89] The public opening to passengers took place[90] on January 21.

The opening of the new part of the line led to a complaint by the Superintendent of the Swansea Sunday School Union, a Mr William Davies.[91] An excursion from Ynysygeinon to Swansea, supposedly in connection with the Sunday Schools of the district, had been advertised for a Sunday in early September. The local Sunday School superintendents wished it to be known that they had nothing to do with such an infringement of the Sabbath. One correspondent roundly denounced the Railway Company for speculating for trade in this way. He repeated the question asked by Mr Davies, addressing it to the Directors:

> By what law, human or divine, do they allow excursion trains to run on Sunday at all, which only help to ensnare the unwary, encourage drunkenness and demoralise the rising generation?

86   Bradshaw's Manual, 1860
87   Board of Trade Inspection PRO MT6 21/9
88   C Feb 24 1860, p 5
89   Board of Trade Inspection PRO MT6 23/5
90   C Jan 25 1861, p 4
91   C Sept 6 1861, p 8

43 St. Thomas Station, Swansea, 1962   Photo: Michael Hale

44 Pontardawe Station, 1962   Photo: Michael Hale

45 Ystalyfera Station, 1963   Photo: Michael Hale

He was glad to say that only three people had got on the train although the Company had sent six carriages to Ynysygeinon Station. He had to admit, however, that this might have been mainly because of the bad weather.

Another critic, 'Observer', claimed that, had the Swansea Vale Railway been in the hands of a powerful company, it would by then have linked up with Aberdare instead of only talking of an extension to Ystalyfera.[92]

Less controversial was the cheap excursion train put on for the benefit of the Cambrian Institution for the Deaf and Dumb on Monday, September 30, leaving Swansea at 11 am for Ynysygeinon, calling at all stations, for a return fare of one shilling.[93] This may have been its proudest moment as the Ynysygeinon station was to enjoy a relatively short life.

Meanwhile, the SVR obtained another Act on July 22 1861, which authorised an extension, some 6 miles long, to Brynamman, where a junction was to be made with the well established Llanelly Railway.[94] In addition to traffic from collieries along the route, the attraction here was the Brynamman Ironworks.

Colonel Yolland was back again on November 2 to inspect the line to Ystalyfera and its important ironworks. He was not very happy about the unprotected state of a level crossing, which had been pointed out by James Palmer Budd, managing partner of the ironworks. However, when the Company agreed to erect a footbridge and place a watchman there, he permitted the line to be used for passengers.[95] It was publicly opened on November 20 1861. This additional link in the chain was marked by a reception for sixty guests given by the Budds at their home, Ynysydarren House, as well as by celebrations of a more general kind.

The special train from Swansea, decorated with flags and evergreen, left St Thomas at noon and arrived promptly at 1 o'clock in Ystalyfera where it was greeted with cheers and the firing of cannon. In his speech of welcome, James Palmer Budd referred in jest to the lack of anyone of influence to greet the Directors of the SVR, the highest civil authority in the district being the local police constable.

Nevertheless all the leading industrialists of the district were present at the lunch, and, in responding to the toast to the Members for County and Borough, Mr Vivian underlined the importance of the SVR's role in opening up the locality to the Midland and Northern districts, a point taken up by Mr Budd. He recognised they had been caught up in the fight between narrow and broad gauges, and was delighted a local line (ie the narrow gauge) had won. He felt they were indebted for the extension to Mr Benson, and foresaw that, having got to Ystalyfera, they would soon reach Ynyscedwyn. He hoped that, before long, the SVR would form a junction with the Llanelly Railway, thereby opening up access to the Midlands and the North. In proposing 'Success to the SVR' he coupled with it the name of its Chairman, Starling Benson.

---

92   C Sept 13 1861, p 8
93   C Sept 6 1861, p 4
94   24 & 25 Vic *cap* clxii
95   Board of Trade Inspection PRO MT6 24/36

J W James, Vice Chairman of the Swansea Harbour Trust, attributed to the SVR much of the success of the North Dock in handling the increased trade of the port. The railway had been responsible for sending down between 250,000 to 300,000 tons of freight a year. If the new lines being opened did as much for Swansea as the SVR, trade should be doubled again within ten years.

Anticipating some of the criticism, Starling admitted they might be charged with slowness, but that had to do with the terrain more than the Company. They had had to contend with the two gauges, the South Wales wanting the broad, the SVR, the narrow. The South Wales Company had been to Parliament twice without going any further, but now that the smaller company had opened narrow gauge track to Ystalyfera, the larger proposed converting to it on their own line. He foresaw developments whereby the SVR would have direct communication on the same gauge with all parts of the Kingdom.[96]

It was not therefore surprising that the Company should soon be applying to the Harbour Trust for an extra siding to be allotted them near the Corporation Quay in connection with the low level railway being laid down, of which we shall hear more in the next chapter. As Chairman of both Railway and Trust, Starling tactfully kept a low profile but, in spite of some initial hesitation on the part of the Corporation who claimed the ground was theirs rather than the Trust's to dispose of, the application was eventually granted.[97]

The Company continued to associate itself closely with the life of the Valley in a way no larger company working lines in the area was doing, a point anticipated by Mr Vivian in his speech at the opening of the line to Ystalyfera in November 1861.

There were frequent instances of its involvement in local activities. On Saturday, August 9 1862, the Company conveyed members of the Kilvey Company of the Sixth Glamorgan Rifle Volunteers under the command of Major Grenfell to Ynysygeinon. From there they marched through Ystalyfera to Glantwrch by the special invitation of Mr and Mrs Price who entertained the riflemen in the grounds of their home while a party of invited guests was entertained in the house.

The following Wednesday and Thursday, August 13 and 14, special trains were run between Swansea and Ystalyfera for the Family Fair and Bazaar held in the grounds of the Budds' home, with Mr Mortimer, the General Superintendent of the Company, not only safeguarding the transport of a large number of 'excursionists' but also rendering valuable aid in setting out the articles for sale on the various stalls.[98]

The following year, on July 14 1863, the Vale of Neath Railway line across the Crumlyn Burrows to Swansea was opened officially. This initially had broad gauge rails, but additional rails on the narrow gauge were soon added.[99] The SVR was connected to this line by a short branch which crossed over Fabian Street by a bridge. As the SVR had not constructed its proposed extension to Fabian's Bay, the course of which was now blocked, a goods shed was erected on this

96 C Nov 22 1861, p 8
97 C May 16 1862, p 6
98 C Aug 15 1862, p 8
99 Swansea & Neath Railway Minute Book PRO RAIL 678/1

connecting line. The addition of narrow gauge rails to the Vale of Neath system provided the SVR with a link to narrow gauge railways in other parts of the country, as predicted by Starling two years earlier. That custom was increasing is shown by the Company's need to invest in two new engines.

Work on the Brynamman extension led to the building of an engine shed at Gurnos, from where the Palleg Branch diverged up the side valley of Cwm Twrch. In addition, tanks and cranes for the supply of water to engines were to be put up at both Brynamman and Glais; nothing spectacular, but all helpful to the work of the line. Goods and mineral traffic began working to Brynamman on January 1 1864, giving the SVR another link with the outside world.[100] By that time, G B Strick of the Brynamman Iron Works had joined the Board.

The prospect of another route over which traffic could flow to and from the SVR appeared with the promotion of the Swansea Vale & Neath & Brecon Junction Railway. An Act of July 29 1864 authorised a line from Ynysygeinon to Capel Coelbren on the Neath & Brecon Railway, which was then under construction, as far as the Brecon portion was concerned. The SVR and N&BR Companies were to give each other running powers over the whole stretch of line by an agreement of June 16 1864, signed by Starling on behalf of his Company.[101]

Although work on building the new line began, unfortunately the contractor failed as a result of the financial crisis of 1866, and the project ground to a halt. Eventually the N&BR obtained powers to take over the company in order to complete the line, but it was a long drawn out business.

Relations within the Company remained excellent. At 'a most substantial supper' provided for the officials and all employees of the SVR at the Assembly Rooms in January 1867, the toast of the evening, 'Success to the SVR', was proposed by Mr Mortimer, the General Superintendent of the line, who took the Chair. He recalled the time when the Company had only two locomotives and receipts were about £50 a week. Now they were nearer £500 a week, the result of a united effort by directors, managers and workers. The Company was not very large nor the line very long, but it brought down a quarter of a million tons of coal and other goods, and the prospects were for an increase in trade. No company had a finer body of men on its Board and it was with pleasure he gave the health of the Chairman, Starling Benson, and of the Directors, Charles Smith, Pascoe St Leger Grenfell, A M Story Maskelyne, G B Strick and H J Bath.[102]

The SVR Act[103] of June 17 1867 authorised the construction of a loop line from Upper Bank to Morriston and Clydach, rejoining the parent line at Glais. The Swansea Canal Company, which had been one of the petitioners against it, had withdrawn its opposition to the Bill on condition that the SVR accepted a clause restricting them from opposing any line the Canal Company might apply to make in order to accommodate all works to the west of the Tawe.[104]

100   Bradshaw's Manual, 1865
101   27 & 28 Vic *cap* ccxciii
102   C Jan 4 1867, p 5
103   30 Vic *cap* xcviii
104   C Mar 15 1867, p 8

Towards the end of 1867, the SVR prepared to open the Brynamman branch to passengers and after numerous improvements had been made, on February 29 1868, the Board of Trade gave its approval.[105] There were intermediate stations at Gwys and Gwaun Cae Gurwen Colliery Halt (later Cwmllynfell). The opening took place in March, but seems to have been a very subdued affair compared with the earlier celebrations.

By the beginning of 1868, the Directors were keen to begin work as soon as possible on the Morriston branch but were held back by the current depression. Dividends had continued to be paid half-yearly on preference shares, but those on the original shares had been on ice for a number of years. The Chairman regretted that capital had not been raised on the original rather than the preference shares as he considered that would have put them in a stronger position. Nevertheless he believed they were now getting into better working order, while trade was increasing and would be further enhanced by the development of new branch lines.

His optimism was countered by one of the more critical of the shareholders, Richard Richards, who felt they should welcome any offer from another company to lease the line as he had little faith in their own company's future ability to pay a proper dividend. The Chairman assured him that they would consider any *bona fide* offer from another railway company, but Mr Grenfell, speaking as one of the Directors, could offer him no evidence of interest shown by any of the big companies like the London and North Western or the Great Western Railways at that time.

It was here Mr Richards revealed the sting in his remarks. He felt those trading on the line should not be Directors of the Company because of their vested interest. Asked to explain the inference, he suggested preference would naturally be given by them to their own business. This, the Chairman felt, was a very serious charge. Mr Richards was entitled to receive a list of shareholders and he could be sure if any of them brought a *bona fide* complaint, the Directors would give it their careful consideration.[106]

During 1869, a party of Midland Railway directors and officials inspected various lines and locations in South Wales. Probably talks were held with Starling because at the SVR Board meeting of December 13 an agreement with the Midland Railway was approved.[107] The MR had already taken a step towards South Wales by taking over the working of the Hereford, Hay & Brecon Railway from October 1.

There had been a cloud on the horizon on account of a heavy lawsuit brought against the Company by the Ystalyfera Iron Company in connection with the purchase of land. Fortunately the case was decided in favour of the SVR. In February 1870, dividends were declared payable at 6, 5 and 4% on preference shares and at 1% on the original shares. In answer to an original shareholder pressing for 2% or at least 1½ in view of the increased earnings of the line during the past half year, the Chairman maintained the Directors had exercised a wise discretion in keeping the dividend to 1% because there was much work still to

105   Board of Trade Inspection PRO MT6 50/12
106   C Feb 28 1868, p 6
107   SVR Minute Book PRO RAIL 679/8

be done. Until that was completed, it was advisable to keep as much money in hand as possible.[108] Work on the Clydach branch had been completed so far as to connect the Upper Bank Spelter Works with the main line.

There was talk of the Midland Railway coming to Swansea although, in reply to Mr Glasbrook at the SVR half-yearly meeting of August 1870, the Chairman admitted there was nothing definite as yet. There had been delay caused by difficulty with the Neath and Brecon Company, but he still believed it was the Midland's full intention to go down to Swansea. He would be only too glad if the Midland link-up could be effected.

A note of weariness may well have crept into the Chairman's voice at this point. The meeting had been a gruelling one with close questioning from Richard Richards who persisted in querying every item of expenditure, including increases in salaries and the payment of six months' salary to a secretary who had been removed, instead of the six months' notice which he considered should have been given.

Another bone of contention was the delay in issuing the statement of accounts which had not, it was claimed, appeared in time for shareholders to have the statutory seven days to scrutinise it. The Secretary explained that the Act merely provided for a statement to be prepared seven days before the meeting but it did not have to be issued to shareholders except on application. Anxious ever to appear compliant, the Chairman assured Mr Richards the Directors were ready to supply the statement of accounts as early as possible, whether shareholders were entitled to it or not, but as they would have received their statement on August 17, and the meeting was not until August 24, he did not think they had much to complain of.[109]

In August 1870 F W Mortimer, the Superintendent of the SVR, was appointed, out of a large number of candidates, to become General Manager of the Midland Company for the whole of South Wales. In paying tribute to him, Starling pointed out that their manager was leaving the smaller company to enter on 'the more onerous duties' of the larger. These he was sure he would discharge with the same efficiency as he had always shown.[110] The occasion of his going was marked by the presentation to Mr Mortimer of a 'handsome and valuable silver tea and coffee service, suitably inscribed'. About sixty subscribers were present and in thanking them, the new General Manager of the South Wales Midland line paid tribute to his former associates on the SVR as 'a Board of Directors second to none'.

> With gentleman like Mr Benson as your chairman and with Mr Grenfell, Mr Bath and others whose names are household words as your directors, you have nothing to fear as long as you remain on the Swansea Vale.[111]

At the SVR half-yearly meeting of February 1871 Starling reported that a contract had been entered into by the Neath and Brecon Company to complete

---

108   C Feb 25 1870, p 5
109   C Aug 26 1870, p 6
110   C Nov 4 1870, p 5
111   C Jan 6 1871, p 5

a branch line to Ynysygeinon by the end of the year, thus connecting the SVR line with the Neath and Brecon by which access would be obtained to Brecon, Hereford and the North. He said that the line to Morriston would be open in about two months and that the contract had been let for work on the remaining part of the branch from Clydach to Glais.

The role of Chairman was not always an easy one. Even a close friend could occasionally cause embarrassment. In thanking the Directors for their past services, J W James expressed his pleasure at hearing the GWR broad gauge was about to be converted to the narrow gauge, which would be most conducive to the prosperity of the SVR.

Starling explained that he had not alluded to this in his report as it had not yet been passed by the GWR Proprietors. Believing the information to be still a secret, he did not feel justified in making it known. If this did indeed materialise, nothing could be more beneficial to the SVR in the production of future traffic or in the conduct of present traffic, enabling trucks to go up to the works where they would be discharged, thus obviating the inconvenience of a break in gauge.[112]

In the meeting of the following August it was still Richard Richards who asked the most awkward questions such as, 'Why did the SVR pay higher rates to its contractors than either the GWR or the Vale of Neath Railways?' The Chairman explained that this applied only to one contract which had entailed unusual risks for which the contractor himself was responsible. On the bridge on the Morriston loop line alone, he had lost £100. It therefore seemed only fair to pay him on a higher scale.

In general, the state of the Company was improving. At last, after years without reward, the original shareholders received a dividend of 3% a year. Mr James even began to entertain hopes of their being able to afford hydraulic machinery for the bridge crossing the New Cut. This would both increase and improve the conduct of trade, doing away with the need to close the bridge for some three or four hours each tide.

Richard Richards was obviously satisfied with the report, as he proposed a gratuity for Mr Morley, the new Secretary, whose efforts he thought had brought about a distinct improvement in the Company's affairs. Starling cheerfully responded that he was glad Mr Richards had brought this up because, as a rule, he was critical of the Directors for their lack of economy. The spirit of *bonhomie* must have been infectious. Mr Richards said he was happy to leave the matter in the hands of the Directors and thanked Mr Benson for his past and present services.[113]

There was good reason for such satisfaction. On September 13, the long delayed Morriston branch was inspected by Colonel Hutchinson. A special train was provided and Colonel Hutchinson, accompanied by the engineer of the line, Mr D H Jones, and 'the indefatigable secretary, Thomas Morley', travelled the new stretch of track which was to be served by four trains running each way daily, independent of the main line service.[114]

112   C Feb 24 1871, p 8
113   C Aug 25 1871, p 5
114   C Sept 22 1871, p 5

Board of Trade approval was sent at the end of the month, and the branch line was opened for passenger traffic on Monday, October 2. The enterprise had been carried through smoothly by the praiseworthy efforts of the contractor, Mr Francis Rummens, as well as through the diligence of Mr Morley who had ensured, by careful advertising, that the general public was well aware of the times of the trains.

To mark the occasion, on the Tuesday, the permanent way men were treated to 'a substantial collation' with plenty of *'cwrw da'* at the Upper Bank station, which left the recipients with an excellent impression of the 'liberality of the Company'.[115]

By February 1872, the original shares had reached a 5% dividend, possibly their highest yet, although 'The Cambrian' believed there was still greater potential to be realised. This improvement was no flash in the pan. At the half-yearly meeting trade was reported to be improving in every part of the line. Once the Glais project was finished, the whole development would be complete, although, if there was a demand for a line to the collieries in the Caelliau district, the Chairman said they could still supply it.[116]

On April 17 1872 Starling met a group of Midland Railway directors to discuss and agree terms on which the SVR could be taken over by the larger company.[117] From the Midland's point of view, the transaction had its disadvantages. Mr Noble, the assistant General Manager of that Company, realised when he came to inspect the line that the SVR Company was completely overwhelmed by its present volume of traffic. They had insufficient rolling stock, and to put the line in proper condition for public service would take a very large sum of money. The doubling of the line, indispensable for the proper development of a through route, would cost over £100,000, which the SVR could not possibly afford.

Nevertheless, the Midland needed the line and were therefore prepared to make it their own by a perpetual lease and by guaranteeing a dividend of 6% per annum on a capital of about £145,000. This was something the SVR, as we have seen, had been unable to do until recently, after years with no dividend or, at best, 1, 2, or 3% for their original shareholders. The business minds of the SVR had no doubt about the practicality of the proposed link-up. Pascoe Grenfell knew from personal experience the necessity of a through line to the North. His firm needed such direct communication to send off its copper manufactures via Birmingham to the Northern ports such as Hull in order to ship them out to Russia or the Balkans. Trucks of block tin worth £1000 or South Wales anthracite would reach their destinations more rapidly when conveyed by the Midland. Thus the case for a through line was of paramount importance to the trade of the area. Even the mere prospect of a merger with the Midland had, as Starling himself conceded, enhanced their prosperity, making it possible for the Company to pay the long awaited dividend of 6%.[118]

The Company's record had been singularly free of serious incidents, with nothing like the accident on the Vale of Neath line at the North Dock to mar its

---

115   C Oct 6 1871, p 5
116   C Mar 1 1872, p 3
117   Midland Railway Minute Book PRO RAIL 491/21
118   C Aug 23 1872, p 6

reputation. There had been two unfortunate deaths in the tunnel on the Morriston line near Upper Bank, but for this no negligence at all was attached to the Company. The two men had been walking along the line on their way home on a stormy night to Miers Street in St Thomas from the Landore steel works when they were struck by a passing train, the sound of its approach having probably been drowned by the wind. It was, however, recommended at the inquest that a road be made between the works and the railway to avoid future fatalities.[119]

The SVR continued to hold its own half-yearly meetings, although it was felt appropriate that someone connected with the Midland should now sit on the Board. As a result, Mr George Braithwaite Lloyd became a Director in February 1873. In moving the reselection of Mr Benson and Mr Maskelyne, the retiring directors, Mr James said that it was impossible to have a more efficient director than Mr Benson or one who paid more attention to the interests of the Company. He regretted that Mr Maskelyne could not attend more regularly now that times were better, in view of his loyalty during the difficult days they had had to come through.

He pointed out that it would probably be the next session before the formal agreement with the Midland would take effect. That would happen once the necessary Parliamentary powers had been obtained. The working agreement, however, was already in operation. Nor did the Chairman foresee any difficulty in getting Parliamentary sanction. In any case they were in the happy position, even if the arrangement with the Midland were to be rejected, of earning alone as much as, or more than, the Midland had engaged to pay them.

The need was now once more felt for increased siding accommodation of their own. Large numbers of trucks brought down by the GWR for shipment at the various wharfs stood blocking the harbour line. Mr J W James, as Harbour Superintendent, thought railway companies should find standing room for trucks until they were shipped rather than leave them on the line, but Mr Morley explained through the Chairman that the fault lay with the works in sending out their cargoes before the ships were ready to receive them. For the distances involved, it was not to the Company's benefit to provide trucks. Freighters should be prepared to find their own.[120]

The Chairman's report to the Half-Yearly meeting of August 1873 stated that the loop line was open for mineral traffic as far as Clydach and the remainder of the line to Glais was ready for the laying of the permanent way. The contract for the Caelliau branch had been let.[121]

The much delayed line from Ynysygeinon to Coelbren on the N&BR was opened[122] on November 20 1873. The Brecon Company began to exercise its running powers by working trains through to Swansea.

A Special General Meeting of SVR shareholders[123] was held on March 25 1874 to approve the terms of the Midland Railway (Swansea Vale Railway Lease)

119   C Jan 10 1873, p 8
120   C Feb 28 1873, p 8
121   Railway News, Aug 23 1873
122   Bradshaw's Manual, 1874
123   SVR Minute Book PRO RAIL 679/1

Bill. The Act[124] was passed on July 30 1874, authorising the Midland Company to hold under lease in perpetuity the undertaking of the SVR, the arrangement to take effect from July 1 1874. This gave the MR the running powers over the N&B Railway which had previously been granted to the SVR.

The increasing level of SVR expenditure was one reason why financial assistance from the MR was welcome. At the 39th Half-Yearly meeting of the SVR in August 1874, it was reported that the receipts of the previous six months were down by £3000. This was not the fault of the Company management but was due to strikes and lock-outs at the collieries and works on the line. It was also reported that the expenses had been exceedingly heavy. They had been increased not only by wages and cost of materials needed for the usual repairs, but more especially by an outlay in relaying and improving a considerable portion of the line, required by the heavier engines and trucks now using the permanent way, and by the addition of trains to Brecon put on to open up the future traffic to the North.

After charging to revenue a portion of the cost of the improved permanent way, a balance remained of £6280 19s. 11d. The dividend on the preference shares would be paid at once, but the dividend on the original shares would be left in abeyance until the Company had closed their accounts and arranged the details of transfer with the Midland Company.

From and after July 1, the SVR would incur no liability but would receive from the Midland a rent of £9452 per half year, as equivalent to the payment of the usual dividend on preference shares and of 6% on the original shares in the Company.[125]

Although these details were advertised in 'The Cambrian' of August 21, giving advance notice of the 39th Half-Yearly meeting, not a single shareholder turned up to the actual meeting itself, evidence, as Starling interpreted it, of their complete confidence in the Directors.[126]

Towards the end of 1874 the line from Morriston to Glais was inspected several times but failed to obtain Board of Trade approval for a passenger service although it was opened for goods traffic on January 17 1875. On the same day MR signalling regulations were brought into use on the SVR. It was the intention of the MR to open the line for passenger traffic on March 1, but Board of Trade approval was not given until the 8th, so there may have been a delay.[127] Passenger services over the original route via Llansamlet were discontinued at this time.

Two years later, by an Act of August 11 1876, the MR obtained powers to absorb the SVR completely, subject to the consent of its shareholders.[128] At a Special General Meeting on December 14, it was proposed by Starling, seconded by G B Strick, and resolved that the Swansea Vale Railway undertaking be vested in the Midland Railway.[129]

124 37 & 38 Vic *cap* clxx
125 C Aug 21 1874, p 5
126 C Aug 28 1874, p 5
127 Board of Trade Inspection PRO MT6 132/16
128 39 & 40 Vic *cap* ccix
129 SVR Minute Book PRO RAIL 679/9

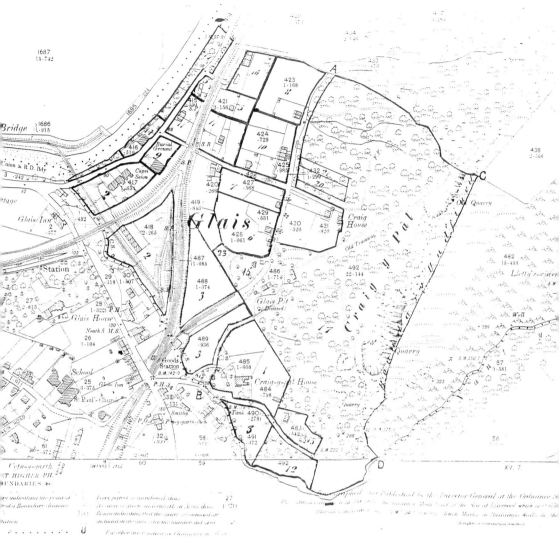

46   The Midland Railway at Glais. Also shows part of Glais Estate (plots 1 - 23) sold by the
Bensons in 1917   D/D SB 12/123, WGRO

This left the sixty-eight year old Starling with one less commitment to take
him away from the tranquillity of his home in Gower. It had been a long haul
since his step-mother had first recorded his visits to London 'on railway
business', and he must have savoured the chance to relax, knowing both industry
and passengers had profited by his efforts down the years.

Through Starling's canny stewardship the humble local project which began
with C H Smith's tramroad was to spawn a variety of lines. These
communications with the Midlands and the North were to prove vital to the
continuing buoyancy of Welsh trade over many years.

Chapter XIII

Starling and the Harbour Trust

A subject as comprehensive and detailed as the history of the activities of the Swansea Harbour Trust during the forty-four years of Starling's association with it demands a whole book to itself. All one can possibly do here is to touch on various aspects of the contribution he made to its work, first as a Proprietary Trustee and then as its Chairman, and trust that those who are interested will pursue the subject in greater depth for themselves. For the general reader the appeal will probably lie in the cut-and-thrust of Harbour politics and what it shows of the man who shouldered much of the responsibility over a longer period than any other Chairman of the Harbour Board.

The painful nature of the Bensons' earlier relations with the Swansea Harbour Trust, of which Starling became a Proprietary Trustee in 1834 and his father in 1836, might well have inhibited a lesser man than Starling from persisting in its deliberations. He had, however, in the years between 1838, the time of the Tyrllandwr case, and 1856, when he became its Chairman, obviously made a deep impression on his fellow Trustees by his sincere concern for the prosperity of the port and town of Swansea and his ability to deal with the various problems resulting from its development. Their respect for him remained until his retirement from the office in 1878.

By 1856 Mr Pascoe St Leger Grenfell had served as Chairman of the SHT for nine years. They had been years which covered many advances in the development of the port. After the opening of the New Cut had come the completion of the North Dock by 1852; there was still, however, the half-tide basin to accomplish. Another venture was the construction of the South Dock begun by a private company but, by 1856, well on the way to being taken over by the Harbour Trust.[1]

In all the deliberations regarding these developments Starling had played a full and active part, bringing to the Trustees' meetings a wide and varied experience. Many of the meetings had been stormy but none so acrimonious as those in which Francis Philip Hooper, the Duke of Beaufort's agent, found fault with the Trustees and the progress of their undertakings.

Proprietary Trustees with interests along the Tawe had been subjected to constant niggling. In 1845, the Duke had threatened litigation against those who had built wharfs in the New Cut. Among these had been the Bensons.[2] Although this threat had later been withdrawn, the situation had undoubtedly coloured the attitude of the younger members of the Benson family towards the Duke. Starling, unlike his stepmother, was no respecter of privilege for its own sake. As

1   W H Jones, *op cit*, p 236
2   C Dec 8 1845, p 3

a result, he was soon to prove himself one of those least likely to be intimidated by the Duke's hectoring agent, Francis Hooper.

At the June meeting of 1855 Hooper had arrived too late to hear the report on the progress of new works being undertaken in connection with the creation of the much needed half-tide basin. In the ensuing discussion, he had reacted violently, threatening action against those responsible for pressing on with the completion of works at the Pottery without sufficient reference to the Duke. Starling, with Pascoe St Leger Grenfell, Sydney Hall and J W James, retorted that they had been placed on the Board as Trustees to further the general trade of the port, not to promote the particular interest of the Duke of Beaufort.[3]

The respective responsibilities of the Trustees and the Duke in relation to the carrying out of work on the half-tide basin were laid down in the 1854 Harbour Act. The Sections referring to the erection of Quay walls were to cause particular difficulty:

> The Trustees may and shall and are hereby required to construct on both Sides of the existing New Cut, from the existing Wharf Walls at the Hoist Bridge to Fabian's Bay, proper and substantial Foundation Walls, to the Height of Six Feet above the lowest Depth of Water in the new Cut; and may fill up any vacant Spaces behind these Foundation Walls; and may and shall make and maintain that new Cut of such Depth as that the Water therein up to those Foundation Walls shall in all Places be of the same Depth as in the Centre. (Part of Section 60)

> The Duke of Beaufort, His Heirs or Assigns, may and shall, within Twelve Months after the Completion of the Foundation Walls on both Sides of the new Cut, construct proper and substantial Quay Walls upon those Foundation Walls so far as they front the Lands of the said Duke, and to a Height of at least Three Feet above High-water Mark, and the Trustees may fill up any vacant Spaces behind those Quay Walls to the Level thereof. (Section 61)

> The Duke of Beaufort, his Heirs or Assigns, may and shall, within Six Months after the Completion of the Foundation Walls on the Eastern Side of the Half-tide Basin construct, and shall for ever thereafter maintain, proper and substantial Quay Walls upon those Foundation Walls, and, to a Height of at least Three Feet above High-water Mark, and the Trustees may fill up any vacant Spaces behind those Quay Walls to the Level thereof. (Section 62)[4]

The implementation of these different requirements was to cause friction between the Trustees and the Duke for a number of years.

In 1856 Grenfell decided to retire as Chairman of the Harbour Trust. This led to the consideration of a successor at the Harbour Trust meeting of August 15. By this time Starling's personal dedication to the cause of the port and its trade

3   C June 8 1855, p 5
4   Swansea Harbour Act 1854, 17 & 18 Vic *cap* cxxvi

was acknowledged by his fellow Trustees. The Mayor, E M Richards, spoke highly in favour of Starling as 'a gentleman who had for many years been connected with this port'. He would venture to say that no one knew better the trade and harbour affairs of Swansea than did Mr Benson. He added that his business habits were well known to the Trustees and were 'sufficient guarantee for the able discharge of the duties of the chairmanship.'

Starling had no illusions about his new role. It was not one 'to be coveted, as it involved much trouble and responsibility'. All the same he would endeavour 'to carry on the duties of that office faithfully and he trusted satisfactorily, relying as he did on the co-operation of the officials of the Trust, as well as of the members of the Board'. The proposal was carried unanimously and Starling took the Chair.[5]

Since 1844 the Board had had its own solicitor and in Lewis Thomas Starling found an able and staunch ally. His task was further lightened by the appointment for the first time of a Vice-Chairman in the person of J W James who now occupied a position similar to that held, under the old Swansea Harbour Act, by his father, Christopher James, one of the early pioneers in the development of the town.

Nevertheless, the work of the Trust, largely involved at this time with the troubled question of the half-tide basin, was fraught with problems which necessarily weighed upon the Chairman. Hooper, on behalf of the Duke of Beaufort, was making difficulties over the question of the foundation of the walls, while G G Francis and, to a lesser extent, J C Richardson, were both adopting delaying tactics.[6] In a controversial move, G G Francis, no longer a Trustee, sought permission in the meeting of August 15 1856, to read a letter advocating the abandonment of the half-tide basin, an idea supported by Mr Richardson. Hooper, on the other hand, wanted the speedy completion of the works and held the Trustees responsible for the delay. The Duke's neighbouring Beaufort Dock, finished by 1852, could not function fully until the half-tide basin had been constructed.[7] Finally, however, on October 14 1856 the Duke, the Corporation and the Trust came to an agreement on the sharing of cost and responsibility, but only after a letter from the Duke himself had helped to draw some of the sting out of his agent's constant sniping.[8]

The Harbour Trust's preoccupation over several months with the Swansea Harbour Bill of 1857, allowing for the dissolution of the Swansea Dock Company and the transfer of its powers to the Swansea Harbour Trust, overshadowed other concerns, both of the Trust and the Town Council. Eventually, in spite of the last minute panic over the retention or otherwise of the Dry Dock, the issue was brought to a successful conclusion in August 1857.[9]

As a result of the passing of the Act, it was now proposed in the September meeting of the Trust that work on the half-tide basin of the North Dock be

---

5   C Aug 15 1856, p 8
6   *Ibid*
7   Swansea & Neath Railway Bill, Select Committee, June 17 1861
8   C Oct 17 and Nov 14 1856, both p 6
9   *Vide* pp 69-72

47 Harbour entrance between East and West Pier-heads from a print by Newman & Co.,
1850s   Courtesy of Mr W C Rogers

48 Beaufort Dock, 1851   Courtesy of Mr W C Rogers

deferred until the South Dock and the Railway to it were completed. The very suggestion of even a three months' delay met with strong protests from those representing the Duke's interests, mainly the quartet of Hooper, Price, (the Duke's local agent), Gaskoin and Glasbrook. They saw this suggested postponement as a way of shelving the work indefinitely. Starling was not to be intimidated. Although he had not originally been over enthusiastic about the creation of the South Dock, he now believed that, since it had been started, the work there must be prosecuted with determination. He pointed out firmly from the Chair that no one was more interested in the completion of the half-tide basin than he, and, indeed, had it not been for delays caused by the Duke over the foundation of the Quay walls, the work would have been finished long before.[10]

He suggested that one way out of the delay over the half-tide basin would be for the trade of the existing float to be carried on during its construction by means of a channel from the New Cut into the existing lock instead of sending vessels round the New Cut. He accordingly asked Mr Abernethy, the Engineer-in-Chief, to report on the feasibility of the idea.[11] This, however, was not pursued.

No amount of hard work on the part of the Trust and its Chairman could appease Mr Hooper who continued to harass them over the half-tide basin. In addition he made numerous other complaints about real or imaginary infringements of the Duke's rights. The Duke's claims, he felt, had been postponed 'most unceremoniously and unhandsomely' as a result of their dilatoriness. Starling reminded Hooper that it was the Duke's objections, amounting at one point to the threat of an injunction if they went ahead, that had obstructed the work of the Trust. Mr Hooper retaliated that that was because they were not proceeding in a proper manner. He did not bother, however, to specify what was 'improper' about it.[12]

Unfortunately Mr Hooper's obstructionism meant the Trustees had to give notice at the end of 1857 to Messrs Jones & Morris, contractors for the half-tide basin. As a result, the firm claimed payment for the twelve months they had virtually lost through the delay caused by the controversy with the Duke, with £12,000 for breach of contract. To meet this claim it seemed that the Harbour Trust would have to abandon either the half-tide basin or their scheme for extending the piers.[13]

To defer the work on the former until 1859 would land the Trustees in an extra expense of £4,000 for a renewal of their Parliamentary powers. Such delay would also give the Duke's agent some genuine ground for complaint, as Starling well knew. All things considered, Starling felt it expedient to proceed with the half-tide basin, and, backed by such unusual bedfellows as Messrs Price, Gaskoin and Glasbrook, as well as J P Budd, Pascoe Grenfell, Richard Aubrey and Sydney Hall, he was able to overcome what resistance there was.[14]

10   C Sept 4 1857, p 6; *cf* Editorial, p 4
11   C Sept 18 1857, p 8
12   C Oct 16 1857, p 8
13   C Dec 18 1857, p 8
14   *Ibid*

As we have seen, the Trustees were responsible for the walls in the New Cut from their foundations up to a certain height, while it was the Duke's responsibility to complete the upper portion of the walls. When the Trustees' appeal to the Duke to fulfil his obligation in this respect was ignored, in April 1858 they instructed the Clerk to apply for a *Mandamus* of the Queen's Bench.[15] Blame for the failure in communication was inevitably attached to the Duke's agent and so the following month a direct approach was made to the Duke himself.

Matters came to a head in the June meeting in 1858 when the Vice-Chairman, J W James, accused Mr Hooper of trickery. Whenever they had direct contact with the Duke, he maintained, it was possible to transact business 'as became a nobleman, a gentleman or a commercial man', but 'directly they had Mr Hooper to deal with, new difficulties were thrown in the way ... and their public business was impeded.'[16]

Mr Hooper countered by accusing the Trustees of going behind his back and surprising the Duke into a correspondence he would never have entered had he known the full facts of the case. 'Trickery' was therefore on their side, not his. He had come to Swansea seeking an amicable solution to all the questions in dispute which he was anxious to have disposed of together, whereas the Trustees wanted individual items dealt with separately.

While assuring Mr Hooper of no personal hostility on the part of the Trustees, the Chairman explained that they had sent their letter of May 5 1858 to the Duke in person as direct contact was vital. They wished to be conciliatory but, speaking for himself, Starling had learned from past experience. Whenever they were within sight of an agreement, some new difficulty was created. That was why it was necessary to have each separate agreement with the Duke on a firm footing, not all mixed together, irrespective of their connections, as Mr Hooper wanted.[17]

Earlier in 1858 a new crisis had arisen with the suspension of the Harbour Master, Captain Pixley, under circumstances shrouded in mystery, his resignation being accepted by the Executive Committee without reference to the General Meeting. The charge, one of great negligence and impropriety in the management of the affairs of the Harbour, was sufficiently serious to cause the Mayor, John Oakshot, grave doubt about the way they were handling the case. He felt someone in a less influential position would have had action taken against him whereas Captain Pixley was being sheltered by influential friends on the Board.[18] John Oakshot was a man who had worked himself up in the business world from a humble draper's apprentice and his sympathies were naturally with the less privileged.

John Rolley Tripp wanted the shorthand notes of the previous meeting read as some of those present did not know the nature of the charges. The Chairman was prepared for this to be done if anyone so moved; he was anxious to guard against the impression that matters had been dealt with covertly, but even so, he hoped

---

15   C April 9 1858, p 8
16   C June 18 1858, p 8
17   *Ibid*
18   C March 12 1858, p 6

the Trust would accept that the case had been thoroughly investigated by the Executive.

The general cloak and dagger atmosphere surrounding the resignation gave rise to public suspicion, scathingly satirised in a letter by 'T H C' to 'The Cambrian', in which he imagined the scene of:

> this solemn farce ... where those ubiquitous individuals yclept reporters, are never allowed to show their noses, much less their pens, ink and paper, and consequently the public remains in the most profound ignorance of what transpires ... The books are opened with becoming reverence - the Chairman rises with more than usually thoughtful countenance - he addresses the members almost in breathless silence, imparting something too sacred for ears profane to hear - the members express their surprise, and some express their determination to sift the matter to the bottom.

He describes another meeting which is called - this time with a short-hand writer present. An investigation proceeds, but no report emerges.

> The various members of the fraternity slyly slip out of the committee chamber, run up dark lanes and alleys on their way home (in order to avoid being questioned) and then bury themselves and their thoughts for the rest of the week.[19]

A further instance of misuse of influence came to light in connection with the appointment of Captain Pixley's successor. It was found some over-enthusiastic friends of one of the candidates, a Captain Thomas Thatcher of the Merchant Service, had been canvassing various Trustees, including the Chairman, who had simply ignored the letters. Sydney Hall revealed that he had been asked by one gentleman to use his personal influence with Mr Benson; 'but', he added, 'the writer could not have known the Chairman, otherwise he would have known he would never be influenced by anything of the kind.'[20]

After much discussion, it was decided Captain Thatcher should still be interviewed for fear a good candidate's position be compromised by the folly of his friends. Starling offered it as his belief that the Trustees would vote conscientiously for the best man.[21] His confidence in them was fully justified by the appointment of Captain Herbert, a commander in the Royal Navy, who served the Trust most competently until he moved to Sunderland some three years later. Only the awkward quartet of Hooper, Glasbrook, Gaskoin and Price, together with the Mayor and J J Strick, continued to support the suspect Thatcher.

Although by this time Starling had moved from Russell House in Swansea itself to Fairy Hill in Gower and had, on account of the distance, retired from the

19   C March 12 1858, p 8
20   C April 9 1858, p 8
21   *Ibid*

Town Council, he continued to serve the Harbour Trust as Chairman. Of his re-election in the summer of 1858, 'The Cambrian' wrote:

> Since his occupation of the chair, and long before that, he has taken a warm interest in the affairs of the harbour, and although always keenly alive to matters connected with his own side of the river, he has nevertheless, by his extensive experience, business tact, straight-forward conduct and gentlemanly bearing, been at all times a most valuable member of the Board.[22]

Now, however, he was driving a frequently unwieldy team of horses. The Docks and Railway Committee, appointed in August 1857 to oversee the construction of the South Dock and the railway to it, had taken upon itself, without any mandate from the General Board, to increase the Clerk's salary from £300 to £500, as was revealed in the monthly meeting of October 1858. The application for a rise in salary had come from Mr Lewis Thomas himself who claimed the procedure was perfectly regular and legal, a view hotly contended by Mr Tripp. In support of the Committee's recommendation, Mr James argued that the Docks and Railway Committee had already dealt with large amounts of money in their transactions with the contractors for the South Dock, Messrs Tredwell and Co., and, in any case, the Committee had merely recommended the increase. It was up to the Trust to accept or reject.[23]

Because of his father's death on October 6 1858, Starling was away for this contentious meeting. During his absence at Teddington, a new disaster overtook the Trust. Its Harbour Offices were destroyed in an extensive fire at 1.30 am on Wednesday, October 12. Fortunately some valuable documents were saved though many, including plans and bonds, were lost.[24] The destruction of these premises led G G Francis to write to 'The Cambrian' suggesting the siting of any new buildings away from 'the Seven Dials of Swansea'.[25] For the time being, the Trustees met in chambers in the Post Office rented for £50 for one year,[26] though by October 1860 they were able to move into fine new premises in Mount Street, in the immediate vicinity of the new Docks, town float, Custom House and principal merchants' offices. These, 'containing every necessary convenience', had been completed at low cost by Messrs Evans Bros. of London, from plans by Mr Richards, a local architect.[27]

For some while, consideration had been given to the possibility of Mumbles becoming the Harbour of Refuge for the Bristol Channel, a development strongly recommended by James Abernethy and the Bristol Harbour Master, Captain Claxton. In August 1857 a petition had been drawn up by the Trustees in support of a similar request from the merchants of Swansea, signed by both John Oakshot, 'shipowner and Mayor of Swansea' and Starling Benson, 'coal shipper and harbour trustee', together with many other prominent businessmen.[28] Some

---

22   C Aug 13 1858, p 4
23   C Oct 15 1858, p 6
24   C Oct 15 1858, p 5
25   *Ibid*
26   C Nov 1 1858, p 6
27   C Oct 12 1860, p 5
28   C Aug 14 1857, p 6

dissatisfaction had been expressed with Mr Dillwyn's dilatoriness in bringing the issue before the Select Committee of the House of Commons then actually dealing with the subject. As a result no mention of Mumbles was made in the first Report in Parliament.

The following year a visit by the Commissioners reporting on the best site for such a Harbour of Refuge led the Swansea Mercantile Marine Service to request the Trust to be ready with full scientific and nautical evidence on the advantages of the Mumbles Roadstead over the other sites proposed.

Jealousy of Mumbles had already surfaced at a meeting in Newport where it was decided to support Clovelly, a decision prompted by the fear that the proximity of Mumbles to Swansea would present a threat to the trade of both Newport and Cardiff.[29] Stung by such opposition, G G Francis wrote to 'The Cambrian' in June 1858, to rally support for Mumbles, warning of 'the survival of prejudices and jealousies in favour of out-of-the-way places'.[30] Starling was commended for having 'with his usual tact and discretion' authorised an engineer to be fully prepared with all the facts relevant to the subject, but it was seen as a failure on the part of the other Trustees that a question of such vital importance should be left to the Chairman alone.[31]

The next obstacle was to be trouble with the Town Council over the contractors' sudden decision to change the proposed line of the Harbour Railway, thereby diverting the Oystermouth tramway on to the public Quay without prior consultation with the Corporation. This contravened the Surveyor's report of March 12 1857 which had called for free and unrestricted passage between the parts of the Corporation land taken by the Harbour Trust for the Dock railway.[32] The Trustees were now asked to desist or pay adequate compensation. They were accused of having shown 'a discourteous and ungenerous attitude' by having failed to respond to a previous approach by the Council.

This charge particularly hurt the members of the Trust. They were anxious to explain that part of the trouble had been caused by the destruction of important documents in the recent fire. These had now been replaced and the Chairman looked forward to future co-operation, though he added, with his strict adherence to the truth, 'being realistic, he had to admit it was difficult to carry out large public undertakings without some unpleasantness occurring'.[33]

As a result of slow progress in the half-tide basin, the New Works Committee had had to apply to Parliament for an Act for an extension of the time allowed by the Swansea Harbour Act of 1854. This was granted by the short Harbour Act of 1859, extending the time until June 1 1860, and the Act of July 3 1860 for a further period until November 1860. The Trust was authorised to borrow extra money, £10,000 of which was to be set aside to complete simultaneously the half-tide basin and the Harbour Railway. The initial application was, foreseeably, opposed by the Duke of Beaufort who, in his petition to the House of Commons, accused the Trustees of slackness. He had already paid them £3000 on account

29   C April 2 1858, p 8
30   C June 2 1858, p 5
31   C Sept 17 1858, Editorial, p 4
32   C Dec 17 1858, p 6
33   C Dec 17 1858, p 8

of the expenses of the quay walls and, if granted an extension, he feared they 'would not vigorously prosecute the same, to the great loss and prejudice of the Petitioner unless clauses were inserted in the Bill to protect him'.[34]

During a second period of absence on Starling's part, caused this time by his stepmother's death on July 3 1859, less than a year after her husband's, the New Works Committee was able to report that the Duke had withdrawn his opposition.[35] There still remained, however, recurrent brickbats. In the first meeting of 1860, Mr James, deputising for Starling, this time away through illness, reported that, without giving any prior warning, the Duke was taking legal action over an excessive amount of soil deposited from the South Dock on the seashore.[36]

There had been achievements to offset their troubles. On September 23 1859 the South Dock had been opened,[37] as we have already seen. Nevertheless the half-tide basin of the North Dock continued to cause problems so, after their difficulties with Jones & Morris and the lost momentum caused by earlier delays, the Trustees had set up their own committee to supervise the work, with powers to sub-contract. This committee comprised the Vice-Chairman, E M Richards and Sydney Hall.[38] The decision was generally welcomed by the Shipowners' Association and the Corporation at a special meeting convened to consider the matter.[39] Initially the Duke had opposed the move, but it was hoped that once he saw, by an expeditious completion of the foundation of the much debated walls, that the change was in his own best interests, he would come round to acting quickly to supply the funds needed for the work.[40] By now, however, Jones & Morris were showing open hostility and it became necessary for the Trustees to file a Bill in Chancery to prevent the firm's interfering with the execution of the work.[41]

Winding up the affairs of the now defunct Dock Company brought its vexations too. In order to be reimbursed for their debts of £33,000 and the arrears of interest which had accrued, the Trust had to take proceedings against the Company. There was also the suit brought against the Trust by Mr Joseph Pickering who, as both contractor to and investor in the Dock Company, had sought to retrieve the large debt still owing to him. The case had been decided in his favour, granting him £27,329 with expenses and the costs of the case. For these the Trustees could hope to be reimbursed out of the Dock Company's assets, provided they were sufficient to meet the demand. To ascertain the amount of their debts and liabilities it had been necessary for the Harbour Trust to file a Bill against them in Chancery; and all this cost money.[42]

The completion of the South Dock brought its own problems. One of these was the inadequate provision made for conveying the coal. The Trustees were

---

34   C April 15 1859, p 8
35   C July 15 1859, p 8
36   C Jan 13 1860, p 3
37   C Special Supplement, Sept 23 1859, p 2
38   C April 20 1860, Editorial, p 5
39   C April 20 1860, p 6
40   C May 18 1860, p 6
41   *Ibid*
42   C June 15 1860, p 6

particularly anxious to attract back colliery proprietors, especially in the Aberdare and Merthyr areas, who were now using other ports. The general dissatisfaction with the existing situation was clearly shown at the first meeting of the Swansea Coal-Trade Association on January 3 1860:

> It should be remarked that the wretched state of things which has existed in this Port, in connection with the Railway-borne coal trade since the date of the opening of the South Dock, is now a fact patent to the world at large, vessels belonging to all countries having spread the intelligence far and wide. Aberdare Colliery Proprietors have found their trade so impeded and their interests so damaged at the port in connection with matters over which they have not the slightest control that it has become to them a serious question whether they should bring coal to Swansea at all when they can ship to greater advantage in every respect elsewhere.[43]

To win back their lost customers it was necessary to provide adequate means of handling the coal and to establish a more efficient network of railways. To this end, it was vital to convince the various railway companies of the Trust's credit-worthiness. It was therefore all the more unfortunate that Mr Hooper should now imply that, because they were reluctant to spend money on providing a temporary structure for the removal of goods from one part of their new low-level railway to the other, they were in financial difficulties.

Even Starling could not preserve his usual equanimity under such misrepresentation. He felt that a great many things said in Board meetings were being misinterpreted. That they were not inclined to spend their money on this particular piece of work did not mean they were in financial difficulties. There was no deficiency of funds to carry out anything they considered of permanent benefit to the Harbour.[44] The Trustees had recently decided on installing hydraulic machinery at the new dock,[45] which gave Swansea a distinct advantage over the other Welsh ports.[46]

The long-awaited opening of the half-tide basin took place on Monday, November 26 1860,[47] but this in no way improved Mr Hooper's temper. The 'Local Events' column in 'The Cambrian' of December 14 described a peremptory letter from the Duke's agent as a *'fulmen brutum'*.[48] To complete the quay walls on behalf of the Duke it had been necessary for the Trustees to occupy a triangle of his land. They had previously been warned against using it for any purpose other than building these walls, a restriction they had conscientiously observed. Now they were suddenly notified that, after December 1, they would be charged £20 a day for occupation of the land.

The Trustees' first reaction was to abandon the walls, leaving the Duke to make his own arrangements for finishing them. On second thoughts, they decided

43   Michael Hale, 'The Origins of the Swansea & Neath Railway', Welsh Railways Archive, p 167
44   C Oct 19 1860, p 6
45   C July 20 1860, p 3 & Aug 16 1861, p 8
46   C July 4 1862, p 5
47   C Nov 30 1860, p 5
48   C Dec 14 1860, pp 4 & 6

that, having accepted the commitment, they preferred to honour it, while protesting to Mr Hooper about his claim.[49]

The resignation of Captain Herbert as Harbour Master on his appointment to a similar, though better paid, position in Sunderland[50] led to the decision to combine the vacant post with that of General Superintendent of the Harbour. Its occupant would concentrate on the administrative side, while the purely practical aspects of the work would be left in the capable hands of Captain Rosser, the deputy Harbour Master. The new appointment went to the Vice-Chairman of the Trust, J W James, upon whom so much of the business of the Trust was devolving now that the Chairman lived out of town. This was not without opposition from Messrs Oakshot, Gaskoin and Price, the last named being anxious to propose George Grant Francis as a candidate.[51] There was feeling in certain quarters too that the Trust need never have lost Captain Herbert's outstanding services had they been more ready to accede to his quite reasonable request for a rise in his pay and more convenient living accommodation.

Although Starling - often conservative by nature though Liberal in politics - was at first averse to a change in the system of managing the Trust's affairs, he had come to see that the present situation made such a change necessary. They could not go on expecting Mr James to give of his private time without emolument, especially as negotiations with the railways were becoming increasingly time-consuming.[52]

An important change affecting the Trust's relationship with the Duke of Beaufort came before the end of the year with the death of Mr Hooper on September 29 1861, and the assumption of his duties by Mr Charles Baker of the firm of Watkins, Hooper & Co.[53] As Chief Steward to the Duke, Mr Baker took his seat on the Board and immediately created a good impression, leading to improved relations with the Duke. Mr Vivian referred to the 'friendly and kind manner' in which he had met them in negotiations over land south of the new Docks which they required for coal drops. There had been 'no hair-splitting niceties or theoretical views attempted' to bedevil the arrangements.[54] Even a year and a half later, when permission was needed from the Duke before they could act on a report from Mr Abernethy concerning the extension of the Western Pier, Mr Tripp assured the Trust that anyone dealing with the present agent would be met 'in the most fair and candid and straightforward spirit.'[55]

The three issues now occupying the Trust were the sorting out of the railway system, the deepening of the South Dock and the extension of the Piers.

After the opening of the North Dock the SWR had extended its line from the Brewery premises to coal drops along the dock. Under the Harbour Act of 1857, as we already know, the Trustees had been authorised to make and maintain a railway from there to the South Dock, to be called the Swansea Harbour Railway.

49   C Dec 14 1860, p 6
50   C Aug 16 1861, p 8
51   C Aug 30 1861, p 5
52   *Ibid*
53   C Oct 18 1861, p 3
54   C March 14 1862, p 6
55   C Oct 16 1863, p 3

W H Jones describes in detail what had been entailed in its construction:

> For this purpose much property and wharfage had to be acquired; the character of the quays along the north dock was altogether transformed by the erection of the substantial arches; the canal wharves, the Brewery premises, Richardson's dry dock and repairing yard, the Landore, Cameron's, and Swansea wharves, and particularly the Corporation quay, suffered considerable encroachment.
>
> Some ancient houses on the east end of the Strand were removed, as, too, was the western side of Quay Parade, where stood the Ship Inn, one of the rendezvous of the press-gang, a great many old houses on the east side of Little Wind-street (formerly Watchet-row ...), including another press-gang resort, the Beehive public house, and the spacious gardens of these houses, which reached to the present line of the Victoria-road front of the Sailors' Home, paid heavy toll to the great mass of masonry which formed the viaduct upon which the railway was to be laid. It cut through the ground of the Royal Institution of South Wales, and the wedge-like premises between York-place and Victoria-road narrowly escaped obliteration, which would have meant the loss, earlier than its eventuation, of the familiar sculptor's shop of Mr Levison, wherein had long been carved the attractive and highly-coloured figure-heads which, to the pride of generations of gallant seamen, adorned the prow of many a wind-jammer whose well-set-up lines had been fashioned upon the banks of the Tawe ...
>
> The harbour railway was completed and opened simultaneously with the south dock, the contractors being Messrs Tredwell & Co. of London and Gloucester, and the cost about £70,000. The low-level harbour railway was then put in hand, and in October, 1859, the Trustees contracted with Messrs Tredwell & Co. for the formation of the line from the New-cut-road to the south dock, joining the Oystermouth railway near Bath-lane and branching away from it near the Royal Institution of South Wales, through whose grounds it passed on to the dock.[56]

The Trustees now sought to let the Harbour Railway, either on lease for a term of years or in perpetuity, or to sell and transfer it, to the South Wales Railway. After careful negotiation an agreement was reached containing the condition that such power was to be vested in the South Wales Railway Company to the exclusion of all other companies.[57] Later, as a result of failure to meet this condition, the SWR withdrew.

Relations with the SWR were frequently strained in spite of the presence of such influential members of the SWR Board on the Harbour Trust as H H Vivian

56   W H Jones, *op cit*, pp 201-203
57   C July 19 1861, p 5

and L L Dillwyn. It had been assumed by the Trustees that, once an agreement with the SWR had been formalised, the railway company would meet its financial commitments to the end of the previous year 'for leasing the Swansea Harbour Railway and the Coal Drops and Sidings belonging to it at the South Docks'. All seemed well when, up to June 28 1861, the South Wales Company had paid off £5000. Unfortunately, this compliance did not last, the Company refusing further payments until the value of the land taken by the Trust to form a junction between the Harbour Railway and the SWR at the South Dock had been assessed and paid for.[58]

Up until this time, the Vale of Neath Railway had been using the SWR line from Neath to Swansea via Skewen to provide an outlet for coal from the Aberdare area at the North Dock. This arrangement entailed serious practical difficulties which the Chairman of the Vale of Neath, H A Bruce, described to a House of Lords Committee. Because of delays and dangers caused by a steep gradient at the Skewen incline and also interference from the ordinary SWR traffic, the Vale of Neath Co. favoured an easier route along the coast from Neath to Swansea. An Act of 1861, introduced by the Swansea & Neath Railway Company and fully supported by the Vale of Neath, was passed, authorising a coastal line from a junction with the Vale of Neath, to a junction with the Swansea Harbour line to the South Dock. The Act also authorised running powers over the Harbour line.[59]

There had been opposition from Francis Hooper as traffic on the proposed route would affect adversely the business of the Duke's warehouses alongside the Beaufort Dock, possibly threaten their foundation on the quay walls, and also create a hazard in crossing the two bridges.[60] Nevertheless, the new line was opened on July 14 1863. Coal traffic began on the following day and a passenger service on August 1, with a station serving the line at Wind Street. On August 5 the Swansea & Neath Railway Co. was taken over by the Vale of Neath.[61]

Negotiations between E M Richards and Joshua Williams, the General Manager of the Vale of Neath Company, led to an agreement for a platform at the Wind Street station on the Harbour Railway.[62] This platform overhung land leased by the railway company from the Corporation at the peppercorn rent of a shilling a year for a period of five years.[63] The arrangement for the land was confirmed by a contract with the Corporation, whereas the SHT understanding was merely verbal. In any case the station was considered a temporary structure.

General opinion in South Wales was strongly opposed to the absorption of other lines in a powerful monopoly. In 1863 the GWR and the SWR had amalgamated and when, in the winter of 1864-65, the GWR introduced the Vale of Neath Transfer Bill in order to take over that Company, including running

58   C Feb 14 1862, p 8
59   Michael Hale, *op cit, passim*
60   Swansea & Neath Railway Bill, Select Committee, June 17 1861
61   *Ibid*
62   C April 17 1868, p 4
63   Gerald Gabb, SWWIAS Bulletin Number 13, July 1976

powers over the Swansea Harbour Railway, the Harbour Trust was deeply concerned.[64] The Trustees felt that the unopposed passage of the Bill could well lead to further encroachment from an amalgamated company in the future. P St L Grenfell, for one, was appalled at the thought of entrusting the affairs of the district, so conscientiously conducted by the Trust, 'to one gigantic Company extending everywhere without any good to itself or its shareholders.' They should strive to prevent at least their own harbour and railways being handed over to a Company which 'over thirteen years had done little to gain confidence or deserve support.'[65]

A committee to oppose the Bill was set up, consisting of Starling, Mr Sterry (another local colliery owner) and Mr Budd, supported, if necessary, by Mr Hall and Mr Jenkin. Mr Vivian, speaking as a Director of the Vale of Neath Company, although with a stronger loyalty to the Harbour Trust, was prepared to give the GWR the benefit of the doubt, especially as the South Wales section would be in the hands of the Secretary of the Vale of Neath Company, Joshua Williams, 'liberal, energetic and enlightened'. Starling, on this occasion, was inclined to be more sceptical. He was all for a committee to get the best terms they could as the Bill passed through Parliament.[66]

The Trustees had constructed the Harbour Railway, at a loss to themselves of £1800 per annum, for the benefit of the mineral trade. Further they had accepted responsibility for building bridges over the New Cut and the Float-lock in order to encourage the development of the coal market. It was necessary, therefore, to prevent a passenger-carrying service like the GWR from interfering with the smooth running of this mineral traffic and with shipping in the Harbour.[67]

The hazard of trains crossing the high-level bridges across the New Cut and the North Dock was foreseen by G G Francis in a forcible letter to 'The Cambrian' of February 3 1865.[68] The reality of his fears was brought home to the public all too starkly before the end of the year when in November a coal train on the Vale of Neath line plunged into the lock of the North Dock, killing both the driver of the train, William Cole, and its fireman, Clement Langstaff. The guard, George Gerrish, seeing the red light at the bridge over the North Dock, managed to jump clear. According to the Inspecting Officer's Report, the bridge had been left open the previous night in readiness for the early morning tide. The signalman, however, had been told that the bridge was closed and so gave the train the 'all clear'. The driver failed to see the danger signal at the bridge and the train plunged into the lock, badly damaging the engine and ten of the trucks, as well as killing the two men.

Huge crowds visited the scene of the disaster, many appearing to take a ghoulish delight in the *macabre* spectacle. It was inevitable that, however morbid the thought, onlookers were bound to speculate on how much more serious the accident could have been had the train been carrying passengers.[69]

64   C Jan 27 1865, p 6
65   C March 17 1865, p 6
66   *Ibid*
67   C Jan 27 1865, p 6
68   C Feb 3 1865, p 8
69   C Nov 30 & Dec 8 1865, both p 5

There now developed one of those apparent molehills of controversy which was, in time, to become a mountain. The GWR considered that they had inherited the platform at the Wind Street station when they took over the Vale of Neath line. As the Trust, unlike the Corporation, had no written agreement, the Railway Company was now claiming the Trust had foregone its right to it.

The Trustees, however, were adamant that, upon the expiry of the contract made by the Corporation for the land,[70] they were entitled to call for the removal of the platform on the grounds that it seriously inconvenienced the trade of the Docks for which the Harbour Railway was specifically built. As many as ten trains a day stopped there. At an approximate delay of half an hour each, this caused a reduction of trade amounting to anything between five to seven hours. Mr Strick, of the firm of solicitors with whom Florance Benson had had close links during his time in Swansea, pointed out that the Trustees had not spent £90,000 on the Harbour Railway to set up a passenger station at Wind Street. In any case, their relationship with the GWR was now very different from that with the Vale of Neath Railway whom they had done their best to accommodate.[71]

Unfortunately the GWR Company was in breach of agreement with the Trust over another matter, a compensation claim pending decision in the Court of Chancery. In spite of the Chairman's anxiety to keep the two issues separate, it was implied in certain circles that the question of Wind Street Station was being used by the SHT as a stick to prod the GW Railway Company. The Wind Street platform was the only Vale of Neath passenger station in the area, and its removal would cause considerable inconvenience to the public. This view was shared by those usually most loyal to the interests of the Trust, Messrs Vivian, Grenfell and Richards. To Starling, on the other hand, the issue was perfectly straightforward. The lease was about to expire, the platform hampered the trade of the Docks; now was the time to remove the obstacle.

A memorial purporting to come from a number of important traders in the area protesting against the removal of the platform was found, on closer scrutiny, to include in some cases two or three names in the same writing.

The signatories came mainly from Merthyr. Their interests, according to Starling, were easily counter-balanced by those of local traders to whom the platform was an impediment, a view queried by Mr Richards though he was willing to concede that Mr Benson was 'accurate in his own opinion'.[72]

In spite of official approaches by Lewis Thomas, the GWR Company continued to ignore any claim to the platform on the part of the Trust. It seemed nothing short of legal action would have any effect, but the day before proceedings were due to begin, an arrangement was offered whereby the GWR undertook to remove the offending platform within two years from July 1 1868, and, in the meantime, pay the Trustees £50 per annum.[73] Although agreement had been reached, the issue with which many of Starling's critics had linked it still

---

70   C Dec 13 1867, p 6
71   C April 17 1868, p 4
72   C Jan 17 1868, p 4
73   C Aug 14 1868, p 6

remained. The money owed to the SHT by the GWR amounted to £3,317 12s 1d. This had been deposited in the Glamorganshire Bank until a decision about it had been reached in Chancery. When it came, the decree entitled the Trustees to receive the said sum with accumulated interest.[74]

The GWR agreement to close the platform had not been implemented by December 1871. J J Jenkins was at that time still protesting at the SHT meeting. Eventually, however, on March 1 1873, the passenger service came to an end.[75]

As far as the two other questions went, the Chairman had pointed out as early as September 1861 that the extension of the Piers and the deepening of the channels were interrelated. A report from Mr Abernethy confirmed that the latter was both practical and expedient, and in the meantime, regular clearing by dredger would help to give added depth of water.[76] This, however, was not so easy to carry out effectively, and when, some time later, in July 1863, a letter was received from the Vale of Neath Railway Company complaining of loss of trade through lack of water at the entrance to the Harbour, some members interpreted it as a direct criticism of the Trust. Starling refused to adopt this view. He appreciated the Railway Company's dilemma and suggested that the solution, after all, was for Mr Abernethy to devise some plan for extending the West Pier.[77]

Eventually, on October 26 1863, a special meeting was called to consider the application to Parliament for powers to extend the Piers and deepen the channel. This involved borrowing £30,000. Mr Baker foresaw no difficulty over land required from the Duke, and the Chairman was optimistic about the standing of the Trust in relation to its bondholders. He had bonds himself and thought them 'first rate security'. 'I can only say for myself and as a Trustee for others that it is one of the safest investments which can be made.'[78]

By November 1863, an application had gone to Parliament for the necessary powers to carry out Mr Abernethy's proposals, now somewhat revised since their original form. It was at first contemplated that the Trust could achieve its purpose through an application to the Board of Trade whereby the procedure would be considerably shortened and the cost reduced,[79] but the idea had to be abandoned as unsuited to their situation, thereby making it necessary to obtain an independent Act of Parliament.[80]

All opposition having been dropped, the Bill went before the Select Committee of the House of Commons shortly after Easter 1864. The Chairman wanted work to begin as soon as possible but the question was whether it should be undertaken in its entirety or piece-meal. The latter method, with sub-contracting under the control of the Trust, had the advantage that it could be paid for little by little.

74   C Feb 19 1869, p 5
75   W H Jones, *op cit*, p 267
76   C Oct 18 1861, p 3
77   C July 17 1863, p 6
78   C Oct 30 1863, p 8
79   *Ibid*; *cf* C Nov 13, p 4
80   C March 25 1864, p 8

The Bill became law on June 3 1864. By July the Trust had accepted the lowest tender submitted for the extension work from Messrs Batchelor Bros. of Cardiff, and a committee was set up to negotiate the purchase of the land.[81]

Here relations with Mr Baker rapidly deteriorated through an unfortunate mistake. The Clerk had written to the Duke about the purchase of the required land in the hope of avoiding an application to Parliament for an Act to permit this, a course which seemed to both Mr Vivian and the Chairman a mere preliminary to reaching an amicable arrangement. Mr Baker took it that only an acre was being applied for - the amount of land referred to in Mr Thomas's letter as needed for the Pier - instead of the twenty acres needed for the entrance to the harbour. When his mistake was brought to his attention, he felt he had been deliberately deceived, and accused, if not the Trust, at least the Clerk, of 'a breach of faith'.

Mr Baker now demanded that the entire correspondence should be read before a General Meeting of the Trust, in spite of Mr Vivian's reminder that the whole matter had already been before Parliament when the Duke's advisers had had ample opportunity to object to the quantity of land required, had they so wished.[82] Mr Vivian further pointed out that, had Mr Baker stopped to reflect, he would have been bound to realise that an acre or two would hardly answer the needs of an entrance to the harbour.

There was a new complication when it was discovered that part of the land required was leased to Mr Tennant.[83] To avoid further friction, the Trustees decided to forego that particular piece of land, only to incur fresh criticism. One minute, it seemed they were under attack for wanting too much land, and the next, for cutting back on their requirements. It seemed they just could not win with Mr Baker in his present mood.[84]

'The Herald', always anxious for sensation to promote its sales, prophesied the inexorable doom of town and port that would follow this bitter warfare. This gave the less volatile 'Cambrian' ample opportunity to ridicule its rival when it emerged that the controversy between the Trust and the Duke ('no, not the Duke but his litigious agents') had been settled the previous week.[85]

Another issue now arose to exacerbate feelings between the Trustees and the Duke's representatives in the autumn of 1864. Mr Vivian and Mr Gilbertson had acquired Docks Purchase Bonds, originally valued at £67,000, for a mere £10,300 at a sale under a decree in the case of the Swansea Harbour Trust versus the Swansea Dock Company. These they wanted the Trustees to have at purchase price, subject to their obtaining the necessary Parliamentary powers for the transaction. The offer had to be provisionally accepted within two months, and the purchase made within two years. Although reluctant to speculate at that time, the Trustees saw the offer as one too good to miss, especially as it prevented the Bonds falling into the hands of those hostile to the Trustees' projects.

81   C July 22 1864, p 6
82   C Sept 16 1864, p 6
83   C Oct 21 1864, p 8
84   C Nov 18 1864, p 6
85   C Nov 25 1864, p 6

Accordingly, they set up a Committee to consider the offer, a procedure sharply criticised by Mr Baker since no notice of the matter had been given and discussion should not therefore have been allowed.[86]

To silence any trace of dissent, the Chairman called a special meeting for the following Monday, although the Clerk had assured the Trustees they were well within their rights under Section 49 of the Commissioners' Clauses Act. Mr Baker failed to attend but there was strong opposition from Mr J T Jenkin who, as former Secretary to the Dock Company, pointed out that the Company stood to lose a good £87,000 of the money invested in the undertaking. He submitted that, should any surplus accrue, as he hoped it might, the original company might share in that advantage.

The Chairman conceded that the case for the Dock Company had been put 'very temperately and on the whole very fairly', but he was anxious to remind the meeting that, if the Trust now appeared to be enjoying some advantage, it had for a long time borne the brunt of years of loss, including the award against it in the Pickering case. He obviously convinced his hearers as the acceptance of the shares was approved, with only Mr Price against and Mr Jenkin abstaining.[87]

It was only two years since the Trust had had to face another heavy award against it in the action brought by Mr George Byng Morris over payment for land taken for the construction of the Harbour Railway. The Trustees had refrained from handing over the money decided by the arbitrators until it had been established that Mr Morris was indeed the person entitled to receive it, as the lease had originally been granted to several parties.

A sympathetic hearing by Mr Justice Turner led to an adjournment for both sides to reach an equitable agreement,[88] but in a subsequent hearing in the Vice-Chancellor's Court, judgment was given against the Trust, Byng Morris being granted a decree for payment with 4% interest from the time of the defendants' taking over the land. Starling might well have had a feeling of *déjà vu*! The sting came in the tail, with Lord Justice Knight Bruce's comment that the Trust's conduct had been 'vexatious',[89] a charge generally resented but especially so by Mr J P Budd, who wanted their solicitor to answer the accusation. Both the Chairman and the Clerk, however, felt the matter best left to rest.

Meanwhile there were more immediate issues to be dealt with. As the result of the inadequacy of the lighting and policing of the docks there were frequent accidents. One tragedy which aroused public interest was the death of a young woman, Annie Watts, whose body was found in the water. It was presumed that she had become involved in a scuffle while following her now-reluctant sea-captain lover back to his ship. Both had fallen into the harbour, but the man managed to attract attention and was rescued. No mention, however, was made of the woman. Her body was not discovered until three days later, and by then the evidence was too scanty for more than a verdict of accidental death to be

---

86 C Sept 16 & Oct 4 1864, both p 6
87 C Oct 21 1864, p 6
88 C Aug 1 1862, p 5
89 C Aug 8 1862, p 5

returned.[90]

Although in this instance insufficient lighting may not have been the main cause of the incident, the case attracted the attention of the Trust to a recurrent problem. There had been six deaths in the docks since Christmas and it was only February. Mr Vivian suggested ropes along the side, and Mr Tripp, chains, as was done in Cardiff. The Mayor, G B Strick, undertook to bring the matter before the Council, although there was some feeling that, as the docks were private property, the payment of rates did not automatically entitle them to support from the Corporation. This applied not only to lighting but also to policing, loss of property being another constant problem in the area.[91]

Occasionally there were less serious moments in their transactions. The Swansea Canal Company had replaced the Trust's mooring posts by others marked 'SCC' on the quay opposite the Company's wharfs near the Town Float. Mr Price's suggestion that, if the posts encroached on the river, they were on the Duke's ground was greeted with an outburst of laughter. The Chairman, in playful vein, rejoined that Mr Price could be sure that, whoever owned the ground, it was not the Duke.[92]

Mr Price had obviously not forgotten the incident when, in a subsequent meeting, without having first obtained the ducal blessing, the Trust sanctioned Mr Vivian's request to erect a drawbridge over the Tawe opposite the Cambridge Alkali works. Mr Price rose to refute the Chairman's claim that, as trade in that area was comparatively small, the land there was not worth much. He remarked acidly that, had Mr Benson been the owner of property there, he would have considered it very valuable and have taken every precaution to improve and develop it.[93]

For a long time the local Board of Guardians had been pressurising the Trust under the Poor Law Amendment Act 1834 (4 & 5 William IV, *cap* lxxvi) for payment of poor rates. In September 1868 an appeal was pending and until a decision had been reached the Trustees were asked to pay £2000 without prejudice to the outcome. The Chairman accepted that they were liable for wharfs, lands, etc, but queried their liability for tolls on goods and vessels. These were levied for the good of the port and, as such, the Trust received no benefit from them. To make further demands on traders would be counterproductive; in Mr Strick's words, killing the goose that laid the golden egg. The high tolls and other charges at Swansea were being constantly quoted as a reason for shippers using other ports, and pressure for their reduction came regularly from such prominent industrialists on the Trust as James Palmer Budd, with Starling seeking to reassure them that, as soon as it was practicable, there would be a thorough overhauling of all port charges - but not yet.[94]

When the assessment by the Poor Law Commissioners eventually came, it was considered by J T Jenkin to be 'favourable'. Starling would only go so far as to allow it was 'fair'. The Trustees had had to yield on several points to get matters

---

90   C Feb 16 1866, p 6
91   *Ibid*
92   C May 17 1867, p 6
93   C Sept 13 1867, p 6
94   C Sept 18 1868, p 6

settled amicably, but it was agreed that possibly it was a good thing that they were not being seen as recipients of 'favour' in this instance.[95]

The payment of arrears eroded the Trustees' finances for the rest of the year, but fortunately trade was picking up and it was a matter of great satisfaction to Starling, when he was re-elected Chairman the following August, that the Trust had never had to increase the dues of the port. Moreover, on his suggestion, they had 'recently ended the capital account so that every farthing now came out of revenue.'[96]

An important part of this revenue came from tolls payable for crossing the bridge across the Tawe. When these had been introduced after the 1854 Harbour Act, it had been generally assumed, even by the Mayor, they would be payable merely until the bridge was paid for. Only on reading the Act for himself did he realise his mistake. The tolls could, if so required, become part of the ongoing revenue of the Trust for the upkeep of the Harbour. A request from the people of St Thomas for some alleviation of this burden elicited a good deal of sympathy from those who, like Mr Grenfell and the Chairman, had occasion to cross the bridge frequently. Starling wondered whether the question of bridge tolls and Corporation tolls could be looked at together to see if both might not be knocked on the head at the same time.[97]

The Mayor accordingly brought the question of bridge tolls before the Corporation. A committee was set up to confer with the Harbour Trust to consider the abolition of tolls from 12 midnight on Saturday or during such hours on Sunday as might be deemed desirable.[98] Starling's position was that the Trustees were bound, under the express terms of the Act of Parliament, to reduce or abolish tolls as soon as they could afford it, but then there was the question of making good the loss. Personally, he was anxious to do that, but, as Chairman, he had a duty to safeguard the revenue of the Trust in the interests of the Harbour. The best that could be done at the moment was for a committee consisting of Messrs Grenfell, J J Jenkins, H J Bath and Alfred Sterry to confer with the Corporation and report back.[99]

Relations with the local Gas Company were also causing concern. Although the Trust had installed its own gas mains, the Company insisted on positioning the meter where it appeared to be registering, not only the amount used by the Trust, but also by the GWR. Frequent letters to the Gas Company had produced no response. Starling was among those who, as a result, wanted the Trustees to consider manufacturing their own gas and a resolution by J W James was put to that effect. Admittedly it would be less pure than the Gas Company's product, but suitable enough for the lamps around the Docks.

The suggestion aroused powerful opposition. Those in favour were reminded that several firms who had sought to be independent were now giving up manufacturing their own gas and were returning to the Gas Company. In spite of the letters to the Manager, it appeared the Directors of the Company had only just

95   C Jan 15 1869, p 8
96   C Aug 13 1869, p 6
97   C Oct 14 1870, p 6
98   C Dec 16 1870, p 6
99   C Jan 13 1871, p 6

learned of the situation. Because of this, Mr Richardson proposed delaying a decision and this was carried in spite of the Chairman's desire to settle the issue once and for all. A fuller attendance than usual would have enabled them to reach a representative opinion. Now, by deferring a decision, they had lost that opportunity for good.[100]

The previous year, 1868, the Trust had been approached by the Harbour authorities of Sunderland and Stockton-on-Tees to support an application to the Government to extend the provisions of the Harbour and Passing Tolls Act 1861, so that loans might be considered retrospectively instead of being limited to new work only. The Chairman proposed that the Clerk should present a memorial from the Trustees to the Lords of the Treasury in support of this application and, within a fortnight, a deputation representing various northern and western ports was received at the Office of the Board of Trade.[101]

Swansea's direct link with Sunderland had been severed by the death of Captain Herbert in June 1868, seven years after he had left the town to become Harbour Master at the northern port.[102] Now, in April 1869, an opportunity for joint action by various Harbour Trusts was offered the port by an invitation to join a proposed Association of Public Harbour Authorities, issued by the Clerk of the River Wear Commission, Mr J S Robinson. It seemed highly desirable to Starling that authorities should unite in this way, especially as the subscription would not exceed 5/-![103]

The common interests of trading ports were again uppermost in the minds of the Trustees when, in 1870, Parliament was considering a measure for the abolition of compulsory pilotage. The control of pilots and their conduct had caused the Trust more than one headache over the years although conditions in Swansea made their services indispensable. The peculiar nature of the approach to the harbour entailed definite danger from vessels entering without pilots. Like Liverpool, Glasgow and other mercantile ports, the Trust was anxious to be represented before the Select Committee.[104] The Bill was happily withdrawn before the end of the summer, only to return the following year, when Mr Dillwyn as MP for Swansea and Mr Vivian as MP for the County were asked to intervene.[105]

With the growth in size of vessels coming into Swansea the Corporation was constantly receiving complaints from ship-owners about the inadequacy of the port. An important public meeting at the Guildhall in the autumn of 1870 again pressed for the deepening of the Harbour. What was needed, it was said, was either a Marquess of Bute or a Board of Harbour Trustees more alive to the problem. That the Duke of Beaufort was no Marquess of Bute was all too obvious from the flow of niggling complaints over such petty annoyances as dredgers coming too close to the Duke's property without his consent![106]

100 C Jan 15 1869, p 8
101 C March 13 1868, p 5
102 C June 6 1869, p 6
103 C April 16 1869, p 6
104 C March 18 1870, p 6
105 C Aug 12 1870 & April 14 1871, both p 6
106 C Nov 4 1870, p 6

Improved relations between the GWR and the Harbour Trust had led in June 1869 to a meeting of coal-shippers with the Chairman and Directors of the Railway Company who undertook to provide the greater part of the facilities required by coal-traders for the transport of coal. This outcome was most welcome to Starling who warmly congratulated his fellow Trustees on their success in establishing an improved climate for negotiation.[107]

Nevertheless the general lack of facilities continued to cause problems. During a visit of the Chairman of the GWR, Sir Daniel Gooch, to Swansea in November 1870, questions of extra siding accommodation, narrow gauge communication between the South and North Docks and more coal drops in the latter were all raised. One source of trouble, of which the secretary of the GWR, Mr Saunders, had been notified, was the accumulation under the shipping places in the South Dock of small coal, thrown overboard by the trimmers.[108]

In March 1871 'The Cambrian' reported an action which had been brought against the Trust by Messrs Livingston & Co. when one of their vessels failed to discharge its cargo on time in the South Dock, owing to an accumulation of coal. Judgment was given for the plaintiffs. When approached, the GWR not only refused to accept liability but warned that they would hold the Trustees responsible for any damage incurred. The latter had cleared the Harbour once under protest and could only hope now that any expenses would be refunded by the Railway Company.[109] The GWR, on the other hand, excused themselves by saying each shipper, jealous of his own independence, employed his own trimmers and it was they who caused the nuisance, which could only be alleviated by the GWR's being authorised to use their own trimmers.[110]

The name of Livingston was now coming to the fore in the public life of Swansea. Already a presence in Corporation meetings, James Livingston was a comparatively 'new boy' in the affairs of the Harbour Trust. In January 1872, he gave notice of a motion calling for greater facilities for the larger type of shipping now frequenting the port and, the following month, moved the resolution before the whole Trust, calling for a report from Mr Abernethy on (1) how to get extra depth of water and (2) the method and cost of carrying out such improvements.[111]

He was supported by Frank Ash Yeo whose firm, like Mr Livingston's, exported about a third of the total goods sent out of Swansea. Steam shipping was becoming increasingly important, although some still regarded it as a nuisance, likely to inconvenience the sailing ships with which the Docks were constantly overcrowded while they waited for wind and tide. The advantage of steamships was that they were able to come into port, unload and move off, irrespective of weather conditions. But lack of space was discouraging owners of steamships from coming to Swansea. On the other hand, with improved access to accommodation in the Harbour, Swansea could attract trade now going to Cardiff, Bristol or Liverpool.

---

107 C June 18 1869, p 6
108 C Nov 18 1870, p 6 & Dec 2, p 5
109 C March 24 1871, p 6
110 *Ibid*
111 C Jan 12 1872, p 6

The chief opposition to Mr Livingston's ideas came from Captain Thomas Davies who played down the future importance of steam. To him the recession was due to shortage of wharfs. Mr Budd's was another discouraging voice, fearful of any venture that would entail future expenditure. He was, however, soon reminded by both Mr Grenfell and Mr Glasbrook of earlier days when the Trustees had taken on colossal commitments with barely enough money for official salaries; they had grown over-cautious in their grey hairs. Starling too supported the resolution. It was essential to examine the possibilities and their cost, but the Harbour Bonds were sound, and he was sure the Corporation would help them in an emergency, seeing expansion as being in their own best interest.[112]

In spite of, or perhaps because of, his opposition to Mr Livingston's resolution, Captain Davies now came up with his own scheme: to float the tidal acres of Fabian's Bay, a scheme likely to cost some £500,000. It was opposed by G G Francis, favouring Mr Vivian's more modest scheme of placing gates at the exit of the New Cut together with the Tawe itself to give floating accommodation to his own and other works on the north banks of the river. The whole scheme was likely to cost only about £50,000.[113]

As an outcome of James Livingston's resolution, Mr Abernethy was asked to report on the best way to achieve the shipping facilities needed.[114]

'The Cambrian' of December 13 1872, more critical than usual, attributed Swansea's decline as a trading port to three factors: the failure of the Railway Companies to provide more coal drops, siding accommodation and engine power; the failure of the Harbour Trustees to provide greater depth of water and more dock area; and, lastly, the failure of colliery proprietors and merchants to provide themselves with an adequate number of railway trucks to convey coal to the port.[115] These criticisms had already been expressed in the meeting of shippers and others involved, convened by Mr Livingston the previous September.[116]

A cordial meeting with the new GWR Manager, Mr Lambert, led to an undertaking to remedy the shortage of coal drops[117] but, welcome though these might be, they could not remedy Swansea's basic weakness as a trading port, its congestion. This only a new dock would relieve.

The remainder of Starling's term in office was to be taken up with the struggle to convince councillors, traders and residents that his early vision of a dock on the eastern side of the Tawe could be a profitable reality. It would seem that the wheel had turned full circle from the time of his letter to 'The Cambrian' of November 1846.[118]

112   C Feb 16 1872, p 8
113   C April 12 1872, p 8
114   C Aug 16 1872, p 3
115   C Dec 27 1872, Editorial, p 5
116   C Sept 27 1872, p 8
117   *Ibid*
118   *Vide* pp 56*ff*

Chapter XIV

The East Dock

As we have seen, the 1870s were dominated by the call for improved shipping accommodation at Swansea. In accordance with Mr Livingston's proposition in February 1872, Mr Abernethy produced his report in May. Here he suggested that enough additional water could be obtained at the entrance to the Channel for the largest class of vessel using the Port and if thorough dredging were carried on, the improvements could be completed in three years at a cost of approximately £67,000. In addition he selected 'as the site of any future dock, the whole of Fabian's Bay and the greater portion of Port Tennant.' These, he felt, would offer 'facility of access and the best means of affording railway communication.' The total estimate for the whole of the channel and dock works was given as £305,827.[1]

The project of a new dock needed to gain general support if it was to succeed, as Starling well knew. To that end, in September 1872, James Livingston requested the Mayor, Mr Glasbrook, to call a meeting of ratepayers, which resulted in the formation of the Swansea Chamber of Commerce. Although Starling did not attend, other members of the Harbour Trust were present, among them Frank Ash Yeo[2] who followed this up at the October meeting of the Harbour Trust by putting forward his own scheme. He proposed 'that application he made to Parliament next session for powers to float the New Cut and River Tawe ... and to provide additional wharfage on both sides of the river'.

This fell far short of Mr Abernethy's proposals and produced mixed reactions. J J Jenkins and Captain Thomas Davies wanted the necessary notice to be given for both the construction of docks and floating the river so that, if the one did not come off, the other would. To Mr Strick this involved the risk of falling between two stools, a view endorsed later by Mr Vivian. Starling's opinion was that, if they went to Parliament for both, they must be able to show *bona fide* intentions of executing both, with sufficient money to carry out the two.

A strong argument in favour of the Fabian's Bay scheme was the availability of land belonging to the Tennant estates which had recently changed hands at a sale held by order of the Court of Chancery. Captain Davies felt the Trust would be wise to acquire floating accommodation in the part of the estate within the Swansea area while the terms were likely to be to their advantage.[3]

Another section of land required for the new dock belonged to the Duke of Beaufort. This had been formed as a result of an agreement as far back as the 1836 Act and the subsequent purchase of land for the development of the New

---

1 Abernethy Report, May 1872
2 C Oct 11 1872, p 6
3 C Oct 18 1872, p 3

Cut. A substantial part of the ground needed at that time had been purchased from the Bensons at Tyrllandwr, as we already know. The rest of the land required belonged to the Duke who gave the Trustees the option of paying £5000 or of paying only £500 but on condition that all the spoil from the New Cut would be deposited on the beach at Fabian's Bay. The Trustees had chosen the second option thus providing the Duke with a valuable reclamation of land. It was this land that was now needed for a part of the proposed East Dock. (*Vide* Appendix A)

Starling had always envisaged a dock at Tyrllandwr. Now, ironically, part of the new East Dock, although not on the Tyrllandwr Estate, would be built on Tyrllandwr soil!

The Special Committee appointed to consider the question of additional harbour facilities had been sufficiently unconvinced by Mr Abernethy's suggestions to call in one of the leading engineers of the day, John Hawkshaw. Unfortunately Mr Hawkshaw had mistaken 'deepening' to refer to the river above Fabian's Bay, with additional wharfage accommodation to be provided along the general frontage of the river, and so the plan given in his first report in November 1872 had to be redrafted completely.[4]

His second report a month later was still more disappointing. Even exclusive of land and compensation, he calculated the work envisaged would cost £280,000. Appalled by the magnitude of the sum involved, the Committee could merely present the figures to the Trust, without making any recommendation. Starling admitted that, in supporting the scheme, he had expected some £50,000, or possibly £60,000 to be sufficient. He was dumbfounded by the discrepancy which, without further details, he was quite unable to explain. In any case, he could not see how they could proceed with the scheme, a view supported by Mr Vivian, both 'as a prudent man and a Trustee'.

Mr Vivian felt he could at least offer two practical suggestions in order to make the best use of their current resources for the good of the harbour. One was that they should try to get the advantage of borrowing at 4% like other public bodies, instead of the 5% they were used to paying. The other was that they should apply to Parliament to amend the existing law which limited loans by the Public Loan Commissioners to Harbour Trusts to the carrying out of future works. With help from the Commissioners they could pay off existing debts. To this Mr Strick moved an amendment that they should apply to Parliament for powers to borrow £50,000 upon security of the Harbour Fund in order to deepen the river, as previously recommended by Mr Abernethy. This would also allow them to pay off the existing liabilities of the Trust, while utilising the dock accommodation already available. This amendment Mr Vivian was happy to incorporate in his proposition.[5]

In the meantime it seemed the most they could do was to dredge the channel in the hope that the extra depth of water would lead to an improvement in trade, involving a demand for increased accommodation.

In spite of the shock of the Hawkshaw report, James Livingston, however, was anxious to press ahead. He believed that it was not too early to set up a

4   C Nov 1 1872, p 6
5   C Dec 13 1872, p 6

committee to consider the creation of a new dock which would, in any case, take four or five years to construct. This, he suggested, should be made up of the Chairman, Messrs Vivian, Glasbrook, Bath, Yeo, J J Jenkins and himself. Mr Richardson asked for the name of Lewis Llewelyn Dillwyn to be added to the list.[6]

Others were less supportive of Mr Dillwyn whose popularity was suffering through his association with the GWR. There had been widespread objection to the Company's lavishing money on a large central station for Cardiff while doing nothing for Swansea,[7] a view shared by many of the Trustees, including the new Mayor, Capt Thomas Ford. In a paper to consider the question of a site for a new station with an improved route for the GW Railway into Swansea, he called for the screw to be turned on the Company by a boycott of its lines wherever feasible, as in the cases of London and Liverpool, though not of Aberdare or the Vale of Neath.

In a Chamber of Commerce meeting in September 1873, this stance was condemned as a 'querulous and nit-picking attack' by an up-and-coming young councillor, Dr James Rogers, who had taken upon himself to defend the GWR. He felt a more conciliatory tone would have achieved more. His call for a route that would avoid the Landore Viaduct, which he felt might break at any minute,[8] brought Starling into the debate. Because of his interest in another local railway, he had come to the meeting intending to listen rather than speak. Now, however, he felt constrained to defend the Viaduct which he saw as 'a feat of engineering ingenuity' and to offer his views on improved railway communication with the town. He hoped for better relations between the GWR and the L&NWR so that trains coming in to Swansea via Landore would be able to go on to Gower Road. To him it hardly mattered where the main station would be; once one was in a cab a few yards made little difference.[9]

A correspondent in 'The Cambrian', writing under the pseudonym 'One Who Has Long Known Swansea', felt Mr Benson had a truer view of the case than Mr Rogers who had betrayed his lack of engineering know-how or, presumably, the Mayor when he called for a boycott of the GWR:

> Having been long on the stage of local railway affairs and much behind the scenes, this is but natural. He understands that the interests of a great railway company like the Great Western and a great town like Swansea must be practicably inseparable.

Nevertheless Mr Benson's suggestions had the same disadvantage as the Mayor's; they offered no alternative to skirting the North Dock and going through Hafod and Landore.[10]

Starling's 'conciliatory' attitude did little to appease James Rogers who, in a follow-up meeting the next week castigated the Harbour Trust for their

6 C Sept 12 1873, p 8
7 C Oct 4 1872, p 5
8 C Sept 26 1873, p 8
9 *Ibid*
10 C Oct 3 1873, p 8

dilatoriness, to which he attributed Swansea's decline as a port. He suggested that any scheme for increased harbour accommodation should be in the hands of a Dock Company. That name, however, still carried unhappy memories for many older townspeople, as Mr Richards reminded him. A Dock Company would have to make out a strong case if it was to supplant the Harbour Trust with its established powers and great experience.[11] A better suggestion would be a Committee representative of both Trust and Corporation to meet the Directors of the Railway Companies. Someone even made the facetious remark that, as one large company was cheaper to run than two small ones, the SHT might be merged with the Corporation![12]

Whether stung into action by James Rogers' stringent criticisms of the inertness of the Trustees or as the result of protracted personal consideration, at the next SHT meeting the Chairman formally proposed that the Fabian's Bay site be adopted for the new dock. He had long been satisfied about the suitability of the site. It was sheltered and easy of access to both the GWR and Swansea Vale lines. As yet, however, he advised against communication with the major Railway Companies lest they opposed the scheme in Parliament. Once the dock was established in the proper place, they would be sure to accept it as a *fait accompli*.

Support for a dock at Fabian's Bay came from Mr Bath. This had been proposed years before but had been swamped by local influence bent on promoting the South Dock, a mistake not to be perpetuated. Mr Grenfell also favoured the east side; he had always opposed the South Dock. To Mr Yeo, however, the immediate course was to improve and extend the South Dock as far as the engineer considered feasible. In this he had the support of Mr Glasbrook whose attitude was that, whatever the drawbacks of the South Dock, they were lumbered with it and must make the most of it.

The two Members of Parliament were divided. Mr Vivian saw a dock at the natural terminus of the GWR coming from the east as likely to give them an advantage similar to Cardiff's. Mr Dillwyn, on the other hand, was in favour of Mr Yeo's more economical solution. Eventually, after much further discussion, the Chairman's resolution was adopted, and a committee set up to further the planning with a view to applying to Parliament for the necessary Bill.[13]

Arrangements for this went ahead reasonably smoothly. Terms were agreed in a friendly spirit with the Duke of Beaufort, while Mrs Tennant had granted them the required facilities on the understanding that she would, instead of payment, be given a wharf in the proposed docks, for which she would receive dues. The Earl of Jersey had also withdrawn his opposition, realising the development would be to his advantage. In addition, agreement had been reached with the GWR with respect to the land required by the Trust for the purpose of the railway authorised by the Bill.[14] The L&NWR had similarly withdrawn its petition, so the Bill went to its third reading without opposition and was passed in July 1874.

11   *Ibid*
12   *Ibid*
13   C Oct 17 1873, p 6
14   C May 15 1874, p 6

Another source of satisfaction was the welcome prospect of relief from the monopoly of the GWR which was being offered by the application of the Midland Railway for an Act to lease the SVR, a move which had the whole-hearted support of the Trust as a means of bringing the larger company into Swansea. Running on the east side of the river, it would act as an important feeder to the future docks there.[15]

Mr Grenfell, in proposing the re-election of the Chairman in August of that year, at a time when continuity of experience was especially important, congratulated the Trust on having someone who united thorough business habits with the necessary leisure. If the projected works were to be carried to a successful conclusion, it could not be done better than under the chairmanship of Mr Benson, although he did not envy him the task before him. Mr Benson would, he believed, live to see the great undertaking carried out, but he doubted whether he would be still alive himself.

Starling, in responding, said he had hoped by now to be succeeded by a younger man, but he would endeavour to conduct the meetings and business of the Trust with cordiality, seeking to promote the further prosperity of the harbour, the extension of the docks and whatever else was connected with the future success of Swansea. In spite of the depression of trade it seemed prudent to him to make a start on the new dock while labour was cheap.[16] He continued to believe that, given improved shipping facilities, the Railway Companies would co-operate. Indeed, it seemed the 'cordiality' he had undertaken to bring to his office was paying dividends when he[17] and Mr Vivian[18] had very satisfactory interviews with the GWR Management in connection with the docks. Starling had also seen the Midland officials who were even more interested than the GWR, so the prospects of help from both companies were excellent.

In spite of temporary hitches when negotiations with the Midland were held up by the illness of Mr Allport, the General Manager,[19] and when the GWR failed to respond to repeated communications from Mr James, his optimism remained unshaken. Thomas Ford still wanted the Trustees to ignore the GWR. Mr Vivian, on the other hand, insisted that they needed the greater experience that the company could provide. He advised patience, reminding the Board that the GWR Directors were busy men and needed constant prodding.[20]

Such confidence was justified. When the Railway Companies next met the Committee, they agreed to take wharfs at fixed yearly rates, in exchange for which the GWR and Midland would be entitled to exclusive rights to wharfage in lieu of wharfage rates in respect of goods handled there. Nothing had been done about the L&NWR as the Trustees considered it less important than the other two.

There were still brickbats, however. The Committee was criticised for failing to consult the general body before giving instructions to the Clerk to prepare and deposit before the next Parliament a Bill which would enable the Trustees to

15   C April 17 1874, p 6
16   C Aug 14 1874, p 6
17   C Nov 13 1874, p 8
18   C Jan 15 1875, p 3
19   C Sept 17 1875, p 3
20   C Nov 19 1875, p 3

grant and the Companies to take up leases of wharfage etc, and to effect such other objects as the Committee deemed desirable. J J Jenkins was not convinced that their haste in bringing matters to a successful conclusion was, in this instance, justified. He insisted a special meeting should have been called.

The Committee was fortunate in having the support of Mr Vivian. He pointed out that, between them, the undertakings of the GWR and the Midland should give an income sufficient to enable the Trust to borrow close on £200,000. Even that, however, would not be enough if they were to proceed with work on the piers and the channel as well as the new dock. He therefore brought before the Board a resolution he had received, asking that an application be made to the Corporation to find out what help they might offer, an idea supported by Mr Glasbrook who had mellowed considerably with the years.

The simplest plan seemed for the Corporation to become, like the GWR, lessees of a certain frontage in the completed dock. That would enable the Trustees to borrow £100,000 without any risk to the Corporation who would in turn receive a substantial property for the £4000 they would be asked to guarantee.[21] Unfortunately, even before the matter had been laid by Mr Yeo before the Corporation, the proposal had been distorted in a letter from the volatile Dr Rogers. In it he discussed the current outlay of ratepayers' money and warned strenuously against incurring liabilities for the new docks, a course which, he suggested, would benefit only the Railway Companies, large traders and mine-owners.[22]

The ferment of popular opposition led to a meeting of the burgesses of Swansea, summoned by Alderman Thomas Phillips to consider the dangers of the proposed dock development. Even though the protesters had come, in the main, to support James Rogers's views, it was some time before he managed to make his voice heard by the noisy and bad-tempered gathering. Eventually, the judicious intervention of another James, James Livingston, that year's Mayor, succeeded in restoring order. He assured the meeting that no action would be taken before the matter had been brought before the burgesses and pointed out that public property should be used for the extension of local trade, which would be seriously limited without the creation of another docks. In what sounded remarkably like an echo of Starling's words thirty years before, the Mayor reminded the meeting that Fabian's Bay was no further from the centre of the town than the South Docks. He had every confidence in the success of the scheme and merely asked them to give the matter their disinterested consideration.[23]

'The Cambrian' came out strongly in favour of the 'new opportunity to find increased accommodation. If the Railway Companies were interested, the Corporation could be sure it must be a sound speculation'.[24] 'The Mining Journal' referred enthusiastically to the Corporation's responding 'cheerfully' to the requirements of trade, and to the willingness of the Great Western and Midland Railway Companies, 'two of the most powerful and far-seeing

21 C Dec 17 1875, p 3
22 C Dec 24 1875, p 8
23 C Jan 7 1876, p 3
24 C Jan 14 1876, p 5

companies in the Kingdom', to help local authorities 'in the most substantial pecuniary manner.'[25]

In reporting a further meeting of burgesses held in the Town Hall, the Editor of 'The Cambrian' drew attention to the support given to Corporation involvement in the Dock scheme by 'men of the greatest acumen', such as Messrs Vivian, Charles Bath and E M Richards.[26]

But Dr Rogers had not finished yet. Mr Yeo brought his fellow Trustees news of a rumour that a petition against the scheme had been presented to the Treasury and this without any reference to the Chairman and Clerk of the Trust who both had to confess they had heard nothing about it. Starling was not unduly dismayed; he did not think such a memorial would have any effect.

Nevertheless, the rumour was proved true when a letter from Dr Rogers was printed in the current edition of 'The Cambrian', giving a copy of his memorial. This sought to prevent the Treasury's consent 'to the alienation of the Corporation reserves from their legitimate purposes,' and 'to cause an official enquiry into the administration of the Corporation estate.' He emphasised the consistent deficit in the Trust's financial statements up to the last two months and, in spite of a substantial majority in favour of the Corporation's becoming lessees in perpetuity of frontage wharfs at the new docks, he besought the Lords of the Treasury not to let this resolution carry weight, especially as those who had proposed that resolution were themselves members of the Harbour Trust.[27]

It appeared at one point that James Rogers's campaign had succeeded when the Secretary of her Majesty's Treasury communicated with the Mayor, informing him that the Lords of the Treasury declined to sanction the proposed arrangement between the Corporation and the Swansea Harbour Trust.[28] In order to overcome opposition, alterations were made in the wording of the Bill, 'a term of 999 years' having been substituted 'for a lease in perpetuity' and the words 'consent of the Lords of the Treasury' having been deleted. On discovering this, Dr Rogers wrote again, asking for further intervention to prevent Corporation revenues which belonged to the whole body of ratepayers from being diverted to 'serve the interests of a wealthy and powerful class who had never contributed their fair share to local rates.'[29]

Ultimately this opposition proved fruitless. The Bill passed both Houses and received Royal Assent on July 24 1876. Agreements were confirmed with the Great Western and the Midland Railway Companies for leases of wharfs 'in perpetuity' for an annual rent of £4800 and £3540 respectively, and with the Corporation for 'a term of 999 years' for an annual rent of £3999. At the end of July the Engineer-in-Chief visited Swansea with all the contract drawings necessary for carrying out the works. He was of the opinion that the time was now favourable for proceeding with the project.[30]

'The Cambrian' was positively euphoric about the achievement of the Harbour Trust, singling out Lewis Thomas and J W James for special praise. By this new

25 C Jan 21 1876, p 3
26 C March 17 1876, p 3
27 C April 14 1876, pp 3 & 8
28 C Aug 11 1876, p 8
29 *Ibid*
30 C Aug 18 1876, p 7

development, the Swansea Harbour Trustees 'should at last reap the fruits of their labours as a result of their foresight and exertions'.[31] The Chairman endorsed this view, attributing the success of the scheme to the long experience of the Clerk and to the diligence of the General Superintendent. The only reference to his own unflinching faith which had done so much to bring it about was a passing reference to his forty years' association with the Trust, twenty of them as its Chairman. Now seemed the time for him to be thinking of relinquishing office. By August 1877 he hoped some younger member would have prepared himself to take over.[32]

Several of those who had borne the burden and heat of the day had already come to the end of their labours. In March 1876 Pascoe St Leger Grenfell announced his resignation on account of age and other engagements which prevented his regular attendance.[33] The following month Alfred Sterry retired through ill health. Mr Dillwyn had already left. Appreciation of the services of all three was duly put on record.[34]

The latest moment of triumph was soon to be overshadowed by the death of the man who had perhaps done most to engineer the success of the new Harbour Act, Lewis Thomas.[35] At a special meeting on Monday, October 16, enthusiastic tributes were paid to his thirty-two years of conscientious service as clerk and solicitor, during which he had so successfully steered the fortunes of the Trust by his great knowledge of parliamentary procedure.

At the same meeting two candidates were interviewed for the position, one of whom was Francis James, the son of J W James. At the time of his death Lewis Thomas had been about to conclude an arrangement to receive the young man into his business as a partner. Now Francis James found himself applying for the post of 'clerk and solicitor' to the Harbour Trust as Mr Thomas's successor.[36]

Starling admitted that he found himself in an unusual situation. It was rarely that the Chairman of a public body proposed that one particular candidate should be appointed. Here, however, peculiar circumstances prevailed whereby much of the work consequent upon the passing of the new Act would devolve on Mr J W James, and it was most convenient that the secretarial work should be done by his son. This proposal was seconded by Mr Strick who had first-hand knowledge of Mr James Jnr's fitness as a member of the legal profession. Mr Vivian felt they were fortunate to have a gentleman so thoroughly identified with town and harbour through his father and his grandfather whom Mr Vivian remembered as a most active member of the Trust.[37]

Appreciation of the work entailed in J W James's added responsibilities was shown by an increase in his salary[38] which, unfortunately, he was to enjoy for only three months. 'The Cambrian' of January 19 1877, in announcing his death,

31   C Aug 25 1876, p 7
32   C Aug 18 1876, p 7
33   C March 17 1876, p 3
34   C April 14 1876, p 3
35   C Oct 13 1876, p 5
36   C Oct 20 1876, p 3
37   *Ibid*
38   *Ibid*

praised his services over the last twenty-five or thirty years, again recalling the distinguished record of the James family, including that of his father, Christopher James, and of his brother, Lord Justice, formerly Vice-Chancellor, James.[39]

Nevertheless a desire for change was in the air. 'The Cambrian' suggested abandoning the post of General Superintendent. The Trustees as a whole were a 'picked body of our ablest men', among whom, 'the Chairman might fairly be considered one of the ablest that Swansea ever possessed' . Even so, the Editor was sure Mr Benson would be the first to recognise that 'the creation of what could be called "the corpus of the Harbour Estate" was due principally to the labours of Mr James and Mr Lewis Thomas'. Nevertheless, it seemed to him that the body of the Trustees should, in the present circumstances, be able to provide such administrative services as to obviate the need of another such post as Mr J W James's. He further proposed that the Chairman, so as not to be unduly taxed, should have the assistance of a deputy-chairman, the role occupied by Mr James himself before his appointment as General Superintendent.[40]

In spite of the views of 'The Cambrian' a new General Superintendent was felt to be necessary, but until the position could be filled, his duties would be carried out by the Deputy Harbour Master, Captain Rosser. Starling's desire to maintain continuity[41] was shared by George Grant Francis who had worked closely with Mr James on Trust affairs many years before. He immediately offered his services to fill the gap created by the loss of the two senior officials. When the short list appeared, however, without his name on it, Grant Francis lost no time in writing to the Press to make it clear that he had never been a serious 'candidate' for the post. He hoped this would put an end to any insidious suggestion that he had been overlooked.[42]

Almost two hundred applications were received. In order to whittle them down, it was decided, on a suggestion from Mr Vivian, to eliminate all those over forty-five. The advertisement, however, had made no such proviso, and Starling himself was unhappy with the move. The setting of an age limit led to sharp exchanges in the meeting convened to make the actual appointment. J J Jenkins hoped none of the five candidates to be interviewed was over forty-five or otherwise the Board might find itself in an embarrassing situation. If objections were raised, there might have to be a new selection process. Fortunately the meeting was able to go ahead. The final choice lay between two candidates, Robert Capper of London and F W Mortimer of the Midland Railway, formerly of the SVR. Mr Capper was eventually appointed at a salary of £600 pa.[43]

It must have been a matter of singular satisfaction to J W James during the last months of his life that the working of the General Harbour Estate had shown a surplus of £1362 7s for the last four months of the current financial year as compared with the corresponding period of the previous year when there was a deficit of £1271 5s 10d.[44] Nevertheless questions of finance still loomed large for the remaining Trustees. One recurrent query was about payments to the Engineer-

39 C Jan 19 1877, p 5
40 C Jan 26 1877, p 5
41 C Feb 16 1877, p 3
42 C March 9 1877, p 8
43 C March 16 1877, p 3
44 C Nov 17 1876, p 6

in-Chief. In reply to a question from Mr Glasbrook, Starling explained that Mr Abernethy was paid the usual percentage, half of which he gave to the local engineer, Mr Schenck.[45] Later it was Mr Abernethy's commission of £2000 which came in for criticism from Captain Davies. Mr Yeo pointed out that this was a small amount in view of what was due to him. Mr Abernethy had already paid £400 out of his own pocket for the preparation of bills and quantities. Both the Chairman and Frank Yeo, as Chairman of the New Docks Committee, further reassured Captain Davies that there was no extra charge for preparing plans in addition to the 5% for superintending them.[46]

That Mr Abernethy was anxious to spare the Trustees too great a financial burden can be seen from his suggestion that the contract for the work should be divided. The dock and lock with the tidal entrance basin as per Plan B should be completed first, thus allowing for an earlier opening of the dock for traffic, as had been the procedure with the North Dock. Such a plan would, according to Starling, have the advantage of saving them the interest payable if they laid out the whole £300,000 at once.[47]

In the August meeting of 1877 Mr Livingston had pressed for a deeper entrance to the South Dock. He hoped they would divert some of the resources available to them under the Act of Parliament for that purpose. In this he was supported by a comparative new-comer to the Trust, Lawrence Tulloch, a native of the Shetland Islands. He had been asked by the Northern shipowners when there would be deeper water in Swansea as docking there obviated the dangers they had to face when going on to Cardiff or Newport.[48] By the October meeting, however, James Livingston had dropped his concern with the entrance to the South Dock to concentrate on the New Dock. The urgency of the need to complete it was shown by the fact that some shipowners were already issuing circulars by the dozen to all ports where coal was sent, saying they now intended giving preference to Swansea as a shipping port.[49]

Even so, there were still the doubting Thomases. J J Jenkins was so concerned by the fluctuations in receipts over the last year that he again wanted to defer the project,[50] while Captain Davies, who had been so keen at first to have a new dock in the area, now had doubts about Fabian's Bay as the right site for it. The question of altering sills, which Mr Abernethy had raised in the adaptation of his plans, had made him aware, as an old salt, of difficulties likely to be encountered.[51] This persistent questioning gave the impression of dithering and made some onlookers suspect that nothing was being done.[52] It fell to the Chairman of the New Docks Committee to reassure his critics that negotiations were going ahead and to convince them that the present members of the Trust were capable of carrying out the undertaking.

45   C March 16 1877, p 3
46   C Nov 16 1877, p 7
47   C April 20 1877, p 3
48   C Aug 17 1877, p 7
49   C Oct 12 1877, p 7
50   C July 20 1877, p 7
51   C Sept 17 1877, p 7
52   C Oct 12 1877, p 7

49 Frank Ash Yeo Esq., Starling Benson's successor as Chairman of the Harbour Trust

The Cambrian, Special Supplement, Oct 1881

50 James Abernethy, Engineer-in-Chief to the SHT October 21, 1880

The Cambrian, Special Supplement, Oct 1881

In July 1877 Starling had written to the Secretary of the Trust indicating his intention to resign at the August meeting. He had been in office for twenty-one years and felt they now had a month to consider his successor.[53] He was dissuaded, however, by a letter from his colleagues, stressing their conviction that, in view of the recent losses of J W James and Lewis Thomas, 'an experienced and able man was still required at the helm.'[54] The present officers were 'not yet ready to grapple with the multifarious and intricate questions' which were for ever facing the Trust.

As a result Starling was prevailed on to remain one more year as Chairman. He explained he had done so simply because there was no one else ready to sacrifice the time needed for the proper discharge of the duties involved although others were quite capable of filling the office. Seeing everything was prepared for the meetings as well as attending to other aspects of the office took a good deal of time.[55]

The Editor of 'The Cambrian' obviously had a higher opinion of the Chairman's contribution to the success of the Trust than Starling had.

> We feel confident that the whole town, more especially the commercial and shipping community, will be glad Mr Benson has kindly consented to comply with the request of the Trustees, and that we thus retain that great experience, ability and zeal which Mr Benson brings to bear in the discharge of his important official duties.[56]

In the September meeting following, it became clear that the man appointed as Vice-Chairman would become Starling's successor. In view of this, J J Jenkins, who had declined nomination, proposed Frank Yeo as Starling's deputy. Since he was already Chairman of the New Docks Committee, he would be able to communicate fully with Mr Benson and 'get the full benefit of his wide and long experience in readiness for the time when it would be his duty to conduct meetings for the ensuing year.' This proposal was adopted unanimously.[57]

Starling's sagacity still proved valuable. Dredging had already made a vast difference in the shipping accommodation available at Swansea and some of the Trustees, in their enthusiasm, wanted the world to know of their achievements. Starling shrewdly warned them against broadcasting too much information about the latest depth of water lest a careless vessel, striking the bottom, might claim damages. Better for Mr Schenck to prepare a section of the depth of the channel and lay it before the Trustees before they rushed into publicity.[58]

During Starling's absence from the January meeting of 1878, probably on account of the weather - the road from Reynoldston could be difficult in the heart of winter - Frank Yeo admitted he was at a loss to answer questions on sensitive

53   C July 20 1877, p 7
54   C Aug 10 1877, p 8
55   C Aug 17 1877, p 7
56   C Aug 10 1877, p 8
57   C Sept 14 1877, p 7
58   C Dec 14 1877, p 7

issues such as dealing with pilots, which still involved the unwieldy body of the whole Trust. Then there were the present rates for ballast, which were causing a loss of money the Board could ill afford. Both were matters with which Mr Benson, who well understood such long-standing practices, would have been quite *au fait*.[59]

The old order was fast changing. Even so when the Proprietary Trustees came up for re-election, J P Budd, who had been a member of the Trust for over twenty-five years, was the only one not to offer himself for a further term of service. Now in failing health, he felt the time had come to withdraw from office where, by his conscientious, sometimes even ultra-cautious stance, he had frequently acted as a brake on hasty decision making.[60]

The time soon came for Starling himself to step down. 'The Cambrian' yet again paid tribute to his long and distinguished record of service.

> Mr Benson has ... been identified with the very infancy of the port, and has nursed it to its present prosperity guiding its affairs and expanding its resources.

Without any of the financial advantages enjoyed by other ports and communities, the Trustees had constructed docks, railways, extensive piers, purchased costly hydraulic machinery and provided all the other necessities of a large, rapidly developing port involving necessarily a vast expenditure of money. Although the bonded debt at the time of Starling Benson's retirement had been £670,000, they had still been able to borrow £500,000 more for the purpose of the new docks at St Thomas.

> The present bonded debt of the Trust has been raised from the public without any collateral security. This fact alone shows the confidence which the investing public have in our Harbour Trust nor has this confidence ever been abused, for never has the Trust failed to meet its liabilities or to pay with promptitude the interest when due. For this happy and satisfactory state of things we are mainly indebted to the late Chairman, Mr Benson. If his management was destitute of that dash and boldness which some would like to have seen carried out, it was characterised by sound judgment and discretion, with a steady advance in those matters which enhanced the material welfare of the port.[61]

Similar views were expressed by his colleagues. Pascoe St Leger Grenfell recalled how he had advised his successor to treat the business of the Trust as if

59　C Jan 20 1878, p 7
60　C Feb 22 1878, p 5
61　C Aug 16 1878, p 5

it were his own private business, and this Mr Benson had done throughout his years of office. To Mr Vivian it seemed only yesterday that Starling Benson had assumed office on the retirement of his old friend, Mr Grenfell. Although very much Starling's junior, Mr Vivian could re-people the chairs round the table with their previous occupants who were no longer with them but who had been associated with the great works which had made town and port so prosperous. 'These,' he added, 'were all men of the honesty, ability and perseverance which had always marked the public men of the nation and which were at the bottom of all great commercial concerns and the very prosperity of the nation itself.'

He recalled how, during Starling Benson's period as Chairman, the Trust had passed through a most important period of its history; the accounts of the harbour bore testimony 'with what marked ability Mr Benson had administered it'. Admittedly he had been ably assisted by the officials who served with him but Mr Vivian was in no doubt that the Chairman himself had taken a leading and active part in the management. 'No member ought to feel otherwise than grateful for the way in which he had discharged the duties and the interest he manifested in this harbour.' This was no small praise from one whose paths lay through the nation's corridors of power.

A resolution to put on record the Trust's appreciation of their former Chairman's services was moved by Mr Strick. In replying, Starling did not know how to respond to the kind manner in which the resolution had been passed. Whatever he had done had been a service of pleasure. He thought the greatest good he had been able to do for the port was to leave it in good credit and in a thoroughly sound commercial state. The wish had been expressed the previous year, when he had been re-elected for a last term of office, that when the time actually came for him to retire, he would not sever himself from the Trust but would continue to give them advice and experienced assistance. This he hoped to do.[62]

Although the late Chairman took part in the next two meetings, his name was not included in the list of those attending the December meeting of the Trust. He had, however, been present on January 13, 'with all his accustomed cheerfulness'. Within four days he was dead in the tragic circumstances we shall see in a later chapter.[63]

Only three months later the ever supportive Mr Grenfell died himself at his daughter's house in Nottingham.[64] Once more the harbour was plunged into mourning. October 1876; January 1877; January 1879; April 1879 - in less than thirty months, four giants of the Harbour Trust had departed. Nevertheless the work went on. The East Dock was begun in July 1879. By March 1880 it was sufficiently far advanced for the Trustees to arrange for their oldest member, H H Vivian, to lay the central stone of the masonry in the presence of a large and distinguished gathering.[65]

62   *Op cit*, p 3
63   Feb 14 1879, p 7
64   C April 4 1879, p 8
65   W H Jones, *op cit*, p 213

On October 18, 1881, nineteenth century Swansea enjoyed what many regarded at the time as its finest hour. 'The Cambrian' of October 21 brought out a special edition to mark the visit of the Prince and Princess of Wales (later King Edward VII and Queen Alexandra) to open the new East Dock. It carried a magnificent full page illustration, showing the head and shoulders of His Royal Highness, surrounded by those of the Members for the County (C R M Talbot and H H Vivian), the Mayor of Swansea (J J Jenkins), the Chairman of the Swansea Harbour Trust (F A Yeo), the engineer (James Abernethy), the Harbour Superintendent (Robert Capper), and the contractor (T A Walker).[66]

The three men without whose dedication there might not have been an East Dock at that time were sadly absent. Lewis Thomas, John Williams James and Starling Benson were now dead and no one seemed to recall their gigantic effort to establish the dock at Fabian's Bay. All the local newspapers of the time, as well as 'The Illustrated London News' of October 22 and 29, were full of the day's proceedings. These were to be prefaced by a Masonic Ball in honour of the royal visit on the night of Monday, October 17, and culminated the following night in the Grand Royal Ball in the Music Hall, to which invitations were issued in the joint names of the Mayor and Mayoress and the Chairman of the Harbour Trust and Mrs Yeo.[67]

The royal couple stayed at the Vivians' home in Singleton Park, where the Princess of Wales planted a lime tree in the grounds to commemorate the first royal visit to Swansea. The route for their arrival was via the Oystermouth Road which was lined by a thousand Sunday School children who greeted the Prince and Princess in song. The royal couple later left along the Sketty Road on their way to the Mayor's Residence, prior to attending the Royal Ball. All the principal streets were elaborately decorated, with triumphal arches at High Street, at Castle Bailey Street and at Mansel Street.[68]

The Benson family was not entirely unrepresented at the celebrations. According to 'The Cardiff Times and Weekly News', General Benson and Mr W D Benson were among the guests at the Luncheon in a large pavilion specially erected on the east side of the Dock where some nine hundred or a thousand guests were entertained.[69] The same paper listed General and Mrs Benson and the Misses Benson as being present that same evening at the Grand Royal Ball, although 'The Cambrian' of October 21 mentioned only Mr and Mrs W D Benson in that connection.[70]

Perhaps it was dramatically right that Starling was not there. He would possibly still have enjoyed the dancing, but, never one for thrusting himself forward, he might well have felt himself by now too old to have focussed upon him the glare of publicity due to the Chairman of the Harbour Trust. He would have considered it sufficient reward that he had laboured and other men had entered into his labours. Yet one cannot suppress a certain feeling of regret that, in the special edition of 'The Cambrian' high-lighting the Swansea Harbour

66   C Oct 21 1881, p 7
67   Illustrated London News, Oct 22 & 29 1881
68   *Op cit*
69   The Cardiff Times and Weekly News, Oct 21 1881, pp 2 &3
70   C Oct 21 1881, p 7

51 The Royal Visit to Swansea: the Prince and Princess of Wales opening the
new dock, Oct 18 1881
Illustrated London News

Trust's contribution to the life of the town, there was only a single passing mention of his name.[71] In some respects his adopted town had, and continues to have, a short memory concerning those who, in Mrs Benson's quaint phrase, 'dreaded notoriety'.

71 C Special Supplement, Oct 21 1881

Chapter XV

Exits and Entrances

His father's death on October 6 1858 had left Starling with a stack of problems. T S Benson had died intestate, with effects less than £16,000, and there were a number of mortgages and other debts to be repaid. The legal business was in the capable hands of the family solicitor, Alfred Turner, but the complicated state of his father's affairs involved constant pressure on his eldest son, to whom Letters of Administration were granted on November 20 1858. Starling must often have wished Florance was still alive to share the responsibility. For the first year after their father's death, Henry was in India while Richard was more of a liability than an asset in practical matters.

During the short period of her widowhood, Mrs Benson had sufficient means left to her personally under the terms of her own mother's will to enable her to to live comfortably. She was anxious to leave Teddington and repeatedly appealed to Richard to find her somewhere suitable to live in the Oxford district so that she could be near him. Richard may well have preferred his mother's presence in small doses. Her close and often over-enthusiastic identification with his work and the lives of his parishioners could well have become oppressive if unrelieved by periods spent elsewhere. Nevertheless, just after Christmas 1858, he managed to secure convenient 'lodgings' for her in Beaumont Street.[1]

There was, however, a respite for Richard the following March when his mother was invited to stay at Theobald's Park, Hertfordshire, the house of her cousin Henry's son, another Henry, who had inherited the baronetcy on his father's death. Unfortunately the second Baronet had quite recently suffered a stroke which made conversation impossible, apart from an occasional word such as 'All dead! all dead!' when he saw Mrs Benson dressed in deep mourning. The poignancy of the situation involving her relative, his young wife and small son made a deep impression on Elizabeth Benson's inherently sympathetic nature, especially at a time when her emotions were more than usually tender through her own loss.[2]

With the death of her husband, Elizabeth Benson had lost the mainspring of her existence, and within the year, on July 3 1859, she died at her new Oxford home in Beaumont Street. That she also died intestate must have added to Starling's problems as he sought to deal with the two estates, though in his step-mother's case, the heavier responsibility would naturally fall on Henry who was now home from India, having arrived just too late to see his mother alive.

Family finances, never completely straightforward after the problems which had come to light in 1852 at the time of Emma Bishop's marriage settlement,

1   All remaining family letters are from UCS/BC; EMB to RMB, Dec 12, 26 & 27 1858
2   EMB to RMB, March 29 1859; EMB to HRB, March 30 1859

253

were still being disentangled in 1860. Some idea of the problems involved can be seen from a letter written to Starling by Alfred Turner on August 31.

My dear Benson,

I send you separately the Drafts of the Deeds I have prepared that your brother Col Benson and yourself may look over them.

The transfer of the Mortgage etc - on the £10,000 security and the release from the deed accompanying it speak for themselves, as does the assignment from you of the Leaseholds.

On the conveyance of the Glais Farm to you I have to remark that the Estate forms part of the mortgage securities affecting the Tyrllandwr Estate - that it will be for you to consider whether your two Brothers ought not to execute an Indemnity to you to protect you in respect of these mortgage debts.

What plan is referred to (in) the Deeds to the Atlas office with the Numbers - is it the Tithe Commutations Map? I have in the Schedule to the Conveyance of the Glais farm taken these particulars from the prior deeds but it wants an explanation on this point also as to the first two pieces which are Woodland and stated to be in hand - is this so or do they form part of Llewellyn's farm?

The remaining Draft has been a matter of some little difficulty. You are Heir at law to your Father and as such of course entitled to the freehold portion of Vogans holding subject to Furnells Mortgage and your Father's other debts and no Conveyance would be wanting as to this - but the leasehold portion subject to Miss Salmon's Mortgage would form part of your Father's ... residue whereas this consisted ultimately of ... (these two words are indecipherable) amongst his next of Kin - you yourself being one - your brothers can now assign their interests - and I presume the shares of Thomas Florance and Sarah all vested in your Father in his life time but not Mrs Usborne's—

As you will see I have made the Draft a recital of the acts and intentions of the parties making your Brothers release all interest in their properties, your covenant to provide for the Mortgage debts ... [3]

The situation was not made easier by Richard's impatience to be off to India where he planned to set up a devotional college in the North West Provinces. Those involved with him in this scheme would all be expected to live on their

---

3 Alfred Turner to SB, Aug 31, 1860

own funds; hence his concern with the speedy completion of his parents' financial affairs, notably his inheritance under the terms of the wills made by his great grandfather, Henry Roxby, and his grandmother, Elizabeth Meux. In a little over a month after his mother's death he was discussing leaving England 'as soon as certain matters of business set me free'.[4]

Before leaving, however, he hoped to see Reynoldston Church renovated. He had obtained plans of a country church suitable for Gower which he sent on to Starling. He wanted to know how much money was available for the purpose and entertained hopes that Mr Talbot 'might be inclined to do it altogether'. In any case he had borrowed £500 for a building scheme in his present parish of Cowley. As the development there had been delayed, he saw no objection to appropriating this money to further the work at Reynoldston, being quite sure he would be able to manage the Cowley project out of his future income.[5]

All the same, he wanted to see the new Cowley building completed before going abroad, and for this he would need £2000. Accordingly, he was making enquiries in London about a life insurance, possibly for £10,000. This, he believed, would go a long way towards effecting his schemes, which included the church at Teddington as well as Cowley and Reynoldston. He hoped Starling would not find him very extravagant in his notions … Starling probably did. His mind did not work in the same way as his half brother's. Happily he was saved the shock of learning the full extent of Richard's extravagance which Henry had to face alone some twenty years later, in 1891, long after Starling's death.

By that time Richard had got to India. Before leaving England Richard had given Power of Attorney to a fellow clergyman at Cowley, the Revd R L Page. Nevertheless it was to Henry he now wrote from Poona in December 1890, asking him to clear a heavy financial commitment which urgently needed to be settled. This Henry had undertaken to do, thinking the first figure, blurred by a blot, to be a '1' and the total amount, £1000; only to discover later that the blotted figure had been an '8'.[6]

The debt Richard wanted paid was, therefore, £8000 while his other liabilities amounted to £45,000! As Henry pointed out, this was 'more than the value of your share of the property left by our grandmother'. It certainly was far more than a family man like Henry, with four unmarried daughters and an invalid son, could afford to pay. He had earlier, to prevent his father being declared bankrupt, 'cut off' the entail which, under the terms of his grandmother's will, had bound the Tyrllandwr property and he now blamed himself for an action which, however well meant, had restricted his own position and encouraged Richard in his quixotic habits. No wonder he signed his letter to Richard, 'Your Affec but Broken-hearted Brother'. Even after nine months of concentrated negotiations through the family solicitor, now Sharon Turner, unforeseen demands were still perplexing Henry. His letter of September 24 1891 ended with the *cri du coeur*, 'Where is the money to come from?'[7]

4   Letters of Richard Meux Benson SSJE (London, Oxford & Milwaukee; A R Mowbray & Co., Ltd, 1916) p *3ff*
5   RMB to SB, July 9 1860
6   HRB to RMB, Jan 27 1891,
7   HRB to RMB, Sept 24 1891

This, however, was well into the future. At the time of his parents' deaths, Richard was still a parish priest in Cowley, and for the next three and a half years he continued to agonise about his work there and what he could do for it out of the money he had inherited. In deference to the wishes of Bishop Wilberforce ('Soapy Sam' of the debate with Huxley over Darwin's 'Origin of Species') he gave up his plan to go out to India in order to concentrate on the spiritual needs of the new suburb springing up within the boundaries of Cowley, an area very different in its requirements from the old village.

The Iron Church, which he founded in this new part of his parish and named after St John the Evangelist, was to become the focal point of the so-called Cowley Fathers, a religious order instituted by Richard under the inspiration of the American R C Grafton and Father O'Neill of Eton. Its aim was to deepen the dedication of the clergy, and in its interests Richard was later to travel widely, not only in India, where branches were founded in Poona and Bombay, but also in America and South Africa.

Starling, in the meantime, was pursuing many of the interests which had provided him with relaxation in the course of his long and busy life, even though the distance into Swansea from his new home made him more selective than formerly. Unlike Henry Lucas, an earlier inhabitant of Fairy Hill who had moved out of Gower because it was too far from the Swansea Race Course on the Burrows, Starling did not see this as deprivation.[8] Admittedly, his name did appear as a subscriber in the announcement of the forthcoming races in 'The Cambrian' of August 13 1847[9] and, as we shall see, he did once borrow an analogy from racing to spur on apathetic supporters of the Swansea Regatta[10] but, in the main, race courses were places where one could lose money, and Starling was too cautious to be caught by the gambling fever.

More to his taste would be an activity practised by the leading families of the County 'without entailing any heavy expense upon any one person'. This was a reference to the second Grand Bow meeting of the Glamorganshire Archery Club, held at Singleton in August 1858, the first meeting having been held at Dunraven Castle. Starling was present at Singleton, though as a non-participating guest.[11] By the time it was next held there, five years later, the event had obviously gained in popularity; the 'toxophiles of the County' numbered over a hundred and fifty. Major Pendarvis Vivian's Band was in attendance, and this time Starling had company, as Colonel and Mrs Benson were also among the guests.[12]

Henry had, by now, gone on half-pay from the Army and he, with his family, was spending much of their time at Fairy Hill. The company of his young nephews and nieces ensured that Starling did not settle too deeply into 'retired leisure' or slough off too many of his earlier interests. When two Grand Concerts were held on Whit Monday and Tuesday 1864, to mark the opening shortly before of the new Music Hall (later to be renamed the Albert Hall), Starling's name was among the honourable patrons.[13] The building had been started in 1861

8   Robert Lucas, A Gower Family (Lewes, Sussex; The Book Guild Ltd, 1986) p 47
9   C Aug 13 1847, p 2
10   C Aug 7 1857, p 8
11   C Aug 15 1858, p 5
12   C Aug 28 1863, p 5
13   C April 22 1864, p 4 (Announcement of forthcoming event)

on a piece of ground donated by Calvert Richard Jones to replace the site of the fast fading Assembly Rooms, and was opened in the Spring of 1864. Later in the year, the Music Hall was the venue for a Festival of Choral and National Music when Starling was again among the patrons.[14]

One function in the Music Hall Starling was not likely to forget was on October 1878, towards the end of his life. Some years before, a tract of land at Knapllwyd, on the top and sides of the hill near the Old Flats commonly known as 'Morris Castle', had been given to the town by John Dillwyn Llewelyn. At the instance of the Mayor, Mr Willlam Thomas of Lan, the official handing over had been marked by a public holiday. Twelve thousand buns were distributed among the school chlldren of the district and a grand display of fireworks was shown in the park at night. It took four years to complete the project. This was celebrated in October 1878, by 'a cold collation', served to special guests in the Music Hall. Here Starling was to propose the health of Mr Talbot, Lord Lieutenant of the County and, by this time, as the country's longest serving MP, the 'Father of the House'. Unfortunately those serving made such a clatter that the voices of the speakers were 'quite drowned', thus ruining the early stages of the banquets. Only after the Mayor had restored quiet among the waiters could the speeches continue, among them that of Starling himself.[15]

It was not often Starling severed a link with the past but one of the few he did break was that with Free Masonry. Most of the leading townsmen of the day were Masons, and as early as 1834 Starling had been installed as Worshipful Master of the Indefatigable and Beaufort Lodge. He again passed through the chair in 1847. Notice had been given of his forthcoming Installation as Worshipful Master Elect to celebrate the Feast of St John the Evangelist on December 27 1846[16] but, as it happened, Starling was not installed in this office until January 26 1847. F D Michael, who should have conducted the ceremony, was absent in December while Starling himself was away from the following meeting early in January. The 'Indefatigable' was then still in temporary accommodation at the 'Cameron Arms'; by the time the Lodge eventually crowned a protracted odyssey through the inns, halls and coffee houses of Swansea by moving into its own Masonic Hall in Caer Street in 1872,[17] Starling had long since left its ranks. Possibly it was the threat of bankruptcy hanging over his father's affairs at the time that led him in 1852 to withdraw from masonic circles.

There was one function, however, where he had no such worries. That was the Swansea Regatta, which he supported with unflagging loyalty until well on into the 1870s. Year after year, he acted as one of its stewards. To him, as he pointed out in his speech responding to the toast of 'The Patrons and Stewards' of the 1857 Regatta at the Ordinary held in the Mackworth Arms, the event was of prime importance to the life of Swansea, reflecting the flourishing trade and prosperity of the port. That year the Regatta had not been particularly well supported by the tradesmen of the town, but the stewards were still determined to ensure it was sufficiently supplied with funds to be able to offer large money

14 C Dec 9 1864, p 1
15 C Oct 4 1878, p 5
16 C Jan 1 1847, p 3
17 W H Jones, History of the Indefatigable Lodge, pp 71-72, 96-99; *cf* C July 7 1871, p 5

prizes. He hoped too that there would be a much better turn out at the annual dinner with gentlemen in future bringing not only their yachts but their friends, as they did in horse racing, without worrying about the increased competition.[18]

The following year, 1858, it fell to him as Chairman at the Ordinary to propose the toast of 'The Army and Navy'. He reminded his audience that, although the Navy was not involved in hostilities, the Army was fully occupied. Undoubtedly prompted by Henry's experiences in the aftermath of the Indian Mutiny so graphically described in his letters home, Starling went on to claim, with unwonted fervour, that the present generation of soldiers 'had proved by their valorous deeds' that they had lost nothing of the heroism which had characterised the British army in the past. His remarks were greeted with cheers, and in proposing the health of the Stewards, coupled with the name of Mr Benson, the Vice-Chairman, E M Richards, said they knew, whoever was absent from the Regatta, Mr Benson was sure to be present.

> Whenever the services of any gentleman were required in Swansea, either for a regatta or any other object which was for the benefit and advantage of the town or port Mr Benson was always ready and willing to extend his aid and co-operation.

Although he would be shortly leaving the town, went on Mr Richards, it was good that he would not be so far away that they would be unable to claim his services as steward for future regattas, a reference to his forthcoming removal to Fairy Hill.[19]

The opening of the new Pier increased public interest in the event as it made it possible to get a full view of the whole bay, although the difficulty of getting up Channel through lack of sufficient depth of water still affected the number of yachts competing, as Starling pointed out in a later speech at the Regatta Ordinary on July 23 1866. Even so, the Regatta had been attended by thousands of sight-seers as a result of the proliferation of amusements, sideshows, waxworks, the fat woman, the fat man who was heavier than an elephant, midgets, cheap-Jacks, Aunt Sallies, roundabouts, the lot. The Editor of 'The Cambrian' had to admit the majority had no appreciation of the finer points of the yachtsman's skills, but 'who could begrudge workers the time off to enjoy their innocent pleasures?'[20]

Those in charge of arrangements for 1867 did not seem to have taken this plea into consideration when they fixed the Regatta dates for the Friday and Saturday. As Friday and Saturday morning were particularly busy times for business people, the only opportunity for them to visit the Regatta was on Saturday afternoon.[21] As a result, the event was less well patronised than usual, and in spite of good prizes, there was little competition. Happily, from Starling's point of view, the one event not adversely affected was the pilot-boat race, which took place on the Friday, when a stiffish breeze made conditions ideal for those

18 C Aug 7 1857, p 8
19 C July 9 1858, p 5
20 C July 27 1866, p 8
21 C July 26, p 5 & Aug 2 1867, p 6

competing. This annual test of skill was of special interest to Starling who saw it as a way of ensuring pilot-boats were kept in order. He made sure the Harbour Trust sent its annual subscription of £20 for this particular race, making, with £25 from Mr Vivian and £15 from Mr Dillwyn, a total of £60 prize money.[22]

Gradually, however, Swansea Regatta began to yield ground to Mumbles whose inhabitants were more accustomed to earning their livelihood by fishing or cruising with pleasure boat parties along the coast, unlike Swansea people who were primarily immersed in trade. Moreover, the position of Mumbles was better for viewing 'the beautiful and exciting spectacle' so that from its advantage spots the race could be followed by all. In addition the drunken junketings which had become a feature of the older event had led to pressure for its being abandoned.[23]

The pilot-boat race, however, continued for years to come, by which time the two events had become combined as the' Swansea Bay and Mumbles Regatta',[24] later shortened to the 'Swansea Bay Regatta' with a common fund into which the Harbour Trust continued to pay its customary £20 donation.[25] Still later, the Bristol Channel Yacht Club joined in the organisation of the races, and by 1876, 'The Cambrian' could give a lively account of the first of the two days' activities, comparing them with the Virgilian description of the boat race from the 'Aeneid'. Here, 'The Benson' continued to hold its own against such other pilot-boats as 'The Vivian', 'The Grenfell' and the 'John Williams James Boat'.[26]

Parallel with Starling's support for the Regatta ran a very different interest, that in the Royal Institution of which, as we have already seen, he had been an enthusiastic supporter since its earliest days. Over the years its activities had not found uniform favour with Swansea residents. 'The Cambrian' in particular had frequently belittled its speakers, so that it had become increasingly difficult to get people to lecture there at all. By 1856 it seemed necessary to overhaul the whole system, possibly by introducing some broad-based scheme to counter the recurrent charge of exclusiveness. L L Dillwyn's brother-in-law, Matthew Moggridge, suggested, for instance, that the Royal Institution should provide some sort of educational service to the community, with a committee, comprising Dr Nicol, the Secretary, George Grant Francis, Starling, Evan Davies and Matthew Moggridge himself, to investigate the possibilities.

Starling had reservations about such an idea. He felt they had already done everything in their power to make the Royal Institution attractive to the public, and considered the provision of elementary education was outside their jurisdiction, although he would be glad for them to lend any equipment necessary for such an attempt. Nevertheless Moggridge's resolution was adopted, although members were warned that the income needed for such a venture was poised precariously upon their ability to build up their subscription list rather than depend on donations; it had not been long since Mr Vivian had had to bail them out of financial difficulties.[27]

22 C Aug 30 1867, p 5
23 C Sept 4 1868, p 6
24 C Oct 7 1870, p 1
25 C Oct 20 1871, p 1
26 C Aug 18 1876, p 5
27 C June 6 1856, p 8

During the next two years the situation improved. In the summer of 1858, a Grand *Soirée* was held with the object of stimulating fresh interest and hopefully leading to an extension of the accommodation available. One immediate difficulty caused by a shortage of space for books had been met by the President, Mr Grove, who had presented the Institute with two handsome mahogany bookcases to match those already in the reading room; but such relief could only be temporary, and more room was necessary if the scope of the work was to expand.

The evening's arrangements were under the direction of the Mayor, W H Michael. He was assisted, among others, by Starling, who was also responsible for the display of Natural History and Botany. For the occasion an attractive collection of curious and valuable objects had been put on display. The staircase was dressed with evergreens 'and the place generally graced with flowers and choice exotics'. In the centre of the large room stood a fountain with gold fish surrounded by aquaria ferns and rockwork.

In the course of the evening Starling and Major Wood of Stouthall received high praise for their explorations in the fossil caverns of their neighbourhood. Dr Falconer's opinion that 'seldom had examinations been better conducted and rarely followed with better results' was echoed by Mr Vivian in his speech accepting the presidency for the following year. He claimed his reason for accepting office was that he regarded it as 'a sacred trust that the institution should be handed down to their successors as a monument to Science', a hope he believed to be well founded in view of the growing reputation of many Swansea men in London scientific circles. Swansea should be proud of possessing an institution unrivalled in any other town in the Principality. 'They could not but feel endebted to Mr Benson for the most perfect *(sic)* collection of the geology of this district which he now exhibited'. This was to be found in an adjoining room.[28]

It was the practice to elect annually a well-known figure as President. This unfortunately did not always enhance that position. Too often the President appeared only to deliver his inaugural address - in some cases he did not even do that - and then was not seen for the rest of the session. This was true of L L Dillwyn's year of office from 1861-62 when pressure of parliamentary business was pleaded to excuse his non-attendance. On the assumption that Starling would have more time on his hands, C T Wilson proposed him in his absence as the next president, a suggestion which won general approval.[29]

The outcome was highly satisfactory. At the 1863 Annual General Meeting the society was able to report a sound financial position. In moving the acceptance of the report and paying tribute to the retiring President, the Revd G B Brock recalled that he had been asked to propose the same resolution some twenty-five

28 C June 4 1858, p 8
29 C June 6 1862, p 6

years earlier. Throughout the intervening years, Starling Benson had continued to feel a deep interest in the welfare of the Royal Institution and he was sure they appreciated the liberality and earnest zeal he had shown for so long. This interest had been 'munificently evinced' by his presentation of a set of eight valuable volumes to the Royal Institution.

As an acknowledgement of his loyal support, at the end of his term of office Starling was unanimously elected Vice-President for the ensuing year. In returning thanks for this honour, he assured the members that his interest in the Institution was as keen as on the first day of its foundation. He had to remind them, however, that he was now residing some miles from Swansea - 'almost the equivalent of forty to fifty miles of railway' - and this prevented his attending as regularly as he would have liked,

A welcome tribute must have been that by G G Francis, not always an unreserved admirer of the Bensons! He took the opportunity of expressing the gratification he felt on seeing Mr Benson in the Chair. He could most heartily endorse what had already been said with respect to the services he had rendered the Institution. It was never easy to find a worthy successor to a gentleman who had filled the Chair with such distinction, but in the present instance, they had been fortunate in persuading Mr H A Bruce (later Lord Aberdare) to accept this office, provided they made allowance for the many engagements which might have to take priority.

In his presidential address, curtailed because the meeting had lasted so long, Starling reviewed the scientific discoveries of the past year, especially in relation to the recent beds in which remains of early man had been found and also to the findings of Dr Falconer and Sir Charles Lyell, some of them relevant to Colonel Wood's examination of Bacon Hole. So many able men were now working on the subject that a clearer solution of the problems relating to the age of Man was bound to be reached. There were always three stages in the popular reaction to any new discovery, as outlined by Professor Agassiz.

(1) It cannot be true
(2) It is contrary to religion
(3) Everybody knew that before.

This light-hearted conclusion was greeted by applause and laughter from his audience.[30]

The difficulty mentioned at the end of L L Dillwyn's presidential year was more evident than ever during Mr Bruce's year of office, resulting in the presentation of a memorial pointing out that it had become the exception rather than the rule for the President to attend. It conceded that the blame attached less

---

30 C June 5 1863, p 8

to Mr Bruce than to those who, knowing of the heavy demands upon his time, had still elected him. It was now imperative that they no longer went in for ornamental names but elected gentlemen who took an active part in the affairs of the Institution. The previous year, when Mr Benson had held office, he had delivered a very able address on the geology of the district, the only regret being that time had prevented his going into the subject at greater length.[31]

The zeal of the members to secure a fully participating President led unfortunately to an embarassing situation where two gentlemen were approached, but eventually Dr Thomas Williams withdrew in favour of John Gwyn Jeffreys, FRS, FLS, one of the stalwarts of the Institution.[32]

Starling was soon to have a devoted companion in those interests which had coloured his contributions to the Royal Insitution. This was his niece, young May Benson. Henry's return from India soon after his mother's death in 1859 had coincided with his promotion to Colonel Brevet and Starling's removal to Fairy Hill. Now, with Teddington no longer the home base, he and his family spent ever longer periods in Gower. The four girls and young Henry Wightman were henceforth to be an integral part of their uncle's world, with Starling Meux joining them from Radley and Willy from Eton for the holidays.

May Benson shared to the full her uncle's interest in the wild life of Gower. Examples of its flora formed the subject of many of her paintings, and it is significant that, on the very morning of her early death in 1895 at the age of forty-three, she had been out in the grounds of Fairy Hill gathering flowers. During her uncle's lifetime her company must have given him endless hours of pleasure, and there is a certain poignancy in her having been buried in the same grave as Starling in Reynoldston churchyard.

Of his other nieces, the eldest, Alice, was the outdoor girl who enjoyed riding, while Margaret (Madge), the third sister, was the 'domestic' one, with special interest in her beehives and the work of the local church. The youngest, Charlie, as Charlotte was generally called, was the family archivist, taking charge of the scrapbooks and photograph albums. All four practised the usual accomplishments expected of Victorian young ladies, especially art, for which they had a special aptitude inherited from their father. Since June 1862 when he had gone on half pay from the Army, Henry Roxby had been free to enjoy the life of a country gentleman at Fairy Hill. This gave him the leisure to round off the pictures he had hastily sketched while on his travels in the Crimea and India, as well as some which dated from his Continental honeymoon when, family rumour had it, he had arranged for brother officers to keep Tiny amused while he went off sketching on his own!

Starling's world must have been revolutionised by the advent of this large clan. He certainly had no lack of company now. It would have been tempting to sit back and enjoy life vicariously through the experiences of the young people around him, to become once more the boy he never seemed to have the time to

31 C June 3 1864, p 8
32 C June 3 1864, p 8 & Ed. p 4

52 Fairy Hill   UCS/BC Courtesy of JREB

53   Starling entertaining his guests at Fairy Hill
     Standing: Hon E Vaughan, Lizzie Gulston, Col. Benson, Miss Pryse Pryse
     Starling Benson, Mr Pemberton, Mrs Biddulph, Miss Chambers, Mr Daniels
     Seated: Mr Biddulph, Mrs Benson, Mr Martin
                                                      Courtesy of JREB

be in his youth when others depended on him at every turn. But old habits die hard and he continued to find fresh avenues of service right to the end of his life. In some of these he was joined by other members of his family; in others, he continued to walk alone.

Chapter XVI

Gower Days

Placid as life in Gower must have seemed on the surface, there were growing pains even there. Changes which were coming slowly but surely in such fields as education were to have a permanent effect on the community. When Starling first moved to Fairy Hill, Reynoldston had only a Church school, its activities still very much under the wing of the local Vicar and the Lord of the Manor. The annual school treat for its sixty or seventy pupils was given at the invitation of Mrs Wood of Stouthall who provided the tea and cake. After Henry's family joined Starling at Fairy Hill, Mrs Benson and her daughters were also invited. For such occasions the room was 'appropriately decorated with texts, festoons and wreaths of evergreen and floral devices, artistically designed and arranged by the young ladies of Stouthall, under their governess, Miss Bryn'. There was brimstone, however, as well as treacle on such occasions; the Rector of Llanmadoc, the Revd J D Davies, was invariably present to examine the children on their lessons.[1]

There were also Christmas parties when about fifty children of the Manse School were regaled with tea and cakes by Miss Wood. The contribution to the festivities made by the children of the Big House was described with suitable respect; the Christmas tree had been 'tastefully got up and loaded with an endless variety of presents, the handiwork of the young ladies'. Colonel and Mrs Wood, Miss Wood and the young ladies of Stouthall, Colonel and Mrs Benson, Miss Benson and the young ladies of Fairy Hill were all in attendance, together with Mr Starling Benson and the Vicar and his wife, the Revd and Mrs Glascodine.[2]

Starling had been involved with education in Gower long before moving to Fairy Hill. According to the 1847 report, S Benson, Esq, of Swansea, and C Morgan, Esq, of Llanrhidian, had in 1843 founded a Church school in Penclawdd 'in a good and commodious room'. Here, in 1847, a Mr Bennett was found to be instructing seventy-four children in the 3 Rs and the Scriptures, though not too skilfully, according to the Assistant Commissioners. At least the accommodation in this case was spacious, unlike the room occupied by a Mrs Gronow in another part of Penclawdd where she taught twenty-eight younger children to read in a room 13' by 12'.[3]

Even more scathing had been the report on the school sponsored by the Rector of Cheriton, the Revd Lucas Collins, in a house in Landimore. Here the master was said to be ill-educated and the children unruly. On his retirement, the parish

1 C Nov 22 1867, p 5
2 C Jan 27 1871, p 5
3 Henry Simons, Early Education in Gower, Gower Journal XX1V, 1973, p 68

had been combined with Llanmadoc under the Revd J D Davies whose controversial reforms in Church ritual were to change the whole character of worship in the two parishes. His fervour extended to the education of his parishioners' children, and by the 1860s, the school had moved to a building close to Stormy Castle, high on Llanmadoc Hill, where the efficiency of the teachers, a young couple, William and Jane Hall, was some compensation for the inadequacy of the building.[4]

The Rector had full responsibility for the management and finances of a Church school, and as money was often scarce, the children's pence had to be eked out by the sale of the Rector's own wood carvings and by concerts and other entertainments. By 1870, however, he had interested Starling in financing a new school on a site of three-quarters of an acre on the Penrice estate just below the Castle, to be built complete with cloakrooms, toilets and separate playgrounds for boys and girls.

Its situation on 'the open hillside with the foxgloves and the scent of gorse in summer, the vast panorama of the Burry estuary with the little ships sailing to and fro from the old Llanelli docks; the mountains along the northern horizon, and the tearing winter gales' left a vivid impression on teachers and pupils alike. About sixty children, drawn from Llanmadoc, Cheriton, Landimore, Burry Green and Llangennith attended the Hill School, as it became known, receiving there, among other things, a sound education in the 3 Rs and scripture. Here, as in Reynoldston, there was the annual Christmas party, organised by the Rector and the Benson family, with a Christmas tree and presents for all. As there was no kitchen, pupils normally brought sandwiches for lunch. These were washed down with cold tea, reheated in cans on the classroom stove. Now, for the party, cooking stoves had to be set up in the open school courtyard and here a 'splendid meal' was prepared. This was served by the Bensons' Cockney maid who, according to one former pupil, 'plied the children with a choice of "cike or jam".'[5]

This semi-feudal order was not to continue long. The establishment in 1839 of the Committee of Council on Education (later the Education Department) led to the inspection of schools to ensure that subsequent Government aid was wisely spent. For Church schools like those in Gower, operating on National Society lines, there was to be no rate-aid until 1902, even though they had now to be inspected by her Majesty's Inspectors. For their support such schools continued to depend largely on the generosity of neighbouring gentry, eked out by sums from regular subscribers and the 'school pence' provided by the parents of pupils.[6]

Nevertheless, the official Government move was for the provision of free elementary education throughout the country. With a view to staving off Government interference for as long as possible, a meeting was held in the spring of 1861 in the Board Room of the Gower Union, perhaps not the happiest of choices but one at least that represented neutral ground. Among those present, in addition to several parish guardians and local clergymen, were Starling and

4   R L T Lucas, Parson Davies, Gower Journal XXVIII, 1977, p 5*ff*
5   *Ibid*
6   Henry Simons, *loc cit*

Henry Benson, as well as Mr Penrice, who was voted to the chair. As a result it was decided to set up a Voluntary School Board.

A previous report by one of the Inspectorate, Mr Bowstead, had caused some hard feeling among the Clergy by emphasising that in such a stronghold of Non-conformity as Wales, it would be necessary to formulate a system of education on 'a scriptural, though not a doctrinal, basis.' The two South Wales bishops took exception to this, wanting the Government to ensure any single school in a village too small to have two schools should be under the sole jurisdiction of the clergy.[7]

Nor was opposition confined to the clergy. At a meeting in the winter of 1870 Mr Talbot, as a major Gower landowner with considerable influence in the area, was shown to be opposed to anything to do with Government intervention in education, while the ordinary Gower resident was even less likely to take kindly to the idea.

Accepting Government aid would involve the appointment of a Clerk and Treasurer, with other related expenses. These would necessitate an extra rate, something to which the man in the fields had a positive aversion.

Many parents indeed failed to see the need for education at all, regarding it as a waste of time in a community where they felt their children would be better employed helping out on the farm, in the works or in the house.

In 1870, the Llanmadoc, Cheriton and Llangennith parishes, with a united population of 854, had one school capable of holding eighty children. The Rector spoke of enlarging the school himself with the help of friends but, as one of those friends, Starling felt the insecure tenure of the school house precluded this and suggested instead that they apply for a grant just for a building, leaving support for the teaching costs to individuals as at present, a characteristically Starling compromise.

The needs of the other parishes were similarly reviewed, including Llanddewi and Knelston, which were still nearer Fairy Hill. The Vicar, Mr Glascodine, considered they were well catered for, although the Rector had found only one school, which was held in the Baptist Chapel in Knelston. Eventually, in spite of opposition from the Vicar, it was accepted that more accommodation was needed.[8]

The recent passing of the 1870 Education Act by Gladstone's Government meant another inspection was imminent, and there was already some apprehension about the outcome. One correspondent to 'The Cambrian' expressed the wish that Her Majesty's Inspectors would take into consideration the 'intellectual size of the masters', as the Voluntary School Board seemed to think only in terms of the size of the building. He implied that Mr Benson had called a meeting of ratepayers to consider the effect of a new rate, whereas what people needed was to be shown the advantages of an efficient system of education to bring out potential talent among the children of Gower. He claimed that yet another meeting had been convened and saw this as a device on Mr Benson's part to hinder the advance of education.[9] Stung by this unfair

7 C May 3 1861, p 4
8 C Dec 2 1870, p 3
9 C Dec 2 1870, p 4

accusation, Starling was quick to spring to his own defence by proving, in a letter to 'The Cambrian' of December 9, 1870, that there had, in fact, been no such meeting.[10]

It was July 1872 before the expected inspection took place. As a result, the Government Inspector of Returns, Mr Percival Balmer, suggested uniting the parishes of Knelston, Reynoldston and Llanddewi with a central purpose-built schoolroom to serve all three, while the three parishes of Llangennith, Llanmadoc and Cheriton, which had previously shared a central school at a site chosen by the ratepayers, were to be divided into two school districts of (1) Llangennith and (2) Llanmadoc and Cheriton.[11]

A long and bitter wrangle followed, mainly between the Clerk to the Voluntary Board, Mr Harris, and the leader of Nonconformist opinion in the district, Mr Samuel Wilson, who accused the Clerk of being both self-appointed and of acting as 'the nominee of priest-craft in Gower'. Mr Harris retaliated by claiming that it benefited Mr Wilson to have the Knelston school continue as it was, as the *ad hoc* Voluntary Board, which had sprung into being in advance of Government sanction, was renting the Baptist premises, thereby providing a source of revenue for Mr Wilson's chapel.[12]

The Inspector, however, found the Baptist schoolroom unsuitable for purposes of education, and eventually the bemused inhabitants of the district decided to contribute towards a voluntary non-sectarian school, with a £60 salary per annum for a trained and certificated teacher in a new school accessible to the seventy-five children in Reynoldston as well as those of the other parishes.[13]

Another development almost as unpopular as the establishment of Government controlled education was the establishment in the 1860s of a Gower Union to oversee the state of the poor in the area. This discontent was reflected in a letter from C D Morgan of Park Mill, protesting against the scheme which he estimated would cost the district over £4000. He saw a Union as 'the crowning monument of degradation' and suggested instead selling the building when the present aged occupants died off and investing the money to establish a fund through a payment of 4d a week which he considered likely to raise £104,000 in twenty years. That would give elderly people a weekly amount payable out of their own savings, thereby helping them to throw off the stigma of pauperism.[14]

In spite of Mr Morgan's ingenious scheme, the Gower Union continued to function along the lines of the 'New' Poor Law Act of 1834. This operated under the guidance of a Board of Guardians, with an Assessment Committee comprising such distinguished local figures as Thomas Penrice, C R M Talbot, N P Cameron, the Rector of Penmaen (the Revd E K James) E R Wood and Starling.[15]

The Workhouse in Penmaen was also the venue for the Gower Petty Sessions. There, for example, as a magistrate, Starling in September 1870 shared with

10   C Dec 9 1870, P 3
11   C Sept 13 1872 p 3 & Nov 28 1873, p 5
12   C June 12 1874, p 8; *cf* June 19 & 26
13   C July 3, 10, 17, 24 & Aug 7 1874, all p 8
14   C Sept 26 1862, p 8
15   C April 19 1867, p 5

Thomas Penrice, N P Cameron and H S Horman-Fisher responsibility for selecting those qualified to serve as jurymen from lists submitted by overseers in the several parishes in the hundred of Gower.[16]

Many of the cases which came before the Gower magistrates must have reminded him of his early days on the Bench in Swansea. Mary Ann Jenkins had been abused and attacked by Elizabeth Eaton who suspected her of enticing the latter's husband from her. The defendant was bound over to keep the peace for three months, with her husband as surety for £10 and two others for £5 each.[17]

William Tucker snr, of Reynoldston, was charged with attacking William Davies at the Rising Sun. Tucker claimed he had been unwell and had taken a couple of whiskies. These had made him behave in a way he would not have done when sober. Nevertheless he was fined 30/-, while in another case of drunkenness, at Park Mill, a fine of 15/- was imposed, including costs.[18]

In September 1876, John Evans, a local man, was accused of raping Mary Walters, a single woman of the same parish. She had been collecting bottles of barm and beer which she was carrying home in her apron when she saw Evans ahead of her on the road from Landimore near Stembridge. She had gone into a neighbour's house in order to avoid him, but on coming out, she was confronted by the accused who had come down the lane to intercept her.

The stile where she was attacked was near Fairy Hill. She had struggled against her attacker, but had been overcome. Although he had told her to make no noise, she claimed to have shouted 'Murder', but no one had taken any notice, even though there were people passing quite near. On getting up after the attack, the complainant said she had gone home to bed and, as she had no money to take proceedings at the time, she had said nothing about it for a week or a fortnight. Probably, indeed, the matter would have rested there had she not been threatened by the defendant's wife who had come to her house and bullied her 'awful'. This was on the day before Mr (Willy) Benson's marriage, 'when there was a great deal of coming and going in the area',

One witness testified that she had seen her passing with Evans and had heard her making a noise, although she had not heard any cry of 'murder'. She had thought Mary Walters was well able to look after herself. The case was dismissed by the Magistrates, N P Cameron, R A Essery, Starling and Thomas Penrice, whose daughter, Jane, had been about to marry Willy Benson at the time referred to in the evidence.[19]

Most cases before the Gower Petty Sessions were rather less dramatic. William Davies, charged with being drunk and disorderly, was ordered by Starling and his fellow Magistrate, R A Essery, to pay costs. Mr Dolling, Llanmadoc, was fined £5, including costs, for selling beer on unlicensed premises. An old lag, Henry Morse, was sent to prison for three months for assaulting P C Shatlock at Llanmadoc on the Saturday night.[20]

16　C Sept 30 1870, p 5
17　*Ibid*
18　*Ibid*
19　C Sept 1 1876 p 3
20　C July 20 1877, p 5

As late as October 1878, in the company of his brother Henry and R A Essery, Starling heard a quartet of cases which epitomised in many ways the issues over which he had presided throughout the years from his earliest experiences as a Swansea magistrate, reflecting the four major aspects of crime with which he had had to deal - dishonesty, drunkenness, violence and immorality.

John Williams of the Railway Inn, Killay, was fined 20/-, including costs, for selling intoxicating liquors at illegal hours on a Sunday, while William Howells, a farmer, had to pay costs for being on the premises. Daniel Williams, also of Killay, and Philip Hopkins were fined 10/- costs for drunkenness. William Thomas of Llanrhidian was bound over to keep the peace towards John Williams of the same place in his own surety of £20, and two other sureties of £10 each. Lastly came an affiliation case between William Gammon of Mumbles and Margaret Llewellyn. This was settled out of court.[21]

Another way in which Starling had come increasingly to identify himself with his Gower neighbours was through his support of The West Glamorgan Agricultural Association.[22] During 1865, the first year he appears to have subscribed to its funds, he had, as a magistrate, been seeking to alleviate the rigours of Government action in forbidding the movement of stock because of widespread outbreaks of Cattle Plague. As we have already seen, Glamorgan was not directly affected by the disease, but the restrictions were causing distress among farmers who could not take their animals to market or put them on show. This had led to divided opinion over the wisdom of holding the West Glamorgan Agricultural Society's December Show. Even sheep breeders had been loth to enter. This had severely limited the scope among the exhibits, even though the gate had been fairly good. Some £20 had been taken but that was no compensation for the lack of atmosphere in the ring.

Starling voiced his ideas about widening the scope of the Agricultural Society at the dinner in the Cameron Arms which followed the Show. The toast to 'The Town and Trade of Swansea', proposed by the Chairman, Thomas Penrice, was again linked with Starling's name. In responding, he outlined the benefits likely to accrue to the Society if its operations were extended to include the whole county by linking up with the East Glamorgan Association and the Cowbridge Agricultural Society.[23]

His idea was taken up by the Association when it met early the next year to consider the feasibility of an enlarged County Agricultural Association. In addition to some of the leading men of the County, Theodore Talbot, Iltid Thomas, John Dillwyn Llewelyn, N P Cameron, Robert Eaton, and Starling himself, many of the principal tenant farmers from Gower were present. They, however, were averse to the whole idea and made it clear they would neither exhibit nor subscribe to the new association.[24]

Nevertheless the principle was adopted. As a result, the Annual Meeting of the Glamorgan Agricultural Society was held at Cowbridge on Tuesday, September 24 1867. There was some dispute about the Society's right to the use of the title,

21   C Oct 25 1878, p 6
22   C June 2 1865, p 1
23   C Dec 21 1866, p 8
24   C March 1 1867, p 5

as only local interests were represented. Few of the major landlords seemed to consider themselves involved, probably because the meeting was taking place in what was dubbed 'one of the most inaccessible towns in Glamorgan'. Nevertheless, Mr Penrice, in his double capacity of High Sheriff and Chairman, was still able to say with satisfaction that there were some Gower people present, and he hoped that, in return, Bridgend and Cowbridge farmers would attend and compete in the Swansea Show in December.[25]

That show, held in the Swansea Market Yard, and followed by a dinner at the Cameron Arms at which Starling was present, proved to be a great success, owing to the tireless efforts of Mr J M Harding of Town Hill Farm. This established a precedent for future years. In 1868 it fell to Starling to propose the health of their 'worthy President', Mr Penrice, of whose private qualities and virtues he felt it unnecessary to speak. Two things, however, had to be mentioned; his contribution to the Society by his support of it, and also the improvement he had effected to his own property and to the neighbourhood generally. This could not fail to be of advantage to local farmers.[26]

The success of the closer relationship between the East and West sides of the County was especially evident the following year when the principal exhibitors of sheep came from Bridgend and Cowbridge. There were, of course, the usual exhibitors from Gower, including Mr Penrice himself, who continued to be most enthusiastic in his praise of the organising genius behind the Show, saying he had never worked with greater pleasure with anyone than with Mr Harding.[27] That evening, at the dinner at The Cameron Arms, Mr Harding occupied the Vice-Chair, with Mr Penrice in the Chair and all the usual notables, the Mayor (J J Jenkins), J D Llewelyn, J T Jenkin, L L Dillwyn, the Ex-Mayor (C T Wilson), Hywel Gwyn and, inevitably, Starling, in attendance.

Side by side with Starling's support for local agriculture went his interest in horticulture, shown by his becoming a patron of the well-established Swansea and Glamorgan Horticultural and Floral Society, under whose aegis he had displayed some of the choice flowers and fruit produced by the greenhouses at Fairy Hill.[28]

In the August of 1866 a new society set up a rival organisation, the South Wales Association for the Exhibition of Poultry, Flowers, Fruit and Vegetables, which arranged for its annual show to be held a week before its older counterpart. The reason given for this was that the latter had appeared defunct. Also some of the exhibitors at the previous year's Horticultural and Floral Show had been so incensed at their treatment by one of the officials that they had refused to enter any of its competitions again. In any case, the newcomers claimed, they had declared their intention of holding a show before the Horticultural and Floral Society had done so.[29]

The new society succeeded in presenting a splendid show in the Music Hall towards the end of August, suggesting, according to 'The Cambrian', 'that Fairy

25 C Sept 27 1867, p 8
26 C Dec 11 1868, p 5
27 C Dec 10 1869, p 5
28 C Aug 31 1866, p 1
29 C Aug 10 1866, p 8

Land was a gay reality'.[30] Even so, the older organisation, which functioned 'in Union with the Royal Horticultural Society in London', managed in turn to produce in the Music Hall 'a scene of magnificence ... unparalleled in its previous history.' The weather had not been kind to them, but the ladies had still braved the elements, though not in 'their gayest apparel'.

There had barely been room in the hall for 'the varied and extensive' exhibits pouring in from the resident gentry and those from surrounding districts. As a result the vegetables had had to be put on display in a tent behind the hall. Among the principal prizewinners were the professionals like the Treseders of Cardiff, but also Pegg of Birchgrove, G B Hermann of Swansea and W T Holland of Llanelly. In the competition for a collection of dessert fruit, not less than six dishes, Starling was awarded second prize, pipped at the post by R T Crawshay of Cyfarthfa.[31]

The following year Starling again figured among the patrons but seems not to have exhibited.[32] By 1871, possibly to attract back some of those who had gone over to its rival, the Floral and Horticultural *(sic)* Society was taking advantage of the early closing day to offer a reduced entrance fee in the afternoon, leaving the earlier part of the day to the more select exhibitors and spectators, with Starling among the latter.[33]

Over the years Starling had had other things on his mind beside the vagaries of rival organisations. In December 1867, his twenty-one year old nephew, Star, after only two years in the Lancers, had, without the consent of his parents, married Elizabeth Tawke, the very lovely daughter of Arthur Tawke of The Lawn, Rochford, Essex. His attachment to her had been previously discussed in the family, when Henry and Tiny had tried to dissuade Star from committing himself to an early marriage. The young couple, however, had gone ahead with their plans.[34]

Star's parents were furious, 'not', as his father tried to explain, 'that we have any objection to the Lady you have married ... All we said was merely for your good as well as hers as you are too young and have not money enough at present to enable you to marry.'

It took all the diplomacy of the supportive Willy and his sisters to bring them round gradually to speak less angrily of the miscreants. The girls, Willy told his brother in a letter from Belgium where the family was spending Christmas, were 'immensely excited', although a little disappointed at losing the fun of being bridesmaids.[35]

Mamma had sent the disgraced pair part of Aunt Wood's letter expressing the general feeling in the family that what they had done was 'most discreditable and dishonourable'. Caroline Elizabeth, wife of the Revd Peter Almeric Wood of Devizes, was Tiny's elder sister, and obviously the family 'conscience' now that grandmother Benson was no longer there to be consulted. There is no record of

30 C Aug 24 1866, p 5
31 C Sept 7 1866, p 5.
32 C Aug 23 1867, p 5
33 C Aug 11 1871, p 8
34 EMB from l'Avenue de la Toison d'Or, Brussels to Starling Meux Benson, Dec 27 1867
35 William Denman Benson, also from l'Avenue de la Toison d'Or, Brussels, to Starling Meux Benson, no date; c Dec 27 1867

what Uncle Starling said, but he certainly did not allow the grass to grow under his feet. By January 3 1868 Henry was answering Starling's letter of December 30 1867.

The Colonel (as Henry then was) had sent his brother by Book post a copy of the proposed settlement on Star's wife. Of this, as Star's father, he did not at all approve. There was, at least, the consolation that her father, 'old Tawke', was rich, but he was extravagant, fond of display and loth to part with his money to his family. He had previously broken off three of his daughter's engagements and one of his son's, as he was not prepared to settle any money on them.[36]

Henry consoled himself with the thought that, fortunately, the Tawke estate was entailed and if anything happened to the brother, who was delicate, it would come to Elizabeth. In addition, there was the Mother's settlement, so eventually there should be plenty of money available, provided the contract was carefully drawn out. 'Old Tawke' had originally wanted four Trustees while Henry had considered two to be enough. He had then been told he need have only one if he liked, but, as 'old Tawke' had now settled on two, Henry thought he had better have the same, himself and Starling, to whom he was now sending the relevant documents. He hoped that, when he returned them, Starling would add any suggestions of his own.

In spite of the initial furore, the marriage proved a happy one, lasting until Elizabeth's death in September 1902, not long after the tragic loss of their only son from dysentery while serving with the Coldstream Guards in South Africa during the Boer War.

It did not take long for the young couple to be reinstated in the family circle, but meanwhile Willy had felt something of the backlash. He had matriculated at Balliol on October 21 1867, just two months before his brother's precipitous marriage, and during his first Christmas vacation, obviously with a legal career in view, he had followed in his maternal grandfather's footsteps by going on circuit through the Northern towns. During his travels he had fallen violently in love with Violet Brett who was there with her mother, and had thoroughly enjoyed himself in their company. Once the story about Star's unorthodox behaviour came out however, Lady Brett took fright and forbade Willy's seeing Violet, for fear that he might prove as rash as his brother.[37]

Undoubtedly Tiny would have understood Lady Brett's feelings. By the summer of 1868, however, she herself had succeeded in putting the whole 'discreditable' episode sufficiently far behind her to be able to face up to serving on the Committee for the Fancy Bazaar which was to be held in connection with the New Hospital on Wednesday, Thursday and Saturday, August 5, 6 and 8. As a comparative newcomer, she had not yet graduated to being a Stall Holder or a Lady Receiver, like Mrs Budd or the Misses Grenfell,[38] but at least she had the pleasure of knowing that many of the luscious grapes, pears, pineapples and melons came daily from the greenhouses of Fairy Hill.[39]

36   HRB to SB, Jan 3 1868
37   William Denman Benson, *vide* n 35
38   C July 3 1868, p 4
39   C Aug 14 1868, p 5

In addition to the contribution made by the Grand Fancy Bazaar to the finances of the New Hospital, the need for increased revenue led to a proposal of a Grand Ball to augment its funds. Although by then in his sixties, Starling served as one of the stewards at the first Ball on January 20 1869. This proved an agreeable evening which 'The Cambrian' hoped would become an annual event.[40]

This wish was realised the following year, with Starling's name in the 1870 guest list second only to that of Thomas Penrice and ahead even of that of the Mayor (J J Jenkins) and his wife. Having young people around him in Fairy Hill for at least part of the year had undoubtedly rejuvenated Starling. Dancing went on until 4 am and, according to the report in 'The Cambrian', it was 'generally acceded that on no previous occasion had the whole arrangement been more perfect or a more agreeable evening spent.'[41]

Starling attended the 1870 Ball alone, but in 1871, he was accompanied by the Colonel and his wife with Alice, May and two of their sons, Willy and Harry, forming part of the company euphorically described by 'The Cambrian' as

> ... wave after wave
> Of fair women and brave men.[42]

The event continued to grow. The Sixth Annual Ball on January 16, 1874 attracted large parties of the leading families, about two hundred and forty in all, among them the Morrises, the Bruces, the Vivians of both Park Gwern and Singleton and the Gulstons of Dirleton, who were to become close friends of the Benson girls. Henry, now Major General Benson, and Mrs Benson were there with the Misses Benson and Mr Starling Benson, but no mention was made of Willy or Harry on that occasion.[43]

Willy, now practising as a barrister in Swansea, was forming new friendships. He had attended the 1872 Ball as a member of the Parkwern party.[44] It was not long, however, before his interest was moving in another direction.

The Christmas period and early January 1876 was a busy time for the younger generation from Fairy Hill. The week after the 1876 Hospital Ball,[45] there was a double event held at the Bridgend Town Hall, the Bachelors' Ball on the 11th and the Hunt Club on the 13th. The principal houses in the neighbourhood were filled with guests staying over the two nights. Both functions attracted over a hundred and fifty, among them the party from Kilvrough. Mr and Mrs Penrice and their daughters, Louisa and Jane, as well as Willy Benson, were staying at Miskin Manor. At last Willy had succeeded in escaping the curious eyes of his sisters who, with Harry, were in another party accommodated at Court Coleman with the Dillwyn Llewelyn family.[46]

By January 1877, the Kilvrough party included Mr and Mrs William Benson.[47] In August 1876 Willy had married Jane Penrice in an idyllic ceremony in the

40   C Jan 22 1869, p 5
41   C Jan 14 1870, p 5
42   C Jan 13 1871, p 5
43   C Jan 23 1874, p 6
44   C Jan 12 1872, p 5
45   C Jan 14 1876, p 3
46   C Jan 21 1876, p 8
47   C Jan 12 1877, p 8

fairy-tale setting of Pennard Church, the bridal party passing through arches of greenery that had been erected along the route from the bride's home. The tenants of the estate were entertained to a liberal celebration of the event at the Gower Inn, but the actual wedding breakfast at Kilvrough Manor was mainly a family affair, attended by the Penrice and Howman relatives on the Bride's side, and on the Bridegroom's, by all the Benson family (apart from Star and Bessie) with other family members, such as his mother's youngest sister, Aunt Gina, and William Wightman Wood, Willy's barrister cousin. There were in addition a few close friends, the Grenfells, Harry Dillwyn, William Crawshay and his wife, and her sisters, the Misses Wood of Stouthall. Later, in the evening, these were joined by extra guests, including Lady Morris with her son and daughter, Miss Vivian and her brother, Graham, the Wilmots and the Camerons.[48]

There were to be no wedding bells for any of Willy's sisters. Mamma saw to that. Eligible young men might be invited to Fairy Hill but none was allowed to get too serious, as she had made it quite clear her daughters were all to remain single to look after her in her old age. But in the meantime there was no shortage of potential admirers, among others, Robert Wilmot, the Gulston boys and Aubrey Vivian, significant for his presence in the 1878 Hospital Ball when all the other members of the Parkwern family (apart from his father, present in an official capacity) were absent because of the death of his step-mother's father. May Benson was there too, the most vivacious of the daughters, as well as her elder sister, Alice, their father and mother, the newly weds, Willy and Jane, but, for the first time for many years, no Uncle Starling.[49]

Perhaps age was beginning to catch up with him. In October 1876, his old friend, Colonel Wood, had died. Starling had been among the family mourners at the funeral service in Llandilo. The coffin had been brought by road from Stouthall to Killay Station, and from there it was conveyed by the L&NW Railway to Llandilo. As young men Starling and Colonel Wood had shared their geological pursuits, and of latter years, they had been close neighbours. Neither had cared much for ostentation, and it was in-keeping with the dead Colonel's character that he should request that there would be no mourning, no plumes on the hearse, no hat-bands or scarves, just the coffin covered with a handsome pall of violet and gold.[50]

Starling, however, was not one to brood over the flight of time. He had plenty to occupy him, even though he had largely wound up most of his business concerns. Gower, in many ways, was a microcosm of the wider world, and his neighbours there looked to him for guidance. Henry might be the artist manqué, Richard, the philosopher and theologian, but Starling remained to the end the clear-headed man of action.

48   C Aug 11 1876, p 5
49   C Jan 11 1878, p 5
50   C Oct 6 1876, p 5

Chapter XVII

The Final Curtain

On January 2 1879, Starling Benson revised his will.[1] His executors and trustees were his brother, Henry, and his barrister nephew, William Denman. The latter and his brother Star were two of the principal beneficiaries under their uncle's will. Starling had obviously retained a very special affection for the two little boys he had taken to the Vauxhall Gardens and to the sands on Swansea Bay.

There were substantial legacies of £3000 each for his younger nephews, Harry, Richard and Florrie, and of £2000 each for his four nieces. He had remembered too his god-sons, William Henry Bishop and Edward Florance Hobling, grandchildren of his dead sister, Emma Usborne, but there is no mention of his brother, Richard Meux, or of Jean Gaufridy, the 'son' of his sister, Sarah Jane, who, it would appear from later correspondence with his uncle Richard, had grown up in Italy.

This is strange as provision is made for Star's son, Richard Arthur Starling, though only after his father's day, and for William Denman's first son or, failing a son, for any daughter of the marriage, should Willy not survive his uncle. By a cruel irony Star's son died, as we have seen, during the Boer War, and Willy's eldest son was killed in the first month of the First World War, both predeceasing their fathers.

Much of Starling's money was invested in Railway stock, Midland, Great Western (Vale of Neath) and Dublin, Wicklow and Waterford, but the bulk of his wealth lay in the land, much of it rich in mineral deposits. In the County returns for February 1876, he was shown to have been one of the wealthiest, though not one of the largest, landowners in Glamorgan.[2] Others might own more acres, but his comparatively small acreage yielded a greater return per acre than that belonging to men far better known than he. Even the 1215 acres of the Duke of Beaufort brought in only £4356 and the 2064 owned by Sir John Morris, only £3478, while Starling's 256 acres were worth £6470.

Absolute discretion in the management of his 'mines, quarries, beds and strata of coal, ironstone, fire clay, common clay, stones and other minerals whatsoever lying within, under or upon or otherwise forming part of the said hereditaments, either with or without any houses or lands convenient to be held or occupied with the same and either with or without the surface of any land under which the same or any part thereof shall lie' was vested in his executors, though 'all his freehold Messuages tenements Lands and hereditaments situate in the higher division of

---

1 Copy of will of Starling Benson, proved at Carmarthen, March 10 1879, by oaths of Henry Roxby Benson, brother, and William Denman Benson, Barrister-at-law, nephew
2 County Returns, Feb 18 1876, WGRO

the Parish of Llanrhidian' were bequeathed to Willy and his heirs. After the payment of his funeral and testamentary expenses, the legacies stipulated in his will and any debts outstanding at the time of his death, all the rest of Starling's personal estate (except estates vested in him in any trust or by way of mortgage) was to go to his brother Henry. He knew he could rely on Henry to act circumspectly, unlike Richard whose fecklessness in the management of this world's goods must have been a sore trial to Starling.[3]

This business having been settled, Henry and Tiny went off with May and Charlotte for a brief winter holiday in Folkestone, leaving Richard Erle (Dickie) and Florrie with Uncle Starling in Fairy Hill. Later on in the month, the parents had occasion to return to Gower though they had arranged to retain their lodgings in Folkestone. Tiny had locked up her store cupboard and left the key with May who had stayed on with Charlie until such time as their parents would re-join them.

When the General and his wife reached Landore, a porter came up to them with the news that Starling was dead. At Swansea, an old friend, Mr Francis (presumably W H Francis) was waiting for them, and then, the Station Master, Mr Kendall, and various porters came up to sympathise. 'Everyone,' in Tiny's words, was 'so shocked and concerned.'[4]

The previous morning (January 16), Starling Benson had gone out shooting rabbits with Dickie and the Fairy Hill gamekeeper, William Lewis. He and his sixteen-year-old nephew had left Lewis with the understanding that when he had reached his usual position on a three foot ledge jutting out above a precipice, he would whistle to let the gatekeeper know. Nothing was heard for about fifteen minutes and then William Lewis heard a double report and Starling's voice calling for Dickie.

His nephew went to him at once and then rushed over to the gamekeeper to say, 'Uncle has shot himself'. This was the natural impression one would get from the way in which the gun had gone off. When, however, Lewis reached the injured man, he could see the damage had been caused, not by the gunshots, which were purely coincidental, but by a fall of some eleven to twelve feet, in the course of which his master's head had struck a sharp stone protruding from the side. There was still hair sticking to the stone which had caused a massive wound to the side of the head.

When William Lewis reached him, Starling's first words were, 'How did this happen?' to which the gamekeeper replied, 'You have fallen off the bank, sir.'

'What a simple thing it is; it is a nasty place' was Starling's only comment. He complained, however, of being cold and his hands felt like ice, so Lewis sent Dickie to his cottage for a blanket. His uncle was now trying to sit up but fell back immediately.

As a temporary measure, while the carriage was being sent for from Fairy Hill, his head was tied up with a handkerchief. Unfortunately the staff at the house, not grasping the full extent of their master's injuries, had allowed the young Florrie, always delicate as the result of a childhood illness, to come up with the

---

3   Copy of will of Starling Benson
4   MHB to her daughter, May; no date, but probably Jan 17 1879

carriage; and so the boy had a full view of the harrowing sight which awaited them.

As soon as the carriage arrived, the wounded man was put to lie in it but once it began to move, its jolting exacerbated the acute pain Starling was now feeling. Instead a stretcher was improvised out of a door and on this he was carried back to the house. Dr Vaux Ellis had been called out and had gone straight to Fairy Hill, but on finding the party had not yet returned, he set off on foot to meet them.

When the party reached the house, Dr Ellis examined the wound which stretched from the right eyebrow to the top of the head and back down towards the nape of the neck, with a large piece of the scalp hanging loose over it. The skull was fractured, and, in addition, there were two or three minor scalp wounds and a cut on the chin.[5] With such massive injuries, recovery could not be hoped for, and that same afternoon, Starling died.

The news was received with genuine distress throughout the area. Flags in the Harbour were flown at half mast, while the announcement of his death in the weekly edition of 'The Cambrian' for Friday, January 17, the day after the tragedy,[6] and the report of his funeral, the following week, were both printed between heavy black lines,[7] as was the practice for important public figures. There had not been time before going into print for 'The Cambrian' of January 17 to check on the exact details of what had happened and they also made the natural error of attributing his death 'to a shooting accident'.[8]

'The Western Mail' as a daily paper, was better placed to keep astride of events and get its facts right. Reporting his death on Saturday, January 18, it paid a warm tribute to Starling's public service.

> For upwards of a quarter of a century he had presided over the Harbour Trustees, and so great was the experience he had gained, and the assistance he gave to the Trust in the onerous position he held for many years that when he signified his intention of retiring he was persuaded to continue office.

It went on to pay tribute too to his other spheres of service, for example, as a magistrate for the petty sessional division of Penmaen where his 'business-like abilities gave great assistance to his brother magistrates.'[9]

An inquest into the circumstances of his death was held that same Saturday when the body was identified by his brother, Henry, and evidence given by his nephew Richard, the Fairy Hill gamekeeper and the local doctor. This was fully reported in 'The Western Mail' of Monday, January 20.[10]

In the meantime the family was trying to come to terms with the shock. On the day of the inquest, his sister-in-law, obviously deeply shaken by their 'most cruel loss', was attempting to sort out funeral arrangements with her two

5 C Jan 24 1879 p 7; *cf* The Western Mail, Jan 20
6 C Jan 17 1879, p 5
7 C Jan 24 1879, p 5
8 C Jan 17 1879, p 5
9 The Western Mail, Jan 18 1879
10 The Western Mail, Jan 20 1879

daughters who were still in Folkestone.[11] She had been 'too knocked up' to write to them at once, and was still feeling 'so bewildered and upset', concerned not only for her dead brother-in-law but with the effects of the gruesome happenings on her two young sons who had witnessed the scene. 'What poor darling Dickie has gone thro' is too dreadful to think of', and then there was Florrie who 'unluckily had come up in the carriage and seen his uncle in that terrible condition. My head aches so dreadfully I hardly know what I have written.'

Nevertheless there was some relief in planning their mourning. The two absent daughters, now in their mid-twenties, could stay on in Folkestone until the funeral. Otherwise they could go to Star's wife, Bessie, who 'would be very glad to be of any use', or to Janie, Willy's wife, in London. They could please themselves but the last suggestion seemed to their mother the most convenient. Charlie would want a hat; otherwise her black silk dress, trimmed with a little crepe, and the black alpaca she wore of an evening would do very well. May could get her mourning in London, and she was also to take her mother's black silk dress and get Miss Woods, presumably the family dressmaker, to put crepe on it. She was then to send it down with the other things they wanted as Madge was having a jacket made like her dress. Tiny herself wanted her little bag and also more pocket handkerchiefs.

She was not concerned only about what her daughters would wear. 'Woods' would also have to be suitably attired. She could either buy herself a black dress in Folkestone or get the material in London and make one. Charles, most likely the butler, could go up with them to London and 'call on the chance of his things being ready, or take them if he wants measuring or any alteration'. He was to get a black arm-band and come down to Swansea by the 5.15 train. He was much needed at the house as they would be such a large party for the funeral. Uncle Richard was already there, and Star and Willy were expected the following week.

The General had written a separate note to his daughter, enclosing a cheque for £10, asking her to give Charles £4 to cover his travelling expenses. Mrs Benson's idea was that Charles could spend the night in Swansea and go on to Fairy Hill in the morning, 'bringing anything with him that may be at either station.' She suggested he should ask if anything had been ordered to be brought out as, if there was, 'he could come in that way', presumably by having a lift on the delivery van, thus saving on time and expense.[12]

The arrangements for the funeral on January 24 were in the hands of D J Jones of Castle Square, Swansea. Rarely could the quiet churchyard at Reynoldston have seen such an impressive array of carriages. The cortège was preceded, first, by that containing Messrs E and G B Strick, W H Francis, Dr Ellis and the Rector of Reynoldston (the Revd J E Jones), followed by that of Mr Vivian and then of Captain Miers of Stouthall who was accompanied by Mr Robert Wilmot of Norton House. They were followed by members of the household staff.

The mourners were met at Reynoldston Green by the Chairman, members and officials of the Harbour Trust, the Clerk and members of the Gower Board of Guardians and the Clerk and members of the United School Board of

11 MHB to her daughter, May. No date, but probably Jan 17 1879
12 *Ibid*

54 Reynoldston Church, 1995   Photo: D M Bayliffe

55 The Benson graves, 1995   Photo: D M Bayliffe

Reynoldston, Knelston and Llanddewi. These passed into the Church ahead of the coffin which was carried by employees on the estate and followed by family mourners.

The coffin was covered with a violet pall with white and gold fringe and a white cross in the centre, together with wreaths of azaleas, primulas, lilalia, albuda and quantities of various fern. The name plate read simply: 'Starling Benson, born August 30th, 1808, died January 16th, 1879'.[13]

After the service, conducted by the Rector of Reynoldston, the coffin was lowered into 'a deep grave', the first family interment in the plot which now contains six similarly shaped graves. The wreaths and cross which had been removed from the coffin were then 'dropped gently into the grave by those whom the deceased had loved so well in life'.

Ironically, the Mayor of Swansea, heading the representatives of the Council, was one who had not perhaps always loved Starling well in life. The redoubtable Dr James Rogers, who had been one of his toughest opponents over the question of the New Dock, was that year's holder of the office, supported on this occasion by a large number of former Mayors, William Thomas of Lan, John Ivor Evans, John Glasbrook, J J Jenkins, G B Strick, Charles Bath and E M Richards.

The Harbour Trustees were led by Starling's successor, F A Yeo, with the new Superintendent (Robert Capper), the new Clerk (Francis James, son of Starling's life-long ally, J W James), the Deputy Superintendent (Captain John Rosser) and his assistants, Captains George Rosser and William Ritchie. Among other members of the Trust were Lawrence Tulloch, E R Daniel, and one who had so frequently crossed swords with Starling in verbal battles over the Duke of Beaufort's rights, Francis Price.

F W Mortimer, who had been a colleague in the days of the SVR, was there representing the Midland Railway while, prominent among the large contingent of Gower Guardians, were the Clerk, John Beynon, the Revd S B Westhorp, R A Essery and that pillar of Dissent, Samuel Wilson. Mr Wilson was also present in another capacity as a member of the Reynoldston School Board which, despite recent controversy, was continuing to operate with E J Harris as its Clerk and Henry Bevan and David Hughes as its other representatives.[14]

As each of the bodies on which he had served held its meetings, moving tributes were paid to Starling Benson. At the next Harbour Trust meeting, in moving a vote of condolence to his family, his successor expressed his deep personal sense of the loss of so able an adviser. He had assumed the responsibility of office 'encouraged by the conviction he could rely on Mr Benson's assistance, and his counsel and experience would be ready at hand', as it had been whenever Frank Yeo needed to fall back on his 'larger wisdom'.

Mr Vivian recalled their first meeting over forty-five years before, thirty of which had been in connection with the Trust. He was relieved that Mr Benson had enjoyed health and strength to the last day of his life, and that there was no prolonged suffering at the end. He only hoped 'so bright a career would be an

13   C Jan 24 1879, p 7
14   *Ibid*

example to many to emulate the pure spirit in which he carried out all he did, summed up in the phrase *'suaviter in modo, fortiter in re'*.[15]

Mr Grenfell had written from Maesteg House to convey his sympathy and his esteem for the dead. He had been able to leave office secure in the merits of his successor whom he summed up as 'one who never made an enemy and never lost a friend'.

> His calm and sober judgment, his temperate and conciliatory manners, and sound sense fitted him especially for the important duties of his office which he discharged so efficiently and advantageously to the harbour and trade of Swansea.[16]

Perhaps one of the most sincere and moving of these tributes came from the Gower Board of Guardians at their meeting in the Penmaen Workhouse on January 23. In this the Board wished to express their sorrow at the loss they had sustained in the sudden death of their Chairman, Mr Starling Benson.

> They feel they have lost in him one whose attention for many years as an *ex officio* guardian, especially during the time he held the office of Chairman, has been of the greatest service. Mr Benson's thorough acquaintance with business and the manner of carrying on the business of a Board of Guardians, the good counsels he was able and always ready to give and the courtesy with which he ever took his part in the business of this Board render his loss one which the Guardians deeply feel and which they desire thus to record.[17]

The sorrow felt at his passing was personal as well as official. 'The Swansea and Glamorgan Herald' of January 22 said of him that

> he won the regard of the farmers of Gower, whose attachment became so strong that very few would undertake any important matter without first seeking his advice. This was at all times freely given, and his neighbours feel now that they have lost in him their best and most valued friend.[18]

Another local journal, 'The Ferret' went one step further:

> None who lacked advancement; none who suffered from the cruel shafts of poverty; none who had to bear the sorrows inseparable from this life; none who needed a steadfast friend - looked to him in vain.[19]

Other Bensons had been buried in various churchyards in England, but for Starling there could be no other resting place. He had lived for over fifty years

---

15 C Feb 14 1879, p 7
16 *Ibid*
17 C Jan 24 1879, p 5
18 Sw and Glam Herald, Jan 22 1879 (Taken from a cutting in a scrapbook belonging to Col. J R E Benson)
19 'The Ferret', January 25, 1879 (from a cutting, *loc cit*)

in Wales; Glamorgan was his home, the place where he belonged. Copper smelter, colliery owner, Town Councillor, County Magistrate, ex-Mayor, Chairman of the Harbour Trust, Chairman of the Board of Directors of the Swansea Vale Railway, Poor Law Guardian: he had been them all, yet he was more than the sum total of his many and varied capacities, while seeking to appear so much less. The essence of the man comes out perhaps most clearly in the unpretentious inscription on his plain gravestone of unpolished granite in a country churchyard where it can so easily be overlooked. He was simply

Starling Benson, Esq,
of Fairy Hill,
born 30th August, 1808
died 16th January, 1879.

Appendix A

Duke of Beaufort's Interest in the New Cut

Swansea and Neath Railway Bill
Select Committee on Private Bills - 17 June 1861

Mr Francis Hooper examined by Mr Granville Somerset:

> ... That Act (1836) was passed to enable the trustees to create a new cut, and to turn the old river into a float, which is now called the North Dock. A. Yes ...

> Did that pass through some land of the Duke of Beaufort. A. Yes.

> Was it that triangular piece of land.   A. Yes; a part of it went through it.

> Was an arrangement come to between the Harbour Trustees and you on behalf of the Duke of Beaufort, to the effect that £500 should be given for that land, and that the trustees should put the whole of the excavation for the formation of the new cut on what is now called the "Spoil Bank".   A. Yes; and hence comes its name.

> Are you aware whether or not owners of the upper portion received £11,000 for land taken from them.   A. I understand so.

> That is, above the bridge; and a large portion was taken from the Duke of Beaufort's, immediately contiguous.   A. Yes.

> You gave the Trustees an alternative - an option - to pay £5000 or lay all the excavations from the new cut on the Spoil Bank, and then only £500. Now, are you aware whether or not the Trustees since then have had to pay a considerable sum of money for carrying ballast away from Swansea.   A. They have to pay 2d per ton for carrying it up to a spot on Lady Jersey's property. They pay that to the Railway Company, besides the cost of unloading the vessels.

> Then it was not only a saving to them in hard money, but also an accommodation in having a spot close at hand to throw the spoil on. A. No doubt it saved them £10,000.

... May I take it that the Spoil Bank consists of from 12 to 13 acres. A. It consists of considerably more than that, and is capable of extension from 2 to 3 acres more when we level it down ...

... Are you of the opinion, if these 12 acres were taken, it would be a heavy loss to the Duke of Beaufort.   A. Yes. In 1846 - so far back as that - I was offered £1000 an acre for 8 acres for docks then contemplated.

Was that at the time when floating accommodation was required at Swansea, and public opinion was very much divided as to whether it was most desirable to make Docks on the east or west side of the river. A. It was on that occasion that the offer was made to me.

Mr Benson, who was examined before the Committee, was very anxious the Dock should be on the east side.   A. No doubt.

The Duke of Beaufort of that day, being applied to by both parties, referred to Mr Brunel.   A. He did.

And Mr Brunel made a report ... that the Docks should be made on the west side.   A. Yes

Appendix B

South Wales Railway

Memorandum relative to the working of the level crossing of the South Wales and Swansea Vale Railways

The SWR will put up a signal post and lamp if required.

The gates at the level crossing to be kept open at all times for the passage of the engine on the SVR line.

The up trains on the SW line to run between Landore and the level crossing at such speed as to be able to pull up if the engine on the SV line should be in sight, but should the SV engine arrive in sight after the signal is given to the SW engine to come on then the SV engine is to be brought to a stand to enable the SW engine to pass.

For the down trains on the SWR the gates are to be closed five minutes before each train is due, and should it be late until five minutes after time when the gates must be closed to allow the passage of the ballast train and the danger signals put on to the SW line. After the passing of the SV engine the gates to be again shut across that line and so to remain until the SW train then due has passed unless another engine of the SV line has to pass when it will again be allowed to do so.

The gates and signals to be under the charge and control of the SW policeman.

These arrangements are entered into between Mr Starling Benson and Mr Charles Henry Smith as directors of the Swansea Vale Railway and Mr Frederick Clarke Superintendent of the South Wales Railway as a temporary measure for securing the safety of the public, it being distinctly understood by the parties hereunto that nothing herein contained is to prejudice any rights or powers of the Swansea Vale or South Wales Companies.

Swansea, 28th July 1852

Bibliography

UNPUBLISHED MATERIAL

Benson Collection of family correspondence, deposited in the Archives of the University College, Swansea

Bute Papers, MS 75 50 (D), Cardiff Reference Library

Family correspondence and other material lent by Colonel J R E Benson of Dorchester

Family wills issued by Somerset House

National Library of Wales
Nevill Papers

Public Record Office
Files in the PRO RAIL and MT6 series
Documents from the British Railways Board Records Centre via Mr Michael Hale by courtesy of the Records Officer. These documents are currently being sorted and classified for transfer to the Public Record Office.

Swansea Central Library
Tithe Maps and Apportionment
Ordnance Survey Maps

Swansea City Archives
Minutes of the Swansea Local Board of Health

University College, Swansea.
Sale Catalogues No 4, Cameron Estate 1852
Swansea Council Minute Book, 1835
Yorkshire Imperial Metals - Vivian Papers B, Title Deeds, No 2
Rutter, Collected Reports, Swansea Dock Company

West Glamorgan Record Office, County Hall, Swansea
Beaufort Estate Map
County Returns
Neath Abbey Iron Works Collection

Strick & Bellingham Documents
Penclawdd Copper Works Plan
Poor Rate Books
Kirkhouse Correspondence, Jordan Collection
Census Returns
Tithe Maps and Apportionment

JOURNALS AND NEWSPAPERS

Bradshaw's Railway Manual
Cambrian
Cardiff Times & Weekly News
Ferret
Illustrated London News
Mining Journal
Railway Chronicle
Railway News
Railway Times
Swansea and Glamorgan Herald
Swansea Journal
Western Mail

PARLIAMENTARY DOCUMENTS

Swansea Harbour Act 1836, 6 & 7 William
Swansea Dock Act 2 7 1847, 11 Victoria
Swansea Harbour Acts' Amendment Act 22 7 1847, 10 & 11 Victoria
Swansea Harbour Act 1854, 17 & 18 Victoria
Swansea Harbour Act 1857, 20 & 21 Victoria

Swansea Improvement Act 1844, 7 & 8 Victoria
Swansea Local Board of Health Waterworks Act 1852, 15 & 16
    Victoria
Swansea Local Board of Health Waterworks Act 1860, 23 & 24
    Victoria

South Wales Railway Act 1845, 8 & 9 Victoria
South Wales Railway (Amendment) Act 1846, 9 & 10 Victoria
Swansea Valley Railway Act 1847, 10 & 11 Victoria
Swansea Vale Railway Act 1855, 18 Victoria
South Wales Railway (Consolidation) Act 1855, 18 & 19 Victoria
Swansea Vale Railway Extension Act 1856, 19 & 20 Victoria
Swansea Vale Railway Extension Act 1861, 24 & 25 Victoria
Swansea Vale & Neath & Brecon Junction Railway Act 1864, 27 & 28
    Victoria
Swansea Vale Railway Act 1867, 30 Victoria

Midland Railway (Swansea Vale Railway Lease) Act 1874, 37 & 38 Victoria

Midland Railway Act (Further Powers) 1876, 39 & 40 Victoria

Evidence before Parliamentary Committees on Railway Bills

NINETEENTH CENTURY PUBLISHED MATERIAL

Swansea Museum

Annual Reports of the Philosophical & Literary Institution, Swansea, Vol 1, 1835-38; Vol 2, 1839-43

Annual Reports of Royal Institution of South Wales

Annual Reports of Swansea Literary and Scientific Society, 1846-53

Swansea Dock Company Collected Reports (Rutter)

Swansea Harbour & Docks Reports, 1794-1847, (Swansea: Murray & Rees)

Swansea Docks Pamphlets 66/10

DIRECTORIES

Butcher, Swansea Directory 1875-76,

Gamwell, S C, Guide to Swansea, 1848

Hunt & Co, Bristol & Welsh Towns, 1848

Matthew's Swansea Directory, Part II, 1830

The Swansea Guide, Part 1, 1823

Pigot's Directory 1836, 1844

SECONDARY SOURCES

RECENT PUBLICATIONS

The Welsh Railways Archive:

Charles Donovan, Tragedy on the Vale of Neath Railway

Michael Hale, Midland Miscellany, The Midland Reaches South Wales Origins of the Swansea & Neath Railway

Glamorgan County History, Vol V

Ch I, A H John, Glamorgan 1700-1750

Ch VIII, R O Roberts, Industrial Glamorgan - Banking and Financial Organisation, 1750-1914.

Ch X, Robin Craig, The Ports and Shipping, *c* 1750-1914.

Glamorgan Historian, ed Stewart Williams (Cowbridge; D Brown & Sons, Ltd)

Vol VI, 1969; W Gerwyn Thomas, The Coal Mining Industry in West Glamorgan.

Vol IX, 1972; Prys Morgan, The Glais Boundary Dispute, 1756.

Welsh History Review, No 4, 1968-69

R O Roberts, The Bank of England, The Company of Copper Miners and the Cwmavon Works, 1847-52.

Gower Journal
Vol V 1952; J M Davies, The Morris Family and Swansea
Vol XXIV, 1973; Henry Simmons, Early Education in Gower
Vol XXVIII, 1977; R L T Lucas, Parson Davies
Margaret Walker, 'The British Association in Swansea in 1848', reprinted by courtesy of the Gower Magazine to celebrate the BA's visit to the city in 1990.

Journal of the Railway and Canal Historical Society,
Vol XXVI, P R Reynolds, Scott's Tramroad, Llansamlet,
Vol XXVII, S R Hughes, The Development of British Navigational Levels
Vol XIX, T B Sands, Broad Gauge on the Swansea Vale Railway

South West Wales Industrial Archaeology Society Bulletins,
No. 13, Gerald Gabb, Wind Street Station, Swansea
No. 30, Barry Fagg, Coal Mining in Llansamlet Parish.
No. 31, Peter Wakelin & F G Cowley, The Forest Copper Works and its Site
No. 32, Peter Wakelin, The Founding of the Forest Copper Works
Nos. 39 & 40, Paul Reynolds, Railroad from Penclawdd copperworks to Berthlwyd coalpits, *c* 1805
No. 46, Paul Reynolds, Early Locomotives on the Swansea Vale Railway to 1860
No. 47, David Boorman, Early SVR Locomotives

Swansea Museum Factsheets
Lower Swansea Valley
1 Chauncey Townsend, Industrial Entrepreneur
2 The Smith Family of Llansamlet
3 John Scott
4 Notes on Coal-Mining in the Llansamlet Area
5 Early Copper Works
6 Later Copper Works
7 The Rise and Fall of the Copper Industry
9 The Grenfells
11 The Coppermen

Maritime and Industrial Museum Fact Sheets
Railways around Swansea
Introduction
South Wales Railway
The Mumbles Railway
The Swansea Vale Railway

Swansea History Project
Tramroads and Industrial Railways

Canals of the Swansea Area

Neath Borough Council, Canals Information Pack

THESES

Toomey, R R (PhD thesis), Vivian and Sons, 1809-1924, A Study of the Firm in the Copper and Related Industries (Swansea; 1979)

Wright, J F (Thesis 1991, UCS Miners' Library, Hendrefoilan), The Development of Public Water Supplies in the Swansea Area, 1837-1989

BOOKS CONSULTED

D S M Barrie, A Regional History of Railways of Great Britain, Vol XII South Wales (Nairn; Thomas & Lochar, 1994)

Bather, James, Full and Faithful Account of the Life of James Bather, late Boatswain of the Nightingale Brig, Thomas Benson, Esq, Owner (Biographical Tracts, London, printed for P Griffiths in Paternoster Row, 1751)

Baxter, British Locomotive Catalogue (Moorland Publishing Co.)

Benson, Richard Meux, Letters, (London, Oxford & Milwaukee; A R Mowbray & Co, Ltd. 1916)

Blanch, W H The Parish of Camberwell (Ilkley; Scholar Press, 1976; first published 1875)

Boorman, David, The Brighton of Wales (Swansea Little Theatre Co., Ltd. 1986)

Davies, John Henry, History of Pontardawe and District (Christopher Davies, Llandybie, 1967)

Francis, George Grant, Smelting of Copper in the Swansea District from the time of Elizabeth to the Present Day (Swansea, 1867), first published as a series of articles in 'The Cambrian' during 1866; printed London, Charing Cross; Willis & Sotheran, 1867

Gabb, Gerald, The Life and Times of the Swansea and Mumbles Railway (Cowbridge; D Brown & Sons, Ltd, 1987)

Griffiths, Ralph A, Singleton Abbey and the Vivians of Swansea (Llandysul; Gomer Press, 1988)

Hadfield, Charles, The Canals of South Wales and the Border (David & Charles, Newton Abbott, in conjunction with the University of Wales Press, Cardiff, 1967)

Harrington, Bernard J, Life of Sir William E Logan, Kt, LLD, FRS, FGS chiefly compiled from Letters, Journals & Reports (Montreal, 1883)

Harris, Alderman E, Swansea (Cardiff; Western Mail and Echo, Ltd. 1935)

Hilton, K J (ed), The Lower Swansea Valley Project (London; Longmans, Green & Co, Ltd. 1967)

Hughes, John Vivian, The Wealthiest Commoner, C R M Talbot (Port Talbot Printing Company, Ltd)

Ince, Lawrence, The Neath Abbey Iron Company (Eindhoven; De Archaeologishe Pers Nederland)

John, A H. The Industrial Development of South Wales, 1750-1850, (Cardiff; University of Wales Press, 1950)

Jones, R Emrys, The Railways of Wales (Welsh Library Association, 1979)

Jones, W H, History of the Indefatigable Lodge No. 237 (Carmarthen; Spurrell, 1923)

Jones, W H, History of the Port of Swansea (Carmarthen; W Spurrell & Son, 1921)

King, W T C, History of the London Discount Market, (London; George Routledge & Sons, 1936)

Lucas, Robert, A Gower Family (Lewes, Sussex; The Book Guild Ltd. 1986)

MacDermot, E T, History of the Great Western Railway, Vol I, 1833-63; Vol II, 1863-1921, revised C R Clinker, (London; Ian Allan, 1964)

Malloy, Pat, And They Blessed Rebecca (Llandysul: Gomer Press, 1994)

Mathias, Peter, The Brewing Industry in England, 1700-1830 (Cambridge University Press, 1959).

Owen-Jones, Stuart, Railways of Wales (Cardiff; 1981)

Painting, David, Amy Dillwyn (Cardiff; University of Wales Press, 1987)

Phillips, Elizabeth, History of the Pioneers of the Welsh Coalfield (Cardiff; Western Mail, 1925)

Phillips, Martin, The Copper Industry in the Port Talbot District (1935)

Rees, D Morgan, Historic Industrial Scenes, 'Wales' (Moorland Publishing, Ashbourne, Derbyshire, May 1979)

Rogers, W C, A Pictorial History of Swansea (Llandysul; Gomer Press, 1981)

Smith, Graham, Smuggling in the Bristol Channel, 1700-1850 (Countryside Books, Newbury, Berks)

Symons, M V, Coalmining in the Llanelli Area, Vol I, (Llanelli; Llanelli Borough Council, 1979)

Thomas, Norman, Swansea's Districts and Villages, Vols 1 & 2 (Swansea; Qualprint Wales Ltd. 1965)

Walford, Edward, Village London, the Story of Greater London, Vol II (London; The Alderman Press, 1984, first published 1883/4).

Williams, Glanmor (ed), An Illustrated History, (Swansea; Christopher Davies, 1990)

Wood, John George, The Principal Rivers of Wales, 1814

Index